The History of Dutch Jewry during the Emancipation Period
1787-1815

The History of Dutch Jewry during the Emancipation Period 1787-1815

Gothic Turrets on a Corinthian Building

Jozeph Michman

AMSTERDAM UNIVERSITY PRESS

Every effort has been made to obtain permission for all copyrighted illustrations used in this book. Nonetheless, whosoever believes to have rights to this material is advised to contact the publisher.

DS
135
N4
M535
1995

ISBN 90-5356-186-2 geb.
ISBN 90-5356-090-4 pbk.

Cover design: Erik Cox, The Hague
Illustrations cover: 'Vrij en gelijk door de wet gebonden',
Rijksmuseum, Amsterdam.
Typesetting: Nieuwland & Nirk Publishing, Eindhoven

© Amsterdam University Press, Amsterdam, 1995

Contents

Acknowledgements

In the course of the more than twenty years during which I was involved with the subject, I received assistance from several institutions and numerous persons, the latter including several who are no longer active in the functions they occupied at the beginning of my quest. I used to be a permanent guest at the Algemeen Rijksarchief at The Hague, enjoying the generous assistance of E. van Laar and F. van Anrooy. In addition I made copious use of the facilities of the Amsterdam Gemeentearchief, and I am grateful to its director, dr. C.W. Pieterse, and in particular to ms. Odette Vlessing. I also utilized the national archives in Haarlem and Groningen, as well as numerous municipal archives in The Netherlands and the Archives Nationales in Paris. Without the vast collection of the Bibliotheca Rosenthaliana my work would have been impossible, and I owe a vote of thanks to its staff, especially its librarian Mr. F. Hoogewoud.

I have very fond memories of the previous librarian, the late Dr. Leo Fuks, as well as of the many fruitful contacts with Prof. Rena Fuks-Mansfeld during her editorship of the Bibliotheca Rosenthaliana. The numerous discussions with my good friend, the late Prof. Max Gans, enriched my knowledge and understanding.

Many a day was spent at the Central Archives for the History of the Jewish People in Jerusalem, with whose director, Aryeh Segal, I have maintained close and friendly contacts ever since my first days in Israel. The microfilms of the Institute and the thousands of copies of documents from Dutch archives in the possession of the Institute for Research on Dutch Jewry saved me numerous journeys back and forth to The Netherlands. I would like to express my particular gratitude to the former librarian of the Institute for Research on Dutch Jewry, Mrs. Shulamith Vomberg-Samuel, and its present director, Ms. Chaya Brasz, whose assistance has greatly facilitated my work.

Dr. Marion Aptroot (Harvard University) kindly checked the English transcription of the Yiddish quotes. It goes without saying that it has been a profound source of satisfaction for me to be able to discuss any and all aspects of this study with my son Dan.

I very much appreciate that Henk and Ruth Nijk, my collaborators on several previous projects, were prepared to translate the original Dutch text into English. The intense devotion with which they approached their task was evident throughout our discussions.

The English edition of this work could not have been realized without the assistance of the Authority for Research and Development Internal Funds and the Institute for Jewish Studies of the Hebrew University (Federman Foundation) in Jerusalem. I owe a special debt of gratitude to Prof. Joseph Hacker, who devoted much time and effort to solving the partly technical problem of a subsidy.

Ever since our first discussion I have had most pleasant contacts with Ms. Saskia de Vries, director and publisher of the Amsterdam University Press, and her staff and it is a source of particular satisfaction for me to see this book published under the imprint of the publisher of my Alma Mater.

I cannot conclude these acknowledgements without remembering my wife Frederika (1913-1991). Not only was she my support during the many years of our marriage, but she was at all times intensely interested in all my activities. She always critically read and corrected my publications before they were sent to the publisher, and I have been painfully aware of her absence during the preparation of this book.

Jozeph Michman

Foreword

Not long after the establishment of the Institute for Research on Dutch Jewry at the Hebrew University of Jerusalem during the early 1970s, I initiated an ambitious project: the publication of the principal sources of the history of the Jews of The Netherlands, under the title Neerlandica Judaica – accompanied by a translation into English and a scientific apparatus. Similar publications exist in other countries, such as the Gallia-Judaica and the Germania Judaica – even though their structures are different from the one envisaged by me.

With the support of the Jewish Cultural Foundation and the Israel National Academy for Sciences we were able to start off several young researchers on the basis of an outline I developed. I considered it advisable to start with the period of the Emancipation. There were already many publications on the subject available that were familiar to me, from my work on my doctoral dissertation on David Franco Mendes. In addition we were able to avail ourselves of the services of two young researchers, Bertie Half and my son Dan, who had both written university theses on the subject.

As soon as I read the first edited sources, serious doubts arose that my planned framework might be too ambitious, and whether we were in danger of putting the cart before the horse. A closer analysis of the sources showed that they failed to confirm the picture that had become accepted on the strength of earlier publications. Those originating from Jewish authors were written from an ideological perspective that only reflected the views of the proponents of the Emancipation, and the complete integration of the Jews within the Dutch society. Non-Jewish historians, to the extent that they had dealt with the subject at all, readily assumed a development different from the one that had, in fact, taken place.

As a consequence it became clear that it would be impossible to make a responsible selection from the source materials until the editor involved would have obtained a historiographically clear overall picture – different from the traditional, never before critically examined view of the history of the Dutch Jews during the Emancipation period.

It became clear to me that first of all I myself would have to research the source materials, before I could envisage publishing them. This research has taken me more than twenty years, mainly due to the fact that – apart from my professional activities – my attention was claimed by numerous other projects. Foremost among these was the *Pinkas, Geschiedenis van de Joden in Nederland*, a Hebrew edition of which was published in 1985 by Yad Vashem, in addition to an expanded and revised Dutch edition in 1992. The Hebrew edition was prepared together with the late Hartog Beem and my son Dan; the Dutch edition together with J. Sanders and Victor Brilleman. Already in the *Pinkas* I

was able to include much of the knowledge I had gathered about the Emancipation era. The necessity to examine separately each and every city and town for
the Lexicon of Jewish communities that forms a part of the *Pinkas*, proved a
valuable support and a useful check of my conclusions about The Netherlands
as a whole.

On the strength of this study of the initial group of source materias I decided
to apply a chronological and thematic framework for the treatment of the very
extensive material. It seemed evident to me that one chronological narrative
could not possibly do justice to the various primary themes relating to this
period. For example, the manner in which the Emancipation decree was conceived and passed, as well as its practical consequences – or possibly lack of
consequences – are of an entirely different nature from the coincident turbulent
events within the Jewish community itself. The various religious, social and
cultural happenings were of course closely linked to the political events, but
each and every subject had its own causality and consequences.

In the course of the years I have published a number of articles about these
subjects. In 1976 my first article appeared, entitled 'Gothic Towers on a Corinthian Building'. This resulted in a polemic with Prof. A.H. Huussen, according
to whom I had failed to pay attention to the opposition against the emancipation among the Jews themselves [see *BMGN* 94 (1979), pp. 75-83, and my
answer in *BMGN* 96 (1981), pp. 78-82]. Since this article – included as Chapter
2 in this book – now forms a part of the overall research, much of it devoted to
the events within and around the Jewish community, we may assume that the
cause of this misunderstanding will have disappeared.

The modern historian, being a child of his times, realizes that he cannot
claim his historiographic opinions to represent the absolute truth. This does
not absolve him from the responsibility of trying to approach historical truth as
closely as possible. Because of this I have done my utmost to be guided only by
the source materials. Anybody interested in more detailed information about
my analysis of the era may consult an article by my son, Prof. Dan Michman:
'"La Période Batave" et la "Période française" dans l'histoire des Juifs de
Hollande (1795-1813) et son évaluation dans l'historiographie' in: *Tsafon, Revue
des Etudes des Juifs du Nord*, 5, 1991, pp. 3-49.

Most of these chapters were previously published in various scientific collections and journals, particularly in the *Studia Rosenthaliana*. Certain chapters (7,
8) were written especially for this book, whereas others (5, 9) have been completely rewritten and updated. In addition, all chapters were re-edited by me in
order to eliminate repetitions, correct mistakes and where necessary add newly
available data from primary and secondary sources. Concise biographies of the
foremost contemporary Jewish personalities have been included in the footnotes.

This book is not the final word on the subject. Much of the material that is
now available has been given a summary treatment, since I preferred a balanced
overall picture over comprehensiveness. I would be gratified if the text would
inspire others to devote more detailed research efforts to this highly intriguing
field. I also hope that its publication in English will contribute to the vicissitudes
of Dutch Jewry during this momentous period claiming their rightful place in
Jewish historiography.

Chronological Summary of the Political Changes in The Netherlands between the Years 1780-1815

1766-1795	Reign of Prince William V of Orange, Stadtholder of the Republic of the United Netherlands.
1787	Patriot revolt.
September 1787	Invasion of the Prussian army – Restoration of William V.
October 10, 1787	Capitulation of the Patriot government of Amsterdam to the Prussian army.
December 1794	Invasion of the Republic by the French army.
January 1795	William V escapes to England – Establishment of the Batavian Republic.
March 1796	The National Assembly.
August 5, 1796	Adoption of the Law separating Church and State.
September 2, 1796	The Emancipation decree and enfranchisement of the Jews of The Netherlands.
August 1, 1797	Elections for the National Assembly.
August 8, 1796	Plebiscite rejecting the draft Constitution.
January 22, 1798	Coup d'état and installation of government of Radical Patriots.
June 12, 1798	Radical government deposed.
1798-1801	Executive Governmental Authority under five directors.
1801-1805	National Authority of twelve members.
April 29, 1805 – June 4, 1806	Rutger Jan Schimmelpenninck Grand Pensionary.
1806-1810	Louis Napoleon, King of Holland.
July 9, 1810	The Dutch territories annexed by France.
December 1, 1813	William, son of William V, proclaimed sovereign ruler of The Netherlands (from 1815: King William I).

1 Prelude – Parnasim[1] and Patriots

The years between 1795 and 1813, which may rightly be called 'The French Era'[2] in the history of The Netherlands, brought about far-reaching changes in the life of the Dutch people in almost every field. The particularist Republic of the United Netherlands, whose individual regions and cities enjoyed a considerable measure of independence, was replaced by a centrally governed unitary state. As regards its system of government, the dual authority of the States General and the Princes of Orange was substituted by a constitutional monarchy. Despite efforts in many countries to restore the Ancien Régime, the international situation had become very different from that during the Republic, and this was also reflected in the economic and cultural sphere.

Even including the entire course of the French Revolution, it took a mere twenty-five years for Europe to assume an entirely new aspect. Regardless of how revolutionary this period was, there had been clear indications during the eighteenth century that changes were in the offing. This also applied to the Republic, and the status of Jews is a clear example of this. In non-Jewish circles the question arose whether the notion of equality did not require the abolition of the social and economic segregation and discrimination of the Jews, or – alternatively – whether the hoped-for new society allowed room for Jews if they insisted on adhering to their religion.[3]

Questions also began to be asked among some Jews about the feasibility and justifiability of a continued observance of religious precepts in the same way as had been done throughout the ages if this were to prevent integration of the

---

1   Parnasim were the governors of the High-German (Ashkenazi) Jewish community. The Hebrew word is *'parnasim'*. In the Dutch text they are variously called 'Parnasim' or 'Parnassijns' – sometimes even with a double plural ending: 'Parnassims'. We have used the term Parnasim throughout.
2   The expression 'French Era' is certainly correct when describing the history of contemporary Jewry, in view of the major influence exercised by the French authorities during the entire period in question. Similarly, the sub-division into the periods covering the Batavian Republic (1795-1806), the Kingdom of the Netherlands (1806-1810) and the annexation by France (1810-1813) is also highly meaningful for the position of the Jews.
3   For a discussion of the position of the Jews in the Republic at the end of the 18th century, see A.H. Huussen and H.J. Wedman, 'Politieke en sociaal-culturele aspecten van de emancipatie der joden in de Republiek der Verenigde Nederlanden', *Documentatieblad Werkgroep achttiende eeuw*, 1981 (51/52), pp. 207-24.

Jews in the non-Jewish world.[4] Even more than in other countries, some Jews in the Republic had permitted themselves a less scrupulous observance of the religious codex, without however seeking affiliation with one of the Christian denominations – a phenomenon that in other countries would be found only at the end of the eighteenth century.

These and other developments are reflected in the French era. However, a chain of events preceded the invasion of the French army in 1795 which requires a certain insight in order to understand the attitude and behavior of both Jews and non-Jews following the establishment of the Batavian Republic. We are referring to the Patriot Revolt of 1787.

As is known, the Patriots aspired towards a reorganization of the government at both the local and national level: the oligarchic regime of the Regents had to be destroyed and the People had to be enabled to influence the composition of the various authorities, which in turn would be accountable to the People. The societal conception underlying this democratic form of administration differed from the Christian notion of God's intervention in world events. This was in itself a subject of discussion between theologians and philosophers, who had met with widespread acceptance of their ideas.

Nevertheless it would be wrong to assume that the entire Patriot following consisted of intellectuals with a clear conception of, or interest in, social systems.[5] Looking only at Amsterdam, the city that was to occupy a pivotal position in all Jewish affairs, the 'People', who according to the Patriotic view were to be the bearers of the future governmental system, consisted mainly of shopkeepers and craftsmen. The individuals concerned cared first and foremost about their livelihood, and by no means did the national government stand at the head of their priorities. It is exactly this aspect that seriously complicated relations between the people – specifically the Patriot part of the population – and the Jews.

What these shopkeepers and craftsmen desired was not just a free economy, but one that would protect their economic status in the face of the continual impoverishment of the Republic towards the end of the eighteenth century. In practice this meant that aliens should not be allowed to compete with them – and in their eyes Jews *were* aliens.

---

4   Standard works about the changes within the Jewish society under the influence of the Emancipation are: Jacob Katz, *Tradition and Crisis*, Jewish Society at the end of the Middle Ages, New York, 1961; *idem, Out of the Ghetto*, The Social Background of Jewish Emancipation, Cambridge Mass.-New York, 1973. Neither of these works deals with the specific situation in The Netherlands. For this, see M. Bolle, *De opheffing van de autonomie der Kehillot* (Jewish Communities] *in Nederland 1796*, Amsterdam, 1960, pp. 62-78.

5   'From either a geographical, a social, or an intellectual point of view Patriotism is a complicated phenomenon,' is the opinion of E.H. Kossmann (*The Low Countries*, Oxford 1978, p. 43). The Dutch edition of the same work even says: 'verbijsterend complex' ('astoundingly complex'). We do not want to enter into recent discussions about the nature of Patriotism, since we are mainly concerned with their relationship to the Jews, particularly in Amsterdam – an aspect, by the way, that is not referred to at all in the discussions. About the discussion, see *De Droom van de Revolutie, Nieuwe benaderingen van het Patriotisme*, H. Bos- W.W. Mijnhardt (eds.), Amsterdam, 1988.

Exactly what this meant for the Jews of Amsterdam had already been experienced forty years earlier. In 1747 and 1748 a series of insurrections had taken place throughout the country, the most serious of which had occurred in Amsterdam. Then, too, the instigators had demanded the dismissal of the Regents and a democratization of the government. Even though the initiative had been taken by well-to-do burghers and intellectuals, the population of Amsterdam proved to have an entirely different agenda: a far more stringent supervision of the implementation of the charters, i.e. the local by-laws which excluded Jews from most professions. There was an insistent demand for the establishment of a diamond workers' guild, as well as protests against competition from Jewish tailors.[6] For the Jews the establishment of a guild in the diamond industry would have meant the virtual closure of one of the few professions that was open to them, and in which they were strongly represented. The threat was deflected thanks to the fact that Prince William IV who, borne on a wave of revolutionary enthusiasm, had been appointed Stadtholder, had in fact chosen the side of the Regents and – to the intense disillusionment of his followers – refused to depose the Amsterdam magistrates. None of the anti-Jewish measures proposed by the People's Movement were accepted by the sitting magistrates. In light of the above it is not surprising that the Parnasim saw an ally in the ruling oligarchy, and that the House of Orange enjoyed an immense popularity in Jewish circles.

The Amsterdam Patriots of 1787 were no more kindly disposed towards the Jews than their predecessors had been in 1748, and their objectives were basically the same. It is therefore understandable that the Jewish leadership, as well as the members of their communities, had every reason to favor the House of Orange over the Patriots.

Undoubtedly the Patriot Revolt posed a real danger for the Jews, and their dread of a Patriot victory is evident from contemporary Jewish chronicles. Together with the official sources, they present a clear picture of enormous tensions and dramatic events.

One of these chronicles was written by a simple cooper called Zalman ben Moshe Prinz, who evidently barely knew more than what he himself had seen

---

6   For this, see H. Brugmans and A. Frank, *Geschiedenis der Joden in Nederland*, I, Amsterdam, 1940, pp. 574-78; J. Michman, H. Beem and D. Michman, *Pinkas*, (Dutch edition, 1992, pp. 54-55). The *Jiddisje kroniek* of Braatbaart from 1747-1752 mentions the measures taken by the diamond workers and tailors, as well as the pogrom-like mood. The plundering of Jewish homes was only narrowly averted. The chronicler summarizes the actions of the 'Doelists' as follows: 'For all the signatures of the burghers were only intended against us Jews; and sometimes the non-Jews would say among each other when they met in their assemblies: "Why shouldn't we allow the Jews their trade, for soon it will be all over for them." If, God forbid, their plans had succeeded, we Jews would have been exiled and there would have been nobody to come to our aid.' *De Zeven Provinciën in beroering* (ed. L. Fuks), Amsterdam (no year), pp. 50, 93, 118-19.

and heard.[7] The second testimony is that of the Portuguese-Jewish author and poet David Franco Mendes, whose story similarly is no more than a chronicle of the events, and who – even though he belonged to the elite of the Portuguese-Jewish community – was clearly unfamiliar with what was happening behind the scenes.[8] This makes a third and rather unexpected source of even greater interest to us. The Protocol Book of the Parnasim of the Amsterdam Ashkenazi community contains a rare document written by someone who was intimately familiar with all the discussions and dealings of the college of the Parnasim. The lengthy document, composed in a mixture of Hebrew and Yiddish, must therefore have been written by one of the Parnasim or the secretary of the college.[9] Even the title, *Gods werken* ('The Works of God'), evokes the serious danger from which the Jews narrowly escaped. It is derived from a hymn that occupies a central place in the Jewish New Year liturgy, and the author(s)' choice not only invests the narrative with a solemn atmosphere, but also conveys the conviction that only Divine intervention saved the Jews from imminent danger.[10]

7   Published by M. Roest, 'Losse Bijdragen tot de Geschiedenis der Joden in Nederland, Kronijke van de jaren 1787/8' in *Israëlische Letterbode* 1-12, Amsterdam, 1875-1888: I (1875), nrs. 2-6 (hereafter: Prinz), The text, written in Yiddish, is divided into paragraphs. Roest has made a Dutch summary of each paragraph. See also R. and L. Fuks, 'Joodse geschiedschrijving in de Republiek in de 17de en 18de eeuw', *St. Ros.* VI (1972), pp. 159-60, and J. Shatzky, 'The Last Manifestation of Yiddish Language and Literature in Holland', *Yivobleter* X (1936), pp. 254-57 (Yiddish). The events are also told in a Yiddish song of twenty-seven strophes. See H. Beem, 'Oranje Boven Fifa', *NIW*, Jrg. 95, 1-1-1965; the whole text is printed in Ch. Shmeruk, 'Yiddish "Historical songs" in Amsterdam in the 17th and 18th Century', *SDT* 4 (1985), pp. 156-161.
8   A translation of this chronicle, with an introduction, was published by R. and L. Fuks: 'Een Portugese kroniek over het einde van de Patriottentijd door David Franco Mendes', *St. Ros.* VII (1973), pp. 8-39, hereafter quoted: with reference to introduction: Fuks; with reference to text: Franco Mendes.
9   The Secretary during this period was the Chief Beadle Chaim Moshe Cauveren, who died on September 17, 1796. Between 1773 and 1796 the Protocols were written by Isaac Cohen. In terms of learning, either of them could have been the author of the document. See D.M. Sluys, 'De Protocollen der Hoogduitse-Joodse gemeente te Amsterdam,' *BMGJW* IV (1928), p. 123.
10   GAA, PA, *Protokolbuch* Joodse Gemeente Amsterdam 1787/8. The text consists of four parts: 1. 12 Sivan (= May 30, 1787) till the second half of June (fo. 587-590); 2. 15 Elul (= August 29) till 12 Tishri (= September 24), fo. 594; 3. 18 Tishri (= September 30) till 22 Marheshvan (= November 3), fo. 603-6-4) from 20 Adar I (= February 28, 1788) till 27 Menahem-Av (= August 30, 1788), fo. 622-624. Also included in the text are the verbatim proclamations on behalf of the Parnasim, in Yiddish; letters (in Dutch) received by the Parnasim from the municipal authorities; decisions by the Parnasim; and so forth. Part 4 is entirely different from the first three parts. It describes the ceremonies following the restoration of William V and concludes with a detailed report on the visit by Prince William V and Princess Wilhelmina to the Great Synagogue.
     Despite its official character, the document is very entertaining. The doubts, fears and even anger of the Parnasim are described in a lively style. The language is mostly Biblical Hebrew, but the authors do not shrink from suddenly changing to Yiddish or introducing Talmudic expressions. It is clear that the authors were quite familiar with the Jewish sources.
     A Dutch translation of the text was published by D.M. Sluys, 'Uit bange dagen', *VA* IV (1927), pp. 324-27, 340-43, 371-74, 386-88, 407-09, 420-23 (hereafter: Sluys, Uit bange dagen). The Hebrew and Yiddish text of the document, supplemented with the separate Yiddish proclamations in the synagogue, were published by me (including an introduction) in *SDJ*, Vol. 3. Jerusalem, 1981, pp. 1-54.

The Fighting near the House of Deputy Chief Constable Papegaay

There had been riots in Amsterdam from the middle of May 1787, which on May 28 escalated into a proper civil war. On the evening of May 29 the Patriots attempted to occupy Kattenburg Island. This was also the first time they used firearms, the consequences of which were felt in the adjoining Jewish quarter. Simultaneously small bands of people roamed the city, plundering the homes of notables, including magistrates, known for their Orangist sympathies. The gendarmes who either failed to intervene or acted too late, subsequently defended themselves by claiming that they had not received orders to fire.[11] In fact, total anarchy reigned in Amsterdam, and it is fair to assume that as well as idealistic Patriots, also – and in particular – criminal elements participated in the lootings. In this serious and complicated situation all those threatened had to act in their own defense, and some hired people to protect their property.[12]

According to rumors in the Jewish quarter, attacks were being planned on the synagogues of the two communities. Whether such plans did indeed exist is unclear, but these stories were widely believed. As a pre-emptive measure the Portuguese community called up sixty men to stand guard in the courtyard of their synagogue; the Parnasim of the Ashkenazi community engaged thirty men to guard their synagogues.[13] On Thursday May 30, Patriot looters prepared to attack the home of Deputy Chief Constable Papegaay. The Deputy had heard about the plan, and it is a sign of the times that, rather than rallying his gendarmes, he hired a small private army, which included some thirty to forty young Jews.[14] The fighting took a rather unfavorable turn for the Patriots, who apparently had not expected any credible resistance. As soon as they arrived at the house, the defenders made a sally, causing the attackers to take to their heels. Each side left behind one dead.[15]

In the Jewish quarter the outcome of the fight was regarded as a great victory, and the participants received a hero's welcome.[16] This opinion was by no means shared by the Parnasim, who in their protocol call the fighters 'riff-raff' and 'dregs of the populace'. This was because the skirmish had created serious resentment among the Patriot leadership, which also chose to associate the decision of the Parnasim of the two communities to post guards at their synagogues with the relatively large number of Jews who had taken part in

---

11 According to *Nieuwe Nederlandse Jaarboeken* (hereafter: *NNJB*), XX (1788), Leiden-Amsterdam, p. 1069.
12 A typical story is that about an inn-keeper who posted a number of 'bruisers' in front of his establishment, causing the plunderers to steal away. See *Nieuwe Nederlandsche Courant*, no. 71 (June 13, 1787).
13 Franco Mendes, p. 30.
14 The figures differ according to the source.
15 Sluys was able to ascertain (p. 387) that the Jewish casualty was called Leib ben Abraham Hilsum. Prinz as well as Fuks (p. 18) call him Leib Judis (Leib son of Judith), the name by which he was known in public.
16 Even the Portuguese Franco Mendes writes admiringly: '...e os valerosos Asquenazim (que chamou por adjuda) não sommente lhe deffenderão heroicam (en) te mas tambem apaliarão os Amutinad(o)s' (p. 31).

the fight. The Patriots concluded that the Jews, who were known to be almost to a man on the side of the Prince, had formed a small army with the express purpose of actively intervening in a civil war.

The same day the city's Defense Committee dispatched a letter to the two communities requesting that they immediately send a delegation 'in order to discuss ways and means of preserving peace and safety, also among the Nation.'[17] The Ashkenazi Parnasim invited their Portuguese colleagues to send a joint delegation, but this was declined. It is typical of the distant attitude of the Portuguese Jews towards their Ashkenazi co-religionists that the *Mahamad* (as the board of the Portuguese community was called) refused to entertain the proposal.[18] However, they did not object to a mutual consultation prior to the meeting with the gentlemen of the Defense Committee.

In the course of the eventual discussion three members of the Committee, B.E. Abbema, L. Hovy and J.B. Bicker, seriously reproached the Ashkenazi Parnasim, accusing them of conducting anti-government activities.[19] The Parnasim countered that they were not responsible for Papegaay having hired Jews, and they pointed out the fact that the guards they themselves had recruited had not been involved in the fighting. However, they had considered it essential to guard the synagogues in view of the rumors of a planned pillage, which had caused considerable apprehension in the Jewish quarter.

The discussion ended on quite a different tone from the one in which it had begun. An agreement was reached that was to form the foundation of the future policy of the Parnasim. They would do everything in their power to deter Jews from intervening in the conflict in any way. Those who broke this rule would be severely punished. The Defense Committee, on the other hand, would let bygones be bygones and drop the charges against those who had been arrested for assisting Papegaay.[20] Given the well-known sympathy of the Jews for the House of Orange, the Patriots were very much interested in neutralizing them. It had already become clear how dangerous twenty thousand Jews might be if they chose to ally themselves with the Orangists: they might even tilt the balance of power in the city against the Patriots. The Parnasim, on their side, were fearful that Jewish involvement in the conflict might lead to a blood bath.

---

17 During the Middle Ages the word 'Nation' was used to identify aliens from the same country. In the course of time it came to refer exclusively to the Jews. Thus, even without the addition of the word 'Jewish', 'the Nation' referred to the Jewish population of Amsterdam.

18 There are various indications that the relations between Portuguese and Ashkenazim deteriorated during the first half of the 18th century.

19 Balthasar Elias Abbema (1737-1796), Jan Berend Bicker (1746-1812) and Lodewijk Hovy de Jonge (1740-1822) belonged to the wealthy merchants class and they were leading Patriots. In 1796 Bicker participated in the debates about the emancipation of the Jews as a member of the National Assembly, arguing that the Jews were a separate nation, and that as long as they desired to maintain this position, they could not simultaneously be members of the Batavian nation. Even so he pleaded for the improvement of the standard of living and the education of the Jews, and stated that it should be forbidden to insult them (Bolle, pp. 152-53).

About Hovy, see: J.H. Hovy, 'Het leven van de patriot Lodewijk Hovy (1740- 1822), zijn rol als vroedschap van Amsterdam gedurende de jaren 1780-1787', *Jbk. Amstelodamum* (79), 1987, pp. 125-62.

20 Prinz, para. 12.

They issued a proclamation calling on all their members to stay out of the political conflict, and not even discuss it with either Jews or gentiles.

Meanwhile the fighting at the Papegaay residence continued to incite emotions, as illustrated by the following satirical poem:

The Sheeny Parrot

The sheeny Parrot, without Honor and Loyalty,
At a certain moment was not safe in his cage.
Not a Christian soul was willing to come to his aid.
Wherefore it afterwards became publicly known
That he surrounded himself with a sheeny Squealers' band.
Such a bad parrot should have the feathers pulled out of his behind.[21]

We understand why the Patriot's propaganda wanted to exploit the incident and inflame public feeling against Papegaay and the Jews. Yet the question remains why Papegaay had mainly selected Jews to help him. A Portuguese Jewish patriot in an unpublished manuscript claims that the Jews had been seduced by promise of financial gain. 'One should ask oneself', he writes, 'whether a poor laborer, an Ashkenazi Jew or member of whatever nation, who at times earns less than three bits a day, should not be allowed to help safeguard someone's home from violation and plunder if this could earn him two or three guilders'.[22] This of course does not explain Papegaay's predilection for Jews, and why he did not employ Christian working men who would also have liked to earn two or three guilders.

Another contemporary Patriot source has the following story: 'Since Deputy Chief-Constable Papegaay – [was] no less hated because of his at times inhuman behavior – (than Chief-Magistrate Dedel; J.M.) they set out [towards his house],

---

21 **De smouse Papegaay**
De smouse Papegaay, ontbloot van Eer en Trouw,
Was op een zek'ren tijd niet veilig in zijn kouw,
Daar was geen Christenmensch die hem te hulp wou komen.
Dus heeft men naderhand ook openbaar vernomen
Dat hij het Smousenrot van Zingers bij hem had.
Trek zulk een slegte Lor de veeren uit zijn gat.

'Ernstige en boertige vaerzen over de Zaaken des Vaderlands. In Holland 1787.' I owe a debt to the late M.H. Gans of Amsterdam whose collection contains a copy of this booklet, and who drew my attention to this doggerel verse. The same collection also contains a verse entitled 'De Jood Patriot' (The Patriot Jew', p. 17), evidently intended to win Jews for the Patriot cause. The text is in a kind of bowdlerized Dutch intended to represent the Jewish 'gibberish'. A linguistically curious aspect of this text is the apparent assumption that Jews were confused about the correct use of the consonant *h*. Thus: iele = hele (all, whole), or ijgen = hijgen (panting, gasping); yet: Horanje = Oranje (Orange); halsie = als ie (if he); hadem = adem (breath); heksersitie = exersitie (drill, practice), and geheert = geëerd (honored). See also *Memorbook*, p. 277.

22 'Korte en Zaakelijke Verdediging voor de Joodsche Natie teegen een zeekeren brief geplaatst in de Nederlandsche Verlemsche Courant van den 13 Juny 1787 onder de zinspreuk Nihil impedit artis officium.' The author refers to himself as: 'a Portuguese Jew, an upright Patriot and lover of justice.' See J.S. da Silva Rosa, *Bibliographie der Literatur über die Emanzipation der Juden in Holland*, Frankfurt am Main, 1912, no. 1.

but hearing that he had several Jews in his house to assist him, they desisted. (The fight, and the ignominious defeat, is completely passed over. J.M.) It is said that the aforementioned Papegaay had contacted the Jews under the pretext that Roman-Catholics were about to plunder their synagogues, and thus arouse the Jews. He succeeded in his purpose, since many ran to their church in order to protect it, where Papegaay told them about the danger to his own home, and asked them to send a number of Jews to his house, in return for which he would help them, after which it is reliably told some forty Jews repaired to his house to assist him.'[23] What we see here is a somewhat transparent ploy to set Jews and Catholics against each other. Nothing at all is known about Roman-Catholic looters, and the story was clearly invented for propaganda purposes.

A more credible explanation for Papegaay's recruitment of Jews is supplied by an article that appeared in the *Nederlandsche Courant* of June 15, 1787, intended to mitigate another article that had appeared two days earlier in the same newspaper.[24] This second article, printed in the form of a Reader's Letter, states: 'I can assure you gentlemen that Jews who are born in Amsterdam are very clear-thinking people; but that many of them have been misled by what Deputy Chief-Constable Papegaay would have had them believe, [namely] that if the Patriots emerged victorious, the Jews would be forbidden to peddle any of their wares in the city. In light of the foregoing, it is easy to imagine the effect this has had on the minds of so many hundreds of poor and simple people who are trying to earn their daily bread in the city.'

Is it reasonable to assume that Papegaay did indeed use this argument, and that there were plans to curtail or even prohibit Jewish economic activities – particularly those of peddlers and petty merchants? Given the intentions of the 'Doelists',[25] it is clear that the question should be answered in the affirmative. We do not even need to rely on past experience, for there are many indications that events would have taken the same turn in 1787. This is evident from utterances of several Jewish Patriots who in 1795 united themselves in the Jewish club Felix Liberate. During the first public meeting of the club on February 18, 1795, S. de Jonge Meyersz said: 'Would it be sufficient for me to point out that among the many demands made at the time was the following: that the guilds would be restored to their full power? Wouldn't this naturally have meant that the Jews, having been deprived of their livelihoods, would have been reduced to the most abject poverty? How far would the generosity of the Patriots of that time have been extended by quietly tolerating the Jews' pursu-

---

23 'Echte beschrijving van het Tumult binnen Amsterdam byzonder op het eiland Kattenburg voorgevallen 29 May 1787 en eenige volgende dagen met de overwinning van gemeld Eiland uit echte stukken byeenverzameld, Amsterdam (1787)' (GAA). See also the thesis: 'Geschiedenis van de Crewd in Amsterdam 1696, 1747, 1787'. (GAA, no. BB. 0177).
24 For this article, see the main text below.
25 Members of the Amsterdam Civil Guard, who met in the Doelen, a place that would typically include a shooting range.

ance of certain menial occupations remains to be seen.'[26] Someone else lamented: 'Obviously our Patriotism had not yet matured seven or eight years ago,'[27] thereby admitting that the poor Jews had indeed good reason to fear the Patriots. However, the most incisive formulation of the danger to the Jews is contained in an address before the National Assembly:

> *... when a start was made to depose Regents whom the Jews regarded as their protectors, wasn't it only natural that the Jews, who only knew their chains and who had not the slightest notion of the meaning of the word Freedom, would disapprove of all these acts? No wonder, therefore, that the Jews, who in their own way were managing reasonably well, trembled at the idea of a Constitutional revolution that could not possibly bring them any gain, but did involve the risk that they would lose everything.*

It is understandable that the idea took hold among the Jews that 'Patriotism only meant the very strictest maintenance of ancient privileges and customs ... and which, once they were so maintained, would have caused the Jews to lose the few remaining sources of livelihood they had tacitly been allowed'.[28] How justified this fear was became apparent during the Revolution of 1795:

> *... how much effort was invested in preserving ancient, virtually extinct guilds in order to break the little glassware and pottery by means of which destitute Jews and heavily pregnant women with barely enough clothing on their bodies to cover their shame, attempted to earn a crust of dry bread? What kind of frightful scenes have been provoked in the so-called Jews' Corner, especially in Amsterdam?*[29]

After the Revolution such a zealous defense of the loyalty of the Jews to the Orangist regents of 1787 required considerable courage. Despite the opposition of most Jews to the new Republic, the Jewish Patriots regarded themselves as tribunes of the people. They undoubtedly knew what would have been in

---

26　'Aanspraak gedaan in de Societeit Felix Libertate op den 18 Februari 1795 door den burger S. de Jonge Meyersz, Amsterdam 1795' (Silva Rosa, *Bibliographie*, no. 12). Comp. also the 'Zeer interessante briev van een joodschen burger te Amsterdam aan een Joodschen burger te Rotterdam over de tegenwoordige Staatsomwenteling in Nederland' (Silva Rosa, *Bibliographie*, no. 7), the author of which was M.S. Asser. Asser claims that the Jews had been misled into thinking that 'the difference in the ideas of the Patriots and those of the Orangists was that the first-mentioned demanded a strict implementation of the existing laws and ancient privileges which (so they believed) meant that Jews had to reside in closed streets – [and] that they were not allowed to engage in retail trade – so that, if the Patriots should at any time gain a majority, the Jews would in the most absolute sense be ruined and might even be exiled from the country.' Possibly Asser intentionally exaggerated in order to inflate the rumors spread by the Orangists *ad absurdum*.

27　'De zaak der Nederlandsche Jooden verdeedigd door eenen vriend der waarheid en rechtvaardigheid, Het eerste jaar der Bataafse Vrijheid' (Silva Rosa, *Bibliographie*, no. 68, p. 28).

28　'Vertoog overgegeeven aan de Bataafse Nationale Vergadering Representeerende het volk van Nederland door een aantal Joden wonende in de Bataafse Nederlanden en betoog van het onwederspreekbaar recht der Joden om als dadelijke Burgers van het Bataafse Gemeenebest gehandhaafd te worden, den 12 van Oogstmaand 1796.' The Hague, 1796 (Silva Rosa, *Bibliographie*, no. 78). The petitioners included M.S. Asser.

29　*Loc. cit.*

store for the Jewish populace in 1787 if the Patriots had their way without being curbed by the French conquerors. This also explains why it had been so easy for Papegaay to recruit several dozen Jews to give the looters a thrashing. The Patriot leadership, which was of course familiar with the mood among the Christian and Jewish populace, was rightly concerned about the possible consequences of the fighting at the Papegaay residence, both for their Patriotic followers and for the Jews, and it was of vital interest for them to prevent the arousal of the Jewish masses. For this they needed the cooperation of the Parnasim – the only people capable of influencing the Jewish proletarians who were spoiling for a fight.[30] The Defense Committee, on its part, seems to have promised to put an end to the prevailing lawlessness, since no further looting took place after May 30.

Relations with the Various Authorities

If the Parnasim believed that their discussion with the Defense Committee had settled the matter, subsequent developments would soon prove otherwise. That same day an assistant to Chief Constable W.C. Backer (1739-1809) showed up at the Parnasim with the following message: The Chief Constable had heard that the Parnasim had visited the Defense Committee, and that its members had intimidated them. He wanted it to be clearly understood that he was the sole authority whom the Jews could and should trust. In addition, he invited them to come and see him on the following day (Friday, June 1). Nevertheless, the Parnasim decided to go ahead with the announcement they had promised the Defense Committee to make, assuming – correctly, as it happens – that Backer's authority in Amsterdam was less absolute than he would have them believe. The Portuguese Parnasim were of the same opinion. The discussion with the Chief Constable did indeed take place the following day, but was unable to change the situation.

Shortly after receiving the Chief Constable's message, the Parnasim had other visitors. A twelve-man strong delegation from the joint committee of Patriotic Clubs, headed by Zion Quint (1733-1788), came to register a complaint about the Jewish participation in the fighting at the Papegaay residence. After the Parnasim had once again explained their views and read out their announcement, the delegation departed in a conciliatory mood, promising that they too would help to protect the Jews.

With so many protectors, none of whom seemed to trust the other, the Parnasim considered it advisable not to take any risks. Consequently they recruited no fewer than a hundred men to guard the various synagogues. The Portuguese Parnasim, who had been consulted, added some fifty guards of their own. Together with the horsemen who had been sent by the Defense Committee

---

30 The martial sentiment among the Jews even resulted in a plan to organize them in a separate unit. See Chapter **8**.

to keep a watchful eye,[31] this show of force sufficed to deter the looters and avoid any attempt at revenge. The following Sunday the Ashkenazim reduced the number of guards to thirty and the Portuguese their detachment to twenty. On June 9 all guards were withdrawn.

Franco Mendes and Prinz relate only one fact about the period from early June till the end of September: the understandably unpopular collection by the Civil Guards among the citizenry to defray the cost of arming and protecting the city.[32] The kind of pressure exercised on the Parnasim to recommend this collection becomes evident from the following note by B.E. Abbema dated June 8, 1787 that Colonel Croese showed to the Parnasim. It read:

> *I am confident that the Parnasim of the Ashkenazi community, following your courageous person's representation, shall not refuse to make an announcement in the church with a view to the voluntary gifts for the Guards on duty in your district. If necessary I would ask you to make use of this note before the honorable Parnasim. With due expressions of my great respect, I remain your faithful servant,*
> *(signed) B.E. Abbema.*

This appeal for a fitting contribution to the collection had the desired effect. However, there were other and even more serious difficulties. We already mentioned an article in the *Nederlandsche Courant* of June 13 – also called the *Verlemsche Courant*, after its publisher Jan Verlem of the Warmoesstraat.[33] It was entitled 'Copia eens Briefs uit Amsterdam aan een vriend te Leiden', but the Protocol Book shows it to have been written by the printer: Hermannus Koning in de Watergraafsmeer.[34] The author, a Christian, relates that on Thursday afternoon, May 31, the day of the fighting at Kattenburg, he was visiting a relative in de Jodenbreestraat 'who resides there and keeps a shop, and whose subsistence is mainly dependent on the Jews'. The author drew the attention of the gentlemen of the Defense Committee to the dangerous mood prevailing in the Jewish quarter. Several fashionable Jews, among them a Portuguese, had expressed themselves to the effect that '... the matter could soon be nipped in the bud if the rebellious leaders of the Orangist Party would only distribute money among us Jews, for then we could, together with the Orangists, knock all

---

31 Franco Mendes, p. 32.
32 Franco Mendes, *loc.cit.* says that the Civil Guard accepted the gifts with 'hypocritical civility'.
33 Sluys (p. 341) mistakenly believes that the article appeared in the *Politieke Kruyer*, which was also edited by J. Verlem.
34 About Hermannus (or Harmanus) Koning [1735(6?) – May 23, 1788]: 'De ongelukkige levensbeschrijving van een Amsterdammer', verschenen bij Hermannus Koning (1775), bewerkt en ingeleid door M.J. Dekker', Amsterdam 1965, pp. 16-20. Koning was a printer and publisher of the *Ouderkerkse Courier* and, after this publication had been shut down, he printed the *Nederlandsche Courant* together with J. Verlem as publisher (September 8, 1783 till October 4, 1787). Dekker's supposition that Koning was both the printer and the author of the 'Ongelukkige Levensbeschrijving' is supported by the fact that he wrote articles for the *Nederlandsche Courant*. As regards the Reader's Letter of June 15 (*Nederlandse Courant*, no. 72) he himself told the Beadle, R. Chaim [Cauveren], that he had corrected the article in the previous issue. And see: J.H. van E(eghen), *Jbk. Amstelodamum* 52 (1965), p. 143.

those Patriotic devils dead, since our entire Nation stands solidly behind the Prince'. His brother, too, had assured him that 'among a hundred Jews of the two Nations, fewer than ten were of a different opinion'. After citing the example of King Saul that God had given them [the Jews] in His anger, he continues: '... and don't they realize how even now Sovereign princes treat them worse than slaves, and that under the kind and judicious regime of this Government they enjoy every privilege and freedom alongside the Christians?' The latter comment was obviously aimed at countering the rumors about economic measures against the Jews and the curtailment of their rights. In actual fact, the tenor of the article was by no means antagonistic to the Jews, particularly when compared with other Patriot utterances.[35]

It stands to reason that the Parnasim were frightened. Here was a clear suggestion of Jewish collaboration with the Orangists – the very same accusation the Parnasim had faced during their discussion with the Defense Committee. The invitation to forceful intervention in the Jewish Quarter was no less embarrassing. Could the article possibly have been planted by the authorities? The Parnasim decided to inquire with Burgomaster Hendrik Hooft (1716-1794), who advised them to try to prevent the publication of the article (apparently it had not yet been printed). Their next step was to contact the printer and offer him a full refund of all expenses for withholding the letter. Unfortunately, meanwhile the article had been printed, and in reply to the Parnasim's request for a rebuttal, the printer answered that he himself had already decided to write some kind of rectification. He advised the Parnasim to read this first, after which – if they still wanted to react – he would publish an article written by them. Sure enough a letter appeared in the newspaper two days later, addressed to 'Mister Newspaperman', stating among other things that 'the Parnasim are busy advising the Jews to behave in a quiet and peaceful manner, and not to take sides in the presently prevailing divisions'. It looked as though Koning had received inside information, and the phrasing of the article satisfied the Parnasim. Even the paragraph about the reasons why the Jews had come to the aid of Papegaay proved unobjectionable. However, the letter also included the following sentence: 'I do not want to deny that in earlier times many wealthy Portuguese and High-German Jews seemingly rallied to the Prince, but that is politics, in the same way as the present Aristocracy is on the side of the Prince.' Such a hypocritical insinuation could be resented by the Orangist Party as well as by the Jewish masses. The Parnasim held a long meeting and the Protocol Book makes it eminently clear that they were on the horns of a dilemma. In the end they considered it the better part of wisdom not to take up the printer-editor's offer to publish a rejoinder. However, they did decide to inform the Burgomaster and the members of their community that the 'rectification' had not been sent by them.

---

35 In the 'Ongelukkige Levensbeschrijving' Koning's depiction of Jewish types is not unsympathetic either. Towards the end he puts his presumably personal philosophy in the mouth of an agnostic Jew who pleads for mutual tolerance between the different religions (pp. 222-24).

It would have been too much to expect that the proclamation of June 2 would have halted the Jewish participation in the riots – as also becomes clear from an announcement dated June 21:

> *...since it has come to their knowledge that certain persons get out of hand and quarrel, also with the non-circumcised,*[36] *besides entering into discussions in public houses and companies, and provoking and showing partisan behavior...' the Parnasim threaten all those ignoring the prohibition to mix in the political infighting with punishment, to the extent of their power and provided they succeed in tracking down the culprits.*

On July 14 the Parnasim did issue another warning that Jews should keep out of the quarrels and hand over any offenders. This means that there were Patriot sympathizers among the Jews: the repeated warnings of the Parnasim that Jews should avoid being involved in mutual political disputes are in a way clearer proof of this than the article in the *Nederlandsche Courant*. The Portuguese community also had Patriot adherents in its midst, as shown by the *Mahamad's* decision to forbid pupils of the theological seminary (*Medras*) to engage in political discussions.[37] The group of Jewish Patriots was small in number, but they were to become a source of considerable concern for the Parnasim.

On July 27 Chief Constable W. C. Backer was dismissed and in his place was appointed C. van der Hoop Gijsbertz (1752-1817) as Presiding Magistrate and Chief Constable ad interim. The Patriots hoped that he 'would strike the necessary fear into the Orangist Party'.[38] We might well ask whether this was the intention of his summary demand that the Parnasim come and see him – and whether Jewish Patriots could possibly have instigated this most uncivil act. In the course of the discussion Van der Hoop launched into a furious tirade: 'There are very ominous rumors about you. A prayer is said in your synagogues for the success of the Prince, and as a result several Jews have refused to go to the synagogue because they were angered by what they heard.' He insisted that the prayer be deleted, but the Parnasim explained to him that he was referring to a traditional prayer invoking God's blessings on the authorities.[39] They promised to send him an official translation, and when Van der Hoop could not discover anything offensive in it, the ban was rescinded.

During a second discussion on September 1 his tone was very different. He apologized for having sent a low-ranking servant to summon them on the previous occasion, due to his unfamiliarity with the customary ceremonial. The

---

36 'also non-circumcised'. Sluys (p. 373) omits the word 'also' and translates 'non-Israelites'. Regardless whether this is a printing error or not, it changes the meaning of the sentence.

37 *Livro de Resoluçoens*, p. 133 (em 14 Menahem).

38 *NNJB*, 1957, p. 1949.

39 The prayer *Ha-noten teshua...* appears in both the Sephardic and Ashkenazi rites and is therefore of great antiquity. The prayer was put in writing around the 14th century, by the Sephardim in Abudraham, and by the Ashkenazim in Kolbo (1400) (I. Elbogen, *Der jüdische Gottesdienst*, Frankfurt am Main 1924, p. 203; S.I. Bär, *Awodath Jisrael*, Berlin 1937, repr. p. 231). Since the contemporary text always contained a prayer for the welfare of the Sovereign and the municipal authorities, Van der Hoop was unable to object.

Parnasim asked to receive the names of the Jews who had maligned them, but this request was refused. However, Van der Hoop did promise to support the Parnasim in future and quash any further opposition.

Meanwhile the situation became more and more problematic for the Patriots. On September 13 the Prussian army entered the country and soon Amsterdam was the only remaining bulwark of the Revolution. The tense and nervous mood in the city is reflected in the following note by Van der Hoop, dated September 24:

> *The undersigned, having been apprised of the growing unrest in the Jewish Quarter, herewith requests the Parnasim of the High-German Jewish Nation to bring all their influence to bear to counter this as forcefully as possible and within the shortest possible time, and to see to it that there shall be no assemblies likely to disturb the peace.*

Once again the Parnasim issued a public call to the Jews to refrain from any kind of intervention to avoid risking their lives.

The Parnasim's most heated confrontation with the forceful Chief Constable occurred on September 30, the day before the Prussians laid siege to Amsterdam, when he sent them the following note:

> *The Honorable Parnasim of the High-German Nation are herewith most urgently requested, and if necessary commanded, to see to it that members of their Nation shall not perpetrate mischief to any ships lying before this city with incendiary or other materials, and that their houses shall not be turned into storage places for rifles.*

The Portuguese Parnasim received a similar note. The notes' tone and contents might be explained by the fear of a fifth column that is typical of the state of mind of a city under siege. Even so, this time both colleges of Parnasim were unanimous that they could not be expected to call upon their congregants to stay out of the conflict. After all, the Chief Constable had made a very serious and very specific accusation, the mere repetition of which in the synagogues might be construed as an admission of its veracity. In effect it was most unlikely that Jews would have sabotaged ships or stored weapons. During the riots that took place the following month it would indeed become clear that the Jews did not possess firearms. The Protocol Book, while recording several fierce denunciations of activities by Jews that were considered antagonistic to the policies of the Parnasim, also denies the accusation in unequivocal terms. Both the Portuguese and the High-German Parnasim decided to talk to the Chief Constable before committing themselves to any kind of public announcement. It is characteristic of the reserved attitude of the Portuguese Parnasim towards their High-German colleagues that they once again refused to dispatch a joint delegation, and even refused to disclose what they themselves intended to do. They had, in fact, decided to use an intermediary in the person of the broker Samuel de Jacob Saportas (1738-1793), who was on good terms with Van der Hoop. Saportas was requested to have a discussion with the Chief Constable that same night. He complied, and was able to persuade him to withdraw his letter.[40] It is easy to understand the amazement of the High-German Parnasim, when at half past eleven that night they received a message from the Chief Constable informing them that he was sorry about his letter and assuring them that no reaction was needed.

Mixed Rejoicing

On October 1 the Prussians laid siege to Amsterdam, and on October 10 the city capitulated. Article 7 of the Conditions of Surrender stated that the Volunteer Corps would be disarmed by their Superintendent, Baron Van Haren, following which the latter would report to the Duke of Brunswick. Although intended as a placating gesture, unfortunately it didn't work out. The Volunteer Corps refused to surrender their arms, and with the Prussian soldiers bivouacked outside the city gates, there was no one within its precincts capable of enforcing their compliance. Only on October 20 did the Duke of Brunswick send an ultimatum demanding that all arms be surrendered within three days, and by the 22nd of the month they had indeed been deposited at the town hall.[41]

As a consequence of the above, Amsterdam was prey to chaos and total anarchy from October 10 till October 20. Nobody knew to whom they should listen or obey. In the *Nieuwe Vaderlandsche Jaarboeken* it is stated: 'There were those who molested people in one part of the city because they wore orange, and those in another part [who attacked people] for not wearing orange; it even happened that burghers on patrol in the Jewish Quarter (most of the Jews sided with the Orangists) injured and even shot to death a number of Jews, acts which those concerned justified as having been necessary to preserve peace and order, whereas others claimed it was due to hatred of the Jews and of the color orange. In any case, that the vanquished party was forced to withdraw much against its will, shall become clear hereafter.'[42]

As this summary description makes clear, the worst skirmishes took place during this intermediate period. This is also borne out by the protocol of the Parnasim. Meanwhile the composition of the college of Parnasim had undergone several changes (new members were appointed during the Sukkot festival each year). One of the new members was Benjamin Cohen (1726-1800), reputedly the richest Jew in the entire Netherlands. He was a banker and tobacco merchant who had originally lived in Amersfoort, but moved to Amsterdam in 1786. He maintained commercial and social relations with Prince William V and his family, the precise nature and intensity of which have unfortunately not been documented. Cohen was also regarded as a Biblical scholar, and he bore the honorary title of *Morenu* ('Our Teacher') – rabbi *honoris causa*. The protocols consistently refer to him by this honorific. His joining the college added much

---

40 *Livro de Resoluçoens*, pp. 143-144 (em 18 Tisry).
41 For this, see J.M. Vervat, *De Pruisen voor Amsterdam in 1787, verdediging en verovering der stelling,* Amsterdam, 1887, pp.59, 160.
42 Vol. XXII, p. 5376.

to the standing of the Parnasim, but Cohen also displayed tactical and diplomatic qualities that were sorely needed under the prevailing confused conditions.[43]

In the Jewish Quarter the news of the capitulation was greeted with loud cheers, and everyone suddenly sported the orange-colored decorations that had so long been forbidden.[44] As a reaction to the rejoicing, Patriotic civil guards on foot and on horseback invaded the Jewish Quarter. A fierce battle ensued in which, according to Franco Mendes, the Jews defended themselves with sticks and planks – which disproves the earlier rumors that they possessed firearms[45] – whereas the Patriots were of course armed with rifles. There were several fatal casualties on both sides: three Jews and an unknown number of

43 Benjamin Cohen (Amersfoort February 10, 1726 – Amsterdam February 10, 1800) was undoubtedly the predominant Jewish personality during the second half of the 18th century. In 1748 he became a partner in his father's business, contributing greatly to its expansion. He was a tobacco planter and broker in tobacco and grain; in addition he melted coins, owned a silver refinery in Muiden, besides being a shipowner, importer of Brazilian diamonds and a banker. In the latter capacity he was an advisor to the princely couple. In 1786 his residence in Amersfoort was looted by soldiers. In the same year he moved to Amsterdam, where he lived at the Prinsengracht 103 in a house he had purchased for Df. 70,000. In June 1787 the princely couple were guests in Cohen's house, and from here Princess Wilhelmina set out on her well-known journey during which she was detained at the Vlist river, following which she returned to Amersfoort two days later.
    Their friendship with Cohen was of course a favorite subject for satire among the Patriots. The Amersfoort newspaper *Janus* of June 18, 1787 wrote for instance: 'Amersfoort, June 9th... The Prince is coming to Amersfoort. And where will His Highness stay? With the little Sheeny. With the little Sheeny? But [don't you know that] Jews are not allowed to have pork in their homes? Well, that of course is Mr. Cohen's own business; I am no Parnas. But what will His Illustrious Highness do in Amersfoort? Some claim that he has come to have himself circumcised by his host...yet another says: the Dutch Sovereign is coming to Amersfoort to place himself at the head of an army! That is [courageous] language! What do you say about that, you Patriots. Cohen and the Prince leading an army: that starts to look like Saul and his armor-bearer'. The same newspaper insinuates that Cohen, in collaboration with the Prince, is exploiting a gold-mine underneath his house, one lode of which terminates in London and the other in Berlin. (Both cities had branches of the banking house managed by relatives of Benjamin Cohen.)
    Cohen also was a mathematician, who maintained contacts with several other mathematicians and supported the publication of their books. We also owe to him the publication of many books in Hebrew.
    There exists no biography of this interesting personality. Chaim Bermant, *Cousinhood*, New York 1972, pp. 130-131, contains a genealogy of his extensive family; for his business activities, see Ze'ev Bar, *Misjpoge* IV (Jan. 1991); about his position in Dutch society, see Jaap Meijer, *Zij lieten hun sporen achter*, Utrecht 1964, pp. 98-103. He is repeatedly mentioned in the correspondence of the Preger family (G. Yogev, *Hape'iluth Hakalkalith shel hapatriat hayehudi beanglia bamea hashemonehesre* (Hebr.), doctoral thesis, Hebr. Univ. Jerusalem, 1962. Condensed English version: *Diamonds and Corals. Anglo-Dutch Jews and Eighteenth-Century Trade*, Leicester, 1978.)
    David Franco Mendes composed a Hebrew operetta for the wedding of Cohen's daughter: see J. Melkman, *David Franco Mendes*, Amsterdam, 1951, pp. 77-95 About the Cohen's in Amersfoort, see Simon van Adelsberg, *De Joden van Amersfoort*, Amersfoort, 1977, pp. 50-73.
44 On October 11 the municipal authorities published a call for the preservation of peace and order; only on December 9 did it publish a 'Warning ' that people 'should provide themselves with some orange emblem, either a cockade, a bow or a ribbon, as a sign of their true disposition, in order to prevent peace and quiet in the city from being once more disturbed.' (GAA, Tijdgeschriften in het jaar 1787).
45 Franco Mendes, pp. 35-36.

'Heldendaden der blikke Banquetruyters tegen de Joodsche plaatkoekenvrouwen'
(engraving with transparency). Satirical illustration showing a Patriot horseman riding through the Jewish Quarter during the riots of October 1787. The transparency shows his punishment: in Hell he is being ridden by the Devil.

Patriots.[46] The Civil Guards spread the rumor that the Jews had provoked the confrontation, as a result of which the Ashkenazi Parnasim were summoned before the anti-Patriot burgomaster W.G. Dedel (1734-1797), who had mean-

46 Franco Mendes mentions three men and a boy. According to Sluys (p. 387) there were three fatal casualties: Salomon Nathan Presser, also called 'The devil', Jacob Levie Barbirer, and Jacob Wilder, a watchman. This corresponds with the *Protokolbuch*, which mentions that one of the watchmen died of his wounds. It is of course possible that the register of the Zeeburg cemetery does not mention the boy as a casualty of the fighting.

while been reinstated. The Parnasim managed to defuse his initial reproaches and convince him that the Jews had not been at fault. They even demanded: '...that the burghers (i.e. the Civil Guards) would henceforth stay out of the Jewish Quarter, for even if they are the guardians of the city, they bear us ill-will and they are our adversaries, and thus we request that they shall keep guard around their own territory and that the Jews, on their part, shall be absolutely forbidden to leave their district, except with the approval of the Parnasim. The Parnasim shall post their own chosen guards at all transfer points, who shall follow their orders. Besides this, additional guards will be posted in the neighborhood to prevent – God forbid – further accidents. If these conditions are met, we can guarantee that there shall be no excesses in our area.'

Dedel accepted the proposal, but sent the Parnasim to the Defense Committee to ensure their approval. As was to be expected, the Parnasim received a far less cordial welcome from the captains manning the latter office, but in the end they had no choice but to accept. Following this, the Parnasim published an announcement informing the public about the new arrangements, as well as forbidding any public celebration until the signal would be given for the city as a whole.

When at 10 o'clock that night, in contravention of the agreement, several Civil Guards entered the Jewish Quarter, the Parnasim immediately dispatched the *Shamash* (beadle) to the Defense Committee with a message that unilateral infringements of this kind released the Parnasim of all responsibility, and that they should not be blamed if anything untoward happened. The Committee's response was that strict observance of the agreement was indeed intended, and that Guards who had no choice but to pass through the Jewish Quarter on the way to their stations, would do so quietly and singly.

However, by next morning (October 12) the tension had not yet been defused. Civil Guards intercepted Jews who were on their way to Kattenburg to peddle their wares. Another skirmish seemed imminent, and Benjamin Cohen hastened to the City Magistrature, which referred him back to the Defense Committee. There he had a confidential talk with the colonel on duty,[47] which ended with what the Parnasim termed a compromise. It was essentially the same as the existing agreement, except for the addition of more detailed arrangements for the various bridges. A Civil Guard would stand at one end of the bridges, and at the other a representative of the Parnasim, 'who would say which Jews may pass in either direction in order to avoid any conflagrations that might arise from the Jewish Quarter' – thus read the instructions to the guards. Benjamin Cohen toured all the guard posts in his carriage, first to Kattenburg, where he was received by a cheering crowd,[48] and then to the remaining bridge crossings. He succeeded not only in soothing tempers, but also in avoiding

---

47 The Protocol mentions a captain, but the continuation shows that the instructions were given by the Colonels Yperius Wiselius (1736-1793), the father of Samuel (Sluys, p. 408 wrongly read H. Wiselius) and Huib Bastert (1748-1806).
48 Prinz (para. 32) tells that people in Kattenburg shouted: 'Viva the rich Jew.'

excessive public rejoicing and averting any attempts at revenge for the Jewish blood that had been spilt the previous day.

A curious situation had thus come into being. The Jewish population had from the outset enjoyed a measure of autonomy, but never to an extent where the Parnasim exercised factual civil authority in the Jewish Quarter. This is what turned out to be the case now. Instead of merely implementing decisions taken by the municipal authorities, they were partners, to whose views the authorities attempted to defer – provided that the Jews, individually and collectively, refrained from intervening in the affairs of state. This happened to contradict the views of a small group that aspired towards the integration of the Jews into Dutch society. The Jewish religious leadership, on the other hand, was very well satisfied with the arrangement. In their eyes the ultimate destiny of the Jews – even if it would take a very long time coming – did not lie on Dutch soil. Understandably the present arrangement was due to the exceptional circumstances of anarchy and civil disorder, and the fact that the strength of the factions in the city was more or less balanced. Nobody expected this exceptional situation to continue for any length of time. What did remain, however, was the realization that the Parnasim had proven they were able to contain the riotous masses. The Parnasim were aware of their newly acquired strength, and – to quote the Protocol Book – 'they gave thanks to God for having granted them fame and honor among the population of the country.'

Tangible proof of this was to follow soon after. On Sunday, October 21, Benjamin Cohen traveled to The Hague for a business meeting with Prince William V. On Tuesday he was joined by two colleagues for an audience with the princely couple. A delegation from the Portuguese Parnasim had also gone to The Hague for the same purpose. 'And on the third day, namely 11 *Marheshvan* – October 23 according to their calendar – at about 2 o'clock in the afternoon, the three men set out for the court of His Serene Highness the Prince, and when they entered the room called the audience-chamber a dignitary from the court of the above-mentioned Gentleman came and asked in a loud voice: Are there Ashkenazi Parnasim from Amsterdam here, and they answered Yes, and all dignitaries who stood there to greet the Prince were most surprised, and they were immediately introduced into the room in which the above-mentioned Gentleman [the Prince] was seated.'[49]

Prince and Princess received them in a most cordial fashion, before the Portuguese Parnasim who until this day had always been accorded precedence. From the speech made by Benjamin Cohen on this occasion we shall mention two points. He requested a renewal of the promise William V had made at the time of his inauguration (1766) 'to protect our Nation,' in addition to which he commented:

---

49 The use of the figure three in connection with the Sovereign's welcome is not coincidental. It is derived from the Talmud, Shabbat 88a: God gave the Torah to the three-fold nation (priests, Levites ansd Israelites) on the third day of the third month through the intermediary of the third-born (i.e. Moses, who already had a brother and a sister).

> *Our nation rejoices about this (i.e. the restoration of the Prince to his former authority) and regards it as Divine providence, which has averted the threatening dangers against which our Magistrate, however kindly disposed towards us he always is, would hardly have been able to protect us for much longer.*

Cohen clearly hints here at the economic measures the Patriots had been planning against the Jews.

Meanwhile the unrest in the Jewish Quarter continued. During the siege and until the disarmament, the Parnasim had issued four announcements (October 3, 13, 16 and 17), each of which demanded that Jews stay out of the political conflict. On October 17, a new element was added, namely pressures and extortion of the defeated opponents by individual Jews: '...the leaders of the community have heard that people pass by the houses under the pretext of [requesting] contributions towards the cost of illumination, and [visiting] not only the Jewish streets, but also non-circumcised people and even personages of the Magistrature and adversaries.'

For several months afterwards opponents of the Orangists would be molested. The Parnasim complained that their warnings were not being heeded, and that both Jews and gentiles were threatened and beaten (December 8). Even though people had been advised to wear orange, it was strictly forbidden to intimidate those who failed to do so (January 31, 1788).[50] In their announcement of February 28, 1788, the Parnasim copied the entire amnesty declaration that the States of Holland and West-Vriesland had proclaimed on February 1, beseeching the members of their community to act accordingly, adding: 'and let us act together in the spirit of brotherhood and friendship and refrain from provocation, and it is hardly necessary to say that no-one should incite against non-circumcised persons or molest [them] in any other way.'

'Every transgressor,' the announcement continued, 'shall be surrendered to the judicial authorities, in order that he be tried forthwith, and we should thank our God that He has guided us from sadness to joy, from mourning to a day of celebration, that He did not cause our steps to falter; until now He has succored us, may He not forsake and abandon us until we have the joy of witnessing the restoration of our glorious House, Amen.'

---

50 In his memoirs Hovy tells that he refused to wear orange, and he continues: 'Les Orangistes ne manquèrent pas aussi de me faire attaquer à la bourse par une troupe de Juifs et de populace mais j'eu le bonheur de m'en tirer avec honneur'. The incident is related at length in *Vervolg van Wagenaars Vaderlandsche geschiedenis* (vol. XXI, p. 16 etc.): 'Once again riots erupted (connected with the wearing of orange - J.M.), and the Jews in particular showed their intense displeasure with this. In the growing confusion one of them was severely beaten. The entire exchange became wild and tumultuous, and most of the merchants fled from that risky place. As on the previous day, Hovy's friends safely managed to extricate him.'

Conclusion

The supporters of the Amsterdam Patriots attempted to impair the economic position of the Jews by a strict implementation of the existing charters and the establishment of guilds for the remaining free professions.[51] Fear of such measures inclined the already Orangist Jewish masses even further towards active participation in the struggle against the Patriots, together with other groups and in particular the residents of neighboring Kattenburg. Since the Parnasim, even though they were no less Orangist than the proletariat, re-garded this as extremely dangerous, they believed that Jews should observe strict neutrality in the wider political conflict and restrict themselves to self-de-fense. On this basis it would be possible to co-operate with the Patriots, who in turn were not interested in driving the Jews into the arms of their opponents. Jewish patriots,[52] amounting to less than ten percent of the male Jews,[53] attempted to incite the Patriot leadership against the Parnasim, but the former soon realized that it was in their best interests not to undermine their authority among the Jewish public. The sensible and consistent policy of the Parnasim had made it clear that only they would succeed in influencing the Jewish masses.

The events of 1787 had a decisive influence on the developments following the foundation of the Batavian Republic. Both parties entered the new era scarred by the trauma of the past: the Patriots with a hatred of the Jews[54] – from which even Patriotic Jews were not exempted[55] – and the Jews with a fear of anti-Jewish measures. Once again the political leaders found each other due to considerations of 'Realpolitik'. With the exception of a very brief period (the

---

51 The literature about the Patriots only rarely refers to the plans for the local economy of Amsterdam. This is because the movement of 1787 is regarded more as a precursor of the Batavian Revolution than a continuation of the 'Doelist' movement. This is openly admitted by Simon Schama (*Patriots and Liberators*, New York, 1977, p. 68): 'It may be accepted, then, that Patriot ideology was a melange of old and new attitudes towards the Dutch constitution. If I am more concerned with the new, it is not because they necessarily played a more important role in the upheavals of 1781-1787, but rather because the more self-evidently modern language linked the "first" (Patriot) phase of the Dutch Revolution with the second (Batavian) phase in something like a genuine continuity of idea and practice'.

52 Virtually no other source refers to the existence of a group of Jewish Patriots. M.S. Asser, in his – in many ways disappointing – autobiography, mentions his contacts with Herman Bromet, which converted him to a more contemporary point of view, as well as the fact that after 1787 his views caused him certain problems, but he fails to provide particulars about the number of members of the group and their activities. See I.H. van Eeghen, 'Autobiografie van M.S. Asser', *Jbk Amstelodamum*, Vol. 55 (1963), pp. 130- 65.

53 The article in the *Nederlandsche Courant* of June 13, 1787 states literally that 'among a hundred Jews of the two Nations there were not even ten who thought otherwise.'

54 See, for example, the petition of District 15 against the admission of Jews to the Civil Guard: 'We are still aghast at that gruesome murder of one of our brothers-in-arms, committed in 1787, when they cut him off from our patrol; we shudder at the thought of all the consequences, the maltreatments, and even total ruination of some of us following that cursed evolution.' (GAA, Petition of District 15, October 8, 1795, Bijlage tot het Dagblad van de vergadering der Representanten van het Volk van Amsterdam, Vol. I, pp. 275-277, Nieuwe Stedelijke Besturen, 404).

55 See note 21 about the doggerel entitled 'De Jood Patriot'.

radical regime between January and June 1798) the Amsterdam municipal
authorities continued to support the Parnasim in order that they would continue to rein in the Jewish masses.[56] Even in 1807 F. van Hoogstraten wrote to
Louis Napoleon, in connection with the recruitment of Jews to the Civil Guard,
that 'the Magistrates have proceeded with the same circumspection as the
Government of this large and populous city has been accustomed to observe
since times immemorial, with the most favorable effects in most, if not all, cases
concerning police matters, namely by consulting the Parnasim of the High-German Nation and discuss with them everything concerning the Jews.'[57]

Viewed in its historical context the correctness of this statement is somewhat
dubious, but with regard to the last twenty years, Van Hoogstraten was undoubtedly right.

---

56 In 1806 the Amsterdam Magistrates declare that the Parnasim 'have always been regarded and
    respected as sovereign heads of the respective Jewish communities,' and that the Parnasim had
    always been able to control the Jewish public.
57 Report by F. van Hoogstraten to Louis Napoleon dated February 4, 1807, ARA, Staatssecr. van
    Lod. Nap.

2 Emancipation or Pseudo-Emancipation

The Emancipation Decree

On September 2, 1796 the National Assembly unanimously adopted the 'Decree on the Equal Status of the Jews with all other Citizens'.

That same day the French envoy and journalist G.F. Baron de Bosset wrote that it was to be expected that 'as far as they were concerned prejudice would persist for a long time to come, and while they will not be excluded by law, this will prove to be the situation in practice; and possibly this is what the majority of their own followers have felt, and what has motivated the majority of the Convention.'[1]

This would seem a bold assumption with regard to a decision that had been adopted unanimously. History has shown, however, how correct Bosset's prophesy was, and how well he had assessed the motives of the majority of the deputies of the National Assembly. They indeed regarded the declaration as a formal statement, and they never intended that it should be applied in full. Bosset had good reasons for his analysis. A week earlier he had reported that the National Assembly was extremely adverse to adopting the Emancipation Decree, and in any case was loath to go as far as its advocates, including J.G.H. Hahn (1761-1823), had proposed.[2]

---

1   Bosset, Nieuwsbericht van 2 september 1796; Colenbrander, *GS*, Vol. 5 (R.G.P., Great series, 2), The Hague, 1906, p. 286. (G.F. Baron de Bosset was the envoy at the Hague of several German states, in addition to which he distributed newsletters.) Even during the Emancipation period the debates in the National Assembly evoked considerable response in Jewish circles. Already in 1797 a German translation was published: *Actenstücke zur Geschichte der Erhebung der Juden zu Bürgern in der Republic Batavien*, Neustrelitz. A Hebrew translation appeared under the title *Divrei Negidiem*, Amsterdam, 1799. The translator was Zwi Hirsch of Amsterdam, a native of Uhlfeld near Fürth. (A reprint was published in Jerusalem in 1972, with a preface by D. Michman, but without the extensive introduction by the translator and the translation of the Constitution of 1798.)
    Modern historians have also spoken in praise of the debates: 'More than in other places attention was paid in the debates to the question of the future redemption of Israel, the relationship of the Jews to Eretz Israel, and the national singularity of the Jews, even in the Diaspora. And less than elsewhere there was the accompanying element of intolerance, hatred and jealously.' (Benzion Dinur, *Bemifnee hadoroth*, Jerusalem, 1955, pp. 318.) Analyses of the debates, in Bolle, pp. 138-74; S.E. Bloemgarten, 'De Amsterdamse Joden gedurende de eerste jaren van de Bataafse Republiek', in *St. Ros.* I,2 (1967), pp. 46-60; A. Halff, 'The Discussions in the National Assembly of the Batavian Republic on the Emancipation of the Jews' (Hebr.) *SDJ* 1, pp. 201-240.
2   J. George H. Hahn was Recorder of the Van Leeuwen Committee that had been appointed on March 29, 1796 by the National Assembly in order to study the petition in which the six members of Felix Libertate requested equal rights for the Jews. See also Colenbrander, *op.cit.* Vol. 2, pp. 284-85; Nieuwsbericht of August 26, 1796.

François Noël, the French ambassador, had from the outset lent vigorous formal support to the initiative of Felix Libertate, the predominantly Jewish Patriotic club, but he too noted the fierce opposition encountered by the proponents of emancipation, in particular that of the deputies from Amsterdam. The voting on the report by the Van Leeuwen Committee (August 30), which recommended granting civil rights to Jews, had been 45 for and 24 against; thus the unanimity with which the decree was adopted only two days later looks extremely strange.[3] It can only be explained by the pressure exercised by the French ambassador. After all, he represented not only the country that had subdued the Republic by force of arms, but also the ideas of the Revolution.[4]

The adoption of the decree is generally regarded as having concluded the struggle for emancipation in The Netherlands. The practical application is supposed to have happened by itself – even though many historians admit that full implementation was a lengthy process.[5] We shall see, however, that matters were far more complicated, and there are good reasons for joining Bosset in questioning whether even the decree's sponsors intended its practical implementation. A week after its adoption (on September 9) a discussion took place in the Constitutional Committee that seemed to return the entire development

---

3   Bolle (pp. 171-73) mentions a number of factors that are supposed to have promoted the adoption: 1. Six of the 14 representatives from Amsterdam supported the adoption; 2. the representatives were not bound by the mandates they had received from the voters; 3. apparently the Catholics voted in favor of the decree; 4. Hahn was working behind the scenes; 5. 'very probably' Noël made every effort to influence the outcome of the voting. Among all these factors, only the final one would be able to explain the reversal of the vote. This would seem to be borne out by a statement by M.S. Asser. He had been in touch with Noël, who had promised to secure an instruction from the French government ensuring the adoption of the decree. See: 'De autobiografie van M.S. Asser', ed. by I.H. van Eeghen, *Jbk. Amstelodamum* 55 (1963), p. 150.

4   The French ambassador, Noël, discussed the Jewish question in several letters to Delacroix, contemporary French Minister of Foreign Affairs. On March 28, 1796, he writes: 'J'ai cru devoir appuyer ce projet et seconder en cela les vues philanthropiques de notre gouvernement. ' On July 23, 1796 he mentions the many prejudices that have to be overcome: '... mais j'espère que la saine raison triomphera. Je n'omettrai rien pour favoriser son triomphe.' On August 22 he mentions Hahn's report, adding that the matter 'donnera lieu à des débats assez violens'. Two Amsterdam advocates, J.G. Luyken and H. van Castrop, who did not themselves participate in the debates, directed the anti-Emancipation lobby. In the same letter Noël reports that the French government fully supported Hahn's proposal (Colenbrander, *op.cit.* Vol. 2, pp. 46, 50, 59-60, 67).

5   H. J. Koenen, in *Geschiedenis der Joden in Nederland*, Utrecht, 1843, writes that in certain towns the implementation of the agreed principles was considerably delayed (p. 373); H. Graetz,*Geschichte der Juden von den ältesten Zeiten bis auf die Gegenwart*, Leipzig, 1900, 2, Vol. 11, p. 218 ff., whose narrative about The Netherlands is full of mistakes, assumes that all restrictions were lifted from one day to the next. To the extent that people acknowledge problems in the implementation, they usually regard this as the start of a process that would automatically lead to complete equality. Thus, for example, P. Geyl, who compares the Jews with the Roman Catholics – whose elevation from social and intellectual backwardness would prove to be a labor of generations (*Geschiedenis van de Nederlandse Stam*, Amsterdam, 1962, Vol. 6, pp. 1648-49). Colenbrander, too, ascribes the considerable lag in the 'social advancement of the Jews' to the reluctance of the Jews themselves, 'the majority of whom fearfully clung to old customs' (*Schimmelpenninck en Koning Lodewijk*, Amsterdam, 1911, p. 116). He even suggests that only the abandonment of time-honored customs would earn them the right to equal treatment under the law!

back to square one. The protocol of the meeting sounds ominous when it asks 'whether it would be reasonable to suppose that the Jews, given their dissimilarity to all other nations, and taking into account that they curse the Christian religion, would indeed fraternize with Christians; besides which, since they themselves continue to regard themselves as strangers, they could be naturalized by mere domicile. That, even supposing Jews might be given the right to vote, this would naturally mean that they should in all respects be equal to the citizens of The Netherlands, in which case it would remain to be seen whether the citizenry of Amsterdam would agree that – once having been franchised, and having been admitted as electors or themselves having been elected – they would have to be admitted to these same positions as all other Dutchmen.'

Certain delegates argued that 'even if the National Assembly had given this proposal a preliminary (sic) reading', and even if the majority had voted in favor, the Constitution must exclude Jews from the right to vote. Instead of rejecting this opinion as contrary to the decision of the National Assembly, the Committee refrained from including a provision in the Constitution that explicitly excluded Jews, but instead decided to draw up a voters' register in such a way that Jews would not automatically have the right to vote.[6] It is evident from this discussion that the Amsterdam delegates continued to oppose Jewish

---

6   Notulen der Commissie tot het formeren van een plan van Constitutie voor het volk van Nederland, Friday, September 9, 1796 (ARA, Wetgevende Colleges, Inv. no. 463 bis). See: L. de Gou (publ.), 'Het plan van Constitutie van 1796' (R.G.P., kleine serie 40), The Hague, 1975, p. 231.

   Although during the debate about the draft Constitution of 1797 in the National Assembly the opponents of Jewish emancipation acknowledged the existence of the Decree, they tried to restrict its implementation as much as possible. E.J. Greve, a member of the nobility of Gelderland, complained that 'even in certain cities a group of aliens who until then had been regarded as belonging to a different Nation...after You invited them into our Community, have usurped the rights of the Dutch citizenry and chosen our Regents'. He expressed fears about the future 'if evil-minded rabble and aliens and Jews were to be admitted among the franchised Citizenry'. The Amsterdam aristocrat H.D. Van Hoorn evoked the bugbear of the destitute Jews: 'I want to add, Fellow Citizens, that I consider the 18,000 Jews in Amsterdam who are being maintained [at public expense] as equally dangerous.' A.J. Strick van Linschoten, a nobleman from the province of Utrecht, commented sarcastically that '...this Assembly has granted the Jewish Nation something that it doesn't crave itself, and of which it will not avail itself since it runs counter to their principles'. *Het Ontwerp van Constitutie van 1797*, ed. L. de Gou, The Hague, 1983, I, p. 194; II, p. 299; I, p. 191, 625.

   On the other hand, P. Vreede, the leader of the Radicals, believed that the State should also fund the education of the Jews, and A.J. Zubli from Amsterdam went so far as to state that, although he regarded the Jews as a sect that formed no part of our (Dutch) Nation, rabbis ought to be remunerated in the same way as Christian clergymen. J.F.R. Van Hooff, the representative of Brabant, proved himself a hundred and fifty years ahead of his time when he claimed that Jews could not be expected to refrain from working two days a week. *Op. cit.*, I, p. 664, 627; II, p. 477.

GELYKHEID.

'Vrij en gelijk door de wet gebonden'
The various parts of the Dutch population jointly constitute the Batavian Republic in Freedom and Equality. The third person from the left is a Jew, the fifth a Roman Catholic, representing the two discriminated groups in the old republic. Rijksmuseum, Amsterdam.

emancipation, even though it was specifically – if not only – in this city that equal rights for Jews had to be enforced.[7]

During the period preceding the Emancipation decree, patriotic magazines and pamphlets had carried on a lively discussion about the future status of Jews.

---

7   This does not mean that there were no difficulties elsewhere. A typical example is the following incident. David Levy and Raageltje (Rachel) Arons were about to get married, and they wanted to settle in Doesburg. The municipal authorities turned down their request because they were Jews (1801). The couple appealed to the Provincial government, which annulled the refusal and ordered the municipality to accept the newlyweds. (D.S. van Zuiden, 'Het doorvoeren van de emancipatie in het Departement van de Neder-Rhijn', *VA* 1b, p. 143-44). This rejectionist attitude on the part of local authorities, who were intent on perpetuating the situation existing prior to 1795, as well as the conscientious pro-emancipation views of the regional and national government organs, was the customary pattern during this era.

A number of fiercely anti-Semitic articles was published,[8] countered by pleas to accept Jews as social equals.[9] Pieter 't Hoen, one of the most prominent publicists, attempted to steer a middle course by arguing that within the framework of the Rights of Man and the Citizen, Jews were deserving of recognition as fellow-men, but not as fellow-citizens.

Given the visceral opposition by many of the delegates to the National Assembly, a renewed – and even fiercer – debate around the Emancipation decree could therefore be expected, that would further impede its practical implementation. In fact, this did not happen. From the second half of 1796 until the first half of 1798 the infant Republic was overwhelmed by a wave of ideological radicalism that aspired towards solving all problems in the spirit of Freedom, Equality and Fraternity. Among its main beneficiaries were the Jews. Characteristic of the spirit of the times is the following poem 'To the Jews' by Betje Wolff and Aagje Deken, two well-known politically engaged poets, which includes the following strophe:

> *Indeed, Brothers! Also to your discernment*
> *We entrust the Fatherland;*
> *Let prejudice take offense:*
> *[But] the Jew, too, is a Patriot,*
> *and in the servants of one God*
> *We all recognize fellow believers.*[10]

The moment was obviously auspicious for the Jews, and they did indeed gain the franchise. The initial results of Jewish participation in the elections could even be called promising. Two Jews, H. Bromet and H. de H. Lemon, were elected as delegates to the Second National Assembly, whereas a third, M. Moresco, became a member of the Amsterdam Municipal Council. This success has often been acclaimed, since the above-mentioned trio were the first Jews to be elected to a representative body anywhere in Europe.[11] What is not men-

---

8   A few examples from the Patriot magazine *De Domkop*: '...since virtue and merit, which should be the principal requirements for achieving a public office, are absent among Jews.' (No. 136, p. 280) In another article it is claimed that granting Jews the benefits of the Declaration of the Rights of Man and the Citizen would invite an invasion of hundreds of thousands Jews, leading to the conclusion: 'the oppressed people will in turn become the oppressors.' (No. 127, p. 223). Somewhere on the same page is the comment: 'Show me a Jew, and I'll show you a liar.'

9   For a summary of the discussion, see Bolle, pp. 107-111. See also an analysis of several well-known authors in M.J.P. Weytens, *Nathan and Shylock in de Lage Landen*, Groningen, 1971.

10   *Ja, Broeders! ook aan uw verstand*
     Betrouwen wij het Vaderland;
     't Vooroordeel moog' zich hieraan stooten:
     De Jood is ook een Patriot,
     En in de dienaars van een' God
     Zien we allen ook geloofsgenooten.

     The poem is printed in a collection called *Aan de Joden, Gedichten en liedjes voor het Vaderland* ('To the Jews, Poems and Songs for the Fatherland'), published in 1798. The entire poem was reprinted in I. Prins, 'Ons Welkom in de nieuwe maatschappij', *VA* 8a (1931), pp. 140-42. See also Weytens, *op. cit.*, pp. 69-70.

11   Thus Dubnow, *Die neueste Geschichte des jüdischen Volkes*, Berlin, 1930, Vol. I, p. 174.

Moses Salomon Asser, 1754-1826. Historisch-topografische Atlas van het Gemeentearchief, Amsterdam.

tioned, however, is the brevity of their tenure: following the coup d'état of June 12, 1798, all three delegates disappeared from the political arena.[12] Moresco's place in the Amsterdam Municipal Council was taken by Is. da Costa, but he too soon departed to take a seat in the National Assembly. It was not until 1813 that

---

12 De Lemon had been closely involved with the coup of January 22, 1798, by Vreede *c.s.*, and it is understandable that following the coup in July of the same year his role, as well as that of Bromet, was finished. Moresco, too, from this moment on disappeared from the political scene; see the letter dated July 26, 1809, his brother sent to the High Consistory (J. Meijer, *Problematiek per Post*, pp. 28-29).

there would be another Jewish representative in the Amsterdam City Council. Two Jews among the 254 representatives during the period 1795-1813 yields a total of less than 1 percent – whereas Jews constituted eleven percent of the Amsterdam population.[13] Taking into account that the entire term of these two representatives did not exceed four months, the ratio becomes even less favorable.[14] Evidently this was no coincidence.

In the course of the 18th century anti-Semitism became more virulent – at least when judged by its reflection in written sources.[15] We might assume that the Patriots would have opposed such a development, but this did not prove to be the case. They depended on the support of social groups that regarded greater freedom for Jews as a threat to their own economic survival, besides which the majority of the Jewish population had such outspoken Orangist leanings that the Patriots regarded them as their enemies.[16] Two striking illustrations of the relationships during the Revolutionary period of the Batavian Republic are a statement by Gogel during his radical period to the effect that Jews did not deserve to be enfranchised,[17] and a report by A.R. Falck about a Patriot meeting, during which only five or six among several hundred participants joined him in a vote about the question of whether Jews were entitled to the Rights of Man and the Citizen – and therefore should be allowed to join the guilds.[18] As a consequence, the only support for the ideas of the pro-emancipatory group among the Jews was to be found among the democratic Patriots. These were identified with the men who carried out the coup of January 22, 1798, and when on June 12 of the same year their rule came to an end, this also terminated the political activity of the leaders of Felix Libertate. Even worse: they were discredited for good.

It is therefore not surprising that the increasingly reactionary regimes kept Jews out of all public positions. If Roman Catholics were systematically barred, Jews could expect even less consideration. In fact, the moderates as well as the aristocratic Patriots and – following the Peace of Amiens (1802) – even the former followers of the House of Orange progressively emphasized the Christian character of the Batavian Republic, and this automatically implied that Jews were to be denied any influence.[19] We may also add that from an economic

---

13 This information is derived from Joh. C. Breen, 'De regeering van Amsterdam gedurende den Franschen tijd', *Jbk. Amstelodamum*, 12 (1914), pp. 1-130. Moresco was a member from March 15-June 13, 1798, and I. da Costa from June 13-July 27, 1798. M.S. Asser was a member of the Judicial Committee from March 15-June 13, 1798.

14 Between 1795 and 1915 the population of Amsterdam declined from 221,000 to 180,000, due to a number of reasons. (See Herman Diederiks, *Een stad in verval*, Amsterdam, 1982, p. 5.)

15 See for example R.B. Evenhuis, *Ook dat was Amsterdam*, Vol. IV, Amsterdam, 1971, pp. 272 ff.

16 See M. Wolff, 'De betekenis van de regering van Lodewijk Napoleon voor de Joden van Nederland', *Bijdragen voor Vaderlandse Geschiedenis en Oudheidkunde*, 7 (1920), pp. 430-67.

17 Wolff, *op. cit.*, p. 446.

18 Quoted by H. Brugmans, *Geschiedenis van Amsterdam*, Vol. V, Utrecht, 1973, p. 12.

19 For some detailed descriptions of the political developments in the Batavian Republic, see Schama, *Patriots*, pp. 210-464; a summary description is contained in E.H. Kossmann, *The Low Countries*, Oxford, 1978, pp. 90-93. About the insignificance of Adath Jesurun, see the report by the French Commissioners about the Sanhedrin: R. Anchel, *Napoléon et les Juifs*, Paris, 1928, p. 222, n. 4.

point of view, few – if any – of the optimistic expectations accompanying the acceptance of the Emancipation decree were realized.

The Petition of April 11, 1806 – Gothic Turrets on a Corinthian Building

In practice very few changes took place to ameliorate the wretched conditions of the Jews of Amsterdam. Nothing will illustrate better the policies of the Amsterdam municipal government after 1798 than the memorable petition that was submitted on April 11, 1806, by six Amsterdam Jews to 'their illustrious Representative to the Batavian Republic'.[20]

The six signatories of the petition were Joseph Arons Polak,[21] Moses Salomon Asser, Adv. Carel Asser,[22] Samuel Moses Metz, Isaac Senator, and Adv. J.D. Meyer, who – according to their statement – were members of the respective Jewish communities of Amsterdam. This assertion is not untrue, but misleading. In reality four of the signatories were members of Adath Jesurun: father and son Asser, the actual initiators, J.A. Polak and S.M. Metz. During the

---

20 ARA. Archief Bi.Za., 1775-1813, exh. September 10, 1806, no. 1.
21 Joseph Aron (or Arons) Polak became a member of the Provisional Commissioners of the Jewish community (March 17, 1798). On March 19 he suggested asking for a perusal of the religious and financial by-laws of the New Community, in order 'that we may behave in the same manner'. As a member of an ad hoc committee he negotiated with the New Community, and on March 20 (the minutes wrongly state March 19) he announced that the Board of the New Community had 'extended the hand of brotherhood'. Following his appointment as Chairman, he gave a speech (on April 23, 1798) that was attended by M.S. Asser as a member of the Municipal Judicial Committee. During the election of the Board he received 651 votes, against Samuel Mozes Metz 498 votes, but all those elected refused their nomination.
22 Carel Asser (Amsterdam, February 15, 1780 – The Hague, August 3, 1836) was the most prominent Jewish figure during the entire period covered in this book. On 3. 7. 1798 he obtained a doctoral degree in literature from the University of Leiden. The previous year he had established a law practice in Amsterdam. He and J.D. Meyer were the first Jewish advocates in The Netherlands. During his legal career he occupied many high government offices, including those of (unpaid) legal advisor to the Privy Council, Justice of the Peace in Amsterdam, Senior Clerk at the Ministry of Justice (from 1815 onwards), Department Head at the Council of State, Secretary of the National Legislative Committee. He also made an important contribution to the drafting of the Legal Code of 1830.
      Asser began his Jewish activities at the age of fifteen as co-signer – together with his father – of the petition requesting the admission of Jews to the National Guard. During the vote on the Emancipation decree he sat in the public gallery of the National Assembly. He will be featured repeatedly in the course of this book. Until the end of his life he continued to occupy distinguished offices within the Jewish community, including that of Chairman of the High Committee for Israelite Affairs. He married Rosa Levin from Berlin, a sister of the famous Rahel Varnhagen-Levin. From his hand appeared numerous legal manuscripts, as well as a translation of the works of Gabriel Riesser.
      A remarkable, and typical, difference between Amsterdam and Berlin was that Rose Asser-Levin led a far more traditional Jewish life in Amsterdam than she had been accustomed to at home. See Heidi Thomann-Tewarson, 'German Jewish Identity in the Correspondence between Rahel Varnhagen-Levin and her Brother, Ludwig Robert', *LBY* XXXIX (1994), p. 4.
      Lit.: Van der Aa, *Biografisch Woordenboek der Nederlanden*, 1969 (repr.), see under Asser; *Jaarboeken voor de Israëlieten in Nederland*, II (1837), pp. 369-92; E. Carmoly, *Revue Orientale*, III, Brussels, 1843-44, pp. 413-18; I.H. van Eeghen, *Uit Amsterdamse Dagboeken*, Amsterdam, *passim*.

revolutionary period the latter two had been *manhigim* (officers) of the Old Community, but in August 1798, following the counter-revolution by Daendels and the return of the Parnasim, they decamped to the New Community.[23] The only member of the Old Community was the advocate J.D. Meyer, and he joined after the petition had been written.[24]

Meyer, a grandson of the famous Parnas Benjamin Cohen, remained a member of the Old Community, but he was not averse to renewal. The reason why he decided to act only now, together with his colleague C. Asser, who was exactly the same age, was the Peace of Amiens, which induced many adherents of the House of Orange (with which the Cohen family maintained close contacts) to reconcile themselves with the new regime. Isaac Senator, the third of this threesome, was a Portuguese Jew, in which capacity he wanted to show that this community also included those prepared to fight for the Jewish common weal. Even so, the fact that they had to suffice with a basically unknown personality who never played any significant role either in the community or outside shows with how little response the ideas and tactics of Felix Libertate met within the Portuguese community. [25]

Following an introductory statement about the beneficial effects of the Emancipation decree, the petition argued that 'whereas the political face of Europe has undergone changes, the petitioners, to their great distress, have noticed that superstition has exploited the situation to their detriment and that of their co-religionists, with the result that the wall separating Man and his Fellows, which – at least in the city of Amsterdam – had been torn down by the legislated resolutions and decrees, had once again been erected, not slowly, but in an instant.' The petition continued: 'That, whereas prior to the Revolution, the rulers of the city were ceaselessly intent on mitigating the severity of the laws pertaining to Jews, to the effect that many Jews were favored with benefices, now the laws that are so clearly in favor of the Jews are being mutilated.'

Thus, they claimed, the situation of the Jews was even worse than before Emancipation, causing them to express the hope that since 'a new political edifice' is being erected, those who stand at its head 'shall certainly not accept that <u>Gothic towers shall remain standing, or rather be re-erected on a Corinthian building</u>.'[26]

Corinthian temples formed the inspiration for the contemporary 'Empire style', and they were considered an expression of the *ratio* – and therefore truth.

---

23 Samuel Mozes Metz was Chairman when on June 27 – 15 days after the coup – the municipal authorities reappointed the original Parnasim. See *Notulenboek van de Provisioneele Gecommitteerden*, as well as Bloemgarten, *SR* II (1968), pp. 55-63. (On p. 60 Bloemgarten mentions Joseph Arons and Chairman Polak; in both cases Joseph Arons Polak is meant.)
  Samuel Mozes Metz joined the New Community, as shown by the fact that on June 25, 1807, he signed a petition to the king in his capacity of chairman of Adath Jesurun.
24 This is shown by the fact that his name was interpolated at a later date, as well as by several changes in the text.
25 Only in 1823 did Ishac de Jeosuah Senator fulfil an office of any importance in the already small community, namely as 'administradores de Talmud Torah'. See J. Meijer, *Encyclopaedia Sephardica Neerlandica*, A-F, Amsterdam, 1949-1950 (hereafter ESN), p. 111.
26 The underlining is in the original.

Gothic, on the other hand, France's traditional national stylistic language, was rejected as representative of the Middle Ages, with its attendant religious fanaticism and lack of logic. In France itself Gothic churches were even defaced. This line of thinking explains why the Union of Utrecht, the confederation concluded in 1579 between the seven Dutch provinces, which also formed the constitutional foundation of the Republic of the United Netherlands, was described as 'the Gothic monstrosity, the abhorrent constitutional abortion.'[27]

Using esthetic symbolism to describe their ideology, the six supplicants argued that with a modern and rational constitutional form of government there was no place for discrimination against Jews in its present form, or in the way that, as they believed, the Amsterdam municipal government intended it to be enshrined in the new Constitution.

They continued by giving a number of examples of this discrimination. I arrange their complaints systematically for greater clarity:

a. **Financial discrimination**: Jews are obliged to pay their share in the municipal taxes, but the proceeds go to 'the teachers of the previously dominant Church, hospitals, orphanages and almshouses', which do not in any way benefit the Jews – who according to the petitioners constitute one-sixth of the population.

b. **Economic discrimination**: The petitioners give two examples of problems regarding admission to the former guilds: only one Jew was admitted to the Fell-mongers, Tanners and Cobbler's Guild following intervention by the National government, whereas a second, Abraham Levy, had been refused recognition as a master-blacksmith, even though he had completed the necessary education.[28]

c. **Political discrimination**: In the city of Amsterdam Jews are treated 'as if the decree officially granting them the same rights as every other inhabitant did not exist.' This is clear from the following facts: Not a single Jew had been admitted to an official position or benefice; among the 200 persons entrusted with the responsibility of checking tax revenues there was not a single Jew; of the 200 citizens appointed to collect votes for the electoral assemblies, only one was a Jew – and his appointment proved to be due to an oversight.

---

27 Quotes by Geyl, 'De Bataafse Revolutie', in: *Verzamelde Opstellen*, vol. 2, Utrecht-Antwerp, 1978, p. 114.

28 This was a cause célèbre. Abram Levy was a pupil of the club 'Arbeid en Vlijt', which had been established by Jews in 1798 for the purpose of providing professional training to indigent Jews in order to reduce mendicancy. At their meeting of February 8, 1807 the Board revealed that for more than a year their efforts to get Abram Levy accepted by the guild had been opposed. He even had been fined 25 guilders. It required the intervention of King Louis Napoleon and the Amsterdam Magistrates to finally settle the matter. Advocate Carolus Asser, also a member of the Club, acted on Levy's behalf in a voluntary capacity.

The guilds were officially abolished by an order of October 5, 1798, but the edict remained a dead letter; on January 30, 1808, a law was enacted liquidating the guilds. But even then it was difficult for Jews to join the new corporations. See Schama, *op. cit.*, pp. 379, 529.

d. **Ideological discrimination**: The petitioners asked '...whether it was not injurious that in municipal publications Jews are referred to as Jewish Nation, as if the Government emphatically intended to exclude them from membership of the Batavian Republic, and whether this too does not give them good reason to feel greatly humiliated.'[29] Apparently Polak and his colleagues had drawn a lesson from the political developments in the Batavian Republic. They no longer believed, as had been the case in 1796, that they would succeed in convincing their opponents. The principal scourge of the Jews, they argued, was that the municipal governments did not include any Jews. And since traditionally every group looked only after its own interests, Jewish interests were neglected. This is an interesting argument, for whereas Jewish fighters for emancipation wanted Jews to be treated as individuals rather than as a group, their experience thus far had taught them to demand representation of Jews as Jews. They rejected the apparently earlier voiced objection that 'the man-in-the-street' objected to Jewish public officials, since previous appointments of Jewish administrators had never caused problems.

In conclusion, therefore, they requested the Grand Pensionary, R.J. Schimmelpenninck, similarly as had been done in France, 'earnestly to require' all municipal governments – and in particular that of Amsterdam – not only to stop interfering with the exercise of civil rights by those Jews who meet the legal requirements, but also to consider Jewish inhabitants 'when allocating offices and benefices'.

Polak and his colleagues never received a direct answer to their petition,[30] but this does not mean that the document was shelved. The opposite is the case, as will shortly become clear. Several official bodies made a serious study of this indictment of the Amsterdam municipal authorities. It appears that the Grand Pensionary passed the petition on to the Provincial Council of Holland, for on April 22 this body had already requested a reaction from the Amsterdam City Council. The reply, signed by Burgomaster Hermannus Drost[31] and the Secretary F.J. Pelletier, was sent on May 7.

This answer is a curious document, in content as well as style, resembling a polemical pamphlet rather than a formal letter. Burgomaster Drost – or the

---

29 Contrary to the situation in France and Germany, Jewish champions of emancipation usually referred to themselves as Jews, and sometimes as 'Mosaites' (Letter of appreciation by Felix Libertate to the National Assembly, 1796). Only following the annexation of The Netherlands to France does the name 'Israelites' come into use. The term is first used in the decree of March 1808 in France. The Minister of the Interior, J.B. Champagny, had suggested the word 'Hébreux' (U. Hadas- Lebel and E. Oliel-Grausz (eds.), *Les Juifs et la Révolution Française – Histoire et mentalités*, Paris, 1992, p. 135). Later on the change of appelation was justified by the claim that 'the word Jew had a negative association' (see: 'Iets over den naam Israëliet en Jood', *Jaarboeken der Israëlieten* IV, 1838, p. 360).

30 This becomes clear from a petition by J.D. Meyer en C. Asser to Louis Napoleon, dated July 15, 1806.

31 Hermannus Drost was a member of the Municipal Council from April 12, 1796 until January 19, 1798, at which point he was deposed as a result of the coup by Vreede *c.s.* He was reappointed on March 12, 1803, and he served till January 20, 1808. He obviously had every reason for hating the Democratic fraction. See J.C. Breen, *op. cit.*, p. 114.

person who drafted the answer on his behalf – does not take recourse to diplomatic formalities, but enters into every single complaint – proof that the petition had impressed the Amsterdam counselors. As is often the case in polemics of this kind, the author attempted to rebut his adversaries' arguments without asking whether, in so doing, he might fall prey to inconsistencies.

The Amsterdam Magistrates first express their indignation about the fact that the petition had been submitted by only <u>six</u> (underlined in the original) Jews 'none of whom can boast of any particular esteem among his co-religionists.' The Parnasim, the writer continues, know what is best for the Jews, and the Council maintains the most cordial relations with them. The claim of a barrier having suddenly been erected between Jews and non-Jews is utterly untrue. The Jews enjoy far more privileges than before the Revolution.

The petitioners might have a point, when they call the lack of 'functions and benefices' proof of discrimination, but this by no means applies to Amsterdam alone, but also to all other cities, as well as to the highest governing bodies in the State. Besides, it was very different whether a person failed to receive an appointment, or whether he was excluded from the particular position (put differently: the absence of suitable Jewish candidates did not mean that Jews could not be appointed in principle). The criticism that there were no Jewish supervisors among the national and municipal tax collectors was countered with the argument that 'religious regulations and particular times for devotions' prevent Jews from working precisely at those hours that are most suitable for the remaining inhabitants.' With a sly dig at the 'modernists', the Council writes: 'It goes without saying that in speaking of Jews, we are referring to those who are so not only in name, but in all seriousness – [those] who observe their ancestral faith in the minutiae, as opposed to those few among them who, to judge by their indifference, would appear to profess no religion, least of all Judaism.' Polak and his colleagues are therefore accused of being irreligious – a reproach entirely in line with the attitude of the contemporary Regime and the government headed by Schimmelpenninck, but far removed from the spirit of separation of Church and State that was characteristic of the early years of the Revolution.

At this point the Council introduces a highly significant and fundamental comment. To the complaint in the petition about the Council's consistent use of the term 'Jewish Nation', it answers:

In fact, we ought to be surprised – and it almost makes us wonder whether the applicants belong to a different sect from the Jews – that a name that has always been revered by Jews, is now suddenly considered an insult by the petitioners; and in truth, when perusing their statement, and seeing that it frequently interchanges the appellations *Jewish Nation* and *Jewish Community*, and uses them as *synonyms*, one wonders how six so-called Jews dare raise this as a grievance against the authorities of their city and waste the time of the distinguished leaders with such a trivial complaint. This the more so since, even if the foregoing had sometimes been done with intent, it could easily be defended, given the undeniable fact that a people who, despite the country's general laws to which they are subject, continue to maintain their own particularistic Religious and National laws, who never intermarry with persons of other nations and therefore, because of these two facts, always remain a separate people, may quite correctly be designated a special Nation. To regard these people as one and the same, and in no way different from the other Batavian people, might be even more preposterous than to try and view a *Gothic tower on a Corinthian building* as buildings belonging to the same order.

Thus, Polak *c.s.* are hoisted with their own petard – a typical polemic one would hardly expect to see in an official letter from the Municipal Council of Amsterdam to the Provincial Government of Holland. In addition to its vituperous tone, the contents of this paragraph is highly illustrative of the way of thinking in leading circles in Amsterdam. Ten years after the Emancipation decree which granted civil rights to individual Jews, the municipal government of Amsterdam is arguing that Jews are a distinct people who cannot be equated with the remainder of the Batavian nation. In contradiction to the unequivocal declaration by the National Assembly, which in turn was inspired by the French views on this subject, the Amsterdam City Council chose to regard the Jews as a community whose members cannot be considered equals of the Gentile inhabitants of the city.[32]

Although this is not said in so many words – a significant fact in itself – the Council essentially rejected Jewish integration, not only in theory, but also in practice, as will become clear further on. A Jew had been refused entry to the Fell-mongers Guild? The commissioners had no choice, and the Secretary of State of the Interior had expressed his appreciation to the Councilmen. As regards the blacksmith Abraham Levy: 'The admission of new members to the guilds is a cumbersome affair. Applications by Jews are placed at the bottom of the list, since the majority of the member-craftsmen are predisposed against Jews. Following consultation with the Parnasim, six Jews have been registered as master-craftsmen and twelve as apprentices with the Painters and Glaziers' Guild. The same thing will happen with the other guilds.' 'That this has not yet been done with the aforementioned Abraham Levie is due to the fact that the necessary preparations with the Blacksmith Guild have not yet been completed; as well as the fact that there has been some hesitation about accepting a Jew as a blacksmith.' Apparently the problem had formed the subject of a discussion of the Presiding Magistrate and some members of the Council with the Grand Pensionary and the Secretary of State of the Interior, 'and since this conference unanimously agreed that it might be a dangerous policy, no Jew had as yet been

---

32 As is well known, the champion of Jewish emancipation in France, Count S. de Clermont-Tonnerre, argued that '*il faut tout refuser aux juifs comme nation, il faut tout leur accorder comme individus*' (December 23, 1789 in the Assemblée Nationale). In the same speech he said that Jews should not be allowed to establish themselves as a distinct political body or estate within the State. If they refused to become citizens in their own right, they would have to be expelled. On no account should the creation of a 'nation within a nation' be allowed. See for this E. Tcherikover, *Jehudim b'itot hamahpecha* (Heb.), Tel Aviv, 1957, pp. 85-86. Arthur Herzberg, *The French Enlightenment and the Jews*, New York-London, 1968, pp. 360-1. S. Schwarzfuchs, *Les Juifs de France*, Paris, 1975, p. 210.

registered with the Blacksmith Guild.' This proves that the Grand Pensionary himself had approved the actions of the Amsterdam City Council and the guilds.[33]

The Council's true attitude towards the Jews emerges at the end of the letter, when they state that since the Emancipation Jews not only reside in their own streets, but also outside, and that they engage in all kinds of crafts and professions from which they were earlier excluded. 'And frankly, if one of the two – the Jews or the other inhabitants – would have reason to complain, it would surely be the latter, who because of the influx of Jews from other places to this city, and their dispersion throughout its districts, have had to sacrifice a considerable part of their livelihood and prosperity, while being forced to tolerate that the Jews, by combining their activities, seized control of different businesses that used to form the meager means of existence and livelihood of these inhabitants; and who are daily forced to see how these insignificant Jews, who[se ways] are largely unknown and therefore escape scrutiny, see fit to circumvent the observation of certain laws that other inhabitants are incapable of evading, thus enabling them to enjoy advantages and profits that others have to forego.'

The decision to appoint Jews to various positions was not in the hands of the municipal government, but even so the Amsterdam City Council wanted to clarify its position on the subject. It therefore stated that it would be considered a very grave development if 'a Nation is included in the administration that, whether or not one denies this, is so attached to each other, and which – with a few individuals excepted – is so vastly inferior to the other inhabitants in civilization and enlightenment.' In addition, this was expected to create very considerable resentment among the other inhabitants, and 'to convince the far greater and more prominent number of the inhabitants to agree to the petitioners' desires would first require the complete suspension of every feeling of self-respect, superiority of knowledge, self-abnegation and more profound feelings for this country.'

And if this was not sufficiently anti-Semitic, the Council's letter continued: First it would be necessary to convince them that the Jew has taken the events in this country as much to heart as they themselves have done, even if no interest or advantage was to be gained from this. One would have to erase religious concepts that were implanted in these others inhabitants, regardless of their denomination, during their earliest youth, which caused them to consider the Jew as an alien, without fatherland and removed from the land

---

33 R.J. Schimmelpenninck (1761-1825) was generally regarded as a proponent of Jewish emancipation, since he had drafted the decree of September 2, 1796. Besides this, his brother Jan was legal advisor to the Jewish community. For this reason Polak *c.s.* appeal specifically to him in their petition. As shown by the answer from Amsterdam, Schimmelpenninck approved the exclusion of Jews from certain guilds. This accords with his general policies and his close ties with the Amsterdam regents. (Comp. C. de Wit, *De strijd tussen aristocratie en democratie in Nederland*, Heerlen, 1965, particularly pp. 85, 122, 168.) In their letter to Louis Napoleon, Meyer and Asser state that Schimmelpenninck would certainly have approved the request of Polak *c.s.*, but in the light of the information from the Amsterdam Municipal Council this would seem highly improbable.

of his forefathers, before and until they could accept and respect a Jew as their Regent. Finally, one would have to accept the fact that several honorable persons would resign from the Government, and that others would refuse to accept such functions, since not a single member of the Government who values the regard and respect of his fellow-citizens would dare expose himself to the contempt and opprobrium of the majority of the population if it saw him share his authority with Jews.

This, at last, is clear language: The members of the Amsterdam municipal government threaten to resign if a Jew should be appointed to the City Council. The knowledge that they enjoy the support of the voters – and the guilds in particular – on the one hand, and the Grand Pensionary, on the other, makes them feel they can afford this threat. Similarly they can afford to thwart every attempt by the Jews to spread their wings either politically or economically. For this reason we can only concur with J.D. Meyer's conclusion about this period several years later: 'Even though the guilds had been abolished, they continued to exist, particularly in Amsterdam, and to harass, under the protection of the Government, all those who would exercise their rights.'[34]

One month after the Amsterdam Magistrates had sent their reply, Schimmelpenninck was forced to resign, and shortly afterwards Louis Napoleon was invested as the ruler of the Kingdom of Holland. Given such drastic changes in the country's system of government, one might ask whether people were still interested in the problems of the Jewish inhabitants? It seems reasonable to assume that the Provincial Government of Holland believed that the king would have more important problems to worry about than the gripes of a handful of Jewish crusaders. The greater was the surprise, therefore, when on August 17, 1806, the States of Holland were instructed by the Minister of the Interior to submit their recommendations regarding the petition of Polak *c.s.* This demand relates to a follow-up letter that advocates J.D. Meyer and C. Asser, two of the signatories of the original petition, had addressed to the king on July 15, 1806 – three months after the first petition – reiterating the contents of Polak's original petition. It had been adapted to the newly created circumstances, and emphasized the equality of rights Jews had been granted in France and the 'sentiments' which 'the great Napoleon' had evinced towards the Jews. This petition, too, concluded with the request that all municipal governments, and in particular that of Amsterdam, should be put on notice 'to enable and allow the Jews to enjoy the consequences of the decree of September 2, 1796'.[35]

Contrary to the reply from the Amsterdam municipal government, the proposals of the Provincial government, dated September 2, 1806, were formulated in restrained and official language – but its final conclusions were the same. The States of Holland questioned the mandate of the six petitioners to

---

34 'Quoique les corps de métiers fussent abolis, ils ne cessèrent jamais d'exister surtout à Amsterdam, et de harceler, sous la protection du gouvernement, tous ceux qui voulaient se prévaloir de leur droits', in: ARA, Bi. Za.' for 1813, inv. no. 1005 (1-6) 'Mémoire de J.D. Meyer aan Monsieur le Baron d'Alphonse' (February 19, 1811).

35 ARA, Archief Bi. Zaken voor 1813, Inv. no. 246.

speak for their thousands of co-religionists, who 'as it were constitute a special Nation'. However, they also referred to the decree of September 2, 1796, that had never been rescinded or changed, and therefore continued to be in force. The fact that Jews failed to receive appointments did not mean that they were ostracized. Decisions whether or not to appoint a certain person should not be imposed, for which reason notifications to the municipalities to this effect would be detrimental. As shown both by the petition and the reply, Jews were indeed admitted to the guilds, and anyone who believed that he had been wronged was free to submit an appeal. As regards the treatment of the Jews of Amsterdam, the States of Holland referred to the answer of the [Amsterdam City] Council 'without, however, intending to convey the impression that we, too, accept or approve the various contentions and arguments set out therein'. Without openly saying so, the Provincial government was evidently of the opinion that the Amsterdam City Fathers had gone too far. Given the fact that – albeit in somewhat milder terms – they too used the term 'Jewish Nation', we may assume that the States' objections did not so much concern the principle of the issue as the anti-Semitic tone in which it had been phrased. For in the end the Provincial government fully backed the Amsterdam magistrature: '...if it were up to them, they would have no difficulty in turning down the petitioners' request and rejecting it.'

Whether or not the Minister of the Interior, J.H. Mollerus, advised the king about the petitions of Polak *c.s.* and Meyer/Asser is unknown. However, Mollerus, a man of the ancient régime,[36] made his views on the same issue known in another recommendation which he submitted to the king one year later, in connection with two petitions by Adath Jesurun – one, dated May 16, 1807, and signed by the three delegates to the Sanhedrin, C. Asser, H. Lemon and I. Littwak, and a second, of June 25, 1807, written in name of the Community itself, and signed by Chairman Samuel Moses Metz and Secretary C. Asser.[37] The first petition contained a number of requests in connection with the Sanhedrin to ameliorate the conditions of the Jews, as well as requesting particular consideration for the new Community. These points will be dealt with in more detail later on. The second petition asked the king to grant knighthoods to members of the new Community and appoint several Jews to the Amsterdam City Council – with special consideration for members of their Community.

In his recommendation Mollerus pointed to the insignificant following of Adath Jesurun among the Jews. Granting special honors was certain to arouse the fiercest jealousy, besides which there was another side to the coin as well: 'To the extent that ...persons might be found among the Jews whose appointment

36 Jan Hendrik Baron Mollerus (1750-1834), was secretary of the Council of State until the Revolution, following which he refused all offices until 1802. Louis Napoleon successively appointed him Privy Councilor, Minister of the Interior and Minister of Religious Affairs. Under King William I he became Vice-President of the Privy Council, and in 1823 President of the Council of Ministers. See Van der Aa, under Mollerus.

37 ARA, Archief Staatssecr. Lod. Nap., exh. October 3, 1807, no. 23. The recommendation is dated September 23, 1807.

to one position or another would not arouse protests from the public', he still considered this inadvisable at the present moment, since 'the appointment of a Jew – particularly a member of the new Community – in the government of a city such as Amsterdam might well make an unpleasant impression.'

In other words, although Mollerus rejected any preferential treatment for the new community, this did not mean that he was prepared to give members of the much larger older community, or for that matter the Portuguese community, a chance. In fact, his summation points in an entirely different direction. He advised the king to write the petitioners 'that he shall always be pleased to cause them to experience the effects of those principles of tolerance and general justice which Holland has consistently exemplified, also with regard to their Nation.' As far as Mollerus was concerned, the decree of September 2, 1796, simply did not exist: the French king had to deal with the Jews according to the principles that were in force prior to the Revolution.

Efforts to End Discrimination

The arguments and tone employed by the above-mentioned three Dutch official bodies may have differed, but their conclusions were the same: the grievances and requests by Asser and his colleagues were to be accepted for information purposes only. It is significant that Louis Napoleon declined this unanimous as well as unambiguous recommendation. Admittedly the king noted in the margin (of the French translation) of Mollerus' recommendation that he agreed with his Minister's advice, but he added: 'Answer that its (i.e. Adath Jesurun) conflict with the majority of their Nation in the Kingdom at the present moment prevents me from doing something for them'[38] – with the emphasis on *pour le moment*. We have already noted the Amsterdam City Council's reference to its good relationship with the Parnasim of the old community, and the emphasis by both the States of Holland and the Minister on the fact that the petitioners formed a tiny minority. None of these three authorities, by the way, evinced much interest in helping to solve these internal Jewish conflicts. It is true that during the first year following their division continuous efforts were undertaken by the authorities to unite the two High-German communities, but these failed to yield results.[39] Louis Napoleon, on the other hand, regarded the unification of the three communities (including the Portuguese) to be a primary condition for the integration of Dutch Jewry within the general society. The return of the intellectual vanguard of the Jews, organized within Adath Jesurun, to the old community, so he believed, would not only prepare the ground for full emancipation, but also help disarm its opponents, by neutralizing their argument that the vast majority of the Jews were opposed to emancipation and integration. Louis Napoleon forced the unification of the

38 'Répondre que la désunion où ell est avec la majorité de leur Nation dans ce Royaume m'empêche pour le moment de faire quelque chose pour eux.'
39 See Bloemgarten, *op. cit.*, pp. 44 ff.

two communities, and this unified organization did indeed become an important instrument for the implementation of a number of Royal decrees. Even so
– as we shall soon see – the united organization failed to influence the position
of the Jews within Dutch society.[40]

It would go beyond the scope of this chapter to enumerate all the measures
Louis Napoleon took with regard to the Jews. We shall restrict ourselves to those
which contradicted the recommendations of his Dutch advisors. Despite their
opinion that 'no Jews should be admitted to offices and benefices', Louis
Napoleon appointed J.D. Meyer and C. Asser to high offices in his government
establishment. M.S. Asser was elected to the committee charged with preparing
the new Commercial Code, and some three-quarters of the text was drafted by
him. The king's physician, Immanuel Capadoce, was knighted. Polak *c.s.* had
requested the Commissioner of State to compel all municipalities, in particular
Amsterdam, to consider Jews for 'offices and benefices'. Although Louis Napoleon failed to comply, it is most likely due to the above-mentioned and other
petitions that in September 1808 he ordered the Minister of the Interior to
circularize all the bailiffs in the country to investigate whether, and to what
extent, Jews were discriminated against in their bailiwicks. The answers were
sufficiently enlightening to induce him to issue instructions for the cancellation
of all remaining discriminatory regulations in several localities.

We see, therefore, that Louis Napoleon followed an entirely different line
from that recommended to him by some of his advisors. In practice he followed
the guidelines recommended by Meyer and Asser, whose ideas, with two exceptions, are clearly reflected in the king's actions. The king did not appoint Jews
to the Municipal Council of Amsterdam, apparently in order to avoid an open
confrontation, besides which – at least at the beginning of his reign – he acted
with great circumspection with regard to the religious sensitivities of the Jewish
majority. The fact that the new community had the greatest difficulty in depu-
tizing members to the Sanhedrin, which had been constituted with such fanfare
by his brother, as well as the fact that the two other communities could continue
to refuse their participation – the pressures of J.D. Meyer, a member of the old
community, and three important Portuguese Jews (I.M. Capadoce, I. da Costa
Athias and J. Saportas) notwithstanding – reflects the king's seriousness about
safeguarding tolerance and religious freedom in his kingdom. This also explains why he refused to impose the decisions of the Sanhedrin on his Jewish

40 A considerable amount of literature exists about the measures taken by Louis Napoleon and
    Napoleon with regard to the Jews (see Chapter 6). See particularly Wolff, 51-110; D.S. van
    Zuiden, *Lodewijk Napoleon*, pp. 66-88. Also of importance is H. Poppers, *De Joden in Overijssel*,
    Utrecht, 1926, pp. 86-153. Wolff, in *Geschiedenis der Joden in Haarlem 1600-1815* (Haarlem, 1917)
    reproduces Louis Napoleon's order about discrimination. For the notes by Asser and Meyer, see
    J.S. da Silva Rosa 'Bijdrage tot de kennis van de economische en politieke toestand der
    Hoogduitsche Joden te Amsterdam in het begin der vorige eeuw', *Centraalblad voor Israëlieten in
    Nederland* 31 (1916), nos. 50, 51, 52; 32 (1917), nos. 2, 4, 6, 9. Important sources for events in
    other towns are: I. Mendels, *De Joodse gemeente te Groningen*, Groningen, 1910, pp. 72-90; Van
    Zuiden, *'s-Gravenhage*, *op. cit.*, pp. 95-107; H. Beem, *De Joden van Leeuwarden*, Assen, 1974, pp.
    114-26, H. Poppers, *De Joden in Overijsel van hunne vestiging tot 1814*, Utrecht-Amsterdam, 1926,
    and *Memorboek*, *passim*.

subjects.[41] Louis Napoleon not only compared favorably with the Dutch ruling establishment, but he also avoided resorting to the aggressive and in many ways hurtful policies his brother had practised with regard to the Jews.

French Policy Regarding the Jews

Napoleon was intensively involved with the status of French Jewry, particularly between the years 1805 and 1808 – the same period, therefore, during which his brother in Holland attempted to improve the lot of his Dutch subjects. His views about the Jews during the period in which he prepared and enacted the legislation, aimed at regulating the position of the Jews within his Empire, are known to us from various sources. He regarded the Jews as 'the most detestable of people' (*les plus méprisables des hommes*), and in line with the teachings of the Church, he believed in the 'curse with which it has struck this race, which seems to be the only one to have been excluded from Redemption'.[42] If the Amsterdam Magistrates would have known how Napoleon had expressed himself in the course of a debate in the Conseil d'État a mere week before their answer to the petition by Polak and his colleagues, they could have quoted the Emperor: 'The Jews should be regarded as a Nation rather than as a sect', but: '...a disgraced and degraded nation, capable of every kind of knavishness'.[43]

Utterances of this kind might lead one to expect a much harsher policy than Napoleon did in fact conduct. His convening in 1806 of an Assembly of Jewish Notables and, a year later, a Grand Sanhedrin of Jewish spiritual and communal leaders were gestures that, while testifying to Napoleon's organizational genius, were liable to create among the Jews – who were unfamiliar with the Emperor's views – the image of a Messiah who would deliver them from their humiliating state.[44] The prevalence of this view in 19th-century Jewish historiography is due to the predominance of German-Jewish historians, who recognized only the positive aspects of Napoleon's regime. Yet there can be no doubt about Napoleon's real intentions when we read the text of the decree dated March 17, 1808, whereby, initially for a period of 10 years, French Jewry was relegated to an exceptional position. Debts to Jews were canceled or subjected to restrictive conditions; Jews needed special permits to conduct trade, Jews not

---

41 See for this Chapter 5. The decisions of the Sanhedrin were imposed as from February 23, 1813 – some time after the annexation of The Netherlands – in a circular letter of the Consistoire des Israélites de la Circonscription d'Amsterdam (ARA, Berenstein Archive, file 5, no. 41).

42 '...la malédiction dont elle est frappée cette race qui semble avoir été seulement exceptée de la rédemption.'

43 '...une nation avilie, dégradée, capable de toutes les bassesses.'

44 See J. Presser *Napoleon*, Amsterdam, 1946: 'En toch: de Joden vereren de nagedachtenis van Napoleon' (p. 289). Even so, disregarding the byzantine adoration during the period when Napoleon was still in power, this expression is mainly due to Heine. In Eastern Europe Napoleon was considered an enemy throughout his reign. See B. Meworach, *Napoleon utekufato*, Jerusalem, 1968 en R. Goetschel, 'l'Hostilité du monde hassidique à la Révolution française', in *Les juifs et la Révolution française*, Paris, 1992, particularly p. 280: the founder of Hassidism called Napoleon a satan.

already residing there were forbidden to settle in the Alsace, and Jewish recruits for army service could no longer designate replacements. Yet another of Napoleon's decrees instituted a special religious ordinance for Jews aimed at checking their daily activities.

The implementation of these decrees was less draconian than the text would lead one to believe, on the one hand owing to the lenient attitude of a number of prefects, and on the other to the fact that Napoleon himself granted increasing numbers of dispensations – which may be indicative of a certain change in his attitude towards the Jews.[45]

Nevertheless, another aspect should be noted: even though Napoleon conducted a harsh policy towards the Jews in France, the French attitude in the vassal states remained without exception pro-Jewish. Even in the annexed territories, where the laws of the Empire were enforced, Jews were exempted from the most onerous provisions. Although during his visit to The Netherlands Napoleon rebuked the Jews in a most ill-mannered vein,[46] the decree of March 17, 1808, was not implemented in the Dutch 'departements'. Lebrun, who had been appointed Governor-General of Holland following Napoleon's annexation of The Netherlands (1810), claimed that the Dutch Jews were not identical to their French co-religionists and succeeded in getting them exempted from the prohibition of appointing replacements for army service.[47] In so doing, Lebrun honored his promise of January 23, 1811, that 'the Dutch High-German Israelite communities would receive the same rights as enjoyed by all other inhabitants who are governed by the laws of France'. He said that he 'had been surprised... at the distinctions in Dutch civilian society between Israelites and other denominations.' We have no reason to doubt Lebrun's impartiality, for what possible reason could he have had to try and expose discrimination where it did not exist? While admitting that 'the law prescribed some distinctions,' he considered that it was not Napoleon's intention to add still further discrepancies.[48] Here, therefore, is another Frenchman who took offense at the discrimination against the Jews in The Netherlands.

The French era (including the periods of the Kingdom of Holland and the Annexation) has indeed one favorable aspect with regard to the Jews: the genuine desire on the part of the regime to implement full legal and civic equality. Unfortunately, from a material point of view, this same period was the

---

45 See R. Anchel, *Napoléon et les Juifs*, Paris, 1928: '...sont des indices d'un changement intervenu dans l'esprit de Napoléon entre 1808 et 1813' (p. 366). On the other hand we believe that François Piétri (*Napoléon et les Israélites*, Paris, 1965) goes too far in his defense of Napoleon when he shifts the responsibility for his policies, and especially for his 'décret infâme' of 1808, completely to his subordinates, particularly Count Louis Mathieu Molé (p. 140). For Napoleon's comments about Jews, see Anchel, *op. cit.*, pp. 63-93. See also Simon Schwarzfuchs, *Napoleon, the Jews and the Sanhedrin*, London, 1979, especially pp. 27-50.

46 For the rebukes of the 'German' Jews during Napoleon's visit to Utrecht, see Colenbrander, *Inlijving en Opstand*, Amsterdam, 1941, 2, pp. 130-32. For an overall report on the visit to The Netherlands, see J. Meijer, *Het Jonas Daniël Meyerplein*, Amsterdam, 1961, pp. 80-83, and D. S. van Zuiden, *Lodewijk Napoleon, op. cit.*, pp. 85-87.

47 Colenbrander, *GS* Vol. 6 (1810-1813), p. 141; and see Ch. 8, note 55.

48 See Poppers, *op. cit.*, pp. 102-103.

worst that Dutch Jewry had experienced in its entire history in The Netherlands. Economic conditions had been declining since the second half of the
18th century, but the crisis during the years 1771-1773 accelerated the process
of impoverishment. In 1799, even before the economic downturn which characterized the French era in The Netherlands, the number of persons on poor-re-
lief in the presumably 'affluent' Portuguese community amounted to 54
percent, and in the High-German community as much as 87 (!) percent –
against an average for the entire city of Amsterdam of 36.7 percent.[49] But
poverty is relative: those who had been on the dole in 1799 were well-off
compared to the paupers of 1811, whose wretched condition was chronicled by
an outsider, the Privy Counselor Réal, according to whom one discerned among
the Jews of Amsterdam *'les derniers degrés de la misère'*. 'They are virtually naked
or are dressed in rags; many of them live in the streets and sleep on the
pavement...'.[50] The French era so seriously scourged the Jews of Amsterdam
that it took a century before they could more or less catch up with their
Christian fellow-citizens.

What were the causes of this catastrophe? For one thing, the economic basis
of the Jews had traditionally been too narrow. Most of them were engaged in
commercial activities of some kind, and their exclusion from the guilds seriously restricted their choice of occupation – despite the fact that in the 18th
century Amsterdam authorities had frequently shielded them against Christian
merchants and dealers. Many indigent Jews were employed by economically
more privileged co-religionists. As a result the collapse of the Dutch position in
international commerce, as well as the 'Continental system' and Napoleon's
monetary measures, affected Jews far more severely than non-Jews. If after 1796
Jews had been allowed a free choice of crafts and professions, their position
might not have become so desperate. Under the prevailing circumstances their
only advantages compared to the situation prior to 1796 was that they could
settle wherever they wanted (an option exercised by a number of Jews from
Amsterdam), and the admission of a limited number of Jews to the guilds
pending the passage in 1809 of Gogel's bill for the final abolishment of the
guilds. But by then it was too late for the Jews of Amsterdam.

This dialectic with regard to the status of the Jews of Amsterdam made their
economic collapse an important factor in the opposition to their social integration. In 1795 and 1796 the Amsterdam citizenry had already opposed the
granting of civil rights to the Jews, but as economic conditions continued to
decline, Jewish equality came to be seen as a direct threat to the citizenry's own
economic survival. People became alarmed at the thought of hordes of Jewish
paupers invading their professions and gaining free access to every kind of

49 Brugmans-Frank, *op. cit.*, pp. 592-95. About the poverty of the Jews in the 19th century, see S.
   Kleerekoper, 'Het Joodse proletariaat in het Amsterdam van de 19e eeuw', *St. Ros.* I (1967), pp.
   97-104.
50 'pour connaître les derniers degrés de la misère, il faut avoir le courage de se hazarder.... Ils
   sont presque nus ou couverts de haillons; beaucoup d'entr'eux n'ont que la rue pour domicile,
   et le pave pour lit.' Colenbrander, *op. cit.*, p. 96.

commerce. The already mentioned claim by the Amsterdam Magistrates of ferment among the blacksmiths can be readily understood. No less obvious is that the same magistrates were far from eager to undermine the authority of the Parnasim and having to shoulder the latter's responsibilities. It is not surprising that Burgomaster Wolters van der Poll[51] of Amsterdam, in a report written at the request of Louis Napoleon – and intended to offset the reports by C. Asser and J.D. Meyer – commended the Parnasim for their most dedicated care of the destitute among the Jewish population. After all, should the Parnasim have neglected this duty, the Amsterdam municipal coffers would have had to bear the expense of caring for some 18,000 Jewish indigents on an equal footing with the Christian poor – a prospect that must have daunted the City Fathers. Thus the French era, which in theory should have brought political emancipation to the Jews, in effect reinforced Gentile opposition to the social acceptance of the Jewish community.

The French era, and in particular the regime of Louis Napoleon, has been judged extremely favorably in Jewish historiography – and rightly so, in so far as it concerns the good intentions of the latter.[52] The question is, how did these intentions benefit the masses? A few measures offered them direct advantages (e.g. a prohibition of street markets on Saturdays and the king's earnest efforts to eliminate discrimination), but they were insufficient to check, let alone arrest, the economic downturn. A number of measures infringing on the traditional Jewish way of life – often the brainchild of the king's Jewish advisors – naturally aroused considerable opposition (an example is the compulsory teaching of Dutch), whereas the organizational issues that fascinated the king hardly interested the man in the street. The establishment of a Jewish army corps, however fetching it may have looked, was – rightly so – regarded as a catastrophe by many poor Jews.

Thus it was without sadness that the Jews said adieu to the French occupation – without any assurance that the kingdom of William I would be any more promising.

Policy during the Restoration

During the discussions he conducted on November 16, 1813, for the purpose of forming a new municipal administration, A.R. Falck (1777-1843), a captain in the National Guard, was extremely gratified to notice the degree of national unity. Former divisions seemed to have vanished: Orangists and Patriots, Dutch Reformed and Roman Catholics, were universally accepted as long as they were known to be 'honorable and well-meaning persons.' At this point Falck, whose impressions are recorded in his Memoirs, continues: 'My principal purpose was

---

51 See Wolff, *Lod. Nap., op. cit.*, pp. 61-62. The mayor warned the king not to revise the by-laws of the Jewish community or, in fact, deprive the Parnasim of some of the authority over their members, since this was likely to endanger the welfare of the poor.
52 See Van Zuiden, *Lod. Nap., op. cit.* , pp. 87-88.

to include a Jew. This proved to be quite difficult, and my efforts at persuasion, which for logical reasons – and with a view to avoiding offense in so delicate a matter – were based on the example of the French themselves, would have been insufficient if it had not been considered necessary to do something for First-Lieutenant Mendes de Leon, who was both liked and respected among the entire Corps. This is how his father's name came to be added to the list.'[53]

We can see that the participants in the meeting with Falck did not want to carry national unity to the point of also including Jews. Falck tried every type of persuasion, and it is characteristic that, while mentioning the French example, he failed to refer – as had been the case with Mollerus – to the manner in which Jews had been treated prior to the Revolution. The reason why those present finally acquiesced to Falck's urgent request was because they felt they owed a gesture to a younger colleague – by appointing his father. The father in question, Abraham Mendes de Leon, was president of the 'Israelite Consistory within the Circumscription of Amsterdam', and as such the appointed representative of the Jews. However, at the time of the decision this was either unknown or considered unimportant, for Falck fails to make any mention of it.

The next day Falck allowed himself, 'on his own responsibility', to call upon a second Jew to become a member of the City Council. 'Admittedly this second one was Meyer, but although quite as clever in 1813 as at any other time, Meyer, who was the editor of the *Dagblad der Zuyderzee*, had forfeited the sympathy of many people.'[54]

The initiators finally succeeded in getting the list approved *in toto*, and suddenly there were two Jews among the twenty-four members of the Amsterdam City Council. This by no means represented a proportional representation (which would have entitled the Jews to three or four members), but a precedent had been created.

The happiness was to be of short duration. Several Council members, including Meyer, could not afford to work without pay for any length of time and resigned. In a letter dated December 28, 1813, addressed to C.F. van Maanen,[55] the man in charge of 'the administration of justice', Meyer informed him that he could no longer stay on the Council, and he requested Van Maanen to see to it 'that the Jews shall not be evicted from the Council without being replaced by other co-religionists'. Meyer's letter was brought to the attention of the king, who passed it on to Falck, who by now was secretary to William I. Consequently it was arranged that Mendes de Leon would remain a member of the City Council, but only after Falck – to quote his own words – 'had to enter

---

53 A.R. Falck, 'Gedenkschriften' The Hague, 1913, p. 82. Colenbrander, in *Inlijving, op. cit.*, omits in his quote exactly the arguments used by Falck (p. 23).

54 Falck, *op. cit.* , p. 91. Falck and Meyer had studied together in Leiden, and both were members of a literary circle.

55 Colenbrander, *GS* Vol. 6 (1810-1813), 'Vestiging van het Koninkrijk, 1813-1815' (R.G.P., grote serie 23), The Hague, 1914, pp. 427, Colenbrander comments that the place where the letter was discovered indicates that Van Maanen must have brought it to the attention of the Sovereign Monarch. This would mean that Falck, as secretary to the king, was also familiar with its contents.

combat with pistol and sword' against Van Straalen, the Minister of the Interior. Thus, one single Jew remained in a body composed of thirty-six members, a scant representation of circa eleven percent of the Amsterdam population.

In his letter to Van Maanen, Meyer raised yet another point, for he requested the latter's intervention on behalf of Jews 'who quite possibly run the risk that, if not forfeiting their civic rights, they will be subjected to the yoke of the old regulations.' The relevant paragraph continues: 'Mr. Brugmans[56] has informed your Excellency of the spirit in which the Provisional Government of Amsterdam intends to advise, and however much I would want to stop them, I fear that I might not succeed.'

Judging from Meyer's words, we must assume that a majority of the Council supported this plan, but also in this case, presumably either Falck or the king himself intervened, for the status of the Jews remained unchanged. The incident is significant, however, since it demonstrates the prevailing mood. Neither should it surprise us, therefore, that the Council continued to bar Jews from all official offices and functions,[57] precisely as its predecessor had done ten years earlier under the regime of the Grand Pensionary, and which had prompted the first petition by Polak and his friends.

Against this it is often pointed out that J.D. Meyer was appointed Secretary of the Constitutional Review Committee, in which capacity he was expected to strike a balance between twelve Protestants and twelve Roman Catholics. However, when we see how this appointment came about, and what followed in its wake, a far less complimentary picture is revealed. It was Falck who suggested to the king how he might avoid disturbing the balance between Protestants and Catholics: '"Your Majesty," I answered, "by appointing an Israelite," and I described to him J.D. Meyer. This idea immediately appealed to him. He needed a few hours to think it over, but already the next morning I found a letter indicating his approval, and an hour later the resolution of April 22 (No. 80) had been signed. Meyer's behavior in the above-mentioned capacity displeased many people, but I have no indications that anybody ever openly expressed these sentiments, at least in any book or journal.'

We see, therefore, that we are dealing here with a personal decision of the king, taken without consultation with his close advisors. These were opposed, but they did not show it, since among the Dutch it was not considered seemly to show one's anti-Semitism in public. In practice, however, they wanted Jews to be excluded from positions such as these ('Is Article 134 of the Constitution mere window dressing?' Falck exclaimed), and in private those concerned showed the king their displeasure in no uncertain terms: 'The king himself told me that Mr. van Aylva had seriously berated him.' Falck's position was undermined by people such as Van Lennep, Elout and Van de Capellen, and in the end Meyer

---

56 P.A. Brugmans, a member of the Provisional Council of Amsterdam; see Brugmans, *op. cit.*, Vol. V, p. 96. He was a brother-in-law of Van Maanen.

57 Thus J.D. Meyer in a letter dated June 4, 1815 to Jeronimo de Vries. See J. Melkman (Michman), 'Klacht over Amsterdams houding tegenover de Joden', *NIW*, July 16, 1965. De Vries had persuaded Falck to add Meyer to the list of candidates for the Provisional City Council.

was forced to resign. Exactly how this happened we do not know. We only have Falck's testimony, who reports that Meyer was opposed from various sides, whereas his (i.e. Falck's) standing proved insufficient when Meyer's 'fretful' attitude played into the hands of his adversaries.[58]

In other words, Meyer's satisfaction was short-lived, and all his subsequent efforts to secure another government post equal to his abilities were in vain.[59] Meyer's career proves the restrictions to which Jews were subject even in the new kingdom, particularly when taking into account that here was a man who possessed all the necessary qualities for fulfilling the highest government positions. He was rich – a grandson of Benjamin Cohen, the wealthiest Jew in the Republic, who had been on an intimate footing with Prince William V. He was highly intelligent and literate (at a time when many politicians engaged in literary activities); he was ambitious, and he possessed political and administrative experience.[60] All this proved to be of no avail. While his fellow students received assignments to high government posts (as Ministers, Ambassadors, Privy Counselors, and so forth)[61], Meyer was deprived of any further appointments – not even at a university – and he had to be satisfied with his lawyer's practice and his literary and scientific activities. Like many Jews after him, he

---

58 See Falck, *op. cit.*, p. 163 and Falck's letter to D.J. van Lennep, in *Brieven van A.R. Falck, 1795-1843* (ed. D.J. van Lennep), The Hague, 1861, 2, pp. 219-20 (letter 114). The dissatisfaction with Meyer's appointment cannot have been a result of the fact that he had been in office during Louis Napoleon and the annexation, for the same applied to all those who were angry with Falck. Count Hans Willem van Aylva (1751-1827), an Orangist, had accepted offices under Schimmelpenninck and Louis Napoleon. Cornelius Theodorus Elout (1767-1843) had accepted numerous offices during the Batavian Republic, as well as under Louis Napoleon and during the annexation. D.J. van Lennep had been a teacher of Louis Napoleon. Godert Alexander Philip van der Capellen (1778-1848) was a minister under the regime of Louis Napoleon.

It is difficult to understand J. Meijer's claim that J.D. Meyer was a lightweight who owed his reputation to extraneous factors (*Erfenis der Emancipatie*, Haarlem, 1963, p. 68). As a legal mind Meyer certainly was not inferior to his fellow members on the Committee.

59 Falck exerted his influence with Van Hogendorp to get Meyer appointed as Secretary to the Council of State: 'For reasons too obvious to be mentioned here (sic!) I would have hesitated to mention my friend Meyer.' Meyer also hoped to be appointed Recorder of the 'Second Chamber', the Lower House of Parliament. In 1817 he applied for an appointment as Privy Councilor extraordinary. See Falck, *op. cit.*, pp. 371-73. Already prior to his appointment as secretary of the Constitutional Committee, Meyer contacted I.F. van der Meersch, suggesting that he be appointed to a Review Committee for new legislation: 'It is not a very prestigeous office, nor very profitable, and religious prejudice will not deter me, although on this score I know I will have nothing to fear from you, or from Van Maanen and Falck; but others might also be able to influence it.' See Colenbrander, *GS*, Vol. 6 (1810-1813), p. 825.

60 See N. de Beneditty, *Leven en Werken van Mr. Jonas Daniel Meyer*, Haarlem, 1925. Beneditty's biography fails to do justice to the role Meyer played in Jewish affairs. No attention whatsoever is paid to his views on Jewish problems, although during the period 1806-1813 he played an important and at times crucial role in the organization of Jewish life in The Netherlands. After 1813 he indeed withdrew completely, and no longer occupied any leading positions in Jewish organizations. The naming of a central square after him in the Jewish Quarter of Amsterdam flanked by the three major synagogues invests Meyer's name with an aura that is not warranted by his course of life.

As to his literary qualities, Falck relates, among other things, that Meyer and Helmers were the big draw of the Reading Cabinet of Amsterdam. Falck, *op.cit.*, p. 25.

61 For example A.R. Falck, J.M. Kemper, C. Vollenhoven, R.H. Arntzenius.

stood before an invisible, but nevertheless impenetrable wall. 'As for the reasons,' complained Falck in connection with the commotion that Meyer's appointment as Secretary of the Constitutional Review Committee had caused, 'I am still waiting for an explanation.'

Falck, too, was well aware that nobody was prepared to speak openly. In fact, why should they? The rationale for the invisible wall that was supposed to separate Jews and Gentiles had been formulated ten years earlier by the Amsterdam Magistrates and the Provincial Government of Holland: the absence of an appointment did not mean non-eligibility for a given office. Indeed, Jews were not excluded, but neither were they appointed.

Tradition has it that the emancipation and integration of Dutch Jewry proceeded faster and more smoothly than in other European countries thanks to the prevailing benevolent attitude towards the Jews. Romein wrote in this context: '... similarly as at the end of the 18th century the emancipation of the Jews had proceeded in the specifically Dutch manner – without friction and with the tacit approval of the vast majority.'[62]

This statement reflects the kind of smug attitude that enabled the birth of the legend, but which is in flagrant contradiction with the facts and their evaluation by contemporary personalities, who in this case showed to be more discerning than the historians. Formal emancipation only became a subject for discussion through French force of arms and was accepted by the 'Batavians' under French pressure. It was a French king who implemented the integration of the Jews into the Dutch body politic, despite the fact that the Emperor's own inclinations tended to lie in quite a different direction. This policy was continued during the annexation of The Netherlands at the initiative of the French authorities. King William I, who was more profoundly influenced by French concepts of equality than the Dutch social and political establishment, was willing to pursue the policies of his French predecessor, but was ultimately forced to capitulate to his surroundings, with the result that he turned out to be less forthcoming than Louis Napoleon. As a Dutchman, the king was more inclined to listen to the views of his Dutch subjects, very few of whom were prepared to support an active integration policy. The only real proponents were the Radical Democrats, who had been joined by the Felix Libertate group. However, when in 1798 – after less than six months – the government of Vreede was swept away, whatever influence they may have possessed was finished for good. From this moment on only a few individuals, people such as Falck and Jeronimo de Vries, were left to take the side of the Jews.

Their opponents encompassed the entire establishment, including government officials and notables of every stripe: moderates, aristocrats, Orangists, the nobility and the regents, whose rejectionist attitude towards integration could count on the support of the civilian population. Until 1808 the Parnasim and the majority of the Jews, the Rabbinate included, also resisted integration, but there are no indications that their opposition affected the attitude of

---

62 J. Romein, *In opdracht van de tijd*, Amsterdam, 1946, p. 165.

government circles in any way. The question may be asked, therefore, what – under these kind of circumstances – were the prospects for the acceptance of the Jews as equal citizens? When J.D. Meyer drew up a balance sheet after fifteen years of emancipation[63] he was extremely dissatisfied. But let us turn, for a moment, to the situation of 150 years later. When in 1940, following the German invasion of The Netherlands, all Jews were dismissed from government service, it turned out that the number of Jewish civil servants was lower than their share in the general population.[64] In fact, the relevant statistical picture is too flattering and should be adjusted in two respects: in the first place there proved to be no Jews among the senior civil servants, whereas in the second place few, if any, Jews had succeeded in penetrating ministries such as Foreign Affairs and Defense. The academic world, on the other hand, showed a very different picture. The number of Jewish professors did not materially exceed the proportion of Jews in the total population, but their position was far more established, which no doubt helps to explain the heated reactions to their dismissal among their academic colleagues, whereas only few civil servants protested against the sacking of the Jews.

A Hundred and Fifty Years of Emancipation

This summary of 150 years of emancipation illustrates the evolution of the integration of Dutch Jewry since 1796. Both in terms of status and professional opportunities the Jews lagged behind the country's social and economic expansion. This had already been pointed out in 1806 by the Amsterdam City Council. The emancipation process proceeded faster in areas where achievement was a principal criterion for appointments, although – as had been the case as early as 1806 – Jews continued to be denied access to positions of a general representative nature. This explains why until 1940 not a single Jew was ever appointed burgomaster, let alone to the position of Queen's Commissioner in one of the Dutch provinces; it also explains why the Ministry of Foreign Affairs remained hermetically sealed to Jews.

Also when compared with the situation in other Western European countries (with lower percentages of Jewish inhabitants), the conclusions with regards to The Netherlands are far from impressive. In Italy, where Jews comprised 0.01 percent of the population, there were Jewish government ministers, and even a

---

63 According to Meyer (in his *Mémoire pour d'Alphonse*, February 19, 1811), the following Government offices were occupied by Jews: 'médecin consultant du Roi, chevalier de l'Ordre; directeur du journal, membre de l'institut, un auditeur au conseil d'Etat; chef de bureau des requêtes; commis employé à la maison du Roi; commis à la commission de bien ferme; deux à la cours des comptes; deux au bureau du journal; un au bureau de la dette publique.' In total these were 11 persons, including three who were employed by the newspaper of which Meyer himself was the director. Besides this there were six advocates and one notary.

64 See A.J. Herzberg, *Kroniek der Jodenvervolging*, Arnhem, 1956, p. 47. The percentage among Government officials was one percent; even in Amsterdam no more than slightly over 2% of the municipal officials were Jews. See also L. de Jong, *Het Koninkrijk der Nederlanden in de Tweede Wereldoorlog, 4*, The Hague, 1972, pp. 780 ff.

Jewish Prime Minister – as well as Jewish ambassadors and a Jewish mayor of Rome.[65] In France (with only 0.4 percent Jews) in the course of the years the political establishment included some fifteen Jewish ministers, including a Prime Minister. Only in two other countries did Jewish emancipation get underway at a very late stage: Great Britain and Germany.[66] Yet, both countries employed Jews in primary representative positions. The British had Jewish government ministers, town mayors and even a Jewish Viceroy of India; the Germans appointed Jews as Ministers of Foreign Affairs and Finance – not counting the positions occupied by Jews in the short-lived Bavarian Republic. In The Netherlands, on the other hand, Jews were rarely, if at all, appointed to representative positions, notwithstanding their much higher percentage of the population and their far longer emancipatory history. [67]

There is still another aspect that should be recalled, if only because it helps to explain the almost unanimous view among Jews and non-Jews alike that the Jews in The Netherlands were so much better off than their co-religionists in other countries. Until 1933 emancipation was never contested in The Netherlands, and there never existed any movement attempting to invalidate the decree of September 2, 1796. Even the vitriolic riposte of the Amsterdam Magistrates to the petition by Polak and his colleagues refers to this decree when it argues that the Jews are availing themselves of it – an opinion seconded by the Provincial Government of Holland. The sole indication of any intention to nullify the Emancipation decree is, not surprisingly, found in J.D. Meyer's letter to Van Maanen: it was a sign of the times. The French had attempted to introduce legal equality for the Jews in all the countries they had occupied or held under their sway and, with the exception of Switzerland, they had succeeded. Emancipation was implemented in Rome in 1798, and subsequently in most other parts of Italy; King Jerome had introduced emancipation in Westphalia, and in the Grand Duchy of Luxembourg as well as in Frankfurt am Main emancipation had also been carried through. Even the Hanse cities had been compelled to admit Jews. The Prussian kingdom granted Jews the right of citizenship – at least theoretically – on March 11, 1812.

However, following the fall of Napoleon, emancipation had been revoked everywhere, and ultimately – petitions from Jews who had succeeded in enlisting the support of Von Metternich and Von Humboldt notwithstanding – the Congress of Vienna adopted a resolution that returned the Jews to their pre-Na-

---

65 See Cecil Roth, *The History of the Jews of Italy*, Philadelphia, 1946, pp. 75-79.

66 See *E.J.*, Vol. 13, col. 811-814 under Politics. For Germany, see also Siegmund Kaznelson, *Juden im deutschen Kulturbereich*, Berlin, 1959, pp. 531- 89; Werner Mosse, ed. *Entscheidungsjahr 1932*, Tübingen, 1965, pp. 51-85; E. Hamburger, *Juden im öffentlichen Leben Deutschlands*, Tübingen, 1968, *passim*.

67 Martin Gilbert, *Jewish History Atlas*, London, 1969, p. 64, which with reference to The Netherlands mentions one Minister instead of two, but considerably larger numbers of 'Cabinet Ministers' for other countries: Italy, 7; Germany 5; France 16; and Great Britain 11.

poleonic status. A wave of pogroms in 1819 undermined their position even further.[68]

It would therefore not have been surprising if in The Netherlands too, voices were raised to restore the regulations that were in force during the Republican era. That this did not happen was possibly due to the intervention of William I, besides which the ratification of the decree had been an act of elected representatives rather than an enforced decision by an alien regime. In any case it is characteristic of relationships in The Netherlands that the Emancipation decree was never again brought up for discussion, and that not a single political party, great or small, ever included anti-Jewish measures in its platform. With the exception of the Patriots, no mass-incited violence against Jews ever took place in The Netherlands. Certain periods were marked by considerable anti-Jewish sentiment, for example following the Pincoffs' scandal (1879)[69] and the Dreyfus affair; well-known personalities such as Abraham Kuyper[70] and Professor Bolland[71] voiced anti-Jewish sentiments reminiscent of utterances by contemporary German anti-Semites. But these were never accompanied or followed by demonstrations or organized actions against the Jews in general or influential Jewish individuals. Criticism of excessive Jewish influence, which in other countries (such as France or Germany) was accompanied by demands for special restrictive legislation, remained a theoretical issue in The Netherlands. Such expressions may have offended the Jews, but they never caused them to fear for the loss of their civil rights. The most convincing evidence of this is complete absence of organizations aimed at the protection of civil rights or combating anti-Semitism.

This seeming contradiction between existential security, on the one hand, and the restrictions to which Dutch Jews were exposed in fact merely represents

---

68 See C. Roth, *op. cit.*, pp. 421-63; Gilbert, *op. cit.*, pp, 55-56; I. Elbogen, *Geschichte der Juden in Deutschland*, Berlin, 1935, pp. 193-206, and: J. Katz, 'The Hep-Hep Riots in Germany of 1819: The Historical Background' (Hebr.), in: *Zion*, XXXVIII (1973), pp. 62-115, which shows the connection between anti-Semitic propaganda documents, pogroms and anti-Jewish legislation. About the Congress of Vienna, see S.W. Baron, *Die Judenfrage auf dem Wiener Kongress*, Vienna, 1920, and *EJ*, under Metternich.

69 Lodewijk Pincoffs (1827-1911) had fraudulently attempted to hide the heavy losses of his African Trading Company (1879). In 1877 Kappeyne van de Coppello had offered Pincoffs the post of Minister of Finance, but the latter had declined. After the scandal had come into the open, Kappeyne van de Coppello for a number of years consistently scotched the admission of Jews to the First Chamber of Parliament – a characteristically anti-Semitic reaction. In 1866 the publication *Eigen Haard* ('Home Fires') wrote: 'Civic equality of Jews and Christians must as yet overcome certain questions and objections that nobody dares express in public, but which quite unexpectedly surface every now and then with regard to matters that are completely unrelated to religion. For the sons of Israel, even for the most talented and modest among them, the road towards public service is of course open, but public opinion hardly helps them to pave it.' See: A.S. Rijxman, *A.C. Wertheim*, Amsterdam, 1961, pp. 268-69.

70 For the anti-Semitism of Abraham Kuypers, see Ivo Schoeffer, 'Abraham Kuyper and the Jews', *DJH* 1, pp. 237-54; J. Michman, *DJH* 3, p. 15; A.S. Rijxman, *op. cit.* , p. 103. See *Memorboek*, pp. 596-98. L.E. Visser left the Ministry of Foreign Affairs as a result of the anti-Semitism generated by the Dreyfuss affair. See J. Michman, 'The Controversial Stand of the Joodse Raad in The Netherlands', *Yad Vashem Studies* X (1974), p. 13, no. 11.

71 About Bolland, as instigator and leader of anti-Semitic currents in The Netherlands, see L. de Jong, *op. cit.* , I, pp. 284-89.

two sides of the same coin, namely the fundamental stability and continuity of the Dutch attitude towards the Jewish minority, the roots of which can be traced back to the Republic. Rogier[72] noted the 'chronic dichotomy characterizing the Reformed faith in the Northern Netherlands in general, and in the larger Dutch cities in particular' – and, we should like to add, most particularly in the city of Amsterdam. It is this dichotomy that more than any other factor determined the social and political status of dissenters and Catholics in the United Dutch provinces. Regardless of how intolerant Calvinism was in theory, in practice a certain equilibrium was established in The Netherlands between the clerical and liberal tendencies. Existing edicts were honored in the breach 'to an astonishing degree.' Yet this tolerance did not mean parity: the established social order, with an Establishment Church on the one hand, and a non-Establishment Church and dissenters on the other, continued to exist.

How did this affect the Jews in practice? In cities where they were tolerated, the authorities took care to mitigate the 'rigors'[73] of the decrees, which helped to make life bearable at a time when the Jews had not been reduced to penury. There existed a considerable measure of religious freedom, but Jewish communities were far from autonomous. Local authorities permitted themselves to interfere in all kinds of internal matters, besides insisting on approving their by-laws.[74] The Jewish Nation stood under *de facto* tutelage, but this same tutelage also meant effective protection.

It looked as if the Batavian Revolution had demolished this entire structure, a development which – at least on paper – had found concrete expression in the Emancipation decree of September 2, 1796. Yet, following the turbulent years from 1795 till 1798 the pre-Revolutionary pattern was largely restored. The Amsterdam City Council insisted on continuing to regard the Jews as a 'Nation', and it is more than symbolic that this appellation continued to be used for at least another century. The Dutch didactic poet De Schoolmeester ('The Schoolmaster') required no interpreters for the following epitaph:

> *Here lie twenty of the Nation,*
> *Extremely noisy before, but now bereft*
> *of conversation.*[75]

---

72 See L.J. Rogier, *Terugblik en Uitzicht I*, Hilversum-Antwerp, 1964, particularly 'De tolerantie in de Statenbond' and 'Proeftuin der Pariteit'. Rogier's observations have materially contributed towards increasing my understanding of the position of the Jews in The Netherlands. The quotations are on pp. 85-86 and 97.

73 As stated in the petition by Polak *et. al.*

74 The suggestion in the doctoral thesis of M.E. Bolle (Amsterdam, 1960), to the effect that in 1796 the autonomy of the Jewish communities was annulled, is incorrect. Prior to 1795 the communities did not enjoy complete autonomy, because the authorities continually interfered in their internal affairs, whereas after 1795 the Parnasim continued to exercise authority over all Jews for many years.

75   *Hier liggen er twintig van de natie,*
        Te voren vol lawaai, thans zonder conversatie.
      Gedichten van den Schoolmeester, J. van Lennep (publisher), Amsterdam, 1859, pp. 258. 'De Schoolmeester' was the pseudonym of Gerrit van der Linde Jr. (1808-1858), a popular poet at the time.

According to the [City] Council, members of this 'Nation' did not belong in governing or representative bodies. Following the Restoration, The Netherlands became a Kingdom, in which all citizens were equal – but only in theory. 'In practice Dutch society continued to be ruled by a tradition established by the minority dictatorship at the time of the Revolt – a tradition that in Republican days had been considered the life blood of the State.'[76] In this State, characterized by 'Protestant supremacy' and rigid class consciousness, Roman Catholics had to struggle hard in order to gain recognition, which ultimately – and unlike the Jews – they achieved though sheer force of numbers. Within this 'old-fashioned, fairly static and tradition-governed system',[77] the Jews, who belonged neither to the Established Church, nor possessed an aristocracy or regents recognized by the ruling classes, continued to find their access to representative functions in society blocked.

During the entire period from 1815 till 1933 this fact was never openly discussed. This makes the French era even more interesting, since the debate about the status of the Jews was in full force during this period. This was owed to a handful of intellectuals who in the year 1795 opened a two-pronged offensive, aimed at securing full social equality for all Jews and the transformation of the Jewish Nation into a denominational body. We should admire the intellect, energy and perseverance which they invested in this struggle. Both offensives were crowned with success, in a way that would appear to leave no room for doubt: its principles were enshrined in the Dutch Constitution. The initiators could hardly predict that the 'Jewish Nation' would live on indirectly in the 'Jewish communal organizations', and they would have been even more surprised had they known that complete equality for the Jews of The Netherlands would have to wait for so many years.

Even so, when a disenchanted and worn-out Jonas Daniël Meyer withdrew from public life, it brought an end to a twenty-year long campaign aimed at forcing Dutch ruling circles to drop all attempts at anti-Jewish discrimination. This campaign proved a failure, for even though Jews became equal before the law, and even though this equality was recognized and no longer overtly challenged, the Jews remained in certain aspects a restricted religious and ethnic minority, or – as the burgomaster of Amsterdam had insisted in 1806 – a Jewish Nation.

---

76 See P. Geyl, *Geschiedenis als medespeler*, Utrecht-Antwerp, 1958, p. 101. A recent article highlights the discrimination experienced by the Catholics following the receding of the Radical current after they had earlier been received with open arms in Enlightenment circles. The conclusion is that '...the increasing integration of the Nation visible prior to 1795, soon receded following the Revolution. In 1801 Roman-Catholics were once more not only ousted from public offices and political life, but even excluded from the Nation...The new Nation was mainly Protestant and enlightened'. Th. Clemens, 'Terugdringing der rooms-katholieken uit de verlicht-protestantse natie', *BMGN*, vol. 110, 1995, p. 39.

77 See H.W. von der Dunk, 'Conservatisme in vooroorlogs Nederland', in: *Bijdragen en Mededelingen betreffende de Geschiedenis der Nederlanden*, 90 (1975), p.19.

3 Adath Jesurun – The Diskursen

Immediately following the Revolution a small group of Amsterdam Jews, imbued with Enlightenment optimism and convinced of the imminent realization of the ideals of the French Revolution in the Batavian Republic, swung into action to demand the implementation of Freedom, Equality and Fraternity for the Jews as well. They literally emerged from the shadows, for during the insurrections of 1787 they had only acted behind the scenes. Now it became evident that at least the leading figures, particularly Hartog Bromet,[1] Moses Salomon Asser,[2] H. de H. Lemon[3] and the physician Joachim van

1 Harmannus Leonard Bromet (1725-1812) was the spiritual father of the group. He had spent twenty years in Surinam as a coffee merchant. Later he became a business partner of Moses Asser (1775-1780), who related that politics and law were his hobbies. According to Asser, he was pro-American and anti-English, and following the outbreak of the conflict he qualified himself, like Asser, as 'a partisan' of the Patriot party. See I.H. van Eeghen, 'Autobiografie Asser', pp. 150-165. Does this mean that the two were officially members? Bromet had participated in protest actions even before his secession from the Old Community, by refusing to pay his community dues – for which reason he had been refused entrance to the synagogue. There was a rumor to the effect that he contemplated legal steps to enforce his admittance. Bloemgarten, I. pp. 67, 70; Bolle, pp. 86-7.
2 Moses Salomon Asser (1754-1826) was the most active member of Felix Libertate. His original name was Moses ben Kalman Shoukhet, and the Asser family officially adopted this name in 1811. One of the Pregers wrote on 23.5.1786 that he was studying law [G. Yogev (Engl.), p. 145], but apparently did not receive a degree. He was a coffee merchant in the West Indies. However, his legal proclivities were both recognized and appreciated during his term as chairman of the Judicial Committee in Amsterdam during the Radical regime.
    During the reign of Louis Napoleon he, together with Van Gennep and Van der Linden, were commissioned to draft a Commercial Code, for which he was later appointed a Knight in the Order of the Dutch Lion (1819). Felix Libertate delegated him to the assembly of Patriotic [Gentlemen's] Clubs, but during the final meeting, Amsterdam succeeded in blackballing the admission of Felix Libertate. During the elections to the National Assembly he was proposed as a candidate, receiving fourteen votes – two votes short of the required number – even though there were only seven Jewish voters. After 1806, when his son Carel began to occupy a more prominent position, he became less active, mainly restricting himself to writing an occasional letter to the authorities. He had two other sons, Tobie and Hendrik, of whom particularly the former was active within the Enlightenment group. Moses was related to the Van Embden family via his mother Gracia.
    Lit.: I.H. van Eeghen, 'Autobiografie van M.S. Asser', *Jbk. Amstelodamum*, Vol. 55 (1963); idem, *Uit Amsterdamse Dagboeken*; Bloemgarten, *passim*; Bolle, *passim*.
3 Dr. Hartog de H. Lemon (1755-1823), or Hirsch ben Hirsch Wiener, also known as Herts Levi Roufe (= physician), studied medicine in Leiden and in 1778 was appointed physician to the poor by the Jewish community of Amsterdam. He was dismissed in 1795, and reappointed in 1808. He actively promoted vaccination (see Hindle S. Hes, *Jewish Physicians in the Netherlands, Assen, 1980*, pp. 93-4). He supported the Radicals, and following his election to the National Assembly was one of their leading representatives. He had prior knowledge of their plans for a coup d'état on January 22, 1798.

Embden,[4] had been in touch with each other before the victory of the French arms.

In effect, immediately upon the appointment of R.C.P. Krayenhoff as Commandant of Amsterdam (January 17, 1795), he was handed a memorandum arguing that Jews were quite capable of serving in the armed forces, and that they should therefore be admitted to the National Guard. The implementation of this idea would be less simple than it appeared (see Chapter 8) – for as in many other respects, theirs would turn out to be an uphill struggle. For though the enlightened Jews were fervent Patriots, the Patriotic clubs refused to accept them because they were Jews.

Jewish Patriots were refused admittance to the district meetings organized by the Patriots in Amsterdam following the occupation by the French army. Felix Libertate attempted to exercise pressure on the Amsterdam Patriots via the Patriotic clubs in other cities. Following a preparatory meeting on July 22 in Rotterdam the Patriotic clubs on August 24 established a Central Council in The Hague intended as a permanent body, to which Bromet, Asser and a Christian member, Nathaniel Konig, were delegated on behalf of Felix Libertate. When the Amsterdam delegates forced the Central Council to choose between them and Felix Libertate, the Council chose to drop the latter.[5]

Thus the Modernists had no choice but to establish their own club, which explains the foundation of Felix Libertate on February 6. However, from the outset the group emphasized that not only Jews would be admitted to Felix Libertate. Indeed, at the time of its establishment, one-third of the members were non-Jews, including two individuals who were very active on behalf of the

Following the deposition of the Radical regime (June 12, 1798) he was arrested, but soon after released. He was once more arrested on February 13, 1813, for his alleged involvement in an Orangist conspiracy. He was sentenced to two years imprisonment and a fine of Dfl. 1,500, plus legal costs. When the situation in The Netherlands became dangerous for the French, de Lemon was taken to Amiens. He was not released until April 6, 1814. [Colenbrander, *GS* Vol. 6 (1810-1813), pp. 30-34]. He wrote a brochure about this experience: 'Iets over de nooit plaats gehad hebbende samenzweering te Amsterdam in Februari 1813' ('Something about a never-existing conspiracy in Amsterdam in February 1813'). De Lemon was a lover of theater, and he translated a German play, 'Bella', into Dutch. In 1809 he protested to the king about the anti-Semitic manner in which a certain actor in the Hollandsche Schouwburg played his role. A French opinion about him in 1807 stated: 'Juif eclairé d'Amsterdam de beaucoup d'esprit et de connaissances.' ('An enlightened, high-spirited and knowledgeable Jew from Amsterdam.') Colenbrander *GS* Vol. 5 (1806-1810), p. 384. See also E.A. Rodrigues Pereira, 'Een drietal op de voorgrond tredende Joodse geneeskundigen uit het begin der 19de eeuw', *VA* I (July 11, 1924), pp. 244-45; D.S. Van Zuiden, 'Officiële bestrijding van het antisemitisme op het Hollandse toneel (1809)', *VA* Proefnummer (January 11, 1924), pp. 6-7.

4   Dr. Joachim van Embden (1741-1826) or Jochanan Levi Roufe. He belonged to a family which combined medicine with the publishing business. He studied in Leiden, but from 1761 onwards he worked as a printer. In 1771 he entered into a partnership with Jacobus Benedictus as printers and booksellers, and in the same year he married Sara Jacobus Benedictus. His own publishing house (run together with his son Benjamin Joachim) was the official publisher of the New Community. For further details about the family, see Hindle S. Hes, 'The Van Embdens. A Family of Printers in Amsterdam', *Quaerendo*, Vol. XI/I (1981), pp. 46-52.

5   About the Central Meeting, see Schama, *Patriots*, pp. 223-34; about the exclusion of the Jews, see Bloemgarten, I, pp. 88-89. About the speeches by Asser during the two meetings, see da Silva Rosa, *Bibliografie*, no. 45, 52.

Jewish cause. They were J. van Laar Mahuet, a bookseller and printer in the Jewish quarter and the advocate Johan Christiaan Hespe.[6]

The chances for achieving civic rights for the Jews, while simultaneously reforming and democratizing the large (Ashkenazi) Jewish community looked very auspicious, but reality would prove to be different. In the previous chapter we have seen that the formal enfranchisement of the Jews was followed by a regression. Even the attempts at an internal reorganization of the Jewish community in accordance with the spirit of the times foundered. In Chapter 1 we described how in 1787 the Amsterdam municipal authorities granted the Jewish community a large measure of autonomy, after having concluded that only the authority of the Parnasim was able to rein in the Jewish masses. This situation was unchanged in 1795. The excesses committed by the Patriotic Civil Guard against the Jewish population in the same year had caused considerable anxiety among the Jews of Amsterdam, and the City Fathers could ill afford to fan the flames by identifying themselves with a marginal group of Jews who agitated against their administrative and spiritual leadership.

This became evident during one of the first initiatives by Felix Libertate.[7] Members of Felix Libertate undertook to translate the Declaration of the Rights of Man and the Citizen into Amsterdam Yiddish. Next they succeeded in convincing the Vigilance Committee (established by the Amsterdam municipality) to instruct the Parnasim to have this document read in the synagogues – a measure that aroused fierce opposition on principle within both the Portuguese and the High-German communities. The most controversial passage was the one on freedom of religion: how could a Jewish community allow each and every Jew to decide for himself whether or not to practice their Jewish faith? The same problem arose in other towns. A joint meeting was convened in Leiden of representatives of the Jewish communities of Amsterdam, Rotterdam and The Hague – a rare manifestation of unity in the history of Dutch Jewry – in order to decide a common point of view.

The community in The Hague discovered a fairly simple solution. Every civil servant and government official was required to pledge an oath of loyalty to the Batavian Republic, and this oath included recognition of the Rights of Man and the Citizen. Prior to the swearing of the oath, the Chief Rabbi of The Hague and the Parnasim recited a statement formulated by their legal counselors to the effect that the oath would not compel them to do anything that infringed upon the Jewish religion – a phrasing that was tacitly accepted by the authorities.[8]

---

6   Johannes Christiaan Hespe was exiled from 1787 till 1795. He gave a lecture during one of the first meetings of Felix Libertate, which was subsequently published: 'Aanspraak van den Burger J.C. Hespe in de club der burgers de Mosaische Godsdienst toegedaan op den 18 februari 1795.' About him, see Ch. 1.

7   About the schismatic process and the resulting conflicts, see Bloemgarten, *St. Ros.* II (1968), pp. 42-65.

8   Bolle, p. 94-95. The swearing in of the Parnasim took place at the instruction of the court [of justice] since 'within the Synagogue establishment these Gentlemen rank higher than Rabbis'. [GA The Hague, Inv. no. 184, fol. 110 (March 27, 1795)].

Matters proceeded less smoothly in Amsterdam. Chief Rabbi Moses Saul Löwenstamm met with the Vigilance Committee, accompanied by the Chief Beadle, Chaim Cohen Cauveren, who in addition to acting as interpreter, also conducted the actual negotiations, since the Chief Rabbi did not speak Dutch. The Committee asked the Chief Beadle to formulate a version of the text of the Declaration of the Rights of Man and the Citizen that would be acceptable to the Jews.

The text subsequently submitted by Chaim Cauveren stated exactly the opposite of the original offending version. The reference to freedom of religion was replaced by a phrase obliging every Jew to adhere to the Jewish Biblical commandments. This was of course unacceptable to the Committee, until the Parnasim introduced an argument that the Committee members were virtually unable to refute. Since not a single other religious group had been requested by the Committee to read the Declaration of the Rights of Man and the Citizen in their churches, on what grounds did they believe the Jews could be compelled to do so? To lend force to his argument, Chaim Cauveren submitted a petition signed by 600 members of the Jewish community pleading 'in the name of God' to desist from the reading of the Declaration in the synagogues. The Vigilance Committee gave in, and the matter was pursued no further.[9]

Felix Libertate, on the other hand, was not content to let the matter rest. It launched a fierce attack on the Parnasim, which was posted – in Dutch and Yiddish – on the doors of the synagogues and other public places in the Jewish Quarter (March 22, 1795). Permission for this had been received from the Maire – the Burgomaster – of Amsterdam, but not from the Parnasim, which in itself was a serious infraction of the notorious Article 22 of the Regulations of the Jewish community, which forbade any opposition to the Parnasim.

On March 26, four days after the distribution of the poster, a notary public informed the Jewish community of the resignation of twenty-one of its mem-

9   Bolle, p. 95. A Hebrew description of the 'special events' in the Protocol Book of the community relates that when on March 13, 1795, two Parnasim and the Chief Beadle came to see the authorities (no mention is made of which authorities were meant) in order to hear the decision about the recitation of the text (no mention of which text is intended) the President addressed them as follows: 'Something new has happened among us, and since it is a secret, we shall have to consider the matter rather than decide.' (CAHJP-HM 9714).

    On March 28 the clerk of the Court of Justice read to the Parnasim and the Chief Rabbis of the Portuguese and High-German communities the formulation of an oath that they considered acceptable.

bers.[10] Three days later these were joined by another prominent personality, namely Rabbi Yizhak Graanboom. His secession was a truly sensational event, given the fact that he was a recognized rabbinical authority and an orthodox scholar who, following the death of Chief Rabbi Saul, had served as acting Chief Rabbi. There were good reasons for suspecting that his decision was caused by disappointment with the fact that the son of Rabbi Saul, Rabbi J.M. (later Moses Saul) Löwenstamm, a not very distinguished Talmudic scholar, had been elected Chief Rabbi of Amsterdam instead of him. By resigning his offices he cleared the way to joining the *Neye Kille* – the New Community.[11]

Graanboom's defection only shows how carefully the secessionists had laid their plans, and how professionally and quickly they managed to implement them. During the week of their resignation from the Old Community they had already planned a synagogue service, but this was prevented by the burgomaster, who feared a disruption by infuriated members of the Old Community. Thus the first religious service of the New Community took place on April 8, 1797, at the residence of Salomon Cats, with a Civil Guard detachment on hand to quell any disturbances.[12]

10 The complete list of names of the secessionists is contained in a paragraph of the *Yiddish Chronicle of Bendit Wing* (= B.J. Benjamins), published by M.M. Roest, 'Uittreksel uit ene Kronijk van de jaren 1795-1812', [in] *De Israelitische Letterbode* III (1877-8) and copied in Jaap Meijer-Jet Slagter,*Versteend verleden, de Joodse begraafplaats te Overveen*, Haarlem, 1983, pp. 9-10.
    For the convenience of the reader I quote Bendit Wing as published by Roest rather than the transcript prepared in 1846 by A. Dellaville for S.I. Mulder under the title *Sefer jaldei hazeman*. The two versions differ both in text and in contents. Roest omits all paragraphs not dealing with Jews, besides which he complements the text wherever he considers this useful for the reader's understanding (without, however, indicating this). He also omits words he considers irrelevant or incorrect, and he usually does not provide the Jewish date. On the other hand Delaville also appears to have bowdlerized the original text. For example, Roest comments that the chronicler everywhere writes Meijers when referring to Jonas Daniel Meyer, whereas Delaville consistently writes 'Meyer'. I also noticed an interesting paragraph in Roest that is missing in Delaville. Apparently neither Roest nor Delaville faithfully rendered the text of the Yiddish manuscript.
11 R. Isaac Graanboom (1738-1807) belonged to the Swedish Christian Graanboom (originally Granboom) family, which was probably of Jewish extraction. In 1750 Isaac's grandfather Jacob and part of his family arrived in Amsterdam, where they converted to Judaism. In 1763 his son, Isaac's father, also came to Amsterdam and similarly converted, changing his name to Abraham. For some years his family called itself Abrahams, until 1811, when they changed their name to Graanboom. Isaac was a gifted pupil, and he received a thorough Jewish education from several Amsterdam rabbis, including Chief Rabbi Saul. Even so he spent twenty years of his life earning a living as a diamond cleaver. Around 1780 he became a teacher at the Amsterdam Beth Hamidrash, and following the death of Chief Rabbi Saul in 1790, he was appointed as one of the three acting Chief Rabbis. Rabbi Isaac Graanboom (or Isaac Ger = 'convert') wrote an ethical and halachic work called *Zera Yitskhok* ('The Seed of Isaac'; 1789). From the imprimaturs by Chief Rabbi Saul and the Portuguese Chief Rabbi David Cohen d'Azevedo it is clear that the book was written for financial reasons, to enable him to marry off his daughter Rebecca.
    Lit.: L. Lewysohn, 'Eine Proselytenfamilie aus dem vorigen Jahrhundert', *Monatschrift für Geschichte und Wissenschaft des Judentums*, 5 (1856), pp. 37-46; S.I. Mulder, 'Het geslacht Graanboom', *Israëlitische Almanak*, 1856, pp. 45-46; L. Fuks, 'De Zweedse familie Graanboom, een Hebreeuwse familiegeschiedenis', *St. Ros*. I, 2 (1967), pp. 85-106; J. Meijer, *Joodse wetenschap buiten de orde*, Heemstede, 1982; M. Zilverberg-Boas, 'De familie Graanboom', *St. Ros*. XIX (1985), pp. 99-100; Meijer-Slagter, *op. cit.*, pp. 19-26.
12 See Bloemgarten, *St. Ros*. II (1968), pp. 43-44. Bloemgarten incorrectly translates the name Adath Jesurun as 'Community of the Just'. Jesurun is a synonym for Israel, and as such is first used in Deut. 32: 15. Adath Jesurun is a customary expression in the liturgy.

The New Community, which had adopted the name of Adath Jesurun, immediately established two other institutions. As early as April 6, it purchased land for a cemetery in the village of Overveen.[13] In addition it established a 'meat-hall', which entered into competition with the existing one of the Old Community. On June 23 the community inaugurated its own synagogue at the Heerengracht, complete with a ritual bath.[14]

Thus the secessionists had everything needed by a full-fledged Jewish community. The initiators must have been confident that under the prevailing revolutionary climate countless Jews would abandon the Old Community and join Adath Jesurun. The thoroughness and scope of their planning leave no doubt about this.

In practice, matters would take a different turn. The twenty-one founder-members were indeed followed by a trickle of new applicants, and following the restoration of the Parnasim in their functions, another sixteen radically inclined *manhigim* (community leaders) joined Adath Jesurun (August 2, 1798), but no real growth took place. On March 20, 1798, about one year after its establishment, the by-laws of the community were passed, with all the members – no more than 100 in total – affixing their signatures on a separate page.[15] In the course of time people even complained about a decline in membership. Altogether the membership of the New Community never exceeded more than 500 souls, compared with 21,000 of the Old Community.

How can we explain this lack of attraction of the modernist direction? The vast majority of the Jews of Amsterdam hated the Patriots. But even those who were sympathetically inclined towards the Enlightenment and the Jewish opportunities for integration within Dutch society were loath to sacrifice their familiar Jewish environment to some doubtful experimental framework that appeared to have little merit even from a religious point of view. Added to this, the administrative and spiritual leadership of the Old Community did not shrink from the severest sanctions against those 'who severed themselves from

13 Meijer-Slagter, *op. cit.* give a detailed description of the purchase and the history of the cemetery. The book contains a register of all persons buried there from 1797 till 1981.
14 On May 1, 1799, a new building was purchased, situated at the present Rapenburgerstraat 173, obviously in the expectation that the community was about to undergo a considerable expansion. The building was inaugurated on June 23 of the same year, contrary to the promise to a committee from the Provincial Government of Holland which attempted to effect a reconciliation (ARA, Gewestelijke Besturen van Holland, session July 6, 1797, Inv. No. 4558, p. 237). For a detailed report on the solemn inauguration, see the *Nationale Bataafsche Courant* 75 (June 24, 1797). An orchestra played a symphony, there was singing by a duo, a speech by De Lemon and a prayer by the Rabbi. Subsequently the building served as the seat of the High Consistory, and eventually the Dutch Israelite Seminary was domiciled there.
15 See about this, D.M. Sluys, 'Het Reglement van Adath Jeschurun (de Neie Kehillo) te Amsterdam', *NIW*, June 12 and 19, 1931. On October 26, 1798 the Board of Adath Jesurun informed the municipal authorities that their community counted 105 members comprising 445 persons. GAA Nieuwe Sted. Besturen no. 415. Dagblad van de Vergaderingen van de Municipaliteit van Amsterdam, Vol. II, 1798, p.122.

the community'.[16] The names of the culprits were put on a list suspended inside a 'cage' in the main Synagogue. After some hesitation the Parnasim also decided to summon the dissidents to a court of law, imposing a fine of a thousand guilders per member. To counter the claim that these measures infringed the constitutional right to freedom of religion, the Parnasim relied on an ingenious argument provided by their legal advisors. Members of the Jewish community were only those persons who themselves or whose parents had paid a certain entrance fee, the so-called 'immatriculation'.[17] Payment of this fee, the lawyers explained, represented a kind of contract. A person who canceled his membership of the community, therefore committed a breach of contract which, according to the by-laws of the community, carried a fine of a thousand guilders. Unfortunately we do not know whether this argument would have held up in court, since the authorities tried everything in their power to stall the case, and in the end ordered the charges dismissed, for fear that a trial would inflame tempers even more and possibly lead to violent incidents.

It is clear that the Old Community conducted a relentless struggle against Adath Jesurun. Marriages with members of the New Community were invalidated by the Chief Rabbi, exposing the children from these unions to the risk of being declared 'bastards' according to Jewish religious law. Women were refused the use of the ritual bath of the Old Community, and Christian bakers were persuaded not to bake for dissident members – or even accept their pots with Sabbath victuals to keep them hot for the day of rest, when Jewish religious law forbade lighting a fire. With reference to the Biblical injunction (Deut. 13: 7-12), inciters were threatened with Divine retribution. In a memorandum that was obviously adressed to Christian readers, the Board of Adath Jesurun complained: 'They are pointing their fingers at us, saying: "*Crucify them*".' (emphasis in the original!)

How ferocious the argument became can be seen from a lengthy and unique printed polemic. It is worthwhile, for various reasons, to devote special attention to this subject.

16 The measures against the New Community are repeatedly mentioned in the New Community's numerous petitions to the authorities, as well as in the *Diskursen*. The quotation 'crucify him' is taken from a memorandum of the New Community to the Provincial Government of Holland (May 5, 1797), included as annex B to a letter dated July 4, 1798, of the Provisionally Functioning Parnasim (the official name of the Parnasim from June 1798 till 1808) to the Bondt Committee. For the Bondt Committee, see p. 80, no. 14. p. 83, no. 23.
17 See D.M. Sluys, 'Het Instituut van het lidmaatschap bij de Hoogduitse-Joodse gemeente te Amsterdam', *VA* 6 (1930), pp. 326-28; 343-44; 356-60. Sluys also was the author of an official report to the Board of the Jewish Community of Amsterdam on this subject (1930). Immatriculation was relevant, for instance when people were buried. Both at Zeeburg and at Muiderberg members were buried in different rows than non-members.

The Diskursen fun di Neye un' di Alte Kille

Not long after the establishment of Adath Jesurun some pamphlets appeared in Yiddish and Dutch setting out the ideas of the French Revolution for the benefit of the Jewish public.[18] The choice of Yiddish shows that earlier pamphlets in Dutch had failed to bear the desired effect. The average Amsterdam Jew knew very little Dutch, and he was far more familiar with the Hebrew characters in which Yiddish was written than with the customary Latin writing.

The literary form of the pamphlets was derived from a plethora of satirical literature that appeared in the Republic during the 18th century. The first pamphlets featured discussions between two people, one of whom attempted to persuade the second that the Batavian Republic represented a genuine blessing for the Jews.

The fact that these first Yiddish pamphlets dwelt on a constitutional theme can be explained by the political developments in the Batavian Republic. Of course, the fledgling State needed a Constitution, and the nature of this Constitution became the subject of a fierce debate between Moderates and Radicals. The nature of the differences between the two sides are of secondary interest for our argument; far more important is the fact that the Jewish Modernists belonged to the Radical camp, and in fact maintained close contacts with its leaders. In 1797 time was on the side of the Radicals, and the founders of the New Community believed that they enjoyed the support of the Radicals among the Patriots.[19]

During the summer of 1797 the political struggle came to a head. Elections for the National Assembly were scheduled for August 1, and a week later a referendum was supposed to be held on a draft constitution. The Radicals were fiercely opposed to the proposed text, in addition to which a stormy election campaign was being waged. This was the moment chosen by the leaders of Adath Jesurun to start a journalistic campaign directed at the members of the Old Community.[20] The campaign had three purposes: propagandistic support for the emancipatory candidates in the first-ever elections in which Jews would participate; to oppose the draft Constitution; and the dissemination of modern, social and political ideas among the Jewish masses.

18 'Frayndlekhe unterredung tsvischn tsvey gute fraynd vegn di tegenvortige umshtandikhheydn zayr nutsig un noytvendig far ayn yeder tsu visn', Amsterdam, 1797. In total four of these brochures, all with the same title, were published. See J. Schatzky, *Presse sammelbuch zum 250-ten joweil fun der jiddischer presse*, New York, 1936, p. 103. For a Dutch 'dialogue', see Meijer-Slagter, *op. cit.*, pp. 13-15.
19 About the struggles between the parties inside the Patriotic camp, see Schama, *Patriots*, pp. 245-353.
20 Bloemgarten correctly comments that Shatzky's dating (see note 17) is wrong. The first issue appeared at the end of July 1797 – prior to the elections, and probably on a Wednesday.

Genre, Development and Extent of the Diskursen Literature

As already mentioned, the literary form of these polemical pamphlets was derived from the satirical literature already being disseminated in the Republic. As a result they bore a close similarity to publications such as *Het Schuytpraatje* ('Discussion on a Tow-boat' – conversations between passengers during their slow and tedious progress on a horse-drawn barge) or the *Saturdagse Kroegpraetje* ('Saturday Night Pub Talk').[21] In effect, the first 'discourse' takes place on a tow-boat en route from Utrecht to Amsterdam, and the second during the journey from the Gooi district to Amsterdam. The third discourse starts in a public-house, after which the participants exit Amsterdam through the Muyden Gate, to walk to the nearby village of Diemen – arguing all the way. However, the scenes eventually shift to a Jewish public-house – and for a good reason. In the tow-boat the same company remained together, as was the case with the wanderers outside the city precincts. But as the discussions continued, and the *Diskursen* evolved into something resembling a weekly 'opinion magazine', certain changes had to be introduced in order to raise the dramatic impact – for example by introducing additional discussion partners or fading out those whose opinions were no longer relevant.

The pamphlets, printed on cheap paper, were extremely successful. The population of the Jewish Quarter gladly paid two stuyvers (later two-and-a-half stuyvers – a fairly considerable sum in those days) in order to relish the spicy fare the *Neye Kille* succeeded in preparing for them week after week.

When, eventually, it dawned upon the Parnasim that they could no longer leave the field to their opponents, they too decided on the publication of a series of pamphlets – but with a twist. The day prior to the scheduled appearance of the thirteenth *Diskurs fun di Neye Kille* another *Discourse* was published that not only looked identical – including the issue number 13 – but featured the same protagonists. The difference was that its authors were the *Alte Kille* and that it was directed against the *Neye Kille*. In fact, it was Issue no. 1 of the *Diskursen fun di Alte Kille*. From here on two pamphlets appeared each week.

On March 16, 1798, these press polemics came to an end. Due to their influence on the Radical movement, which had come to power in the coup d'état of January 22, 1798, the Jewish Patriots were able to bring about the dismissal of the Amsterdam Parnasim and their replacement by members of the Old Community who – although supporters of Felix Libertate – had stayed loyal to their community. We might say that the producers of the *Diskursen fun di Neye Kille* had the last word. In celebration they published a Victory Issue that concluded the appearance of a total of thirty-five *Diskursen* between the end of July 1797 and the middle of March 1798. This included eleven issues by the Old Community, which on the title pages were numbered from 13 to 23, and on the back pages from 1 to 11. An average issue contained fifteen or sixteen pages (or

---

21 About the satirical literature, see J.M. Buynster-C.M. Geeraars, 'Bibliografie van 18de-eeuwse satirische tijdschriften in Nederland', *Documentatieblad Werkgroep Achttiende Eeuw* V (1969), pp. 126-39.

eight pages according to the Hebrew pagination), although some issues were more voluminous. The total *Diskursen*-literature, including a number of earlier pamphlets, comprised some 550 pages – a very substantial corpus of Yiddish writing that is of great significance for our knowledge of conditions in the contemporary Amsterdam Jewish community.[22]

Dramatis Personae of the Discourses

Three personages are featured in the first *Discourses*, representing three different types of people. Anshel Hollander, a fervent supporter of the New Community, is an open-hearted and rather irascible type (a real 'Hollander'); Gompel Shpanier, a member of the Old Community, is dull-witted and naive; Yankev Frantsman, as yet a member of the Old Community, already in the first *Discourse* informs his listeners that he intends to join the New Community. Like the others, he is a merchant, but he is cleverer and more intelligent than his interlocutors, and he maintains good relations with French government officials (hence his name!).

The eleventh *Discourse* introduces Rabbi Sender, a German Jew. It would seem that the authors required an 'outsider' for a more objective evaluation of the situation in Amsterdam.

Certain other personages appear only incidentally, such as Khone Dreykopf, a fanatical supporter of the Old Community, and Khane Kanteman, a business woman who reveals certain abuses in the *mikve* – the ritual bath. Even publicans, both Jewish and non-Jewish, put in a word edgewise now and then – the latter obviously in order to demonstrate that the Revolution had made Jews and Gentiles each other's equals.

As the publication of new *Discourses* from both sides proceeded, actual discussions receded into the background, to be replaced by increasingly barbed recriminations and mutual insults. Lengthy speeches and letters are interpolated, as well as fake 'news items', not to speak of various other deceptive literary devices. The final *Discourse* consists entirely of long speeches, and the entire series is concluded with two victory hymns.

---

22 Except for the four pages Bloemgarten devotes to the *Diskursen* (*op. cit.*, II, pp. 51-55), Shatzky's article mentioned in note 17 is the only published study on the subject. Shatzky's article contains an extensive bibliography and evaluation of the *Diskursen*. Unfortunately he was unfamiliar with the political developments in the Batavian Republic and therefore was unable to place them in their proper context. Worse is that he failed here and there to understand the meaning of the text, as shown by certain attempts to explain words that were unintelligible to East-European Jews. Thus: *bousn laytn* = country folk; Shatzky: bad people; *kogl* = suet pudding (made with noodles or bread); Shatzky: bullet; *tsaakhenen* = place a signature; Shatzky: look out, search.

Another objection to Shatzky's article is his uncritical acceptance of the views and actions of the Felix Libertate group, without trying to understand the position of the Parnasim. This criticism, by the way, applies to all historians who have written about the emancipation of the Jews in The Netherlands.

The Languages of the Discourses

The Yiddish of the *Discourses* was of course Amsterdam Yiddish, an offshoot of Western-European Yiddish – as opposed to the Yiddish spoken by Eastern-European immigrants.[23] In the course of time this Yiddish became pervaded with numerous Dutch and French words, which were pronounced and written in the Yiddish manner. The *Discourses of the New Community* contain purely Dutch words (such as *zootje* = lot, pack – like in 'a pack of ruffians'; *gebabbeld* = conversed; *lolletjes* = jokes; *met hangende pootjes* = 'with their tail between their legs'), all of which have Yiddish equivalents, even though the authors emphasized that they were writing in Amsterdam Yiddish. At one point Anshel commented about a certain letter: '*dos iz halb taytsh un halb amsterdamsh*' ('that is half German and half Amsterdams'). At a later stage we find more and more purely German items, probably because the authors assumed that the readers would have no problem reading them. The authors of the *Discourses of the Old Community* disagreed, arguing that barely four percent of the residents of the Jewish Quarter had a command of German. The New Community rebutted that every second home possessed works by German authors such as Mendelssohn, Wieland, Lessing, Kotzebue, Rousseau(!) and Voltaire(!). This highly improbable claim is further refuted by the very publication of the *Discourses* in Yiddish, a result of the fact that most Jews were unable to read *galkhes* (Latin script). One of the authors of the *Discourses of the Old Community* provides comical evidence of this deficient knowledge of German when he writes: '*habst du lang geshlafn*' and '*der toyfl habt dayne seele*' ('Did you sleep a long time' and 'The devil take your soul') in a supposedly pure German text. In the next issue of the *Discourses of the New Community* he was mockingly referred to as '*Herr habst gehabt*'.

On very rare occasions we will find Eastern-European Yiddish, such as: '*nun voln mir mal poylish shmuesn*' (Now let's talk Polish [Yiddish]). More common is the introduction of Dutch-speaking persons, particularly by the New Community, which aimed at Jewish integration within the Dutch society. A good example is the following translation of a discussion in a public-house:

> *Landlady: I suppose you are a Jew?*
> *Khone: Did you peek into my trousers?*
> *Landlady: I don't say that to insult you; for me all people are equal.*

From time to time the Old Community would also take recourse to Dutch – only to reveal how poor the knowledge of Dutch was in these circles. One of the participants in a discussion asks a Dutch Gentile: 'Well, citizen, did you read today's newspaper? What do you think about our valiant Parnasim?' To which the Dutchman answers in a hotch-potch of German, Yiddish and Dutch: '*Es komt mir vor oyer parnasins vershtandiger zaynen vi ir, das zi gor nit an storn.*' (Your

---

23 About Western-Yiddish in general, and its Dutch branch in particular, see the publications by H. Beem: 'Yiddish in Holland, Linguistic and Socio-Linguistic Notes', in Uriel Weinreich (ed.), *The Field of Yiddish*, New York, 1954, pp. 122-133; *Jerosche*, Assen, 1970; *Sheerith, Resten van een taal*, Assen, 1967; *Uit Mokum en Mediene*, Assen, 1974.

'Diskurs fun di alte Kille'.
A discourse of the Old Community against the New Community. The lion in the illustration is
holding a balance. In the scale on the right lies the Old Community (the Hebrew letters Aleph Koph),
and in the scale on the left the New Community (Nun Koph). The caption reads: das heist kal ('that
means light', i.e. the New Community has been weighed and found wanting). Universiteits-
bibliotheek, Amsterdam.

Parnasim would seem to be more intelligent than you, that they take no notice of it). Of the seventeen words, only six are real Dutch.

It is clear, therefore, that only a thin upper layer of Amsterdam Jews had a proper command of Dutch, and it would take several decades before Yiddish was replaced by the vernacular.[24]

The Authors

Very little is known about the authors of the *Diskursen*. Schatzky's assumption that the texts were written by the leaders of the New Community, people like Moses Asser, Bromet and De Lemon, cannot be substantiated. The authors of the Old Community claimed that 'Philanthropus', who wrote several contributions in German, was an alias of David Friedrichsfeld, a noted champion of Jewish emancipation, and they bowdlerized his name to 'falderappes' (blackguard).[25] This identification was strenuously denied by the New Community, which of course does not disprove it.

Of two authors of the *Discourses of the Old Community* the names and further particulars are known. One of them was Leib Waag (also Vaagshaal), who had been punished for working as a ritual slaughterer in Nijkerk with a forged license. He wrote *Discourses* on behalf of the Parnasim, but he had to flee to Cleve in Germany in order to escape his creditors. For a time he employed an assistant by the name of Dikje, a son of the Parnas David Dikje, variously known as David ben Anshel Levi and under different family names such as Preger, Kampen and Salomons.[26]

According to the New Community no fewer than 300 persons contributed to the *Discourses of the Old Community*, which is almost certainly an exaggeration. Even so it looks as if in both communities several people were involved in the publications. The weekly collection of subject matter – which often required the use of informers in the enemy camp – as well as the writing, editing and correcting of the texts and their embellishment with jokes, plays on words and other fanciful literary devices, could only have been accomplished by the close cooperation of a sizable staff of experienced collaborators.

---

24 Dutch Yiddish had a tough streak. Sixty years after the Emancipation decree religious subjects at the Dutch-Israelite Rabbinical Seminary were still being taught in Yiddish. See J. Michman, 'De strijd om de benoeming van dr. J.H. Dünner tot Rector van het Nederlands-Israëlietisch Seminarium', *St. Ros.* XXII (1988), pp. 165-85 (especially p. 175). In 1856, S. Bloemendaal (Maastricht) requested the High Committee for Israelite Affairs in The Netherlands to forbid sermons in 'Jewish or corrupted High-German'. As late as 1867 the *Weekblad voor Israëlieten* complains that countless Jews are unable to follow sermons in Dutch. In the same year the Board of the Amsterdam Jewish community objected to the proscription of sermons in Yiddish. J.H. Coppenhagen, *De Israëlitische Kerk en de Staat der Nederlanden*, Amsterdam, 1988, p. 77.
25 For David Friedrichsfeld, see D. Michman, *David Friedrichsfeld – A Fighter for Enlightenment and the Emancipation of the Jews* (Hebr.), *SDJ* I (1975), pp. 151-199.
26 For details about the Preger family, see Yogev, *op cit.*

Contents

The initiative to the publication of the original *Discourses* was taken by the emancipators in an effort to transmit their views and ideas to the Jewish masses over the heads of the Parnasim. Especially in the beginning the didactic element prevailed: explanations of the nature of the parliamentary system, information about voting, and so forth. In addition considerable space was devoted to presumed abuses in the Old Community and various long overdue reforms, such as the democratization of the election of the Parnasim and the supervision of their financial management.

By contrast, the *Discourses of the Old Community* make a rather mediocre impression – and for two main reasons. For one thing, the Parnasim had the ingrained mentality of Jewish regents, meaning that they chose to play their cards as close to their chest as possible. The second and no less important reason was the extreme complexity and delicacy of their position, due to the radical atmosphere which prevailed during the years 1797 and 1798. As representatives of the Old Regime, the Radicals suspected them of being supporters of the House of Orange. Committing their true opinions to print in the course of a polemic with the New Community was quite a risky undertaking, besides which they had to be careful not to hurt the feelings of some of its leaders, especially notables such as Bromet and De Lemon, who were delegates to the National Assembly, and M.S. Asser, who was Chairman of the Judicial Committee of the City of Amsterdam.

This explains why the discussions in the *Diskursen* had a fairly one-sided character. The New Community fielded a large variety of subjects, whereas the Old Community, from its side, restricted itself mainly to the discussion of religious aspects.

General Political Aspects

The initial motive for the publication of the *Discourses* was of a general political nature. Thus they dealt at length with subjects such as the new constitutional form of government, the intricacies of the election system, the significance of the French Revolution in general, and its beneficial effects for the Jews in particular. The readers nearly might have been persuaded that the election of Bromet and De Lemon to the National Assembly heralded the coming of the Messiah. 'Blessed be God's Holy name for ever and ever – two Jews in the Government in The Hague', exulted Gompel. Their vast influence in The Hague, particularly following the Revolution of January 22, 1798, was discussed in considerable detail. Thanks to the Revolution, Jews could be appointed to public positions, the guilds were going to admit Jews, and the attitude of the population in general was said to have undergone a considerable change for the better. The Government even considered forbidding the use of the pejorative '*smous*' (thief, or vagrant) for Jew. The Parnasim, in their opposition to the Patriots, wanted to deny the Jews the fruits of the emancipation. They defended the despicable monarchist system, they maintained illegal contacts with England and attempted to smuggle money to that country. When following the coup all public functionaries were asked to forswear monarchism, anarchism and feudalism, the Parnasim were accused of perjury.

The attacks on the Parnasim grew more and more violent, and towards the end they were not only accused of high treason, but threatened with deposition and even death at the guillotine. All that the Parnasim were able (or prepared) to say in their defense was that they too were good patriots, and only opposed anything that was liable to harm the Jewish faith.

Social Conditions

The first few *Discourses* enlarged upon the wretched social conditions within the Old Community, and this subject remained one of the principal themes.

The membership of the High-German community of Amsterdam could be divided into three categories:

1. *Members*, amounting to some 1,500 persons, whose membership had been acquired through purchase or inheritance (the so-called 'immatriculation');
2. *Guests*, who although not immatriculated, were financially established;
3. *Indigents*, who comprised some 80 percent of those affiliated with the community.

The *Discourses of the New Community*, on the other hand, feature only 'Members' and 'Guests': nowhere do we find a sign that the democratic reforms demanded by the emancipators also embraced the poor, even though expressions of commiseration with their wretched fate are not lacking. Quite within the spirit of the times, we are therefore dealing with a bourgeois revolution aimed mainly at serving the interests of the members and the guests. The latter were also expected to pay dues, but they had no rights.

The very first subject of the *Discourses*, and one which remained a main topic throughout, was the meat-hall.[27] In 1672 the municipality had already granted the High-German Jews of Amsterdam a monopoly for the sale of *kosher* (ritually slaughtered) meat. A surcharge was levied to supplement the municipal welfare

---

27 The attention that is paid in the *Diskursen* to the meat-hall derives from its importance for the well-being of the community. The existence of the two meat-halls – one for the Sephardim and one for Ashkenazi Jews – is a unique feature in Jewish history. Their existence was predicated upon the close cooperation between the city government and the Parnasim. On September 1, 1672 the High-German community was granted a monopoly for the sale of meat to Jews in order to prevent the evasion of national taxes and losses to the community's welfare fund. From now on, anyone who purchased meat outside the meat-hall risked excommunication, as well as punishment by the secular authorities. The two Jewish meat-halls also guarded against mutual competition. Initially their sanctions consisted of fines. In 1730 these were raised due to the large number of infringements, and eventually – when this proved an insufficient deterrent – supplemented by a threat of imprisonment and even flagellation (1737). The surcharges on the meat sold were deposited into the Welfare Fund, and its revenues at times amounted to over half the total income of the community. This enabled the disbursement of social welfare allocations, as well as the part maintenance of an administrative apparatus that included physicians to the poor. For more information, see the detailed articles by D.M. Sluys, 'Het Halwezen bij de Joodse Gemeente te Amsterdam', *VA* VI (1929), p. 39 to p. 254 (in several instalments).

fund. In fact, the entire Jewish social welfare establishment depended on this fund. The New Community was opposed to this monopoly for reasons of principle, but it also exposed the abuses that were rife in the meat-hall administration, such as the preferential treatment accorded to the Parnasim and their families, and the discrimination and humiliation suffered by the poor and others who did not belong to the privileged classes. The New Community rejected the entire welfare system, claiming that instead of doling out charity handouts, the unemployed had to be taught a craft, while young people had to be assisted in finding employment. Begging, in particular, had to be proscribed.

They also criticized the available medical care. Gruesome stories were told about incidents in the Jewish hospital. It was said that patients lay in dank and dark rooms in which they could neither see nor breathe, and that people who entered the hospital had little chance of coming out alive. People were placed in beds in which other patients had died only minutes before. Even the matron was a member of the conspiracy: she was paid twenty-eight stuyvers per week for each patient, so that she stood to profit handsomely if a patient who had been admitted on Wednesday died on Friday.

To all these accusations the Parnasim could only answer that the revenues of the Welfare Fund had declined drastically and that the community was near bankruptcy. This elicited a response by the New Community that the money had been spent on loans to friends of the Parnasim, and that not the Welfare Fund, but these friends had gone bankrupt. Their conclusion: it was not sufficient to change the policy, but that all incapable and corrupt Parnasim and their families had to be ousted from the Board of the community.[28]

Religion

It was not differences of opinion about religion that had provided the impetus for the establishment of the New Community, but the absence of a social and political revolution within the Old Community.[29] According to the authors of the *Diskursen*, the leaders of the New Community, in their effort to adapt the synagogue services, had adopted certain elements of the Sephardi ritual. Even so the Modernists were fully aware that in strictly orthodox Amsterdam even minor deviations from the religious codex would create a storm of indignation, thwarting any attempt at social reform. For this reason the secessionists repeatedly emphasized that they were no less observant than the members of the Old Community.

All this did not prevent their opponents from accusing the New Community of the most flagrant infractions of Jewish tradition. They were said to desecrate

---

28 It is worth mentioning that the same 'incapable and corrupt' Parnasim succeeded within a short period of time in subscribing a loan of Dfl. 250,000 – an enormous amount in those days – enabling them to repay all debts. The *Diskursen* of the New Community vainly agitated against this loan (referred to as a 'negotiation'), arguing that everybody who contributed to this enterprise was certain to lose his money.

29 ARA. Archief Ministerie van Binnenlandse Zaken, 1775-1813, exh. September 10, 1806, no.1.

the Sabbath, violate the laws of *kashrut*, and even promote mixed marriages. '*Kriye iber zolkhe yehudim, zi veln kaatye [Kaatje] un mitye [Mietje] trouen*' (We should mourn such Jews, who would marry Catharine and Mary), exhorts one of the participants in the *Discourses of the Old Community*.

The sole rebuttal of alleged 'modernist' views concerns the questions of reward and punishment in the World to Come and the coming of the Messiah – axioms of the Jewish faith, which the Modernists were said to deny. In practice, there was no evidence whatsoever of manifest unorthodox behavior on the part of members of the New Community, and the accusations of their antagonists were no doubt unjustified. The same cannot be said about certain other aspects of their Jewish world view, since there is no doubt that the emancipationists entertained deist ideas. Articles of the faith concerning the coming of the Messiah or the return of the Jewish people to the Holy Land were indeed not interpreted in the traditional spirit, but in that of the Enlightenment. Nevertheless, in their *Discourses* the New Community carefully steered clear of these and other controversial subjects which, in terms of their propaganda value for the Jewish masses, could only be regarded as slippery.

The Struggle between the Two Communities

Particularly during the initial period various attempts were undertaken to heal the schism. The first twelve *Discourses of the New Community* report on these efforts in considerable detail, charging the Parnasim – as may be expected – with responsibility for the failure to effect a reconciliation. At first the Parnasim refused to receive a delegation from Felix Libertate, since they did not recognize this club. Subsequently they delegated six prominent members to a discussion, including the famous former Parnas Benjamin Cohen, but this delegation was unable to secure a single concession. The Parnasim even insisted on the integral prolongation of the notorious Article 22, which proscribed any opposition to the Parnasim and imposed enormous fines of up to 2,000 guilders on the offenders. For, said one of the Parnasim following a discussion with the burgomaster of Amsterdam: '*Mir behalten unzer kraft*' (We are as strong as ever).[30]

Just the same the Parnasim were hesitant to sue the dissidents. The *Discourses of the New Community* reveal that they conducted serious consultations with their legal counsels Rutger Jan Schimmelpenninck and his brother (known to be very expensive lawyers) about their chances of winning a lawsuit against the dissidents, despite the fact that the Emancipation decree had officially annulled any kind of religious sanctions. The same *Discourses* show that the Board of the New Community continued to reassure the members of the Old Community that they could resign without fear of punishment.

---

30 The remark by the Parnas Joseph Prins can only mean that the Amsterdam municipality had promised the Parnasim not to lift its protection ('sanction') of the Regulations of 1737 – in clear violation of the text of the Emancipation decree and the subsequent letter of the Provincial Government of Holland.

Style, Word Use and Literary Devices

Much of the language of the political pamphlets that circulated in The Netherlands during the 18th century was coarse in the extreme. The *Discourses* are no exception to this tradition. Most satirical literature was characterized by personal invectives and aspersions on the victim's character. The fact that the *Discourses* were addressed at a specific type of public, many of whose members were intimately familiar with the personalities concerned, enabled their calumny to be even more vicious and direct. Gossipy tales whose significance might escape the modern reader were eminently clear to the denizens of the Jewish Quarter. These close relationships between the authors, the subjects and the readers made the *Discourses* both more attractive and vulgar at one and the same time. A few small examples will illustrate this. The earlier-mentioned David Friedrichsfeld was said to have 'a face like excreted peas', and another prominent member of Adath Jesurun is called 'a flea blown over from the East to the West'. The New Community, not to be outdone, pooh-poohed the threatened retaliation by the Old Community as 'excrement with fringes'.

Other favorite subjects were money and sex. One of the leaders of the New Community was said to reside above a brothel, where he had his *mile* (literally 'circumcision', but here – by extension – his male member) washed. A certain Herz, recommended within the Old Community as *ibershoukhet* (chief ritual slaughterer), is said to be more proficient as an *unterstekher* (someone who sticks it in from below), for having impregnated a servant girl. Youkhenen Dokter (Joachim van Embden), dismissed as physician to the indigent members of the Old Community and presently employed by the New Community as a printer, is together with his son called *dalfonim in kompanye* – 'joint down-and-outers'). Thus the invectives flew to and fro, each party accusing the other of swindling their fellow-men, defaulting on debts, bankruptcy, and so forth.

The Chief Rabbi of the Old Community was one of the principal targets of the barbs of the New Community. Rabbi J.M. Löwenstamm, son, grandson and great-grandson of Amsterdam Chief Rabbis, had in 1793 been appointed Chief Rabbi. Because he had received his rabbinical training in Poland, he was continually referred to as a *polnisher maaster* (a 'Polish master'). His small stature was an inexhaustible source of ribaldry: comments such as the little rav, the *nebishe* (wretched) rav, and dunce – in other words a person whom scholars looked down on.

For tactical reasons the Old Community had to go easy on the leading personalities of Adath Jesurun, whereas – given the linguistic level of the *Discourses* – Chief Rabbi Isaac Ger also got off relatively scot-free. He was merely called a hypocrite and a careerist, who tried to introduce new Jewish customs for the single reason that he wanted to be regarded as a great scholar. His children did not get off so lightly: his son was a 'spendthrift' and his daughter 'immoral' (for having exchanged a few words with boys in the corridor of the synagogue after the service).

Even so we would underestimate the *Discourses* by looking only at the coarseness, insinuations and unproved accusations. There is no doubt that the authors displayed considerable ingenuity in continually inventing new tricks in order to fascinate their readers. Besides being the most amusing part, these literary devices are noteworthy from a social and cultural point of view. Some of these aspects are discussed below.

a. *Imaginary News Items*

A good example of an 'invented article' is the following item:

London – housing prices have skyrocketed during recent weeks, due to the fact that numerous residences have been rented by Parnasim from Amsterdam who have decided to settle in this country. The government is busy making preparations for welcoming them... and it has already appointed a deputation to discuss how their smuggled goods can be imported. *Goddammit* (!), we'll manage, says the President.

This item appeared following the coup of January 22, 1798, and therefore insinuates not only that the Parnasim intended to take refuge in England, but planned to take all kinds of contraband goods with them. In effect, they are accused of high treason.

b. *Pseudo-Regulations*

Issue No. 21 of the *Discourses of the New Community* carried an extensive supplement containing the Regulations of the Old Community, preceded by the words: 'Extract from the Tenth Great Memorandum Book, Folio 11, deposited at the Upper House (of Parliament) at London.' This suggested that the British Government had consulted the Prince of Orange. All concerned deplored the schism within the Amsterdam Jewish community because it had disrupted the gold shipments to London. For this reason the British Government decided to send a deputy to Amsterdam in order to announce new Regulations, for publication in the synagogue. The alleged revised text adheres closely to the existing Regulations... except for the fact that every article has an addition that makes nonsense of the article in question. For example: 'Nobody can be elected as a Parnas or a steward unless he is a sworn enemy of the Patriotic system. Besides this he has to be registered with Eik en Linde.' Eik en Linde ('Oak and Linden') was a gentlemen's club in Amsterdam that had been closed down by the Radical regime on suspicion of being too sympathetic towards the House of Orange.

The Old Community responded in kind by publishing a (as yet non-existent) draft constitution of the New Community. The first article read: 'The management of the Community and all its affairs, the synagogue, the Charity department and everything associated with all this, will be the responsibility of twelve *manhigim* (governors), five *gaboim* and six treasurers.' The joke is the total of twenty-three office bearers – a number corresponding exactly to the twenty-three secessionists from the Old Community, which also explains Rabbi Sender's taunt that it was a curse when everyone was a Parnas. An interesting typographical joke is contained in the notorious Article 22, which is copied *verbatim*. In the sentence: ...but not to secede from the Holy Community, the word 'Holy' was printed upside down, to make sure everybody realized that the opposite was meant. The same device is used elsewhere, and in certain places the words 'honorable', 'pious', *'rebetsen'* (= the rabbi's wife) are also stood on their head.

Apparently there were people in the community who believed these jocular Regulations to be genuine. In any case, the Parnasim considered it necessary to insert a notice in their own *Discourses*, informing the public that they were a complete fake, and that 'people should feel free to use the paper on which they were printed for lighting fires and all other purposes'. A surprising indulgence – considering that religious law prescribed that every scrap of paper bearing Hebrew characters had to be treated with the utmost respect, to be buried when its use had come to an end.

c. *Programs and Performances*

No doubt the most amusing and from a social and cultural point of view most fascinating sections are the programs of completely imaginary theater performances. They testify to the fact that theater, opera, marionette plays and concerts enjoyed an extraordinary popularity among Amsterdam Jewry. The Jews of Amsterdam had staged theatrical performances for the last hundred years,[31] and during the period of the *Discourses* there existed a Jewish theater company that performed plays in German, French and Italian. J.H. Dessauer, its founder and director, was a fervent supporter of the New Community.[32] Yet, the fervor with which the *Discourses* entered into the spirit of these kinds of entertainment was surprising, as well as evidence that their audiences were familiar with the particular jargon.

31 See Brugmans-Frank, pp. 490-92.
32 J.H. Dessauer in 1784 founded the High-German Jewish Theater, whose first performances took place in a shed at the Houtgracht. Following the Revolution (on May 6, 1795) he and Dr. Joachim van Embden signed a contract with the High-German Theater for a series of performances during a period of three months. There would be two performances per week, and for each performance Df. 90 would be paid – a total sum of Df. 2,340. The company was called 'Theater der jonge Tonelisten' ('The Young Actors' Theater'). An effort to make them appear in the Municipal Theater was refused by the meeting of People's Representatives (1796). Dessauer staged comedies and operas. In 1824 they had an orchestra consisting of twenty-three musicians (orchestra leaders J. and H. Preger Jr.), eight male and eight female singers and fourteen other employees. Directors were Dessauer and M.J. Hoofien, with H. Binger as musical director. The musical repertoire mainly consisted of contemporary compositions (particularly Mozart). Dessauer himself wrote a play in rhyme called 'Mardochai und Esther oder die geretteten Juden'.
   After May 1807 the company as such ceased to exist, but Dessauer established a theater school exclusively for Jews. Following the Restoration (January 1, 1814) the High-German Jewish Theater once again performed in the German Theater in the Amstelstraat. The evening was concluded with a playlet called 'Wir dürfen wieder spielen', written by Dessauer. The Theater school continued to exist until the 1830s.
   Lit.: Volledige Tooneel Almanak 1806, 'Joods Hoogduits Toneelgezelschap', *Oud Holland*, Vol. 5, 1887, pp. 194-99; I.H. van Eeghen, 'Christiaan Andriessen in zijn jonge jaren', *Jbk.Amstelodamum*, 80 (1988). Hetty Berg, 'Jiddisch theater in Amsterdam in de achttiende eeuw', *St. Ros.* XXVI (1992), pp. 24-27, 34. For a list of plays performed in Rotterdam, see Institute for Research on Dutch Jewry (Hebr. Univ., Jerusalem), no. 062.

It was the Old Community that raised the curtain with an 'advertisement' (in its issue no. 15, in reality no. 3) announcing that the coming Friday night a company from the 'community Adas Kourakh' was to perform a play in its own theater, called 'The Charlatan, or the hypocrite unmasked'. The 'theater', of course, was the synagogue of the New Community, and its name a direct reference to Korah, who rebelled against Moses (Num. 16), whereas the hypo-crite was the rabbi of the community.[33] 'The play will be followed by the performance of a comic operetta and a ballet. At the end of the performance the audience will be regaled to meat and milk, sausage and cheese and even oysters and pork. And for good measure, the host's parlor will be available for smoking tobacco (on Friday night!)'.

Once again their opponents retaliated in kind. Already in the next issue of their *Discourses* the New Community announced the arrival of a Dutch and French theater company who were going to perform at the Houtmarkt (the present Jonas Daniel Meyer Square) in the assembly hall of the Old Commu-nity. The director of the troupe was called 'Pregini', the Italicized form of 'Preger'– one of the Parnasim of the community. The same device was employed throughout when referring to the names of musicians and composers. Our Pregini (elsewhere called David Kampen or David Dikye) had written a tragic comedy called 'The Spendthrift, or the House of Fools', the performance of which was to be followed by a pantomime 'Parnasim or the Violators of Free-dom'. Here, too, the performance was to be followed by a buffet, at which oranges and 'princessebonen' (haricot beans) would be served — alluding to the family of the Prince of Orange. There also were to be rooms where boys and girls could mix together — suggesting that the Parnasim were permitting profligacy.

The various programs are an endless source of vulgar jests and insinuations. The Princesses of Orange were to perform 'The Whoring Aunt and Whoring Daughter'. In another play, called 'Drolliges Figur' (A Droll Figure) the Chief Rabbi takes a French cure accompanied by the symphony 'Ça Ira.' Besides infractions of the Jewish faith, the Old Community ridiculed the impecunious-ness of the Modernists, who were said to be bankrupt and liable to be incarcer-ated in the debtor's prison.[34]

---

33 The site of the 'theater' is also mentioned: 'oyf die H...graft vor di tsvey geyle katsn far di tir stehn'. ('At the H...canal, with the two yellow cats in front of the door'). This refers to the residence of the Cats family at the Heerengracht, where the services were conducted.

34 The members of the New Community were not among the most affluent Jews. The highest assessment for membership taxes following the restoration of unity in the Jewish community (1813) was paid by J.D. Meyer – who throughout had remained a member of the Old Community. He paid Df. 107.-, followed by Awraham A. Prins (Df. 93.10) and Isaac Levy de Vries (Df. 79.-). Among the former members of the New Community the highest assessment was paid by M.S. Asser (Df. 57.-), followed by B.A. de Metz (Df. 50.-). Many of the members of the former New Community do not even appear in the taxation list of 1813, which shows that they had very modest incomes and possessions. The list is reproduced in ARA, 'Minuut verbalen met Relatieven van het Verhandelde van de zittingen van het Consistorie der Israëlieten in de Circumscriptie van Amsterdam', June-September 1813.

In the case of countless titles, names of actors and actresses, dramaturges, composers and ballet masters, we no longer know which persons were intended and who was ridiculed. However, none of this diminishes the impact of this vengeful humor and sheer inventiveness on the modern reader.

d. *Rhymes and Songs*

Dispersed among the *Discourses* are a number of short German poems. They are of little consequence, except to show how poor the knowledge of German was among members of the Old Community. For example, one of their *Discourses* contains the following two lines:

> *Vilkommen ver mit volle(!) kraft*
> *das gude vil, das gude tut.*[35]

The 'Victory Issue' of the New Community contains two lengthy songs. The first is a 'Jewish anthem', set to the melody of the Marseillaise, whereas the second song is set to the music of another French revolutionary song, the Carmagnole. Both are doggerel rhymes, but the following lines – even in translation – neatly encapsulate the aims and principal successes of the Jewish revolutionaries:[36]

> *Di parnosim zayn far nasht*
> *nun kenen mir oukh ambten haben*
> *und verden brave zayn*
> *und krigen flaash ohne bayn*
> *und doch vi yehudim glaben*
> *o, shma, shma yisroeyl*
> *was eyn kharpe far di bul (2×)*
> *triomf hat nu di neye kille shul.*

Conclusion

The *Diskursen*, which started as imitations of existing Dutch satirical pamphlets, soon took on a rather different and even singular character. For one thing, not being addressed to a general public, but to the Jews of Amsterdam, they assumed a more and more personal tone. Everything that happened in the Jewish Quarter was somehow passed on to the authors, who exploited it to

---

35 *Welcome to him who with all his strength*
  desires good and does good.
36 *The Parnasim have been defeated.*
  now we too can have [public] functions
  and be considered honorable
  and receive meat without bones
  while just the same as Jews affirming:
  Hear O Israel..., Hear O Israel...
  What a disgrace for the others,
  but victorious is the New Synagogue.

incite their readers. The regular, virtually weekly appearance of the *Discourses* also affected the tenor of the discussion. From the moment the Old Community decided to join the fray, there was a constant shuttling of accusations, personal insinuations, sordid rumors and strident vituperations. Even so we cannot gainsay the various authors a great deal of imagination and a quite considerable sense of humor.

The *Discourses* are a rich source of information about the closed Amsterdam Jewish community from a social, medical, political as well as religious point of view. It is not a very exalted perspective, for its purpose was after all to place the opponents in the worst possible light. However, this does not diminish the expressive power of the *Discourses*, and in this light they represent a most uncommon – if not unique – phenomenon from a Dutch as well as Jewish perspective.[37]

---

37 An English translation with scholarly apparatus is being prepared by me together with Dr. Marion Aptroot of Harvard University.

4 The High Point of Jewish Political Activity

Jewish Representatives in the National Assembly of the Batavian Republic, 1797-1798

Even after the adoption of the Emancipation decree, opposition continued against the granting of active and passive voting rights to the Jews. It was only the sheer impetus of democratic radicalism during the initial two years of the Batavian Republic that enabled this opposition to be overcome. Even if the Moderates (or 'slijmgasten' – 'slimy fellows' – to use a popular epithet) held many of the key positions, they were unable to withstand the élan of the Radicals[1] who, pursuant to the goals of the French Revolution, aimed at a drastic revision of the constitutional system and structure of the government in The Netherlands as well.

It was in this atmosphere that elections for the Constituent Assembly were held. It was to be the first people's representation in which Jews would be allowed to vote and for which Jewish representatives could be elected. Even so it should be taken into account that the franchise was as yet of a very restricted nature, and that only a small part of the Jewish population, depending upon its annual income, would be eligible to vote and be elected.

The elections were held according to a kind of indirect constituency system. The representatives were elected in constitutional meetings by district, in which all enfranchised citizens of the constituency could exercise their right to vote. These meetings were held on August 1, 1797, which happened to be *Tisha Be'av*, a Jewish fast day in commemoration of the destruction of the Temple.[2] The Parnasim of the High-German Jewish community in Amsterdam and their supporters had thus far refrained from participating in any constitutional meetings, but this time they changed their tactics, if only to prevent the election of one of their hated adversaries of Felix Libertate. Thus, precisely at 11 o'clock on the day of the election they abandoned the Synagogue service and to a man

---

1 In using the term Radicals we follow Kosmann, *op. cit.*, p. 89. Previously the terms Unitarians, Jacobins and Democrats were more customarily used. See also the paragraph concerning the Political Relationships within the National Assembly and an analysis of the historiography of this subject in De Gou, *Constitutie*, pp. XXIV-XL. The author arrives at the conclusion that there were only two parties, the Democrats and the Moderates. As regards the Second National Assembly, Kosmann's appelation seems to be preferable.

2 Not on August 8, as Bloemgarten writes on pp. 48-49. On the other hand, the vote on the constitution took place on August 8 and not on August 1.

proceeded to the constitutional meeting in the Wallone Church in order to pledge their vote to one of the Christian candidates.[3] They almost succeeded in their objective, since none of the Jewish candidates in their district were elected. Their joy – prematurely vented in the election hall by one of the Parnasim – would nevertheless be short-lived. Two candidates, Jacob Blauw and L.C. Vonck, who had been elected in several other districts, yielded their seats to the two candidates who had received the next largest number of votes – namely H.L. Bromet and H. de H. Lemon. Thus Bromet and De Lemon became members of the Constituent Assembly – as well as the first Jews to be elected in any national Parliament.[4] Dutch Jewry had surpassed even the Jews of France, turning the Batavian Republic into a model for other nations. The elections also left a deep impression on the Jewish community of Amsterdam. We can imagine the tears of joy that must have coursed down the cheeks of many of the participants during the solemn farewell service in the Adath Jesurun synagogue prior to Bromet's departure. Countless supporters accompanied him when he embarked for The Hague to take his Parliamentary seat.[5]

In The Hague Bromet and De Lemon exercised far greater influence than could have been expected from any two novice Jewish parliamentarians. The statement by the *Diskursen fun di Naye Kille* to the effect that 'Asser and Bromet could accomplish anything they wanted in The Hague', while no doubt exaggerated, nevertheless contained an element of truth.[6] Bromet and De Lemon belonged to the most dynamic faction, that of the Radicals. More than any other party the Radicals had placed their support behind the emancipation of the Jews in order to draw the logical and practical consequences from the Emancipation decree. The intensity with which the Radicals tried to impose their ideas and oust their opponents among the old regents and moderate Republicans closely resembled the fervor of the attempts by Felix Libertate and Adath Jesurun to replace the Parnasim and haul them before a court of law.[7] There was yet another factor that played a role here: one of the main planks of the Radical platform stated that the Batavian Republic was a single and indivisible entity, which in practical terms meant the elimination of provincial and municipal autonomy. In Jewish terms this was tantamount to destroying the autonomy of the Jewish community, a pivotal point in the program of the Modernists. Even so, as regards the situation in The Netherlands in general, it was evident that the principal opposition against the granting of equal rights to Jews existed among the local authorities, and that only a powerful central

3   *Disk. N.K.* II, p. 3.
4   'Farewell speech by H.L. Bromet in the Synagogue of the New Jewish Community.' (Silva Rosa, *Bibliog*rafie, no. 81); in his autobiography, published by I.H. van Eeghen, *Jbk Amstelodamum*, no. 55, 1963, M.S. Asser writes that Bromet was the mentor of the group. This also emerges clearly in De Lemon's speech during the farewell ceremony in the synagogue of Adath Jesurun on Sunday, August 27, 1797. Although Bromet had been elected the previous week, and had also earlier left for The Hague, they were both installed at the same time on August 31, 1797, ARA, Dagverhaal Constituerende Vergadering.
5   *Disk N.K.* no. 4, p. 3.
6   *Disk N.K.* no. 1.
7   *Disk N.K.* no. 4, p. 3.

administration would succeed in enforcing the rights which the Jews already possessed in theory. On a number of occasions Jews who wished to exercise their civic rights were compelled to appeal over the heads of the local council to a higher authority, usually ending up with the provincial authorities or, as a final resort, with the national government.[8] A final point was that the Radical faction happened to be short of men of caliber, for which reason it was vitally interested in the support of Felix Libertate.[9]

This fact became readily apparent when the Radicals came to power following the coup d'état of January 22, 1798, and dismissed their opponents in the Constituent Assembly. The Party was unable to find sufficient competent personalities for the various government positions they wanted to fill. An example was the Justice Committee in Amsterdam, for which the Radicals could only find several incompetent lawyers, a grocer, a chemist and a cloth merchant. It was therefore not surprising that M.S. Asser, who also had been appointed a member of the Justice Committee, and who, although he was not a lawyer, possessed extensive legal knowledge, stood head and shoulders above his colleagues.[10]

The influence of the two Jewish representatives in the Constituent Assembly is also shown by the fact that De Lemon was a member of the select group that prepared the Radical coup of January 22nd. On the day of the coup, De Lemon was appointed a member of the Committees of Internal and Foreign Affairs, whereas Bromet was appointed a member of the Supervisory Committee for the organization of the Batavian Civil Guard.[11]

In light of the above it is also understandable that Adath Jesurun – the only religious community in the country to do so – immediately addressed a declaration of support to the Radical government. The phrasing of this declaration by the New Community of Amsterdam is so characteristic of the world view of Adath Jesurun in terms of both contents and style, that we will quote some of its contents in translation:

> *Citizen Representatives, the New Jewish community has taken your example and, on the recommendation of the undersigned President, accompanied by the most sacred prayers and under the invocation of an omniscient God, on Friday 11th in their Synagogue swore an Oath of inexorable aversion to Stadtholder-*

---

8   A good example is Friesland, where the Provisional Municipality of Leeuwarden excluded Jews from the right to vote. This resolution was rescinded by the Provincial States of Friesland. See Beem, *Leeuwarden*, pp. 91-92. The Constitutional Committee also received a petition for consideration from Moses Abraham Cohen, butcher, who had been denied his civil rights in Gouda on the grounds of a decision by the Municipality of June 5, 1795 – i.e. after the Batavian revolution – in which 'he of the Jewish Nation did not receive a permit of residence' (ARA, *Dagverhaal*, February 28, 1798).

9   See Kosmann, *loc. cit.* 'But the quality of its followers was generally not outstanding and its leaders, most of whom did not come from Holland, lacked the political flexibility and the cool realism of the skeptical Moderates.'

10 About the composition of the Committee of Justice in Amsterdam, see Breen, p. 89. For Gogel's judgment, see Colenbrander, *GS*, (RGP II), p. 761.

11 ARA. Dagverhaal Constituerende Vergadering, January 27, 1798, pp. 17, 19; Dagverhaal, January 22, 1798, p. 15.

> *ship, Aristocracy, Feudalism and Absence of Government [italicized in the*
> *original] and it is on behalf of said community that the Undersigned have the*
> *Honor to inform You that all of us are ready, while forgoing our most precious*
> *desires, to hasten at the first indication to wherever the interest of our dear*
> *Fatherland and the upholding of your righteous Decrees should call us.*
>
>   *Hail and Respect,*
> *the aforem. Directors and on their behalf*
>   *M.S. Asser, President*
>   *Joseph de Jongh, Secr.*
> *Amst. January 27, 1798.*
> *The First Year of the One and Indivisible Republic.*[12]

Bromet and De Lemon used their position in order to try and organize the
Jewish community in The Netherlands according to their views. It was only
natural that this applied in the first place to Amsterdam.[13]

In its struggle for the democratization of the High-German Jewish community in Amsterdam, Felix Libertate had been defeated by the Parnasim, who
enjoyed the support of the Municipal authorities. Now the moment had arrived
to abandon democratic means and enforce the Revolution with the help of the
national government. Immediately following the coup of January 22, Joachim
van Embden and Carel Asser, respectively President and Secretary of the New
Community, contacted the Uitvoerend Bewind (Executive Authority – the name
of the new government) as well as the Agent van Politie (Commissioner of Police
– an office considered to be on a par with a Ministry), requesting them to
dismiss the incumbent Parnasim.[14]

However, who possessed the required authority to dismiss the Parnasim
when there was, after all, freedom of religion? On March 9 the Administrative
Council of the former Province of Holland decided to raise the matter with the
Commissioner of Police.[15] On March 12 the latter decided that the same
committee charged with reorganizing the Amsterdam Municipal Council
should also intervene in the matter of the Jewish community. Thus, only one
day after a new, Radical-inclined Municipal Council had been nominated and

---

12 Dagverhaal, January 29, 1798, pp. 469-70.
13 For the course of events in Amsterdam, see Bloemgarten, 11 (1968) pp. 55-63.
14 This is apparent from a memorandum sent by Adath Jesurun to a committee charged with
    effecting a reconciliation between the two communities. 'Requeste van Directeuren der Joodse
    Nieuwe Gemeente aan 't Uitvoerend Bewind' (ARA, Exhib. May 2, 1800). The committee
    consisted of J. Bondt, Jacob Walraven and Angelus Jacobus Cuperus, all of them lawyers, of
    whom at least two (Bondt and Cuperus) had earlier been involved in the disputes. The
    committee had been appointed by the Executive Authority on June 15, 1798, but it protested
    against its assignment because of the illegitimacy of the dismissal and the reinstatement of the
    Parnasim. For this reason the Executive Authority decided to charge the Mayor of Amsterdam
    and his deputies *c.s.* with the resolution of this matter, and to reinstate the triumvirate in order
    to arrange a reconciliation, while emphasizing that the separation of Church and State should be
    respected. (ARA, Uitvoerend Bewind, no. 30.) The committee produced numerous interesting
    documents, but it failed to yield any results.
15 ARA, Extract uit het Register der Resolutiën van het Administratief bestuur van het voormaalig
    Gewest Holland, March 9, 1798.

the former members had been dismissed,[16] the ax fell in the Jewish community.[17] On Friday afternoon, March 16, all Parnasim and former Parnasim were
told to present themselves at the Great Synagogue at 5 o'clock in the afternoon.
Both the day and the hour had clearly been deliberately chosen: just before the
onset of the Sabbath, and assuming that the following day of rest would pre-
clude rebellious reactions. If despite all this any of those present would have
wanted to protest or cause a disturbance, they no doubt would have been
deterred by the accompanying military show of force: a company of soldiers, on
foot and mounted, was deployed in front of the synagogue, and for good
measure the procession of dignitaries was escorted by armed militiamen. In a
lengthy speech, Romswinckel, a member of the Reorganization Committee,
enumerated the complaints against the Parnasim – all of which are already
familiar to us from the writings of Felix Libertate and the New Community. At
a given point Romswinckel had to explain the reasons why the Government,
despite the existence of religious freedom, had seen itself compelled to intervene
in the Jewish community's internal affairs. The Parnasim, he stated, had violated
the Laws of the Land, particularly the Emancipation decree of September 2, 1796,
which also included the abolition of the 'sanctions' by the Municipal Council:

> *See here Parnasim! See here, Jewish Community, Brothers, Fellow Citizens,*
> *why we, while respecting your Freedom of Religion, nevertheless saw ourselves*
> *compelled to uphold the Political Government.*

The Parnasim were given until 8 o'clock the following evening (after the termi-
nation of the Sabbath) to vacate their positions. This did not prevent the
Reorganization Committee from unilaterally nominating that very Friday afternoon, in the synagogue, five candidates who had expressed their willingness to
form a new 'Board of Manhigim' (to replace the Parnasim),[18] a move that had
obviously had been decided beforehand. The viewpoints of the new leaders,
officially named 'Provisional Delegates', were closely related to those of the New
Community, and they were expected to restore harmony in the Jewish community, on the assumption that the New Community would for all practical purposes dominate the Old Community.[19]

---

16 This meant the disappearance of Iz. da Costa Athias, the only Jew on the Municipal Council.
    Moses Moresco, one of those who had resigned from the Old Community, was appointed a
    member of the new, Radical Municipal Council. Following Daendels' coup and his subsequent
    dismissal, Moses clearly became impoverished, for his brother Benjamin recommends him in an
    application for a commission as a lieutenant in the Jewish Corps. According to him, the
    government commissioners who had dismissed him had given Moses a verbal promise that, if
    necessary, they would assist him in making an honest living, 'which had indeed been said at the
    time, although it was sufficient to be a Jew in order not to receive anything.' (J. Meijer,
    Problematiek, pp. 28-29.
17 The same Reorganization Committee charged with replacing the Amsterdam municipal
    administration had to carry out the removal of the Parnasim – proof, if necessary, that the
    Government's intervention was politically motivated.
18 The letter of March 12, 1798 (ARA, *ibid*). It seemed obvious that Romswinckel's speech had been
    drafted by or written in consultation with the leaders of Adath Jesurun.
19 S.E. Hartog was nominated President of the 'Provisional Deputies'. The most prominent among
    his twelve 'assistants' was J.A. Polak.

Nothing much came of all this. During their brief regime (all in all three months), the new administrators proved themselves totally incapable. Besides, the rather startling revolutionary behavior of the authorities had stirred up passions among the Jews. One day about fifty young people forced their way into the room in which the new Board was deliberating, creating such a commotion that the President precipitously adjourned the meeting and left post-haste – subsequently enabling him to claim that all decisions taken after his departure were illegal.

On June 12 General Daendels deposed the Radical Republican regime, handing over the reins of government to an Interim Executive Authority that pursued a more conservative policy. These new circumstances made it reasonable to expect that the Parnasim would also be reinstated, but reality turned out to be different. On June 18, Daendels met with several of the deposed Parnasim, as well as with Moses Asser – a sign that the conflict among the Jews of Amsterdam was considered an important government issue. It would seem that Asser made a more profound impression on Daendels than the Parnasim, for the Government reached a decision that, under the circumstances, appeared quite favorable to the New Community. A commission of three persons was appointed, charged with reinstating the Parnasim, who were to be assisted by fifteen elected *manhigim*, as well as to arrange a reconciliation between the parties; at the same time it was clearly stipulated that previous infringements of the law on the part of the Parnasim were not to be forgiven (June 15).[20]

The three-man committee consisted of three lawyers, namely J. Bondt and J. Walraven representing the New Community, and A.J. Cuperus for the Old Community – a composition that might very well have been the brainchild of Asser. Cuperus, who realized that both the terms of reference and the composition of the committee were unfavorable to the Old Community, wrote a letter to General Spoors, who together with Daendels had staged the coup and who was currently President of the Interim Executive Authority (June 20). In it, he explained that one could not expect lawyers to take measures affecting the Jewish Community that were within the jurisdiction of the Government. Neither was he happy with the Commission's mandate, and the implication that the Parnasim had committed illegal acts. His letter resulted in an announcement by the three committee members that as advocates of the two parties, they were unable to implement the required measures and that consequently they were unable to accept their appointment.

Thus the Government was once again forced to intervene. This time it decided to place the burden of reinstating the Parnasim on the Amsterdam municipality. The former triumvirate was re-appointed, but this time their mandate was restricted to bringing the warring parties together (June 22).[21]

20 ARA, Uitvoerend Bewind, exh. June 22, 1798 no. 30. Bloemgarten (pp. 62-63) only mentions
    the conversation with the Parnasim, and immediately after this the decision of June 22 – and
    therefore not what had happened in the meantime.
21 ARA, *ibid.*, no. 29.

The official reinstatement of the Parnasim took place on June 27 in the Great Synagogue, the same site where their dismissal had been proclaimed, and once again with great military pomp and circumstance. This time there was no reason to worry about disturbances: the Parnasim were carried into the Synagogue on the shoulders of their supporters, where the President of the Municipality appointed them as 'Provisional Executive Parnasim', a title they were to bear for ten years. A tentative proposal by the President to have the fifteen chosen *manhigim* elected as a kind of Council next to the Parnasim was rejected with a resounding 'no' by all present.[22]

This was the end of the Radical adventure. The next, far more comprehensive and successful intervention in the administration of the Jewish community would take place ten years later under King Louis Napoleon, but only following extensive consultations and much more thorough preparation. As for the Reconciliation Committee: it continued to pursue its unrewarding task until 1801, without ever achieving anything.[23]

Returning for a moment to the Radical government, it appears that it had also been involved with the Jewish communities in The Hague – the High-German as well as the Portuguese community. As regards the High-German community, this is evident from its handling of a plea by Levy Manasse for the annulment of a bond of Df. 180 owed by his sister Kaatje to the Jewish community, with the argument that ever since September 2, 1796, the by-laws of the Community had no longer been in force. A special committee was set up to deal with the case, but before it managed to reach a decision, Levy Manasse had agreed upon a settlement with the community. More important for us is the announcement by Manasse to the Constituent Assembly 'that this scandalous as

---

22 Bloemgarten, *loc. cit.* The Parnasim who returned were: Benedictus Lemans, Ab. Marcus van Offen, David Levy, Leon H. Keyser, Joseph Aron de Prins, Philip Isaac de Jongh and Simon Zadok Philip. On August 2 sixteen of the *manhigim* who had burnt their bridges to the Old Community joined Adath Jesurun.

23 Dagverhaal, etc., April 30, 1798, pp. 582, 583. The Bondt Committee started its work in high spirits, since both parties had declared to be desirous of a reconciliation. However, this proved to be the opening stance only, for it soon became clear that their real viewpoints were diametrically opposed. The Parnasim also complained 'that the first-mentioned member of this Committee (Bondt; J.M.) served the disaffected members (i.e. the New Community; J.M.) and their Procedures as legal advisor, and the second (Walraven; J.M.) as attorney, a situation that should be regarded as undesirable for both parties'... but they were prepared to cooperate in any way. As customary, countless memoranda were produced, but in the end the Bondt Committee informed their principals, the Provincial Government of Holland, that they had failed in their mission and they wished to be relieved of their responsibility. The Provincial authorities passed the matter on to the Executive, which during its meeting of May 25, 1802 took a far-reaching decision. The preamble of the resolution explains why the dispute between the Amsterdam Jews justified Government intervention: '...That these Quarrels, Rifts and Procedures are extremely detrimental, not only for the Welfare Funds and secured Debts of the earlier-mentioned High-German Jewish Community, but that they could also become extremely dangerous for the Local Peace, the maintenance of Order, and the Policies of the City of Amsterdam.That nevertheless the very prodigious High-German Jewish Community should not be exposed to confusion, dissolution or anarchy'. In short: the Executive Authority ordered the re-unification of the communities. The resolution contained 12 articles, that were meant to resolve the disputed points. But even this decision by the Government was ignored by both communities.

well as inconsistent law (i.e. the Community by-laws) has been annulled last week, thus releasing many of my co-religionists who suffered under this oppression'.[24] The annulment of the old by-laws during the first week of April 1798 necessitated the formulation of a new set of rules, more adapted to the contemporary requirements of the community, and these were passed in October 1799 by a majority of one vote.[25]

The Portuguese community, on the other hand, invoked the assistance of the Constituent Assembly against Moses Cohen Belinfante, one of the most renowned publicists during the emancipation era.[26]

In 1786 Belinfante's father had died, and he had succeeded him as teacher at the Portuguese-Israelite Paupers' school. It was never clear, however, why his career as a teacher came to an end, or why his main activities took place in Amsterdam, to which city he relocated. A petition lodged by him on April 20, 1796, sheds some light on the matter.[27] It appears that in June 1795 he had been summarily dismissed by the Parnasim. The official reason was that he had neglected the school, which, considering his service record, is highly improbable. According to Belinfante the real reason was different: in 1795 he had become a member of the National Club, where he had been assigned to a Civil Guard company. One evening in June, while he was on guard duty, a colleague who was supposed to relieve him before the commencement of the Sabbath had not turned up. As a result he had been compelled to continue patrolling, carrying his rifle – even though in the meantime the Sabbath had commenced. In accordance with the rulings of the Amsterdam rabbinate, the Parnasim had regarded this as a desecration of the Sabbath, and as such sufficient grounds for Belinfante's summary dismissal. April 20, the day on which the request was filed, fell on a Friday and – almost symbolically – the matter was taken up by the Constituent Assembly that very evening. During the debate it became clear that the Jewish representatives' activities on behalf of the Jewish communities met with some opposition on points of principle. When the president proposed that the request be referred to committee, one of the members contended that due

24 Levy Manasse's outrage about the by-laws of the High-German community in The Hague is understandable once we know the circumstances surrounding this liability. In his letter of March 26, 1798, to the Constitutional Committee Manasse relates that his sister Kaatje (Chaya) had had a relationship with Meyer Rekkendorff (son of the cantor of the community). When she became pregnant, they married (February 1796), but already a month later Meyer had died (March 5). According to the regulations, a man who married a pregnant woman forfeited all rights as a member of the community, as was also the case in Amsterdam. To be reinstated the man would have had to pay Df. 200, and even if he had died in the meantime, the Parnasim were entitled to claim this sum from his relatives. Meanwhile the Hague Parnasim refused permission to bury the body, unless the family paid Df. 210. Since the destitute widow did not have that kind of money, she had no choice but to sign a bond, with her mother and her brother as guarantors. Even this did not satisfy the Parnasim: Levy Manasse had to surrender two silver watches as security, which he redeemed later for Df. 30. The debt of Df. 180 remained outstanding, as the widow was unable to pay the installments.

25 Van Zuiden, *'s- Gravenhage*, p. 95. Van Zuiden failed to take into account the connection between the events in the Jewish community in The Hague and the political developments in the Batavian Republic. For this reason his description is unclear and requires further study.

26 About M.C. Belinfante, see chapter 7, pp. 168, footnote 38.

27 ARA, Wetgevende Colleges, 1798, Request no. 310, Inv. no. 316.

to the separation of Church and State, the Assembly was no longer authorized
to deal with a dispute involving a school teacher employed by a Church. Other
delegates proposed to let the problem be decided by the Executive Authority,
which meant initiating a police or a legal investigation on whether the Parnasim
had been authorized to dismiss Belinfante. De Lemon was unable to rebut his
colleagues' arguments, other than saying that Belinfante was known to him as
an honest and diligent patriot, who for several years now had been employed as
secretary of Felix Libertate. He therefore seconded the president's proposal
that a committee from the Assembly should look into the matter. In the end the
president's proposal was accepted, and De Lemon, Fronhoff and Bromet were
appointed members of the committee.[28] No need to guess how this committee,
which was quite naturally on the side of Belinfante, would have reacted to the
defense of the Parnasim, who also invoked the separation of Church and
State.[29] But unfortunately for Belinfante, Bromet and De Lemon would soon
lose their seats in the Constitutional Assembly (June 12, 1798) – with the result
that Belinfante failed to be reinstated in his post.

The unpredictability of the Constituent Assembly was evident in yet another
case that considerably discomfited the two Jewish representatives. On March 17
a petition was tabled by a number of Amsterdam citizens.[30] The first signatory
was Xaverio Bianchi, who had obviously been briefed by the Adath Jesurun
people. The petition contained a serious complaint against the Parnasim of the
High-German community in Amsterdam, but since the latter had been dismissed only the previous day (Friday), De Lemon tried to prevent the reading
of the document – which by the way had been inspired by his own supporters.
However, this was not acceptable to the Assembly, so that the petition was read
in toto. As a result the delegates discovered that the Great Synagogue still
featured a so-called 'Cage of Infamy', containing the names of twenty-four
persons – including De Lemon and Bromet – to whom entry to the 'Church' was
denied, with whose children one could not associate, since they were 'children
of *nidda*' (children conceived as a result of impure matrimonial relations), whose
victuals and dishes were forbidden, and a marriage with whom would be
considered an offense. The president wanted to accept the petition as read,
supported by De Lemon, who noted that the Parnasim had been dismissed and
everything was under control, with Bromet adding that the petition should not
be discussed. The Assembly disagreed, and the president reconsidered, suggesting that the request would be discussed again at a later date. Apparently this
satisfied the Assembly, but it showed its curiosity about the further development
of the matter.

28 ARA, Dagverhaal, etc., April 20, 1798, pp. 521-22.
29 ARA, Wetgevende Colleges, Request no. 320.
30 Dagverhaal, March 7, 1798, p. 147.
    The first signatory of the request (Requ. Wetg. Colleges, 1798, no. 318) was Saverio, and not
    Xaverio as mentioned in het Dagverhaal. Neither he nor the other 53 signatories were Jewish.
    This means that the Jewish Patriots mobilized a considerable number of non-Jews to support
    them in their struggle against the leadership of the Amsterdam Jewish community.

The Rastatt Congress

From the Jewish point of view, by far the most important issue to be discussed in the Constituent Assembly, although not in any way connected with the conflicts within the Jewish communities, was nevertheless of generally Jewish and even international consequence. Felix Libertate, which in The Netherlands had succeeded in promoting such a favorable Emancipation decree, believed that it also could and should pursue the struggle for emancipation outside The Netherlands. On November 14, 1797, 'several distinguished enfranchised citizens of Amsterdam, members of the Mosaic Brotherhood', submitted a memorandum,[31] in which, referring to the equal status achieved by the Jews, they complained about the still existing discrimination in other countries, in particular Germany 'where as yet a distinction was made between Batavian *Jewish* and Batavian *Christian* Citizens, and where '"Mosaites" (and for no other reason than that they are such) were barred from staying overnight or from passing through the town unless escorted by a guard; [and where] in some they were even refused safe passage; [whereas] in others Public Billboards were posted with the inscription: **HERE PIGS AND JEWS PAY TOLL FEES.**' Such behavior, they contended, was disadvantageous for commerce, for:

> *which discerning Jew would leave this free Republic (as many Jewish merchants are wont to do every year, when traveling to the Annual Fairs at Frankfurt on the Main, Leipzig, etc.) to visit such a country, where they are received with indignity and contempt?*
>
> *[This is] hurtful for the National Representation.*
>
> *Assuming that You gentlemen would at any time consider or deem it necessary to dispatch one or more Delegates to that country in order to represent the interests of the Dutch People, and if You gentlemen would charge a Jewish citizen with such a Commission, then this Delegate would not only be obliged to pay this Infamous Toll, but have to endure all those molestations which they habitually inflict on so-called Jews.*

The petitioners stated they had heard that the French republic had for the same reason exerted pressure on the Swiss cantons.[32] They were of the opinion that the time has come – together with or through the influence of the French Republic – to bring about the abrogation of discrimination, either at the next Congress of Rastatt or elsewhere, under threat of reprisals, to wit that otherwise the inhabitants of those countries would have to pay the same tolls when visiting the Batavian Republic 'so that the Foreign Powers will also be made aware and

---

31 Dagverhaal, November 16, 1797, pp. 741-42.
32 In 1797 the French envoy Barthelemy did indeed exert pressure on the Swiss Cantons to abolish the Jew toll. The request was granted, on condition that the Jews would wear no external distinguishing marks of their religion. About the stubborn opposition of the Swiss against any amelioration of the position of the Jews, even during the era of the Helvetian Republic, and the abrogation of the existing concessions in 1809, see S. Dubnow, pp. 189-193; R. Mahler, *History of the Jewish People in Modern Times*, (Hebr.), Vol. I, Merhavia, 1952, pp. 279-85.

will know that this Republic consists of ONE INDIVISIBLE BATAVIAN NA-
TION ONLY.'

The thirteen signatories of the petition were well-known members of Felix
Libertate; De Lemon and Bromet obviously did not sign. At the moment that
M.S. Asser and his faction submitted the petition, the Congress of Rastatt had
not yet convened. The ostensible purpose of the Congress was to determine the
compensation for the German princes in the event that France would annex the
right bank of the Rhine, but Napoleon viewed the matter in a much wider
context: at Rastatt the future of Europe would be decided.[33] This was an
opportunity – the first after the enfranchisement of the Jews of France and the
Batavian Republic – to raise the demand for equal rights for the Jews, or at least
the abrogation of discrimination, before an international forum. It would be
possible to exert pressure on the German States, who since the recently signed
peace settlement between France and Austria at Campo Formio (17. 10. 1797)
were much more dependent on France.

There are clear indications that the advocates of emancipation, Jews as well
as non-Jews, both in the German States and in the Batavian Republic, had
cooperated in order, through meticulous preparation, to achieve the best possible results. During 1797 and 1798 a series of German translations was published of documents relating to the struggle for emancipation in The Netherlands,
including the debates in the National Assembly and the Emancipation Decree
itself.[34] The *Divre negidim*, mainly a translation of the debates in the National
Assembly, but supplemented with other material, similarly made no secret of its
propagandist intent: '... Behold the righteousness of the Batavian people, and
perhaps God will grant you (i.e. the Jewish inhabitants of other countries) the
same success as granted to us by inducing the Nations to be good to them'.[35]

When the Congress of Rastatt opened on December 9, 1797, it seems that
M.S. Asser and his faction were worried that the Foreign Affairs Committee, to
whom their first petition had been submitted, had not been sufficiently active.
In any case, on February 27, 1798, they presented a second petition, in which
the Executive Authority was requested to intervene jointly with the French
government.[36] As a result the Executive Authority immediately instructed the
envoy of the Batavian Republic in France, Caspar Meyer, as well as its envoy in
Rastatt 'to use every opportunity and every means that you shall deem suitable

---

33 According to Napoleon. About this congress, see Louis Villat, *La Révolution et l'Empire
(1789-1815)* I, Paris, 1940, pp. 363, 395, 397-98.
34 *Actenstücke zur Geschichte der Erhebung der Juden zu Buergern in der Republik Batavien*, Neustrelitz,
1797. Within the framework of this campaign two more documents on the Dutch Emancipation
decree were published: Hahn, *Rede über die volkommene Gleichstellung der Juden mit den übrigen
Bürgern*, Frankfurt, 1796; 'Decret über die Gleichstellung der Juden mit allen übrigen
Batavischen Bürgern, den 2 September einstimmig angenommen' (in: *Der Sammler*, Jhrg. 7,
1797, Annex 2, pp. 25-28).
35 *Divrei negidim*, Amsterdam, Ao. 5 der Bataafse Vrijheid, 1975. p. 2.
36 Dagverhaal, February 28, 1798, p. 272 (Silva Rosa, Bibliogr., no. 101). Several citizens from The
Hague sent a request along the same lines; see Dagverhaal, March 16, 1798, pp. 152-153;
request no. 316.

to effect compliance with the Petitioners' request.'[37] The French envoy in the Batavian Republic, Delacroix, was also informed of the entreaty of the Constituent Assembly. Caspar Meyer appealed to the French Minister for Foreign Affairs, Talleyrand, with a fervent plea to intervene on behalf of the Jews in Germany (March 23, 1798).[38] On April 12, the Executive Authority was able to report that the necessary steps had been taken.[39]

This vigorous action by the Dutch Jews[40] was accompanied by the necessary activities in Germany itself. Several appeals were addressed to the delegates at Rastatt, whose authors referred to the rights achieved by the Jews of the Batavian Republic, as well as earlier petitions for the abolition of discrimination in Germany, that Dutch Jewry had addressed to their Government.[41]

Unfortunately all this would come to naught, since the Rastatt Congress came to an abrupt end. On April 23 the French delegates to the Congress were murdered, and a coalition of European countries (the 'Second Coalition') renewed the war against France. For the time being the opportunities for a favorable arrangement for the German Jews were lost. Soon after there would be a setback in the Batavian Republic as well. On June 12, 1798, General Daendels staged his coup d'état, putting an end to the faltering rule of the Radicals. The fall of the Radical regime had serious repercussions for Adath Jesurun: all its representatives at the national and regional level (Amsterdam) lost their positions.[42] Apart from this they had become identified with the Radical party to such an extent that their political future was compromised.

---

37 ARA, Wetg. Colleges, Inv. no. 236.
38 *Ibidem.*
39 *Ibidem.*
40 In *Disk. N.K.*, no. 12, p. 7, the following story appears under the title 'Advertissement' (translated by us): 'According to a written communication from Rastatt a splendid equipage has arrived there. A deputation of several plenipotentiaries from the Amsterdam Parnasim of the old Amsterdam Kehilla [has arrived] to oppose the petition submitted by several personalities of the Adath Jesurun kehilla about the abolition of the scandalous Jew toll. It is said that they have been contemptuously rejected by the entire congress with the question whether their present harassment of their Dutch brethren wasn't enough, that they should again seek to attack Jews, and that they should know that all efforts were being made everywhere to abolish the Jew toll.'
    It seems most improbable that the Amsterdam Parnasim should have sent a delegation to Rastatt. Far more likely is that the authors of the *Diskursen fun die Neye Kille* wanted to ridicule the Amsterdam Parnasim, who had attempted to prevent the Emancipation decree.
41 Volkmar Eichstadt, *Bibliographie zur Geschichte der Judenfrage* (Hamburg, 1938) mentions the following pamphlets:
    294. Cranz, August Friedrich, *Heus und die Juden, oder Nachtrag zu den sämmtlichen paziszirenden Abgeordneten in Rastatt, die Stimme von einem Weltbürger*, Altona 1798; 311. Riem, Andreas, *Apologie für die unterdrückte Judenschaft in Deutschland. An den Congress in Rastatt gerichtet*, Leipzig 1798; 312. Grund, Christophe, *Ist eine bürgerliche Verbesserung der Juden in Deutschland dem Rechte und der Klugheit gemäsz?*, Regensburg, 1798.
    About this literature, see Graetz, pp. 235, 241.
42 De Lemon was even arrested, but released soon after, as shown by correspondence between the Executive Authority and the Arbitrating Legislative Body. In July 1798 the Arbitrating Legislative Body asks if De Lemon is to be regarded as a fugitive (ARA, Uitvoerend Bewind, Inv. no. 31, July 3, 1798). The Executive Authority replies that no instructions have been given to arrest De Lemon (ARA, *id.*, inv. no. 33). Following this De Lemon, as a former member of the Upper Chamber of the Representative Body, started to receive a daily allowance (ARA, *idem*, July 6, nos. 13 and 31).

This does not mean that the Batavian Republic ceased its efforts to abolish the Jew toll in Germany – albeit with little success.[43] But the key role played by the Jews was finished. Many years would elapse before Jews were once more elected as members of European parliaments. Not all Jewish parliamentarians championed the interests of oppressed Jews, and those that did usually practised great circumspection. It is to the credit of Bromet and De Lemon, in their capacity of parliamentary representatives, and of M.S. Asser, as a motivating force, that they fought so valiantly and openly, and with complete commitment of their persons. They considered themselves called to stand up for Jewish rights, not only in The Netherlands, but in other countries as well. The world would not see a second international initiative such as theirs until half a century later, during the Damascus affair (1840).

5 Louis Napoleon's Concern with His Jewish Subjects (I)

Participation of Dutch Jewry in the Grand Sanhedrin

The existing detailed documentation on the Grand Sanhedrin of 1806 contains no indication whatever about who was the first to raise the idea of creating a body to be called 'Sanhedrin'. We may assume therefore that the idea originated in the prodigious brain of Napoleon himself.[1] There is no doubt that he perceived the Sanhedrin in the spirit described in the New Testament. I believe this is borne out in the manner in which its president, Rabbi Joseph David Sinzheim, the Rabbi of Straszbourg, was dressed. His strange headgear, illustrated in a well-known painting[2] resembles a bishop's miter turned sideways – similar to the hat worn by the High Priest Caiaphas in a picture depicting Jesus' trial, a work of the Flemish painter Cornelis de Vos. We could consider this a subtle kind of revenge on the Jews who – now subjected to a Christian emperor – were expected to change their religious laws.

It is quite possible that Napoleon believed the Jews themselves would greet the re-establishment of such an august body with enormous enthusiasm. In fact his Jewish admirers praised him in the most lyrical terms, as though he had finally raised the Jewish handmaiden from the dust. Nevertheless, neither they nor their orthodox opponents would have thought of establishing a Sanhedrin. After all, all that the Modernists could expect from such a Rabbinical Assembly was the rejection of any attempt to abolish or change Jewish religious laws, whereas – as we shall see – for orthodox Jews the idea of a Sanhedrin was reprehensible on principle, which explains why an earlier attempt at planning a new Sanhedrin had come to naught.[3]

The convening of the Paris Sanhedrin was in fact due solely to Napoleon's authority and power. His intensive preoccupation with the Jews had been

---

1 See R. Anchel, *Napoléon et les Juifs*, Paris 1928, pp. 188-189, who also assumes that the Sanhedrin was a brainchild of Napoleon himself. Various aspects of the Sanhedrin are dealt with in *Le Grand Sanhédrin de Napoléon*, ed. B. Blumenkranz-A. Soboul, Toulouse 1979. Here too it is assumed that the idea originated with Napoleon himself (pp. 10-11). Sinzheim's portrait is reproduced there opposite p. 59.
2 See note 1.
3 In 1538 Rabbi Jacob Berab (ca. 1474-1541) tried to re-introduce the authorization of rabbis (*semicha*) in Safed. If his plan had been accepted by his colleagues, the High Court or Sanhedrin could have been instituted, but his attempt failed because of the opposition of the Jerusalem rabbis led by Rabbi Levi ben Habib; see *E.J* under Berab.

triggered by complaints by anti-Semitic lawyers about alleged usurious practices on the part the Jews of the Alsace. Even so, Napoleon saw the problem in a far wider context: he wanted to incorporate the Jews, who were considered to be outsiders, into French society; to cure them of their evil practices and force them to adapt and subordinate their Jewish laws to those of the State. For this purpose he convened an 'Assemblée des députés d'Israélites en France et du Royaume d'Italie', and presented them with twelve questions intended to place the Jews before the unenviable choice of either reconciling themselves totally with the demands of Napoleon and his dictatorial and centralist regime, or to exclude themselves from the community. The Assembly's answers satisfied Napoleon, and he now sought a way to convert them 'through decisions by means of another assembly of an even more important and religious character' – as his commissioner Molé put it to the Assembly of Notables. These resolutions were to be placed 'side by side to the Talmud, and thus acquire the greatest possible authority in the eyes of all countries and all centuries.'[4]

However pretentious this decision might have been, it certainly conformed to Napoleon's megalomaniac nature. Even so, if the emperor and his government were serious about achieving this objective, convening a Sanhedrin should have been accompanied by a widespread activity, not only among the Jews themselves, but also among the governments of the vassal states, aimed at compelling the various Jewish institutions to cooperate with this endeavor. And this general legitimacy could only be achieved if the rabbinical authorities outside France and Italy were invited to participate in the discussions of the Sanhedrin on an equal basis.

However, none of this happened. Molé gave his speech on September 18, 1806, while the Sanhedrin was convened for October 20. How could representatives from so many countries be convened in Paris at such short notice? Besides, what kind of role would they have been able to fulfill there? All the seats in the Paris Sanhedrin had already been allotted to Frenchmen and Italians: forty-six rabbis (or those passing as such) and twenty-five laymen were nominated by the Prefects of France and Italy to constitute the Sanhedrin. Foreign participants were admitted as observers, and at most were only allowed to convey greetings to the Assembly.

Apart from the fact that the French government did not concern itself with issuing invitations, neither did it take the trouble to inform the governments of the vassal states about convening the Sanhedrin. The matter was left entirely to the Presidium of the Assembly of Notables, which also sent the invitations to the various Jewish communities.

Such a letter, dated October 6, 1806, and written in flowery Hebrew and French, was received on October 15 by four communities in the Netherlands. In it, they were requested to delegate 'sages' to participate in the debates to commence on October 20. The lack of an agenda, the vague invitation to send

---

4   '... à coté du Talmud et acquissent ainsi aux yeux de tous les Juifs de tous les pays et de tous les siècles la plus grande autorité possible.' See Anchel, *op. cit.*, p. 128.

'sages', without stipulating how many, the limited time for making preparations for the meeting (in actual fact the Sanhedrin was only opened on February 9, 1807) – all these demonstrated how little value was attached to foreign participation.

The four communities contacted, namely the Portuguese Community of Amsterdam, the High-German communities of Amsterdam and Rotterdam, and Adath Jesurun in Amsterdam, were of course unaware of this, and understandably, the invitation to participate in a Sanhedrin, convened by the most powerful man in Europe, caused quite a stir. A small group was jubilant, but the majority of Jews was dismayed and confused. The members of Adath Jesurun were ecstatic. For them the invitation from Paris proved their recognition as a fully fledged Jewish community by the country that dominated the world. The Community, which between June 1798 and 1806 had led a somewhat withdrawn existence under the increasingly reactionary governments of the Batavian Republic, had turned to renewed political activity in 1805, together with several members of the Portuguese and High-German communities.[5] The convening of the Assembly of Notables signaled their renewal of the struggle for a Jewish religious reform on 'purer' foundations. One indication of this was the publication of a weekly magazine that contained virtually nothing but commentaries, reports and announcements about the Assembly and related subjects.[6] The fact that Adath Jesurun had been invited to send delegates to the Sanhedrin was seen as a 'triumph for the New Community' – organized 'on the principles to be established ten years later by the Great Sanhedrin in Paris.'[7] Adath Jesurun lost no time in dealing with the matter. On the day that the invitation was received, three delegates were appointed, namely Carel Asser, H. de H. Lemon and J. Littwak, the latter's son-in-law, a mathematician and Hebraist. The delegation was chosen carefully: between them the three members were conversant with the three languages of the Sanhedrin: French, German and Hebrew. The mood at Adath Jesurun was optimistic. Even though a certain amount of opposition

---

5   See Ch. 2.
6   *Bijdragen betrekkelijk de verbetering van den maatschappelijken staat der Joden*, The Hague, Belinfante, 1806-1807 (further referred to as Belinfante, *Bijdragen*).
7   '...un Triomphe pour la nouvelle communauté' that had been organized 'd'après les principes qui ont été etablis dix ans après par le Grand Sanhédrin à Paris'. Thus M.S. Asser in a memorandum addressed to Ch.F. Lebrun, the Governor-General of Holland. (Colenbrander, *GS*, Vol. 6 (1810-1813), p. 827). Joachim van Embden, at the time Chairman of Adath Jesurun, expressed himself in the same vein during the celebration of the tenth anniversary of the Emancipation when he said: '...further to bring to the attention of the Community the questions and respective answers addressed to the Assembly of Jewish Notables in Paris by the great Napoleon, and reminding the Community that many of these questions that were raised as objections against the equal status of the Jews during the years 1795-1796 in this country were even at that time answered by the praiseworthy society of Felix Libertate in the same vein as now in Paris' (Belinfante, *Bijdragen* no. 7, September 12, 1806, pp. 61-62). Equally Carel Asser in his speech to the Sanhedrin: 'Tels, docteurs et notables, (nous le répetons avec orgeuil), tels étaient les principes qui nous guidaient quand nous érigeâmes notre communauté en l'an 1796' (Diogène Tama, *Organisation civile et religieuse des Israélites de France et du Royaume d'Italie*, Paris 1808, p. 120).

was expected, they were convinced that the other communities would also send delegates, and that a new era in the history of the Jewish community of the Kingdom of Holland was about to begin.[8]

It did not take long for them to discover that their optimism was unfounded. The Parnasim of the Portuguese and High-German communities had no intention of attending the Sanhedrin. The correspondence of the Parnasim with various other bodies contains all kinds of explanations, all of them inspired by tactical considerations. The real reason can only be found in the secret protocols of the Board of the Portuguese community, the *Mahamad*. It is argued in the secret protocols that during the period of the Temple and the Mishna, members of the Sanhedrin were always elected by co-option, in order to ensure the continuity of the tradition. However, since the chain of tradition had been broken, only Divine intervention, expected to coincide with the rebuilding of the Temple, could bring about the reinstatement of the Sanhedrin. A Sanhedrin established by human intervention during the period of Exile should be denied any authority.[9] Given the sharp criticism of Napoleon's initiative that this argumentation implied, it is understandable that the Board preferred not to state this in public.

The Parnasim of the High-German (Ashkenazi) community were even more alarmed by the invitation than those of the much smaller (2,500 individuals) and more homogeneous Portuguese community. They met on October 16, only one day after receiving the invitation.[10] They too regarded the Sanhedrin as an ax to the roots of the Jewish faith, and the joy among their bitter opponents at Adath Jesurun had not eluded them. But how could they refuse the invitation? The Kingdom of Holland was merely a vassal state of France, and the king,

---

8   This is shown by a letter from M.C. Belinfante to Abbé Grégoire: 'So far we have not heard that the Synagogues of Holland have received the direct proclamation of the Paris assembly, but in the event that this will happen, there is no doubt that the various synagogues, especially those in Amsterdam, will send delegates.' This letter was written on October 19 (in The Hague), in other words three days after the Parnasim of the Portuguese and the High-German communities had held their first meeting and decided on principle not to accept the invitation.
     Belinfante also argues that the delegates after their return 'may be able to introduce beneficial measures for the happiness of the Israelites.' Quoted from Meijer, *Problematiek*, pp. 14-15.

9   *Livro de Segredos* (W.Ch. Pieterse, *Inventaris van de archieven der Portugees-Israëlitische gemeente te Amsterdam*, 1614-1870, Amsterdam 1964, nos. 61-62). The same text, except for the last two pages, appears in the *Bijlagen* bij de Notulen van de President, 1789 and 1806 (Pieterse, *loc. cit.*, no. 64). Actually the Parnasim were somewhat out of their depth, since halakhically speaking there is no connection between the reconstruction of the Temple and the re-establishment of the Sanhedrin. On the contrary: according to tradition the re-establishment of the Sanhedrin will precede the coming of the Messiah. According to Maimonides (*Yad Hahazakah*, 4:11), an undisputed authority for the Portuguese Parnasim, *semichah* can be given if all the rabbis in Eretz Yisrael are unanimously agreed; a person who has received *semikhah* (ordination) may ordain as many others as needed for the re-establishment of the Sanhedrin. However, this cannot be done outside Eretz Yisrael.

10 GAA, *Protokolbuch*. The text of the Protocol book on this matter is reproduced in D.M. Sluys, 'De Amsterdamse Joodse Gemeenten en het grote Synhedrion te Parijs', *VA*, Vol. 3, (1927), February 18, pp. 324-26); February 25 (pp. 338-42). The *Protokolbuch* and the *Livro de Segredos* complement each other. As against this, the protocols of Adath Jesurun, that have also been preserved, do not make any mention about it.

Louis Napoleon, was a brother of the emperor who had convened the Great Sanhedrin. The Parnasim considered this such a dangerous state of affairs that they took two decisions. Firstly, they would contact the Portuguese Parnasim with the express purpose of arriving at a common stand, and secondly, they would propose that the Portuguese Parnasim consult the Amsterdam Municipality, which at that time was headed by a College of Magistrates. The Portuguese Parnasim accepted the proposal.[11] At their meeting of October 19, the Ashkenazi Parnasim already tended towards not sending any delegates at all. This also turned out to be the position of their Portuguese colleagues, but neither side had as yet had the courage to take the decisive step of sending a letter to Paris without the guaranteed support of the Magistrates. However, the meeting with the Magistrates, in which representatives of both communities participated, turned out to be completely satisfactory. Not only did the Magistrates leave the decision entirely to the Communities themselves, since they saw it as a purely religious affair, but – even more important – they promised to support the Parnasim whatever the outcome of their decision.[12] This may reasonably be regarded as an encouragement not to send delegates and thus, after mutual consultation, both communities formulated their separate replies, which were sent to the Magistrates, requesting that they be forwarded to the government.[13]

Although the issue may have been labeled as religious by the Magistrates – and we know that the opposition to the Sanhedrin was indeed based on religious motives – somehow, neither the letter to Paris from the Ashkenazi Parnasim or from their Portuguese colleagues made any mention of them. In fact, the Parnasim deemed it preferable to play a political card, arguing that for centuries the Jews had been so comfortable in The Netherlands that it made no sense to try and 'obtain privileges that they already enjoyed,' besides which this would seem an offense to 'notre gracieux Roi Louis Napoléon.' The Portuguese Parnasim, in their letter, noted that the wise and venerable persons who had

11 *Livro de Segredos*: The Ashkenazi Parnasim requested the *Senhores do Mahamad* to conduct the negotiations since they, the Sephardim, had been longer established in Amsterdam. The *Protokolbuch* merely mentions that the two communities decided to maintain harmonic relations ('in guter harmoni tsu zayn') and to keep each other informed at all times (October 19).

12 According to the *Protokolbuch* the Magistrates called it a private affair ('ayn partikulire zakh'); the *Livro de Segredos*, on the other hand, calls it 'completely religious' ('totalmente ecclesiastico'). The latter view is probably correct. This view of the ecclesiastical character of the invitation probably explains the decision of the Ashkenazi Parnasim on October 25 to consult the Chief Rabbi and the Beth Din. When they suggested that the Portuguese Parnasim do the same, the reply was that it was 'beneath their reputation to consult the Beth Din in a case that was so clear and of such little importance' ('inferior a sua reputaçao de acconselharse com Beth Din per cazo tão claro e de tão pouco momento'.) This shows the low esteem in which the rabbis of the Portuguese community were held.

13 An entry in the *Protokolbuch* on October 19 already contains the draft of the answer (in Hebrew with French translation). Later several minor changes were made. The Hebrew text was published in B. Mevorach, *Napoleon utekufato*, Jerusalem, 1869 (Hebr.), pp. 141-42. The text of the letter from the Portuguese Parnasim was published in Belinfante, *Bijdragen*, 1807, no. 35, p. 317.

been invited 'could very well do without the presence of any delegates that we might have decided to send.'[14]

If the Parnasim believed that with these diplomatically phrased letters the case was closed, they were badly mistaken. By no means did everybody agree with their approach, especially in the Portuguese community which – even though it had not lost any members to Adath Jesurun – had quite a few sympathizers with the Modernist view. One of them, the famous physician Immanuel Capadoce[15], who himself had been a Parnas, approached the president, to inform him that he had received a letter from a certain friend, a member of the Council of State, who had pointed out to him that before giving a negative reply, the king should be consulted. The president deflected Capadoce's warning with the remark that a decision had been taken and the letter was already on its way. Capadoce refused to accept this excuse and asked another Parnas to broach the matter again. The latter was given the same answer, and this time Capadoce demanded to be heard in person. That same day (25 Heshvan) a stormy meeting took place during which the *Senhores do Mahamad* were confronted with expressions not heard since the establishment of the community. The upshot was that Capadoce once again received a negative reply, to which he reacted by stating that many '*Yehidim*' (members of the community) had very serious objections to the Board, and that in the interest of the (Jewish) Nation he considered it an honor to be able to place himself at the head of these malcontents. Faced with this threat and Capadoce's highly unseemly language, the *Senhores do Mahamad* decided that silence was the better part of valor, 'in order to preserve the reputation of the body that had been maintained for so many years'. At which point Mr. Capadoce left the meeting.[16]

It soon became apparent that Capadoce's threat had not been an idle one. Together with Jacob Saportas, a banker[17], and I. da Costa Athias, a former President of the National Assembly, he wrote a letter to Louis Napoleon, arguing that the Parnasim had no right to refuse the invitation without consulting the members of their Community, or at least the Council of Elders. They therefore requested His Majesty to 'instruct the Parnasim as he saw fit.'[18] Although there were only three signatories – collective petitions being forbid-

---

14 '...pourront bien se passer de la présence des députés que nous pouvions les adjoindre'.
15 Immanuel de Abraham Capadoce (1750-1826) had been Parnas in 5561 (1801) and 5565 (1805) (*ESN*, p. 110). Koenen writes (p. 379): 'According to verbal reports it was mainly the Royal physician Iman[uel] Capadoce who managed to avoid that the Portuguese were not compelled to appoint delegates to the Sanhedrin.' From the context is it clear that the word 'not' is superfluous, and Koenen obviously means that Capadoce agitated *against* the appointment of delegates. This statement was copied by almost all historians, including Da Silva Rosa, *Geschiedenis der Portugese Joden*, Amsterdam, 1925, p. 131; J. Meijer, *da Costa*, p. 22. In another book the latter author even writes that Capadoce refused to be appointed a delegate (*ESN*, p. 133).
16 *Livro de Segredos*.
17 Jacob Saportas was one of the most prominent bankers of the time; he was a 'colleague and business associate' of the Minister of Finance I.J.A. Gogel, who served in this capacity in various governments of the Batavian Republic and during Louis Napoleon (see Schama, *op. cit.*, p. 616).
18 '...telles ordres qu'Elle jugera convenables'.

Dr. Immanuel Capadoce, 1751-1826. Rijksmuseum, Amsterdam.

den – they assured the king that 'the largest and most reasonable part of the Portuguese Jewish community' were of the same opinion.[19]

Capadoce still had more arrows to his bow. Five days later the talented young lawyer Jonas Daniel Meyer sent an identical letter in which he requested the

19 '...las plus grande et la plus saine partie de la communauté Juive portugaise'. ARA, Bi.Za., afd. Erediensten, inv. no. 1, exh., November 22, 1806).

king to give the Parnasim of *his* community the necessary instructions.[20] It may be assumed that Capadoce also contacted Adath Jesurun, for on November 10 this community despatched a letter to the king informing him of the appointment of three delegates, and requesting him 'to give some sign of his approval, which would contribute greatly to the respectability of the delegates, both in their own eyes, as with regard to those who would like to be assured that they enjoy His Majesty's patronage.'[21]

It seems probable that the king's retroactive approval was requested in order to provide legitimacy to Capadoce and his faction and J.D. Meyer, after they had voiced the opinion that the invitation to the Great Sanhedrin was such a crucial matter that the king himself should take a decision on the matter. However, at the same time the king's compliance with Adath Jesurun's request would mean that the three delegates would officially represent all Jews in the Kingdom of Holland, propelling a small community like Adath Jesurun into a position of power overnight.

The petitioners must have been fairly confident that Louis Napoleon would accede to their requests. After all, he could hardly disown the initiative of his 'auguste frère' and 'the great conceptions that His Creative Genius appeared to entertain in order to improve the lot of the Israelites.'[22] This suggestion was all the more reasonable since the contacts that especially Asser and Meyer had established with the king[23] had created the impression that Louis Napoleon was also imbued with the desire to ameliorate the lot of the Jews in his kingdom. The country's political dependence upon France also appeared to ensure the king's favorable decision.

It is characteristic of Louis Napoleon that the petitioners misread his intentions. His close identification with his new kingdom ever since 1806 had steadily aggravated the conflict with his brother.[24] He was certainly not prepared to accept without criticism dictates from his brother. Contrary to the emperor, Louis Napoleon was well-disposed towards the Jews and he had absolutely no desire to offend their religious feelings. As a result he did not accept the proposals of either Adath Jesurun, or Capadoce *et al.* and Meyer; he even went so far as to annotate Adath Jesurun's request with the following handwritten comment: 'Returned to the Minister of the Interior, informing him that nobody may be delegated without my instructions. The Minister is to advise me on this matter and the appropriate steps to be taken under these circumstances.'[25]

---

20 *Idem*, inv. no. 1, exh., November 10, 1806.
21 *Ibidem*. '...de donner quelque marque de Son approbation, ce que contribuerait beaucoup à rendre ses députés respectables, tant à leurs propres yeux, qu'à l'égard de ceux qui seront informés, qu'ils jouissent de haute protection de votre Majeste'.
22 '...vastes conceptions, que Son Génie Créateur paraît nourrir pour améliorer le sort des Israélites'.
23 C. Asser and J.D. Meyer already had addressed petitions to Louis Napoleon in the summer of 1806. About this, see Silva Rosa, Bijdrage, Vol. 31, nos. 50, 51, 52; Vol. 32, nos. 2, 4, 6, 9).
24 See Schama, *op. cit.*, pp. 486-90.
25 'Renvoyé au Ministre de l'Intérieur pour lui signifier que personne ne doit aller en députation sans mon ordre. Le Ministre me donnera son avis sur cette démarche et ce que convient de faire dans cette circonstance'.

The initiators of the petitions must have been most surprised about this instruction to the Minister. They had succeeded in getting the king personally involved with the despatch of a delegation, but at the same time the participation of Adath Jesurun in the Great Sanhedrin had been thrown into doubt.

The two other communities also understood that the letters they had sent to Paris were not the last word, so it is understandable that in the days following the royal instruction, both parties made feverish efforts to influence the king's decision. However, it became clear that the Dutch authorities supported the Parnasim of the Old Community. First of all, the Minister forwarded the letter of Capadoce *et al.* to the Amsterdam Magistrates, who secretly passed the original on to the Parnasim for reply. In accordance with the agreement, the Ashkenazi Parnasim were kept informed of every new development, and from then on there were almost daily contacts about the steps to be taken.

For their answer to Capadoce's petition the Parnasim called in the assistance of a lawyer – a gentile, in fact, which is clearly noticeable in the formulation of their defense.[26] It is a verbose document in which, among other things, it is argued that 'nothing is more destructive to the common weal than differences and discord among its members.'[27] The document invokes Article 22 of the Regulations of 1639, which stated that 'nobody may oppose the decisions taken by the said Assembly (i.e. the Parnasim) and those that do so can be excommunicated.'[28] What Capadoce had done was illegal ('illicite'), which as a former Parnas he no doubt knew. Nine-tenths of the Community agreed with the Parnasim. If the Sanhedrin was to pass resolutions binding upon Jews outside France, they would still need the sanction of King Louis Napoleon; and if the decisions were not binding, what harm would be done if they could be studied first?[29] It is the sort of pleading that takes us all the way back to the Ancien Régime, and it is significant for the enormous changes that had taken place since the Batavian Revolution of 1795 that the Magistrates were delighted with it. They did not suffice with merely forwarding the defense plea, but added a recommendation for the Minister which revealed in a painfully obvious manner why they supported the oligarchic Parnasim so strongly. They explained that the 'Parnasim had always been considered and respected as Sovereign Heads of their respective Jewish communities' and that 'a broad hint from the Parnasim had always been sufficient to keep the Jews, who composed a large part of the inhabitants of this city, under control and cause them to observe the laws and regulations of the Police in this city.' In other words, 'maintaining their author-

---

26 The name of the lawyer was Bondt (*Livro de Segredos*). This probably refers to Jan Bondt, a lawyer who several times stood as a candidate for the Amsterdam City Council. See Breen, pp. 10, 28, 48 and 88.

27 '...que rien n'est plus contraire à la prospérité de toute communauté que les dissentions et les discordes parmi les membres'.

28 '...que personne ne pourra s'opposer aux résolutions que prendra la dite assemblée (sc. des Syndics)...et ceux qui le feraient seront sujets à être ex-communiqués.'

29 ARA, Bi. Za., exh., November 22, 1806.

ity' was of the utmost importance and 'absolutely vital for the peace and tranquillity in same (i.e. the city).'[30]

I do not know whether this mutuality of interests of the municipal rulers and the Parnasim has ever been expressed in such an open and forthright manner. All this was grist to the mill of Minister Hendrik Mollerus, a man of the Ancien Régime and an ardent supporter of the House of Orange. In two separate memoranda, one in reply to the Adath Jesurun petition, the other in reply to the letters from Capadoce *et al.* and Meyer, Mollerus pointed out that Adath Jesurun existed only in Amsterdam, that it had a relatively limited following (400- 500 members), and therefore could not be considered representative for the Jews. He also adopted the argument of the Portuguese Parnasim – whose reasoning he highly commended – to the effect that 'either the resolutions of the Sanhedrin are binding, or they are not.' In the first case, Louis Napoleon's subjects would be forced to accept religious and political changes in their faith without the king's permission, whereas in the second case it would be better to anticipate the decisions. Summarizing all this, it was quite unnecessary to send a delegation – the more so since France had not even demanded it. 'The fact that the French government has not issued any invitation or announcement to other countries, may be taken to mean that His Majesty the Emperor's intention has been to leave it to everyone to act according to the circumstances in their respective countries, and the suggestions of their Jewish subjects.'[31]

'If, therefore, there was no reason to send a delegation or to "approve" the delegation already appointed by Adath Jesurun, one might still discuss the possibility of "granting the delegates permission to depart"',[32] but on this point, too, the advice was negative.

One week later the king made his decision: 'I do not wish to be involved in any way in matters concerning religion in the various European countries. I am duty bound and wish to ensure freedom of conscience to everyone and I do not wish to prevent any sect from enacting changes or to alter its specific religious laws, provided that this is done with the unanimous consent of the members of that religion, so that I will never have to fear religious schisms, disagreements or quarrels, and that the complete tolerance and freedom enjoyed by the Dutch in this respect shall never be disturbed. Consequently, permission is granted to the new Jewish community to send delegates to Paris, on condition that all other Jews in the realm are in agreement with this act; without the above, permission is refused – all the more so since they are always free to adopt the changes resulting from the Sanhedrin in Paris.'[33]

---

30 *Ibidem.*
31 'Comme de la part de Gouvernement Français il n'a été fait aucune invitation ou communication aux autres Pays, on peut l'attribuer à ce que l'intention de sa Majesté l'Empereur a été de laisser à ceux-ci d'agir suivant que les circonstances de leur Pays et de leur habitans Juifs le leur suggéroient'.
32 ARA, Bi. Za., exh., November 22, 1806.
33 ARA, *idem*, invent. no. 144, item 34. The decision was taken on on November 30. 'Je ne veux me mêler en aucune manière de ce qui se passe dans les différens pays de l'Europe sur la religion. Je dois et je veux assurer la liberté de conscience à chacun et je ne veux empêcher aucune secte

Three days after the king's decision, the Parnasim of the Portuguese and the High-German communities were jointly invited by the Magistrates, who informed them 'with complete satisfaction the favorable decision of the King.'[34] Profoundly moved, the Parnasim expressed their gratitude for the protection [sic!] the Magistrates had granted them, as well as their hope that they might continue to rely on them in the future, to which the Presiding Magistrate replied that they could rest assured of this. The exultation in the Orthodox camp was as great as the disillusionment among their opponents. Their attempt to get the king directly involved in the matter had achieved exactly the opposite effect. Since it was clear that the condition of unanimity among the Jews had no chance of being fulfilled, they were now explicitly forbidden to send their delegation to Paris, even though its composition had already been announced. We have no information regarding what steps, if any, the advocates of the Sanhedrin took during the month of December, to save at least the deputation from Adath Jesurun to Paris. However, the following facts seem to demonstrate that some pressure was brought to bear on the king to review his decision. On January 5, 1807, Adath Jesurun sent a letter to Louis Napoleon that was supposed to clear away at least some of the obstacles.[35] It had never been their intention, they wrote, to appear in Paris 'in the name of all Jews inhabiting this Kingdom, but...solely in that of the New Jewish Community. The New Jewish Community...can never represent persons other than those belonging to their own community.'[36] Neither did they request the king's 'approval' any longer, but only his permission to send a delegation. The Minister of the Interior, when asked for advice, refused to be moved. Quite rightly, he pointed out that the matter at hand was not whether or not the Adath Jesurun delegation represented all Jews – 'a request that the petitioners never gave me reason to assume – but that all Jews of the Kingdom should be of one mind about this mission.'[37]

---

de faire changemens et de modifier ses lois religieuses particulières, pourvu que ces sortes de choses soyent faites par l'accord unanime de sujets de la même religion, afin que je ne puisse jamais avoir à redouter des schismes, des divisions ou des quérelles religieuses et que la tolerance et la liberté entière dont les hollandais jouissent sur ce point ne puissent jamais être troublees. En conséquence il sera accordé la permission à la nouvelle communion juive d'envoyer des députés à Paris si les autres juifs du Royaume y consentent également et qu'il soyent d'accord; sans cela la permission leur sera refusée, avec d'autant plus de raison qu'ils seront toujours maître d'adapter les changemens qui résulterons du Sanhedrin de Paris.'

34 '...com toda satisfaçao o favoravel Decreto del Rey.' *Livro de Segredos.* The entire text of the Extract, that was sent to the Magistrates, is included in the *Protokolbuch*.

35 ARA, *idem,* State Secr. Lod. Nap., inv. no. 287, exh., January 17, 1807.

36 ...au nom des *tous* les Juifs, demeurans dance ce Royaume, mais .exclusivement de la part de la nouvelle communauté Juive. La nouvelle communauté...ne peut jamais représenter d'autres personnes que celles, qui appartiennent à leur propre communauté.'

37 '...demande que les supplians n'avoient jamais faite, ni donne à entendre, mais que tous les Juifs du Royaume penssasent d'une manière unanime relativement a cette mission.'

In other words, not a single new motive had been advanced to justify changing the unequivocal Cabinet instruction.[38]

It would seem that the Minister had not really grasped the king's real intention. Louis Napoleon's requirement of unanimity was not merely an elegant way of rejecting Adath Jesurun's request. The policies that he was to pursue during the coming years would prove that he viewed the re-unification of all Jews in a single community as a precondition for the amelioration of their lot. It is possible that he expected his decision to urge the Jews to some mutual arrangement. The fact is that he proposed a joint consultation with the representatives of the invited communities (the three in Amsterdam and that of Rotterdam) 'to see whether it was possible to come to an agreement and consequently send delegates to Paris on behalf of all the Jews in the realm.'[39] This suggestion obviously upset the Minister, for in his advice of January 12 he went out of his way to enumerate all the difficulties connected with this plan – including the danger of 'religious schisms, conflicts or quarrels, which Your Majesty has so emphatically declared he wished to avoid.'[40] If at all, it would be preferable to permit Adath Jesurun's delegation, as long as they clearly understood 'that they could not assume any right to extend their representation, or convey the resolutions that would be passed in Paris in any manner liable to commit Jews who did not belong to their community.' [41]

Conforming to this advice, that had most probably been agreed with him in advance, on January 17, 1807, the king decided that 'the Jewish community of Amsterdam going by the name of Adath Jesurun could send freely and unhindered on behalf of this community deputies to Paris, to attend the Grand Sanhedrin in that city. The expression 'free and unhindered' is to be understood in the sense that the above Community has a separate existence, and that as such it has also received a separate invitation to the Assembly of Jewish Notables in Paris; that the members of this Community unanimously agree with its Directors on the despatch of the delegates; that its delegates therefore represent the entire Community; and that they do not presume to extend their representation or to declare anything that might be resolved in Paris and accepted by them as even in the least degree binding for Jews who do not belong to their Community.'[42] In other words, the approval was phrased in such a way that the delegates could neither commit Dutch Jewry, nor even represent it.

38 Mollerus' advice is dated January 6, 1807; ARA, *idem*.
39 '...s'il étoit possible, d'envoyer de concert et conséquemment au Nom de tous les Juifs du Royaume de Députés a Paris,'
40 '...schismes, divisions et quérelles religieuses, que Votre Majesté a si expressement déclaré vouloir éloigner'.
41 See note 37. '...qu'ils ne s'arrogent aucun droit d'étendre plus loin leur Représentation, ou de rendre de quelque manière obligatoire pour les Juifs n'appartenant pas à leur communauté, les résolutions que pourront être prises a Paris.'
42 ARA, Bi. Za., afd. Erediensten, inv. no. 144, item 37.

Thus, after an arduous struggle, the three delegates finally set out for Paris, probably in early February 1807.[43] There a disappointment awaited them. Contrary to the wording of the invitation, neither they, nor the other foreign representatives (i.e. the delegates from Frankfurt am M.) were consulted and nobody took the trouble to ask their advice. It is possible that the leaders of the Sanhedrin, who had been informed that the three Dutch delegates merely represented a small minority,[44] saw no need to recognize them as fully fledged participants. More likely is, however, that the French and Italians were simply not interested in the foreigners. Thus the members of Adath Jesurun had to content themselves with being permitted to address the Sanhedrin as observers. Evidently they had drawn the appropriate conclusions from the king's warning, for even though Carel Asser assured the members of the Sanhedrin that he was authorized 'to vote for the resolutions that would be passed on behalf of his community',[45] he immediately toned down his statement by adding that even his community 'was unable to ratify them as long as they had not obtained the king's approval.'[46]

Following their return, the three delegates hastened to obtain the king's endorsement of the 'doctrinal decisions' of the Sanhedrin, but the king refused to oblige.[47] It must have been clear to him that acquiescence to this request would have resulted in serious conflicts with the High-German and Portuguese communities.[48]

---

43 A memorandum, 'Recherches sur l'Etat de Juifs en Hollande et moyens provisoires de le reformer' mentions the fact that the delegates had left for Paris. Since the memorandum is undated, we believe that it was written in February 1807 (in any case not in November or December 1806, as suggested here by Colenbrander). It is curious how this memorandum presents the struggle for the invitation to the Great Sanhedrin: 'Il est connu à S.M...., que les Parnasim n'ont pas voulu se prêter a cette invitation honorifiante, et comment ont a tramé pour persuader S.M. de défendre à la nouvelle communauté d'envoyer des députés à Paris. Mais grace à ces nobles Français, ces Hollandais intègres qui ont l'honneur d'environner S.M., par qui la vérité a percé jusqu'au trone, les députés de la nouvelle communauté sont partis. Vive Louis Napoleon! le bien-aimé qui leur a donné la permission.'
   In my opinion, this shows that Adath Jesurun must have manipulated influential persons at the court in order to revoke his decision that prevented the sending of a delegation. See Colenbrander *GS*, Vol. 5 (1806-1810), p. 274.

44 This appears *inter alia* from a memorandum 'Coup d'oeuil rapide sur l'État des Israélites en Hollande et principalement dans la Ville d'Amsterdam' in the archives of the Great Sanhedrin (AN F 19-1100/4). It looks as if this document was written after the approval of the delegation to Paris, and it is possible that it was submitted by the delegates. The formulation shows that it must have been written by one of the members of the New Community.

45 '...d'adhérer au nom de notre communauté aux décisions que vous venez de prendre'.

46 D. Tama, *loc. cit.*

47 ARA, State Secr. Lod. Nap., exh., October 3, 1807, no. 23.

48 *Idem.* See formulation by Mollerus: '.quoique qu'une lecture attentive des procès-verbaux ne m'ait suggéré aucune objection contre l'approbation qu'il (sic!) demandent, de la conduite tenue par eux a Paris, cependant comme les décisions du Grand-Sanhédrin dont il s'agit, n'ont été adoptées jusqu'ici en Hollande que par leur société particulière il me parait qu'il suffira d'énoncer cette approbation en termes tres génereux ainsi que les commissaires de S.M. Imp. et Roy l'ont fait le 18 septembre 1806 à l'assemblée des Israélites de France.' This advice by Mollerus is dated September 23, whereas the request for a delegation had already been submitted in May. Mollerus certainly took his time. The king made his decision on October 3 of the same year.

In fact, the Sanhedrin had passed a number of resolutions that were diametrically opposed to the views of the Parnasim. For one thing, it had formally accepted the distinction, introduced by Moses Mendelssohn, between Jewish religious precepts and political precepts,[49] declaring that in the absence of an independent Jewish state the latter were no longer valid.[50] Whereas a State was constitutionally permitted to use coercive measures, a religious community neither desired nor had the right to use compulsion. On these grounds the Sanhedrin declared that the Jewish community was prohibited from excommunicating persons who married non-Jews. This in itself was a concession to Napoleon, but the Sanhedrin refused to endorse mixed marriages, as Napoleon had demanded.[51]

Forgoing the ban (*herem*) was one of the things the Parnasim, who had also used this weapon against the members of Adath Jesurun, were unable to countenance. Another sensitive issue was the new regulation that no Jewish marriages could be celebrated or divorces pronounced unless the corresponding civil procedures had taken place.[52] Certain unions that were common within the Jewish community, such as marriages between uncle and niece, were prohibited in The Netherlands. The rabbis often evaded the pertinent Dutch laws, and the authorities had thus far turned a blind eye to this practice.[53] Finally, the Sanhedrin urged Jews to enlist in the armed forces, going so far as to release them explicitly from the observation of their religious obligations whenever this interfered with their military duties.

---

49 On the distinction made by Mendelssohn, see Altmann, p. 522: 'The state issues laws, religion issues commandments' and p. 523: 'Civil society viewed as a moral person has the right of coercion...religious society neither demands the right of coercion nor can it possibly obtain it by any conceivable contract.' As usual with Mendelssohn, the distinction is based on Talmudic sources. The pronouncement by the Amora Samuel (early 3rd century) that the law of the land is also binding for Jews (*dina de malkhuta dina*), applies to civil law and not to religious law. However, Mendelssohn's formulation did open the door for the subordination of *halakhah* to the laws of the land: 'Although Mendelssohn's distinction did not run counter to traditional concepts of the authority and application of *dina de malkhuta dina*, his language which distinguished between religious and civil law, lent itself to a more expansive reading.' (Gil Graff, *Separation of Church and State, Dina de Malkhuta Dina in Jewish Law, 1750-1848*, University of Alabama, 1985, p. 80).

50 'En conséquence déclarons que la loi divine, ce précieux héritage de nos ancêtres, contient des dispositions religieuses et des dispositions politiques. Que ses dispositions politiques ne sauraient être applicables depuis qu'ils ne forme plus un corps de nation' in: *Organisation civile et religieuse des Israélites de France et du Royaume d'Italie*, Paris, 1808, p. 96.

51 'Le Grand Sanhédrin déclare en outre que les mariages entre Israélites et Chrétiens, contractés conformément aux lois du code civil, sont obligatoires et valables civilement, et bien qu'ils ne soient pas susceptibles d'êtres revêtues des formes religieuses, ils n'entraineront aucun anathème' (*op. cit.*, p. 54). In effect the Sanhedrin used a tautology (after all, civil marriages are civilly binding), and the only concession was that the Jewish community would renounce sanctions against mixed marriages.

52 'Le grand Sanhédrin.défend à tout rabbin ou autre personne dans les deux états, de prêter leur ministre à l'acte religieux du mariage sans qu'il leur ait apparu auparavant l'acte des conjoints devant l'officier civil conformément à la loi' (*op. cit.* p. 53).

53 Occasionally the authorities intervened, but during the last part of the 18th century infringements of the marriage laws in Amsterdam were tacitly ignored or arranged through bribery.

It was these and other 'doctrinal decisions' that were particularly objectionable to the Amsterdam orthodox establishment. Given the fact that it did not recognize the Sanhedrin's authority on principle, vigorous opposition against an attempt at imposing these resolutions was therefore to be expected. Louis Napoleon was not even prepared to try. It was his general policy (as expressed in his decision written in the margins of his Minister's advice) that he did not want to take any actions with regard to the internal affairs of his Jewish subjects until all Jews were united in a single organization. But even after this had become a fact, he failed to impose the resolutions of the Sanhedrin.

Only after the Kingdom of Holland had ceased to exist and The Netherlands had been annexed to France did the situation undergo a change. At this point the introduction of the Sanhedrin's resolutions could no longer be averted.

6 Louis Napoleon's Concern with His Jewish Subjects (II)

Little attention has been paid in the historiography of the Jews in The Netherlands to the establishment of the High Consistory by King Louis Napoleon. Insofar as historians have occupied themselves with the history of its origins, this has almost always been treated as a by-product of the re-unification of the two Amsterdam Ashkenazi communities – the Old Community and the New Community. This is already the case with H.J. Koenen, who did not consider it necessary to discuss the by-laws of the High Consistory, since they were in any event to be replaced.[1] Koenen's text was copied almost literally by Sluys and Hoofien, which shows how little these two typical late nineteenth-century representatives of the Orthodoxy realized the far-reaching significance of the High Consistory, in particular for the Orthodoxy.[2] An important step in the right direction was the detailed article by M. Wolff on the Jews during Louis Napoleon's regime, in which he wrote: 'On the king's own initiative an arrangement was made whose significance, also for the future, can hardly be overstated.' Even though Wolff perceived this significance only in terms of the consequences for the enfranchisement of the Jews, he nevertheless emphasizes the importance of the High Consistory.[3] Da Silva Rosa, on the other hand, only quotes the High Consistory's by-laws as a kind of supplement to the plans for a reconciliation between both communities.[4] J. Zwarts was the first one to realize that the High Consistory derived its importance from the fact that it was the first framework unifying the majority of Dutch Jewry.[5] Van Zuiden's posthumously published essay, actually intended for inclusion in the second part of Brugmans and Frank's standard work, is a serious step backwards compared to Wolff, Da

---

1 H.J. Koenen, pp. 383-84.
2 D.E. Sluys-J. Hoofien, *Handboek voor de Geschiedenis der Joden*, Vol. 3, Amsterdam, 1873, p. 550. There is not even one word of criticism of the report by C. Asser, who condemned the Parnasim in such virulent language.
3 See about this Wolff, *Lod. Nap.*, p. 73.
4 Silva Rosa, Bijdrage.
5 J. Zwarts, *Hoofdstukken uit de Geschiedenis der Joden in Nederland*, Zutphen, 1929, p. 263. Besides correct comments about the High Consistory, the article contains erroneous and improbable statements. For example, he credits C. Asser and J.D. Meyer with the adoption of the Emancipation decree, notwithstanding the fact that in 1796 both were only 16 years old. His comment that they were 'fashionable' young men from 'aristocratic Jewish circles' applies only to Meyer. Louis Napoleon's alleged intention to make the High Consistory 'a Dutch version of the Paris Synhedrion' (p. 263) is contrary to the facts and demonstrates the author's lack of insight into the relationship between Louis Napoleon and his brother.

Silva Rosa and Zwarts: besides being incorrect, it also evinces a serious misconception about the circumstances prevailing at the time.[6]

The most important – although by no means the only – change brought about by the High Consistory was the unification of all Ashkenazi Jews in the Kingdom of Holland into a single organization. This was something new, since prior to 1808 the Jews in The Netherlands, with the exception of the municipal Jewish communities, had not known any kind of organization, either at a national or provincial level. The reason for this was obvious. Since the resolution of the States of Holland and West-Friesland (1619), which was subsequently adopted by the other provinces, left the management of Jewish affairs entirely in the hands of the municipal authorities, these were the only points of reference for the Jewish population. If and when the latter encountered any problems, these were dealt with at the local level, without involving the Jews in other areas. Neither from a legal nor a practical point of view would joint action by the Jews in the Republic or in a specific province have made much sense. In the sporadic instances where broader interests were involved, such as the impediments the Spaniards placed in the way of Jewish commerce, the negotiations were probably conducted by private persons.[7] Interventions on behalf of foreign Jews were in most cases similarly initiated by influential personalities, sometimes in cooperation with the Parnasim of a community. Such was the case with the protests against the deportation of the Jews from Prague, against which Tobias Boas (1696-1782) of The Hague and Benedict Levy Gomperts of Nijmegen, as well as the Jewish communities of Amsterdam, The Hague and Rotterdam (albeit the Ashkenazim only), deployed considerable activity.[8] In 1765 Tobias Boas and the councillors of The Hague community exerted pressure towards the abolition of anti-Jewish discrimination in Surinam.[9] In 1785 the Jewish communities of Amsterdam, Rotterdam and The Hague submitted joint petitions about a matter concerning the Jews of Essequibo.[10] Thus the three main High-German communities were accustomed to coordinating in incidental cases, as also was the case when representatives of these three communities called a meeting to protest the enfranchisement of the Jews.[11] Even so all these discussions were conducted on a voluntary basis, without the existence of any permanent organizational framework. To the best of our knowledge there was even less cooperation between the Chief Rabbis and rabbis of the various communities. In their halakhic decisions the rabbis of the smaller communities were no doubt guided by their illustrious colleagues, especially

---

6   Van Zuiden, *Lod. Nap.*, p. 71. Van Zuiden even writes that the High Consistory was dependent on the instructions of the Consistoire Central in Paris, and he confuses the situation prevailing during the annexation with that during the Kingdom of Holland.

7   See J. Israel, 'Spain and the Dutch Sephardim, 1609-1660', in *Stud. Ros* XII, (1978), pp. 32-34. Idem, 'The Dutch Republic and its Jews during the Conflict over the Spanish Successions (1699-1715)', *DJH* 2, pp. 117-36.

8   See J. Melkman, 'Interventie tegen de verdrijving van de Joden uit Praag', in *NIW*, 'Cultureel bijvoegsel', p. 6, (January 31, 1963) and the literature there.

9   GAA, Copies of letters from the Jewish Community in Amsterdam, 1750- 1796, fo. 163 ff.

10 Idem, B. fo. 880, no. 334 B; fo. 898, no. 335.

11 See p. 56.

those of Amsterdam and Rotterdam. But they were under no obligation to do so, and we have no knowledge of any meetings between Chief Rabbis of different communities. Smaller communities, on the other hand, depended for their spiritual leadership on the nearest larger Jewish population centers. Several local Chief Rabbis regarded themselves as Chief Rabbis of the surrounding areas, but their authority did not formally encompass any specific province. In other words, the Jewish community of the Republic was fragmented: besides the fact that it lacked a national or provincial organization, no need was felt for the existence of such a framework.

The Emancipation Decree and Its Consequences

As we have seen, the Emancipation decree of September 2, 1796, annulled the traditional support of the local authorities for the by-laws of the various communities, such backing being diametrically opposed to a decision on the separation of Church and State adopted by the National Assembly on August 5 of the same year. This decision, too, has been claimed to be of considerable moral significance, but fragmentary and ambiguous in terms of its immediate and practical consequence.[12]

This was not due to any laxity on the part of the authorities. They saw to it that the Emancipation decree was circulated among all the Provincial governments. The Provincial governments of Holland and West-Friesland sent strict instructions to all local authorities to 'rigorously' observe the cancellation of all 'sanctions'.[13] Despite this unequivocal language, not a single local authority complied immediately with this instruction. Isaac da Costa Athias, himself one of the founders of Felix Libertate, in his capacity as advisor of the committee charged with settling the dispute between Adath Jesurun and the Old Community, even went so far as to contend: 'that the by-laws of the communities will remain in force until they are annulled by a special decree.'[14] We do not know whether plans for a nationwide settlement did indeed exist. The fact is that in

---

12 P. Geyl comments with reference to this decree: 'However, what did it mean? Its moral significance was considerable. The principle had been reaffirmed in an impressive fashion ... But the immediate and practical effects were fragmentary and uncertain ... the real, as opposed to the legal, emancipation (of the Roman Catholics, J.M.) ... would turn out to be a labor of generations.' P. Geyl, *Geschiedenis*, pp. 1644 and 1648.

13 ARA, Placard dated September 29, 1796 of the Provincial Government of Holland.

14 In GAA, 'Stukken betreffende de Israëlitische aangelegenheden en bepaaldelijk de Nederl. Israël. Hoofdsynagoge te Amsterdam, geput uit de Provinciale Archieven van Noord-Holland', p. 147; Letter by M.L. de Jongh to the Eerste Kamer van het Vertegenwoordigend Ligchaam des Bataafschen Volks, Amsterdam, July 29, 1801 (Rapt. Besier *et al.*, November 20, 1801. The documents were probably collected by or on behalf of Dr. S.I. Mulder. During my visit to the Provincial Archives of the Province of North Holland the staff was unable to locate the original documents there and then.) The political press also showed an interest in the case of Da Costa Athias. The *Burger Politieke Blixem* (August 18, 1800, p. 191) contains an attack on Isaac da Costa Athias: 'However, since the Church is separated from the State and, let us hope, will remain separated, Jupiter (the author, J.M.) cannot fathom how Da Costa Athias can put forward an alleged legally acquired right, purely ecclesiastical in this case, as an argument.'

practice everything continued on the old footing. The conservative municipality of Groningen acted as if nothing had changed since the Revolution. Following a request by a Jewish citizen to abolish the 'ordinance on the Jewish Community', the municipal authorities decided (April 15, 1798) that all regulations and articles would remain in force. This decision was even taken during the incumbency of the Radical regime. A subsequently appointed committee (1801) advised that 'the regulations should remain in force'.[15]

The Radical municipal authority of Leeuwarden, on the other hand, wanted to compel the Parnasim to hold democratic elections, a decision that was nullified by the Provincial Administration of Friesland. A sadder but wiser municipal government referred the petitioner back to the Parnasim. 'When the latter refused to drop his opposition, the Parnasim punished this Revolutionary in pre-Revolutionary fashion.'[16]

From all this it appears that the various authorities continued in their pre-Emancipatory ways and that, despite the separation of Church and State, even the Radical regime intervened in the Jewish communities of Amsterdam and The Hague. The authorities were hard put to do otherwise, since – in contrast to all other churches – the Jews had no overarching framework and, as we have seen earlier, not even a rudimentary form of provincial organization capable of replacing the municipal authorities in intervening in disputes or approving new by-laws. It soon became apparent that the lifting of the 'sanctions' by the decree of 1796 had been a shot in the dark. It was a negative decision, not only because it failed to indicate any substitute arrangement, but also completely disregarded the fact that not a single body existed capable of formulating such an arrangement.

There was yet another aspect to this absence of a representative Jewish body at the time of their emancipation. The 'enlightened' Jews, encouraged by their success in the struggle for the Emancipation decree, continued to forge ahead. Although supported by only a fraction of the Jews in the Batavian Republic, they nevertheless regarded themselves as the general representative of Dutch Jewry. A curious example of this is a request submitted by M.S. Asser and his son Carel Asser to the 'Representative Body of the Batavian People' (1801). Several merchants in Koog Oost and Westzaandam had requested permission to operate their windmills on Sundays. The Executive Authority was prepared to approve their request, but the Representative Body had turned down its recommendation to this effect. The two Assers now contended that they considered the advice of the Executive Authority very fair and wise, but that, if the request was disallowed and the Sunday recognized as a day of rest for Christians, then 'on the basis of equality' the Jewish Sabbath or Saturday should be accorded the same honor or prerogatives.[17] It goes without saying that the request of the Assers, who were considerably ahead of their time, was turned down. Even so it

---

15 Mendels, *op. cit.*, pp. 75-80.
16 Beem, *Leeuwarden*, pp. 94-96.
17 ARA, Staatsbewind 245, exh. March 9, 1802, no. 69.

would have been more natural if an official Jewish body had submitted such a request.

Thus we see that during the decade following the Emancipation decree the situation was as yet extremely vague and confused. Municipal authorities continued to interfere in Jewish affairs, and rebellious members of Jewish communities in many cases continued to be handled with pre-revolutionary rigor. Those concerned might have appealed to the Provincial or National government, but these bodies were themselves caught on the horns of a dilemma: intervention meant bringing them into conflict with the separation of Church and State, whereas to let matters take their course encouraged the continued festering of internal Jewish disputes. In practice the authorities could scarcely avoid acting, since no pre-revolutionary Jewish body or organ existed on which authority over all the Jews in the Batavian Republic could be conferred. Even after 1796 no such body was established: the Orthodoxy remained totally impervious to the fundamental changes that had taken place in the position of the Jews, whereas the 'enlightened' Jews saw no need for a representative body that would have relegated them to a minority status and curtailed their freedom of action. It was Louis Napoleon, installed as King of Holland by his brother on June 5, 1806, who finally put an end to this chaotic state of affairs.

Louis Napoleon Prepares the High Consistory

Dutch historiography has traditionally paid little, if any, attention to Louis Napoleon,[18] and whatever was written about him has usually been in a condescending vein: a well-meaning figure who failed to understand that he was simply Napoleon's proxy, and whose outraged opposition to the annexation of his kingdom by France has been explained by contemporaries as well as by subsequent historians as evidence of his lack of a sense of reality. The fact that during the short period of his rule in The Netherlands Louis *did* introduce certain changes on which William I was later able to build is either belittled or suppressed. Simon Schama has advocated a fairer historical appreciation in his work on the Batavian or French period,[19] besides presenting a more positive picture of Louis Napoleon as a person: 'candor, moral rectitude and political naiveté he possessed in disarming abundance,' he writes *inter alia* about him.[20]

With regard to the Jews, this character sketch deserves to be complemented and corrected – in a positive vein. Wolff already pointed out the extraordinary importance of Louis Napoleon for the Jews in The Netherlands.[21] But more can be said about this, especially when comparing Louis with his brother the

---

18 For an example, see Kossman, *op. cit.* The Kingdom of Holland is not even mentioned, and Louis Napoleon is mentioned only twice, once at his appointment, and once at his deposition. As against this, some of the successes during his reign are ascribed to Schimmelpenninck, who – contrary to Louis Napoleon – is allowed to achieve 'some very useful results'.

19 Schama, *op. cit.*, pp. 486-490.

20 Schama, *op. cit.*, pp. 489.

21 See note 3.

emperor. When searching for an explanation of Napoleon's anti-Semitism, it has been suggested that this was due to childhood indoctrination.[22] Judging by his brother Louis' feelings towards the Jews, this seems most unlikely. It may or may not be significant that on ascending the throne he declared that under his regime no distinction would be made between adherents of the different faiths:[23] official declarations of this kind failed to be honored in practice. But Louis not only strove to implement this principle, he also took a special interest in his Jewish subjects in The Netherlands and truly sympathized with their lamentable fate. Everything he wrote on this subject in his memoirs is confirmed by the actions of his government.[24] Even before being aware that he would ever play a role in The Netherlands, he arrived one Friday night, in the course of a visit to Amsterdam in his capacity of commander of the Northern army, totally unexpected and unannounced and accompanied by a number of staff officers, in the Great Synagogue, where he asked to be shown around.[25] When, as we shall see further on, he declared that he was genuinely interested in the welfare of the Jews, this was confirmed by his own actions and by the comments of his non-Jewish Dutch functionaries, who themselves would not have been likely to initiate measures towards the amelioration of the lot of the Jews. No ruling monarch, either in his time or subsequently, devoted so much time and attention to the Jews. Neither was this interest motivated by political considerations, intended to neutralize this alien and therefore disruptive Jewish element in society by means of assimilation — as was the case with enlightened despots such as Joseph II.[26] Louis' policy was informed by humanitarian sentiments. It is characteristic of him that he ordered clothes to be purchased for Jewish schoolchildren with the instruction that they should be 'clothed according to their individual measurements, coats of good quality and colorful, so that they will be able to go to church in a proper and respectable manner'.[27]

---

22 See for example Simon Schwarzfuchs, *op. cit.*, pp. 22 ff.

23 'Je ne veux point avoir d'autres guides, il n'est pour moi ni religions, ni partis differens. Le mérite et les services seuls feront la différence', *Documents historiques et Reflexions sur le gouvernement de la Hollande, par Louis Bonaparte* I, Brussels, 1820, pp. 85.

24 'The Catholics were not admitted to a single honorary office, and the Jews to no offices whatsoever. The latter constituted a separate nation: their wretchedness, and the abominable spectacle of their dirtiness and sickness failed to move anyone; they are Jews, these words were the only answer to everthing said about them. The intense torments, the injustices, and even crimes only interested their co-religionists, but the Government failed to intervene.' In other words, like other high French dignitaries in The Netherlands, Louis Napoleon is highly critical of the authorities' attitude to the Jews. *Documents Historiques*, I, p. 100.

25 The visit took place on January 10, 1806. See Bendit Wing III (1877-1878), p. 196.

26 See Josef Karniel, *Die Toleranzpolitik Kaiser Josephs*, II: 'Zusammenfassend ist zu sagen, dasz das Patent ein seltsames Gemenge von scheinbare Gleichberechtigung und Diskriminierung darstelle' (in: Walter Grab. ed., *Deutsche Aufklärung und Judenemanzipation*, Tel-Aviv, 1980, p. 175).

27 GAA, *Protokolbuch*. Dispositie 28, Summer Month, 1809. See also the notification of the Landdrost (Governor) of Amstelland, informing those concerned of the king's desire that the clothing of orphans and inmates of other institutions shall reflect general custom, rather than being multi-colored or red, 'weil zolches ayn distingirt zaykhen iz fun ir shtand' (*Protokolbuch*, fo. 323, dated September 18, 1808).

Jonas Daniël Meyer, 1780-1826. Rijksmuseum, Amsterdam.

The change in atmosphere in favor of the Jews became evident soon after Louis had ascended the throne. In August 1806 the Provincial government of Holland received a note from Louis Napoleon's Minister of the Interior requesting its reaction to the petition submitted on April 11, 1806, by six Amsterdam Jews.[28] Most probably the petition would have been quietly filed away in

28 See Chapter 2, p. 37.

some bureaucrat's drawer, were it not for the fact that on July 15 two of the six signatories had addressed a petition of approximately the same wording to King Louis. The change in signatories is significant: four receded into the background, leaving the struggle for the emancipation of the Jews in The Netherlands and the restructuring and direction of Dutch Jewry in the hands of the two youngest people in their midst. From this moment on Carel Asser and Jonas Daniel Meyer would, each in his own way, but in close mutual cooperation, play a dominant and even decisive role.

Carel Asser's participation in this struggle did not begin with the petition of April 1806. Being a son of Moses Asser, he had witnessed all the developments so far, and we find his signature at the bottom of many petitions and publications by Felix Libertate and Adath Jesurun – but always after that of his father. Now the roles were reversed. From now on, Moses Asser, one of the original six signatories, would only intervene on rare occasions, allowing his son Carel to act in his stead. Carel's ally, Jonas Daniel Meyer, on the other hand, had thus far never been involved in Jewish affairs, and it is significant that his name was added to the petition of April 1806 at the last moment. After all, J.D. Meyer and Carel Asser were of a similar age and equally precocious. How do we explain that Meyer only became involved in the struggle at the age of twenty-six?

Jonas Daniel Meyer, a grandson of Benjamin Cohen, moved in prominent circles and his friends at the University of Leiden belonged to the similar elite among the citizenry. He was no revolutionary, and his dissertation[29] contested Thomas Paine's *Rights of Man*,[30] a highly popular work among revolutionary circles in Amsterdam. Besides this, the leaders of Felix Libertate belonged to the Radical Patriots, who were fierce opponents of the House of Orange. To join them meant being disloyal to the traditions of the Cohen family.

However, following the peace treaty of Amiens (1802), relations underwent a change. The House of Orange, especially the future king William I, began to make overtures to Napoleon, and the Orangists in the Batavian Republic showed a willingness to participate in the new regime. Schimmelpenninck in particular did his utmost to have them placed in important positions, and Louis Napoleon went even further, by introducing people who had traditionally been loyal to Orange into his government.[31] The days of revolutionary anti-Monarchism were past, and there was no longer any reason for Jonas Daniel Meyer to stay on the sidelines.

Rather than restricting himself to the struggle for emancipation, Meyer also embraced the second item on the 'enlightened' Jewish program: the reforms within the Jewish community. Towards the end of 1806 a committee of members of the Old Community was formed under his chairmanship 'for the ameliora-

---

29 The title of his dissertation is: *Disputatio iuris sistens dubia de Thomae Paine doctrina in iure publico civitatum posteros ex maiorum pactis conventis non obligari*. About this, see S. Kalff, 'Een Joodse rechtsgeleerde', in *VA* II (1945), pp. 82-86; N. de Beneditty, *op. cit.*, pp. 9-10.

30 In 1794 *Rights of Man* by Thomas Paine was being discussed in 34 political clubs in Amsterdam and 12 in Utrecht. See R.R. Palmer, *The World of the French Revolution*, San Francisco/London, 1972, p. 165.

31 Schama, *op. cit.*, p. 469 ff.

tion of the political status of the Jews'.[32] The committee approached the Parnasim with a few modest requests.[33] To the latter's great – and most unhappy – surprise the letter was addressed to the 'Parnasim of the Old Community', implying recognition of the existence of another, 'New' Community, whose existence the Parnasim had never accepted. After consulting Jan Schimmelpenninck, their lawyer, they decided against replying in writing, but to ask Schimmelpenninck to advise them, that they might submit their proposals to the Committee of Former Parnasim, the *Kommissie mikahal*.[34] In May Meyer and his committee formulated a new request, suggesting the presentation of more detailed proposals. Once again the Parnasim evaded a direct discussion, limiting themselves to an acknowledgment of the memorandum. Characteristically, this memorandum begins by stating that it was not the intention of the committee to suggest any religious reforms: it did not intend 'to effect any changes in points of religion or belief or, for that matter, modify any existing synagogue regulations, but, leaving everything as it is as present or might in future evolve, exploit the favorable opportunity that has opened up for the Jews to become useful and privileged Citizens of the State'.[35]

The memorandum clearly contradicts the campaign pursued by the New Community to introduce radical changes in the by-laws of the communities; in addition it suggests – no doubt because of King Louis' disposition – that this was a favorable moment for improving the condition of the Jews. This expanded

32 Besides Meyer, the Committee included B. Cantor Is.zoon, Jacob Marcus, M.L. Cohen, Loeb Elias Reis, M. Coopman Jacobs and Jacob Gomperts Emrik. Before long, M. Coopman Jacobs resigned. After Meyer, Reis was the most active member. Jacob Marcus would eventually gain notoriety as a recruiter for the Jewish corps.

33 The committee met for its first meeting on December 21, 1807; on December 28 it sent a letter to the Parnasim touching on the following issues: 1) the discrimination of Jews in the issuing of passports, for which Jews required a recommendation of the Parnasim; 2) a complaint about the fact that Jews were not appointed in public offices; 3) the refusal to admit Jews to the Civil Guard.

    The Parnasim replied: ad 1): Their endorsement was particularly useful for those who were unable to write Dutch; ad 2) and 3): these were issues that did not concern the Parnasim; if someone wanted a recommendation in order to apply for some job, they would gladly oblige. *Protokolbuch*, 1806, fos. 91-92.

34 In the protocols the College of former Parnasim is referred to as '*Kommissie mikahal*' ('Members' Committee').

35 Memorandum Meyer-Reis *et. al.* dated May 31. 5, 1807, *Protokolbuch*, fo. 152. Apart from the issue of the passports, the memorandum discusses a large number of other subjects that are of direct concern to the Parnasim. One of the most important is that of mendicancy, which is not merely ascribed to poverty, but also to laziness: 'The much larger number (proportionate to the population) of Jewish compared to Christian criminals is solely due to this category of idlers.' They suggest that the Parnasim should encourage Jews to open small businesses, to accept employment in the municipal work-houses – provided that they are allowed to conduct their religious practices – to establish a foundation for providing work to the unemployed, to intensify the relief of the really poor and sick, as well as to see to the strictest possible implementation of the laws against vagrancy. In the area of eduation they recommend the foundation of a school that (after a German example) would teach both religion and sciences, and the establishment of a (free) school for the poor and a (similarly free) vocational school where the unemployed could be taught a craft. Finally, they suggested that the Parnasim would lend their assistance to the organization of a committee to elaborate the various proposals. *Protokolbuch*, 1807, fos. 152-154. See also D. Michman, 'Jewish Education in the Early 19th Century' (Heb.), in *SDJ* II, Jerusalem, 1979, pp. 101-2.

report was handed to the lawyer, but the Parnasim were still not prepared to discuss it. They kept on postponing, hoping that eventually the subject would be dropped altogether. But Meyer was a haughty character, whose pride would not permit a humiliation of this kind. Soon the Parnasim would find out what a formidable enemy they had made themselves with their status-oriented policies.

That same month, May 1807, the Parnasim approached the king about the nomination of new Parnasim.[36] When on June 27, 1798, the Amsterdam Municipal council had reappointed the Parnasim of the High-German community, the Interim Executive Authority had determined that their nomination would only be provisional. Nine years had passed since then, and no reconciliation was as yet in view. Meanwhile the same Parnasim continued occupying their 'provisional' seats: they were unable either to resign or appoint new Parnasim, since this prerogative (a far cry from separation of Church and State) was as yet reserved for the government. The Parnasim had no reason to object, until during the years 1805 and 1806 three of their colleagues – David Levy (Salomons), Lion H. Keyzer and Abraham van Offen – died within a short time of each other, while a fourth, B. Leemans, fell ill. Although the Parnasim were assisted by four ex-colleagues (from the *Kommittee mikahal* – the membership committee), these were not authorized to take decisions. Permission was therefore requested for the appointment of three new Parnasim, in accordance with the procedure prescribed in the by-laws of 1737.

For Louis this was yet another reason to scrutinize the affairs of the Jewish communities. In any case the Parnasim were forbidden to arrange for an expansion of their Board (a later request made via the burgomaster of Amsterdam was equally rejected),[37] since this would have implied that the king recognized the existing situation as permanent. Even so his minister J.H. Mollerus advised him to permit the Parnasim either to co-opt three new members, or to wait until a new Municipal Council would be appointed in Amsterdam.[38] At the same time the king received another, contrary, request, namely from J.D. Meyer, who not only asked him to reject the proposal of the Parnasim, but to depose the 'Syndics' and to grant him an audience.[39] A few days later, yet another, very strongly worded, letter arrived, this time signed by all the members of the Meyer committee.[40] The present Parnasim, so it stated, 'do not deserve to be affirmed or to continue in their functions'. The letter went on to refute the arguments of the Parnasim one by one. After having noted that 'for

---

36 *Protokolbuch,* Disp. May 6, 1807, fo. 122.
37 March 6, 1808. *Protokolbuch,* 1808, fo. 236. The letter is also in the collection of J.D. Janssen, the official who was specifically appointed for dealing with Jewish affairs, and who wielded great influence behind the scenes (ARA, Coll. Janssen, no. 44)

    Jakob Didericus Janssen had been Chief Clerk since 1805. On July 18, 1808, he was appointed Head of the First Department of the Ministry of Religion. For more details, see Ypey and Dermout, *Geschiedenis der Hervormde Kerk* IV, Breda, 1827, pp. 497 ff.
38 Recommendation of Mollerus, dated April 26, 1808. (ARA, Coll. Janssen, no. 45).
39 J.D. Meyer's letter is dated September 30, 1807. (ARA, Coll. Janssen, no. 41).
40 The letter from the Committee is dated October 5, 1807. (ARA, Coll. Janssen, no. 42.)

the last nine years the Parnasim have shown nothing but incompetence and malevolence', the request ended on a rather threatening note, namely that if the king ratified the by-laws (i.e. those of 1737), the signatories would have no choice but to cause a new schism, to renounce their faith, or to leave the country. A complication of this kind was definitely the last thing Louis wanted, and it undoubtedly reinforced the decision he had earlier contemplated in another context, namely the difficulties regarding the participation of Dutch Jews in the Sanhedrin in Paris.

This problem, too, had impressed upon him the need to intervene personally, in order to put an end to the Jews' internal squabbles. Or – in a rather more negative formulation, handwritten on a plea by Adath Jesurun to impart the benefits of emancipation to the Jews: '[Hàve] approved the Minister's report, [and] to reply that its dissension with the majority of their Nation in this Kingdom for the present moment prevents me from doing anything for them.'[41] Two things stand out in this annotation: firstly, that despite his sympathy for the ideas of Adath Jesurun, Louis disapproved of the existence of this community; and secondly, that although he was unable to do anything 'at the moment', this did not mean that he rejected their views.

Seen in this light it is understandable that Louis was not in the mood to entertain any proposals aimed at changing the present leadership of the Old Community. J.D. Meyer had sent him a letter on this subject even before the negotiations between his committee and the Parnasim had broken down completely.[42] This letter is written entirely in the spirit of the 'enlightened' Jews, with the customary mixture of complaints about the failure to implement emancipation in everyday life, and criticism of the Community by-laws which, the Emancipation decree notwithstanding, still proved to be in force in all respects (' and actions and decisions are still taken by virtue of the regulations on all occasions that present themselves').[43] However, before undertaking any action, Louis decided to hear some of the arguments of the opposing side. J.D. Janssen, the chief clerk at the Ministry of Religious Affairs, was instructed to collect some information from the Parnasim of the Old Community.[44] In

---

41 'approuvé le rapport du ministre et répondre que la désunion où elle est avec la majorité de leur Nation dans ce Royaume m'empèche pour le moment faire quelque chose pour eux'.

42 Colenbrander, *GS* Vol. 5 (1806-1810), no. 220, pp. 284-86; translation from the French by Silva Rosa, *Bijdrage*, pp. 34-39. The fact that Da Silva Rosa inserts Meyer's letter after that of Asser (even though he indicates that the former was written a year earlier) causes the historical context to be lost and creates the impression that we are dealing with two equivalent memorandums that were composed under the same circumstances.

43 ' et c'est toujours en vertu des règlements qu'on agit et qu'on décide dans toutes les occasions qui se présentent'.

44 *Protokolbuch*, 1808, fo. 165. Amsterdam was instructed to notify the other municipalities in the province that they had to to send their answers before September, either directly or via the Jewish Community of Amsterdam. At the end of September the Jewish community submitted its report, accompanied by the answers received from Enkhuizen, Medemblik, Den Helder, Zaandam, Beverwijk, Thamen, Uithoorn and Naarden. Apparently no replies were received from Hoorn, Alkmaar, Edam, Muiden, Weesp and Hilversum. These were the first reports expected from small communities. During the period of the High Consistory and the Consistories such questionnaires would become more frequent.

addition, the Jewish community of Amsterdam was to gather reports from neighboring local authorities (basically the present province of North Holland), which seems to show that while the Jews of Amsterdam – the various Communities as well as private individuals – were mired in their mutual quarrels, Louis was already planning to tackle the Jewish problem on a national basis.

Another one of the king's informants was the burgomaster of Amsterdam, J. Wolters van de Poll, who sent his memorandum on May 26, 1807.[45] The Parnasim had briefed him in considerable detail,[46] and Wolters van de Poll fully agreed with their views. The Parnasim pointed out that 'due to their policies there had been a considerable improvement in their finances – since in the year 1797 the Community's unpaid debts exceeded Df. 123,000, in addition to annual interest on perpetual loans and annuities in the amount of more than Df. 2800, whereas at this moment, even though some Df. 5000 in annual interest on perpetual loans and annuities must be paid, the remaining debts do not actually exceed Df. 59,300.' This improvement of the solvency of the Community was the result of the so-called 'Negotiation' of 1798, during the climax of the conflict with the New Community. A loan issue of Df. 256,000 – an enormous sum in those days – divided into 1,600 shares, had been fully subscribed within a short time by Community members and outsiders, including creditors.[47] This loan had provided the Old Community, which according to the New Community had been on the verge of bankruptcy, with a solid financial base.[48] Wolters van de Poll warned the king that revising the structure of the Community would have disastrous consequences for its finances and its welfare establishment – a prediction that would turn out to be all too correct. In line with the traditional policy of the Amsterdam municipal government (and

---

45 For the full version of the report, see Wolff, pp. 104-107.

46 For example, in a memorandum called 'Korte schets van de gebeurtenissen in de Hoogduitsche Joodse Gemeente te Amsterdam' (May 12, 1807), *Protokolbuch*.

47 In 1797 the following plan was chosen from among a number of proposals aimed at improving the financial situation of the Community: 1600 shares of Df. 160 were to be offered (in total Df. 256,000), guaranteed by permanent seats in the various synagogues, to be allocated by lot. Each year 100 shares were to be redeemed. A special Directorate was appointed, of which Benjamin Cohen was the first president, to visit personally all eligible members for the purpose of placing the shares. The first placement started on January 21, 1798, and by March 16 no fewer than 1470 shares had been taken up – despite a vigorous campaign by the New Community against the enterprise. The dismissal of the Parnasim on March 16 caused the 'Negotiation' to be suspended, and only in January 1799 did the authorities permit its continuation, after which the remaining shares were quickly sold. On June 1, 1800, the Directorate announced that the Community had already repaid Df. 227,539 to the shareholders (including widows, who were entitled to financial grants). From July 1, 1803 onwards another 100 shares were redeemed each year, but in 1811 the Community announced that it was unable to make futher payments. The Negotiation is proof of the devotion of the members to their community, and their preparedness to make financial sacrifices. The above details are derived from the minutes and financial reports of the Directorate of the Negotiation. (GAA, archives Jewish Community).

48 In their letter to the Minister of the Interior dated October 5, 1807) Meyer *et al.* claimed that the favorable financial position of the Community was due to an legacy of Df. 200,000 from the estate of Jonas Efraim Dresden. This is incorrect, since the legacy ('*Joune Kan*') was destined for dowries for girls, which did not benefit the Community directly in any way. This was the case with a gift by Aron Korijn, a poor teacher at the Beth Midrash, who won Df. 60,000 in the State Lottery, Df. 45,000 of which he donated to the Community (*Bendit Wing* III, pp. 190-91).

PLEGTIGE INKOMST VAN ZIJN MAJESTEIT LODEWIJK NAPOLEON KONING VAN HOLLAND,
in deszelfs Hoofdstad AMSTERDAM op den 20 April 1808.

Tour of Louis Napoleon through Amsterdam. On the right the High-German synagogue, and on the left the Esnoga. Historisch-topografische Atlas van het Gemeentearchief, Amsterdam.

contrary to the Emancipation decree) the burgomaster was exuberant about the prevailing situation during the Old Regime. 'At that time, and notwithstanding the large number of [Jewish] indigents, they never had to be looked after by the government, and although they consisted of a great many different nations, they were never charged with opposition to government regulations; on the contrary, they always behaved in the way of dependable and loyal subjects, who contributed no small amount to the perfect harmony that existed at all times between the Governors of the city of Amsterdam and the Parnasim of the Jewish Nation, as a result of which the latter were assured of the protection of the Municipal Regents and, in turn, were able to maintain peace and quiet among the individuals entrusted to their care.'[49] In other words: as long as the Parnasim are granted unlimited authority over the Jews, they won't bother us, and neither will we be charged for maintaining their poor. This was the kind of language Mollerus – himself a conservative – liked, and he hastened to inform the king 'that in his opinion it would be dangerous and – with special reference to the finances of the city of Amsterdam – disadvantageous to implement or encourage any *innovations* in the administrative *by-laws* of the Jewish communities' [italicised words underlined in the original, J.M.].[50] Louis disagreed with this recommendation, although he did not entirely disregard the warnings. He was looking for a solution that would create the least possible damage; neither did he want his decision to split the Jews into two camps: winners and losers. No doubt he was also inspired by Napoleon's decree for the establishment of the Central Consistory on March 17, 1808.[51] But while Napoleon's intention in establishing the Consistory was to supervise the Jews (it was not for nothing that the Parnasim were given the title of *commissairs surveillans* – 'Supervising Commissioners'), Louis regarded the Consistory as an instrument for promoting the material and moral welfare of the Jews.

In late April rumors started going around that Louis was planning to terminate the schism in Amsterdam. The Parnasim were told by the burgomaster, and the Chief Rabbi also heard about it and asked for details.[52]

Louis Napoleon had indeed worked out a plan. There exists a very detailed memorandum by Carel Asser, dated May 5, 1808.[53] This memorandum must have been drawn up *after* Asser had received a general briefing about the solution. There are several indications for this. Two years later, Carel's father

---

49 'Pendant cet espace de temps et non obstant le grand nombre de leur pauvres, ils n'ont jamais été à la charge du gouvernement, et quoique composés d'un amas de tant de différentes nations, ils ne sont rendus coupables d'aucune opposition aux ordres du Gouvernement, ils se sont au contraire toujours conduits en sujets subordonnés et fidèles, à quoi n'a pas peu contribué la parfaite harmonie, qui de tout temps a regné entre la régence de la ville d'Amsterdam et les Parnasim de la Nation juive, de façon que ceux ci étant assurés de la protection des Régents Municipaux étaient par là en état de maintenir l'ordre et la tranquilité parmi les individus confiés à leur soin' (Wolff, p. 105).

50 Mollerus to the king, September 28, 1807 (ARA, Coll. Janssen, no. 40).

51 Schwarzfuchs, *op. cit.*, pp. 122-7.

52 *Protokolbuch* 1808, fo. 263.

53 Colenbrander, *GS* Vol. 5 (1806-1810) II, no. 272, pp. 406-13; Da Silva Rosa comments that C. Asser 'often quotes entire paragraphs from Grégoire's brochure *Nouvelles observations sur les Juifs et particulièrement sur ceux d'Amsterdam et de Francfort*, that was published in 1806, but without giving the source. (p. 11) This criticism is unjustified. Already Wolff (p. 59) had rightly concluded that C. Asser was the author of an anonymous brochure entitled 'Recherches sur l'État des Juifs en Hollande et Moyens provisoires de le réformer' (Colenbrander, *GS* Vol. 5 (1806-1810), pp. 268-76). As shown earlier, this document dates from February 1807, rather than from the end of 1806. However, it is preceded by a similar anonymous and undated document, residing in the Archives Nationales Françaises (AN F19-1100/4), entitled 'Coup d'oeuil rapide sur l'état des israélites en hollande et principalement dans la ville d'Amsterdam'. This document also shows considerable similarity to Asser's memorandum of May 5, 1808. We assume that Carel Asser was the author of all three texts, and that 'Coup d'oeuil' probably provided Grégoire with the information for his brochure, from which he quoted without mentioning his sources. In other words, why should Asser have had to quote Grégoire, part of whose brochure consisted of his own words?

related that his son had been charged by the king with 'formulating a plan for a reunification, and that he had the inestimable satisfaction of its adoption by the king'.[54] Carel himself also writes that he had been working on an assignment from the king. Even more important, however, are the contents of the memorandum itself. Thus far more attention has been paid to the first two chapters, devoted to a devastatingly critical analysis of the situation of the Jews and the Amsterdam Jewish Community establishment. In fact, however, these two chapters are merely a restatement of points that had been expounded by members of Felix Libertate and Adath Jesurun on countless occasions. On the strength of both content and style M. Wolff has concluded rightly that Asser himself had explained the same thing on earlier occasions, including in two anonymous reports, one of which was evidently intended for the Assembly of Notables in Paris.

The third chapter, on the other hand, reveals a totally new line of thinking, culminating in a constructive solution. Whereas earlier memoranda had urged the dismissal of the Parnasim as a precondition for reunification, Asser now proposed a very different and far broader conception, far less hostile to the Old Community than would have been expected from the preceding diatribe. It is almost unimaginable that at least the general outline of this proposal should not have been discussed with the king, who in fact ratified it one week later.

Asser's proposal contained the following elements:

1. The king (or the burgomaster of Amsterdam) would appoint a Committee consisting of members of both communities, based on parity. Asser wrote: 'to prove the absolute neutrality of the undersigned, he would propose that Y(our) M(ajesty) will appoint to this committee one additional person from the general community, provided that the additional person would not in any way be beholden to the cause of the Syndics'.[55] It is clear that Asser was in fact referring to Meyer, which makes his comment about 'absolute neutrality' sound somewhat hypocritical. Nevertheless, it was important that, contrary to earlier reunification proposals, the leading figures of both Communities (including C. Asser, who had already offered his candidacy) would be seated on the committee.

2. The Committees would not only be charged with formulating a plan for the reunification and its aftermath, but also with drawing up 'ecclesiastical by-laws' and 'establishing a consistory'.[56] Thus far only the conflict between the Amsterdam Communities had been on the agenda; the notion of a nationwide Jewish organizational framework was no doubt Louis' contribution.

---

54 ' de projeter un plan de réunion et il a eu l'inappréciable satisfaction qu'il fut adopté par le Roi'. M.S. Asser to Comte Lebrun, Colenbrander, *GS* Vol. 6 (1810-1813), pp. 827.

55 'Afin de prouver la parfaite neutralité du soussigné il proposerait même à V(otre) M(ajesté) de nommer à cette commission une personne de plus de la grande communauté, pourvu que cet excédent soit composé d'un individu non intéressé à la cause des syndics'. *Idem*, p. 412.

56 ' règlement ecclésiastique et l'établissement d'un consistoire'.

However, the individual articles of the proposed by-laws were reminiscent of earlier demands by Adath Jesurun: reorganization of the slaughterhouse and the ritual baths, early burial and cleanliness, to mention only a few. The French influence, on the other hand, was evident in the prescriptions for the rabbis: ' who should be required to preach love of the fatherland and its defense as a most sacred duty.'[57]

3. The management of the welfare establishment had to be taken out of the hands of the Parnasim; instead, a 'special authority for the poor' would have to be established. The Parnasim's control of the welfare funds, and the enormous hold this gave them on the Jewish masses, was a thorn in the side of the enlightened Jews, and here were the time and the opportunity to put an end to this system.

4. The Committee would be authorized to submit requests for the amelioration of the lot of the 'Israelites', the education of Jewish youths, as well as to make the necessary political arrangements 'in order that the Israelites would no longer be exposed to unlawful harassment' and would be accorded all benefits granted them by the king and the constitution.

The plan is an organizational as well as political program: there is no reference whatsoever to religious matters. As such the document is typical for the way in which the Enlightenment was pursued in The Netherlands, where the pressing nature of social problems permitted reformers only the most vicarious discussion of religious and philosophical issues.

On the face of it, this plan, whose elements combine Louis' objectives with those of the 'enlightened' Jews, seems a resounding victory for the Jewish reformers over their orthodox brethren and the Parnasim. A closer look shows this to be not entirely true. In the process Carel Asser committed himself to the dissolution of his own community and its merger with the Amsterdam and other High-German communities in the country, the vast majority of which were strictly orthodox.[58] At the same time this concession turned out to be insufficient to ensure the implementation of the reorganization plan.

The Personal Committee for the Preparation of the High Consistory and the Elimination of the Schism

Two weeks after the introduction of the Asser Memorandum (May 18, 1808) a Royal Decree was published adopting Asser's recommendations with one minor

---

57 ' qu'ils soient tenus de prêcher l'amour de la patrie et sa défense comme le plus sacré devoir'. The prescriptions for the rabbis correspond with the draft Regulations for a Consistoire that had been adopted at the Assemblée des Notables in Paris. For this, see Schwarzfuchs, *op. cit.*, p.105. Subsequently the Consistoire Central issued corresponding instructions to all rabbis (July 6, 1810), that were to be observed also in the Dutch 'Départements' annexed by France.

58 Among Asser's concessions to orthodoxy – very possibly also due to the intervention of Louis Napoleon – was the absence of any suggestion that the decisions of the Paris Sanhedrin were to be made binding for the rabbis in the Kingdom of Holland.

change.[59] This decision, whose importance was rightly accentuated by Wolff,[60] included one consideration that demonstrates the seriousness of Louis Napoleon's intention to ameliorate the life of the Jews:

> *Having observed with acute displeasure the abject state of poverty and wretchedness in which several communities of [High]-German Jews in our Kingdom exist, and in particular the multitudinous community in our goodly Capital; and being desirous to make an effective contribution towards the amelioration of the lot of this section of our Royal subjects, and to cause them truly to enjoy the same equal advantages as accorded to those professing other religions, advantages that have been vouchsafed them by Law, but which they have been unable to enjoy due to natural and material causes connected with their way of life and the situation in which they have existed thus far; and taking into account that it is important to eliminate the schism which has arisen several years ago between the members of the German Jewish community in our good City, and being desirous that the interested parties shall themselves propose the necessary procedures, as well as the remedial measures to be taken in their favor, We appoint a committee composed of Messrs. Simon Zadoc Philips, Barend Boas and Elkan Philips de Jong, members of the Board of the Old Community,[61] Messrs. Charles Asser, Van Laun, and Isaac de Jonge Meyers, members of the Board of the New Community, as well as Messrs. J.D. Meyer, B. Leemans, and J. Littwak, who are hereby charged with this task and who shall submit their recommendations to Us.*

It cannot be ascertained what exactly was the role of C. Asser in this scheme, but there is no doubt that Louis Napoleon himself was responsible for both the content and the style of the decision. His emphasis on the wretched condition of the Jews in an initiative that dealt only indirectly with remedial measures shows that he regarded a solution to the problem as his principal task. And rightly so, for contrary to the situation in France and Germany, in The Netherlands the social condition of the Jews constituted the crucial aspect of the problem of their emancipation. Louis Napoleon realized that the Emancipation decree had not transformed the Jewish residents into equal citizens. This would happen only after the 'natural and physical causes' of their backwardness had been removed. However, whereas in other countries civic equality was granted on condition that the Jewish residents assimilate within their environment, Louis Napoleon regarded the rights that they had been granted by law as both

---

59 ARA, Staatssecr. Lod. Nap., exh. May 18, 1808; Coll. Janssen, no. 46.

60 Wolff, op. cit., p. 73: 'Thus, at the initiative of the King himself, an arrangement was made whose importance, also for the future, cannot be overestimated, given the fact that it spoke of the firm determination to grant the Jews complete civil and economic equality – not merely as a pretense, according to the model from the era of the Batavian Republic, because this was the contemporary fashion, but true [equality] in all respects.' Although Wolff is undoubtedly correct, he fails to mention the considerable importance of the Royal Decree from an internal Jewish point of view.

61 A mistake appears to have occurred in the division into three groups. Barend (= Ber) Boas belonged to the old Parnasim (Kommissie mikahal = 'members' committee'), whereas B. Le(e)mans (Bendit Wing) was a Parnas.

unequivocal and operative, and he merely cast around for the means to place the Jews into the full and unimpeded enjoyment of these rights. In the course of his decision he repeatedly reverts to this point, adding emphatically that he does not want to infringe upon Jewish religious practice in any way: 'We do not want the slightest attempt to be made to do anything that might in any way be construed as affecting the essentials of the Jewish religion; this would be entirely opposed to our sentiments, which are inclined towards doing nothing that might offend the fullest freedom of conscience.'[62]

In addition, the king's Personal Committee was charged with the responsibility for solving the schism within the High-German community of Amsterdam and to create a 'General Consistory' whose Board would reside in the capital (i.e. Amsterdam) and which would look after the general religious interests of the various 'German Jewish communities' in the Kingdom.

With this instruction the cornerstone was laid for a nationwide organizational structure uniting all High-German (Ashkenazi) Jews in The Netherlands, who prior to this had not known any other, even regional, framework. To this end the Committee was expected to make recommendations for the administration of the various communities, in order that the Jews would be in the same position and enjoy the same protection as any other citizen.

Through his choice of the members of the committee Louis had basically accepted C. Asser's recommendation to give the Old Community one more member than the New Community, even though this was supposed to be 'an objective' person. I have no doubt that Asser meant someone who was opposed to the Parnasim, and from the outset he must have had Meyer in mind for this position. Even so he proceeded with considerable circumspection, by dividing his list of candidates into three parts: three official representatives of each of the two communities, plus three who did not belong to either Board. However, to all intents and purposes B. Leemans and Juda Littwak[63] were Board functionaries, and only Meyer was not a member. On paper the Committee looked more impartial than it was in practice.[64]

---

62 'Nous ne voulons pas que la moindre atteinte soit porteé ce qu'ils pourraient croire tenir à l'essence de la religion Judaïque, ce qui serait entièrement opposé à nos sentimens, qui sont de ne gêner en rien la liberté la plus complète des consciences.'

63 Juda Littwak (1764?-1836) was born in Latvia, which explains his name (and not, as Eduard Asser wrote according to Dr. I. H. van Eeghen: 'He was born in 1751 in Poland in a town of this name' (Asser, *Jeugd*, p. 176). Littwack was a son-in-law of Dr. H. de Lemon and one of the founders of Felix Libertate and Adath Jesurun. He also was a member of the Board of Adath Jesurun.

64 Da Silva Rosa (*Bijdrage*, pp. 39-40) writes on the authority of the chronicle of Bendit Wing that initially the burgomaster of Amsterdam appointed a committee of three persons, who had an audience with the king and eventually co-opted another six members (the first six persons mentioned in the decree of May 18). Despite Bendit Wing's close relationship with the Parnasim and their circle, it is evident that he was unaware of the decision to establish the Personal Committee. It is incomprehensible that Da Silva Rosa preferred the chronicle over the official decree as already reproduced by Wolff (p. 64). Also the information in the chronicle that the committee was divided into three sub-committees is mistaken.

To emphasize this neutrality, the Committee did not convene in a location belonging to either community, but in a rented room in the new City Tavern. Their first meeting took place on June 8, 1808, and the eighth and last on July 18 thereafter.[65] Within the short span of one month the Committee achieved the impressive feat of preparing three documents: a draft of the by-laws for the High Consistory (A), by-laws for the (reunited) Jewish community of Amsterdam (B) – each draft comprising dozens of articles – and an outline for the settlement of the conflict between the two existing communities (C).

Undoubtedly Asser and Meyer must have done a great deal of preparatory work prior to the Committee's first session, besides which the two bright and experienced advocates succeeded in imposing their ideas on their fellow Committee members, the way they were to do on many future occasions. Even so it took another month before the Committee was able to submit its texts to the king, due to the fact that their proposals almost immediately aroused serious opposition in both communities.[66]

Opposition within the Old Community

All authors who have dealt with the establishment of the High Consistory mention the dissatisfaction within the New Community, without devoting even one word to the resulting mood in the Old Community. Yet the protests of the New Community can only be understood in light of the developments within the Old Community and the reactions of the Committee. This void is no doubt due to an inadequate study of the sources, which – as we shall show further on – contain sufficient material about this opposition. However, there is another and no less important explanation, which casts a light on the mentality of the contemporary Jewish community.

The voluminous and even disproportionate space allocated to the views and activities of 'enlightened' Jews in historical accounts is a direct consequence of the plethora of available literature which they themselves produced. Their opponents, on the other hand, failed to publish a single document. The Parnasim were weary of publicity, to the point where they refused to counter attacks on their policies in public.[67] They persisted in their traditional policy of secret discussions with the authorities, to whom they submitted memorandums that had been drafted following consultation with their legal advisors. These docu-

---

65 *Bendit Wing, loc. cit.*

66 The letter containing the various by-laws submitted to Louis Napoleon (ARA, Staatssecr. Lod. Nap., exh. September 12, 1808; Coll. Janssen, no. 48) is undated; however, the commentary by Minister Mollerus is dated August 30 (Coll. Janssen, no. 47).

67 A member of the Amsterdam Jewish community had written an extensive reaction to Abbé Grégoire's brochure *Nouvelles observations sur les Juifs et particulièrement sur ceux d'Amsterdam et de Francfort*, that had also been published in German in *Sulamith* (Vol. II, 1808, pp. 55-68, 90-116) and which contained several vicious attacks on the Parnasim. The Parnasim decided not to publish the reply, but record it in the communal protocols (*Protokolbuch*, 1807, fo. 183-87), which of course rendered it totally useless.

ments defend the Orthodox point of view, which also enjoyed the full backing of the Chief Rabbi and his assessors.

The establishment of the Personal Committee by Louis Napoleon prompted a fundamental structural change in the Old Community. The fact that the Parnasim were themselves represented in the Committee, and since – contrary to the demands of their opponents within the Old and the New Community – they would continue to sit on the Board, from the outset placed them in a different position, one that would inevitably result in their alienation from the Chief Rabbi. Besides this, the attitude of the Parnasim of 1808 was no longer the same as that taken in 1798, despite the fact many of the persons involved might have been the same. Their children had meanwhile grown up to become

Rabbi Jaacov Moses Löwenstamm, 1748-1815.

quite prosperous burghers, with a different outlook on Dutch society from that of their elders. A typical example is Barend Boas, two of whose children chose a career that was applauded by the enlightened group.[68] There is no doubt that these overtures to the Dutch gentile environment were regarded with regret, if not hostility, by the strictly orthodox group gathered around Chief Rabbi Jakob Moses Löwenstamm.

Jakob Moses Löwenstamm was a scion of famous rabbinical families on both his father's and mother's side. He was the brother-in-law and father-in-law of rabbis.[69] Unfortunately this distinguished affiliation stood in stark contrast to the mediocrity of the person entrusted with the spiritual leadership of one of the largest Jewish communities in the world at such a crucial point in time. He was an indifferent Talmud scholar[70] and there were good reasons why the Parnasim hesitated for three years before appointing him Chief Rabbi as successor to his father.[71] It is possible that he was not quite so incapable as his adversaries made him out to be,[72] but even his lack of knowledge of the Dutch language (virtually unimproved after fifteen years in office!)[73] prevented him from conducting negotiations with the Dutch authorities. With the exception of several *haskamot* (recommendations of Hebrew books) he published no works of his own.

---

68 One son (David Samuel) was an advocate and in 1807 assisted in the foundation of the emancipatory associations 'Tot Nut en Beschaving' and 'Mathesis Artium Genetrix'. The second, L.S. Boas, became an officer in the Jewish militia, and subsequently made a career in the Dutch navy.

69 It would be impossible in the present context to enumerate all the rabbis to whom Rabbi Jakob Moses (later Moses Saul) Löwenstamm (1753-1815) was related. Two of his progenitors were his great-grandfather Haham Zvi, Chief Rabbi of the High-German community in Amsterdam, and Rabbi Heshel of Cracov – both founders of rabbinical dynasties. Both his grandfather and his father were Chief Rabbis of Amsterdam. His great-uncle was the famous Rabbi Jacob Emden, and Rabbi Zvi Hirsch, the Chief Rabbi of Berlin, was his uncle; he married the latter's daughter, which made him the brother-in-law of Rabbi Saul Hirschel, a rabbi in Frankfurt am Oder. Rabbi Saul Halevi of The Hague was his uncle and Rabbi Solomon Hirschell of London his cousin. His son, Rabbi Jechiël Arjeh Leib, was Chief Rabbi of Leeuwarden, and his son-in-law Rabbi Samuel Berenstein became Grand Rabbin, whereas another son-in-law, Rabbi Hartog J. Herzveld, was Chief Rabbi of Zwolle. This (and other bifurcations not mentioned here) shows the international ramifications of the Dutch rabbinical families.

70 When he was still a rabbi in Cleve, Rabbi Leib Redisch is supposed to have said: 'That *am ha-aretz* (boor) should become a rabbi here?'(*Disk. NK* no. 9); or: 'I have heard him preach, and then Bendit Chalfon (one of the Parnasim) said to another Parnas: "From which book did he take that sermon?"'(*Disk. NK* no. 15).

71 On August 30, 1790, the Parnasim requested the Amsterdam Municipal Council to extend the period within which (according to Art. 44 of the by-laws) the replacement of a departed Chief Rabbi had to be appointed (Chief Rabbi Saul having died on June 19) from six months to six years 'in order to safeguard the Peace and Unity of the Community'. In the end he was appointed in 1793 by a virtually unanimous vote.

72 From a letter by M. Asser to Lebrun: 'Pour comble des malheurs des Israélites allemands, il se trouve à la tête de ses synagogues un rabbin polonais (sic!), déstitué de toute éducation, sans charactère, sans connaissance, sans talents, sans moyen de s'exprimer dans quelle langue que se soit, enfin dépourvu de tout se qu'on doit exiger dans un ecclésiastique respectable. Ce rabbin s'oppose à toutes démarches que les bienveillans veulent et peuvent faire et les entrave.' (Colenbrander, *GS* Vol. 6 (1810-1813), p. 828).

73 He rarely participated in negotiations, and then only in the presence of a translator. During the crucial discussions about the participation in the Paris Sanhedrin the Parnasim consulted him only once (see Chapter 5, note **11**)

Neither did his followers react in writing to the contemporary events which were critical for them. The only document to emerge from this quarter are the unpublished chronicles by Bendit Wing,[74] but while admitting its importance as a source of historical information, this document is little more than a factual – and for that matter incomplete – record, since the author quite obviously omitted facts that might have proved embarrassing to him and his brothers-in-arms.[75]

We must therefore suffice with the information supplied by their opponents and by various official sources. These contain indications that the Committee encountered opposition from within the Old Community right at the start of its activities. This can be the only explanation for the receipt by the Parnasim of a hand-written letter from the king, dated June 20, whose contents are sufficiently important to be quoted in full:

> *Parnasim of the High-German community, Gentlemen,*
>
> *I have been pleased to notice your willingness to work towards the amelioration of the lot of your co-religionists. However much I welcome these efforts, I want to leave you entirely free to suggest to me the means by which you intend to achieve this. You, gentlemen, are completely familiar with the attitudes within your community, and I have every right to expect from the exalted personalities in this community a discernment of truth, as well as recommendation concerning the means that will likely be most effective in every respect. I am desirous that you shall unite yourselves with the rest of our society, and I shall be grateful for any efforts you will exert towards this end, but I shall not compel you, and in all this I am only intent on your welfare. With this, Gentlemen Parnasim of the High-German Jewish community, I commend you into God's protection.*
>
> *(Signed) Lodewijk.*
>
> *Palace Het Loo, June 20, 1808* [76]

This letter, and the moment at which it was written (following the Committee's first session), must have been aimed at removing any uncertainty about the king's intentions, and thereby securing the cooperation of the Old Community. The Parnasim will no doubt have been flattered to receive a personal letter from

---

74 The introduction of the chronicle (copied by Awraham Dellaville at the request of S. I. Mulder), contains a description of the author, written by one of the two last-mentioned persons. 'Rabbi Bendit Wing was an enemy of anything new for which reason he always exaggerated anything that could shame his opponents, while belittling or even ignoring anything that redounded to their credit Many times he recorded hearsay or items he had read in the pamphlets of the followers of the old direction. But he never went to the root of the issues he wasn't a scholar or intellectual, who searches for the origins of things.'

75 It seems to me that the author was afraid his notes might get into the hands of oppositional elements. Activities by the Orthodox faction within the Parnasim, and actions directed against them (and subsequently against the Consistory) are ignored.

76 *Protokolbuch*, 1808, fo. 287. At the Algemeen Rijksarchief I was told that there is no copy of this letter in Louis Napoleon's Secretarial archives. Even so the letter's authenticity cannot be doubted. It is possible that the king gave the original to Asser or Meyer following a discussion with either of the two.

the king (indeed a unique event), their faith in the monarch's good intentions being further strengthened by a request on behalf of the king to recommend a number of suitable persons for governmental positions.[77]

But even if the Parnasim were reassured, the Chief Rabbi wasn't. On July 4 he met with several members of the Committee[78] and on July 11 – the day before their final session – Chairman J.D. Meyer had a personal interview with the Chief Rabbi. The subject of the discussion is known to us from a memorandum that Adath Jesurun addressed to the king two days later. According to this memorandum the Committee had promised that following the re-unification of the two communities the Chief Rabbi 'would suggest to the Board members functioning at the time that they adopt the rites and ceremonials that are presently practiced within the Old Community, and that, once approved by them, the Consistory that was to be established was absolutely certain to approve them.'[79]

This promise, to which we shall return later on in more detail, also explains the highly unusual proposal by the Committee that all its members were to be appointed to the future High Consistory. It was made in the course of a discussion with the Minister of Religion, and subsequently explained in more detail in a letter that, among other things, stated:

> *Having been appointed by His Majesty in order to put an end to the many divisions and to organize the Jewish Religion, it is only natural that we have considered ourselves extremely honored to be able to work towards this noble goal; we have been fortunate in being able to work speedily and in unanimity. We have had the satisfaction [of seeing] that the Great Community, which no doubt has been indirectly informed of our plans, is awaiting His Majesty's decision with deferent silence; We therefore expect to be able to implement these benefits, and thus assist in promoting further the fatherly insights of His Majesty and [therefore] propose ourselves as members of the High Consistory but we considered that to leave the choice undetermined might give rise to pretensions and possible insults, while there is no guarantee that the same principles that formed the basis of the [new] by-laws, would be implemented in practice.*[80]

---

77 The letter thanking the king is dated June 29. On June 19 the burgomaster had informed them (as recorded in the *Protokolbuch*): 'das adouneynu hamelekh jorum houdou (our exalted Royal Majesty) farlangt um di yehudim gam keyn (also) tsu eplogiren (to employ) in eynige bediningen, veliyes (since) das ho-odoum minister fun eren dinsten farlangt eynige layt an tsu shtelen die bekvam zayn eytsl (at) ministeri sjelov (his Ministry) tsu fungiren, dehayne (in other words) youser (more) als ordinere klerken vaylen zi oukh als shefs muzn kenen kontsiperen di untersheydene zakhen velkhe eytsl minister hanal (the afore-mentioned minister) zolten vorfalen'. For this reason the King requested them to nominate two persons. The Parnasim decided to propose ten persons. (*Protokolbuch, idem.*)

78 *Bendit Wing*, p. 90.

79 ARA, Req. Staatssecr. Lod. Nap. Req. of five members of the Board of Adath Jesurun to Lodewijk Napoleon, July 13, 1808.

80 Letter of the Personal Committee to the Minister of Religion, dated August 11, 1808 (ARA, Staatssecr. Lod. Nap., exh. September 12, 1808).

Even this veiled formulation cannot hide the Committee's fear that a High Consistory composed in any different way (note the word 'silence' with respect to the Great Community) would fail to implement the proposals in the spirit in which they had been formulated and accepted. Knowing that the members of the Committee had given a prior undertaking to accept the Chief Rabbi's proposals lock, stock and barrel, it is clear that the only way to make good their promise was to make sure that they themselves would be responsible for the implementation of their recommendations.

The Objections of Adath Jesurun

The impact on the members of Adath Jesurun of this promise to defer the decisions on religious matters 'to the ignorant and most vicious adversary and hater of the New Community, and the discretion of the Chief Rabbi of the Old Community' was shattering.[81] 'We have been betrayed by our perfidious members on the Committee,' the Board wrote to Louis Napoleon.[82] The worst of their opprobrium was directed at Carel Asser, who was accused of having 'sacrificed our interests to his hunger for power or personal advantage.'[83] He was accused of having 'inveigled' two members of the Committee, H. van Laun and J. Littwak, who had opposed the arrangement with the Chief Rabbi, to sanction the agreement with their signature.[84] During a meeting of the Board of the New Community on July 13 a petition was read signed by twenty-three members protesting the course of events. A much discomfited Carel Asser requested two day's grace before forwarding the petition to the king, promising that he would try to annul the agreement with the Chief Rabbi.[85] Not surprisingly these efforts were in vain, and thus it was decided on June 15 to dispatch the petition of the twenty-three members with an accompanying letter from the Board of Adath Jesurun.[86] A similar letter drawn up by supporters of the compromise, however, was not sent.[87] These supporters, apart from C. Asser himself, included his fellow-committee members Is. de Jonghe Meyersz. and H. de Lemon, M. S. Asser and two of the latter's sons, three others from the De Jonghe Meyersz. family, as well as Joseph Arons and another four persons who had authorized the others to sign in their names. Although forming a small minority, they nevertheless included the most prominent founders of the community.

81 H(ermanus) Salomo in letter to Louis Napoleon (ARA, Staatssecr. Lod. Nap., annex August 30, 1808, no. 6 (Lit. a), dated July 29).
82 ARA, Staatssecr. Lod. Nap., Adres Direction d'Adat Jesurun, September 3, 1808.
83 Letter H. Salomo to Minister of Religion, ARA, Staatssecr. Lod. Nap., annex August 30, 1808, no. 6 (Lit c).
84 Salomo to Louis Napoleon (see note 81).
85 Petition Board of Adath Jesurun, July 26, 1808 (ARA, Staatssecr. Lod. Nap., annex August 30, 1808, Lit B).
86 *Idem.*
87 Petition dated July 22, 1808, first signatory Benjamin de Jonghe Meyers.

A look at the protesting petitions and memorandums by the leaders of the New Community provides us with an unexpected insight into the nature and strength of the community. We read, for instance, that during the past few years hardly any members had transferred from the Old Community to the newer congregation, and that the membership of the New Community had in fact declined.[88] This confirms an impression from other sources that the New Community had lost much of its attraction. The majority accused the minority of having betrayed the oath that all members had solemnly sworn 'in our Holy Synagogue and in the presence of the Supreme Being, around the coffin of our venerable departed Rabbi,[89] that neither we, nor our descendants, will ever abandon these dogmas, rites and ceremonies.'[90] Worse still: Carel Asser, Moses Asser and De Jonghe Meyersz. had at one time accepted the dogmas of the New Community, as shown by a petition that had been sent in 1802 to the National Government and which had been signed by the entire Board.[91] The minority's answer to this accusation was highly revealing: 'Admittedly the New Community had stated in 1802 that it had conscientious objections to re-unification, which statements were of such a nature as to cause the cancellation of the planned re-unification',[92] but on the other hand 'the establishment of the New Jewish Community had not at any time been due to differences on points of religion' – for which reason any theological investigation (as the majority desired) would only cause it to be humiliated. Neither, the minority claimed, was the majority opposed to the rituals of the Old Community when they were still members. The opposite was the case: 'Despite the most strenuous efforts on the part of the founders,' the New Community 'had equally shown very little inclination to introduce new rituals, so that we must regretfully admit that a Christian who would enter either church would observe very few differences.'[93] Wolff and J. Meijer have interpreted this minority document as conclusive proof of the absence of any meaningful differences between the two communities.[94] Even without contesting their conclusion, there are several good reasons for analyzing the religious basis of Adath Jesurun in more detail. In the first place it

88 Petition B. de Jonghe Meyersz. *et al.* (see note 87).
89 Adress July 13, 1808 (see note 79). Rabbi Yizhak Graanboom died March 10, 1807. About his funeral, see *Bendit Wing*, p. 199; Meijer-Slagter, *Versteend Verleden*, pp. 33-40.
90 Address dated July 13, 1808.
91 In the course of 1802 the New Community submitted four petitions: June 25, by the Board, 'requesting support for the unhindered exercise of their religious obligations'; on July 6, a 'Memorandum of amplification'; on July 9 a petition regarding the conflicts with the Old Community; and finally, on September 23, a petition 'requesting that the current conflict between them and the Parnasim of the Old Community should not be taken out of context'. All these petitions relate to the decision of May 25, 1802, by the National Government ordering the re-unification of the two communities. ARA, Coll. Janssen, nos. 20-23.
92 Petition July 22, 1808. This is a confirmation by these prominent personalities in the New Community of the accusations by the Parnasim of the Old Community that the merger had not come about 'due to the fact that the dissenting members had created an entirely new kind of obstacle by declaring that they differed with the Community on points of religion, something they had never mentioned at any time in the past.' Report of the Parnasim dated May 17, 1807, *Protokolbuch*.
93 *Loc. cit.*
94 Wolff, p. 67; J. Meijer, *Joodse wetenschap in Nederland*, Heemstede, 1982, pp. 17-18.

should be taken into account that the contemporary documents had a practical purpose, rather than being intended as a record of historical truths. For this reason researchers should ask themselves what the underlying reasons were for the majority's claim that there existed marked differences between the dogmas, rites and ceremonies of the two communities.[95] In addition, every organization has a dynamics of its own, which means that its original purposes may become tinged by other tendencies. For this reason it is important to question whether – and to what extent – those historians are right who regard Adath Jesurun as the first 'Reform' community – or at least the bellwether of the kind of reform that was to become so widespread in Germany.[96] Graetz, for instance, writes: 'The political division also became a religious division. For the adherents of the new Adath Jesurun community started to introduce a kind of Reform.'[97] The same view was adopted by Dubnow[98] and R. Mahler,[99] with J.J. Petuchowsky similarly calling the New Community a precursor of the German Reform movement.[100] The question is therefore whether the founders of Adath Jesurun, besides political and social motives, also had religious objectives – and whether they aimed at a reform of religious practices.

A contemporary document provides a definitive and negative answer to this question. Even before the installation of the Bondt Committee the Provincial government of Holland had set up a committee to facilitate an accommodation between the two communities. In its session of July 6, 1797, i.e. two months after the founding of Adath Jesurun, this committee reported:

> On this occasion (the discussion with representatives of the New Community) we were very pleased to be given to understand that as regards the Jewish religion they differed on not a single point from their fellow-Jews, but that they merely demanded a reform in several articles relating to the by-laws of the Church and the management of the community.[101]

The Committee's experience is confirmed by the appointment of a strictly Orthodox rabbi as Chief Rabbi of the new community. The person concerned, Rabbi Yitzhak Graanboom, was in fact adamantly opposed to any religious reforms even remotely inspired by Enlightenment ideas. As the spiritual leader

---

95 H. Salomo (see notes 83 and 85) mentions 80 to 90 differences, but fails to specify what they are. Since Israel Graanboom mentions 40 to 41 differences, it would be interesting to know what the other 40 to 50 were. No doubt they were of very little importance, if at all, since Salomo would no doubt have taken the trouble to provide details.

96 See, for example, L. Lewysohn about Yizhak Graanboom: 'Als praktischer Theolog war er zeitgemäßen Reformen nicht abhold, und führte als Rabbiner seiner Gemeinde manche Neuerung ein, die in Deutschland erst viel später versucht wurde.' (*Monatsschrift für Geschichte und Wissenschaft des Judentums*, Vol. 5, 1856, 45). Besides being incorrect, this representation is out of all proportion to the decisions taken by Graanboom.

97 Graetz, II, xi p. 218.

98 Dubnow, VIII, p. 173.

99 Mahler, p. 93.

100 Jakob J. Petuchowsky, *Prayerbook Reform in Europe*, New York, 1968, p. 48-49. Petuchowsky admits that the reforms of Adath Jesurun were extremely modest, but he is wrong when stating that they resulted in the excommunication of the members.

101 ARA, Gewestelijke Besturen van Holland, Inv. nr. 4558, p. 236.

of a newly created community, it was his responsibility to set its theological course. It might have been very tempting for him to abolish certain customs that had annoyed him, and replace them by others more akin to his views. Being the rabbi of a *new* community he might have considered himself released from his obligations towards the *minhagim* (religious customs) of the Old Community[102] – all this, of course, without departing in any way from *halakhah*.

During the first services no fixed rituals as yet existed. Somewhere in the *Discourses of the New Community* it is stated: 'We shall adopt the best from the two *kehillot* (the High-German and the Portuguese)', and in another place it states that the community 'follows the Polish and Bohemian rites.'[103] The Rabbi, it was said, was preparing new *minhagim*. Even so it took considerable time before any changes were implemented, and then – more significantly – often only in order to avoid the danger that the authorities might dissolve the New Community. Such was the case in 1797, after the reconciliation committee had decided that there were no meaningful theological differences between the two (High-German) communities. At this point the New Community argued that such distinctions did exist but, when pressed, it was unable to mention more than five. Simultaneously its rabbi was instructed 'to find more such different tenets'. Five years later, in 1802, the New Community was once again threatened with dissolution, and once again – as a last recourse – it trotted out the religious points of difference. This time there were eight such contentious points, most of them related to the order of the service. Those that related to matters of principle will be dealt with later. In the course of the next few years Rabbi Yitzhak introduced several other changes, eventually resulting in the corpus of *minhagim* in the New Community that is known to us from *Melitz yosher*, a publication by his son Israel.[104] As we shall see, this document was originally written as a report for the High Consistory following the dissolution of Adath Jesurun.[105] The report was provided with critical comments by Rabbi Josef

---

102 In principle *minhag* even has precedence over *halakhah* in Jewish religious law. Jewish religious authorities have throughout the ages attempted to curb this domination of *minhag* by determining at which moment pointless or even foolish *minhagim* might be abolished. For this reason the situation in which Rabbi Yitzhak Graanboom found himself (or believed to find himself) was ideal for a *halakhic* authority. For more information about *Minhag*, see the article in *EJ* XII, pp. 4-26, and the most recent and thorough research on the essence and history of the *minhagim*, D. Sperber, *Minhagei Yisrael* (Hebr.) 1-3, Jerusalem, 1990-1994.

103 *Disk. N. K*, nos. 1 and 5.

104 *Melitz yosher*, Amsterdam, 5569 (1809).

105 That this booklet is identical with the memorandum written by Israel Graanboom at the invitation of the High Consistory (see also J. Meijer, note 94, *op. cit.* p. 16) is also apparent from the text. For this reason it does not contain changes such as the abolition of the *Birkhat hagoyim* that had already been incorporated in the by-laws of the High-German community of Amsterdam.

Asser Lehmans of The Hague.[106] The document composed by Israel is rather disjointed, since he wrote down everything as it came to him or as it appeared in the protocols of the Community. Lehmans correctly criticizes the absence of clear definitions in Israel's report. He divides the decisions about deviations from the Amsterdam Ashkenazi custom (forty-one in total) into four categories, relating to: a) *din* – points of religious law that are inviolable; b) *minhag* – customary laws, which can only be changed by a generally recognized authority; c) local customs, which may be changed by the local authorities; and d) the order of service, which each community is free to determine as it sees fit. The vast majority of the articles in *Melitz yosher* concerned customs and service rituals, which means that they could have been changed by any rabbi in the position of Rabbi Yitzhak. In any case, the numerous revisions in the order of service that had been implemented in course of time, and that in turn were cancelled by Rabbi Yitzhak, were not the fault of the successive rabbis of the Amsterdam congregation. Countless Ashkenazi rabbinical authorities had – usually in vain – fought this continuous process of accretions to the basic service.

It is in this light, therefore, that we should see the articles in Israel Graanboom's document, which by and large were intended to preserve the decorum during the synagogue service. This is in itself a typical aspect of the early nineteenth-century reforms. At the same time, most of the relevant decisions by Rabbi Yitzhak were adopted from the Sephardi rites of the Amsterdam Portuguese community. The Sephardim in Amsterdam exercised an enormous – though not always salutary – influence on the Amsterdam Ashkenazim.[107] Apparently Rabbi Yitzhak was so impressed by the solemnity of the services in the Esnoga, that at least fourteen of his reforms may be traced back to this fact. Most of the latter, for example the cancellation of the *piyutim*,[108] resulted in shortening the service. At the same time there were additions, such as the

---

106 Lehmans' critical notes were published by Maarsen under the title 'Ma'mar Or Ha-emet', *Ozar hahayim*, 9, 1933, pp. 110-20. This document was not written at the request of the High Consistory, for this had asked the Chief Rabbis of Rotterdam and The Hague to give their opinions *without stating their reasons*. This Rabbi Lehmans did in a letter to the High Consistory (see ARA, Minuut Verbalen van het Verhandelde in de gewone en buitengewone zittingen van het Opperconsistorie – Session Friday February 10, 1809). In principle Rabbi Lehmans is of the opinion that all modifications have lapsed automatically, since the members of the New Community had returned to the bosom of the Old Community, whose Chief Rabbi rejected any changes.

107 See about this J. Michman, 'Bein Sepharadim ve-Ashkenazim be-Amsterdam', in *Michmanei Yosef*, Jerusalem, 1994, pp. 27-40.

108 The *piyut*, liturgical poetry, which in course of time gained a permanent place in the prayer book, has traditionally been attacked by *halakhic* authorities – without much success. See about this I. Elbogen, *Der jüdische Gottesdienst*, Frankfurt o/t Main, 1924, pp. 280- 305, and *The Penguin Book of Hebrew Verse*, ed. T. Carmi, 1981, pp. 14-22. The Graanbooms therefore had no problem quoting a large number of important authorities in support of their point of view. Lehmans' criticism is inconsistent, and his statement that *piyutim* were recited as early as the Mishnaic period is completely baseless. It is interesting that not long before Rabbi Eliah, the Gaon of Vilna, had also raised serious objections to the *piyutim*, and that those of his disciples who settled in Eretz Israel abolished the *piyutim*. This explains why the official Ashkenazi as well as Sephardi rites in Israel do not include *piyutim*.

recitation of *Aleinu* between *Minha* and *Ma'ariv*,[109] and the recitation of the Priestly blessing during every Sabbath service. Particularly the latter was a highly controversial decision, since this *minhag* had been introduced in the Portuguese community during the period of Shabtai Zvi, and as such had evoked considerable criticism.[110]

No doubt Enlightenment considerations also played a role in the decisions, but their primary inspiration and legitimization were provided by the Portuguese-Israelite community. This also applies to the one article in *Melitz yosher* that is not connected with liturgy, namely the permission to eat pulses during Pesach – an issue that divides Sephardim and Ashkenazim even today.[111]

The final article of *Melitz yosher* (no. 41) concerns the abolition of the prayer *Makhnisei rahamim*[112] from the Selihot prayers, which invokes the angels to carry the prayers of the community before God's throne. In certain writings about Adath Jesurun this is construed as proof that the community denied the existence of angels. That this is totally unjustified is shown by the fact that no other prayers mentioning angels were abolished. The main problem with this prayer concerned something else entirely, namely the much older question of whether angels possessed the kind of power enabling them to act as intercessors between God and mankind, or whether it was justified to accord them such power. These questions led to conflicts between supporters and opponents of this prayer that continued from the twelfth till the seventeenth century. The opponents included many noted Jewish religious scholars, and Rabbi Yitzhak Graanboom chose their side in the argument.[113]

The conclusion is, therefore, that the liturgy of Adath Jesurun was the outcome of a specific set of circumstances, to wit, a newly established community that was not subject to existing *minhagim*, and therefore felt free to formu-

109 *Mincha*, the afternoon service, and *Ma'ariv*, the evening service – frequently held one after the other with a brief interruption. The inclusion of *Aleinu* is another Sephardi *minhag* that entered the Israeli Ashkenazi rite via Lurian Kabbala and Hassidism.

110 The Priestly Blessing during the Shabbat morning service was introduced in the Amsterdam Portuguese community under the influence of the mystical religious ecstasy of Sabbatianism and Hassidism, and the Parnasim refused to abolish the custom following Sabbetai Zvi's conversion to Islam. Rabbi Jacob Sasportas deals extensively with the subject in his *Sefer Zizat Novel Zevi* [Hebr.], ed. J. Tishbi, Jerusalem, 1954, pp. 211-40. The Gaon of Vilna also encouraged the frequent recitation of the Priestly Blessing, as indeed is customary in Israel.

111 About this, see *E.J* VII, col. 1235, under *Hamez*. The issue of eating pulses on Passover is also discussed in the Responsa of Rabbi Michael Steinhardt (1812) in connection with military service of Jews. See Graff, pp. 98-100.

112 *Makhnisei rahamim* dates from the Geonic era, and can already be found in the sidur of Gaon Amram (9th cent.). See D. Goldschmidt, *Seder haselihot keminhag polin*, Jerusalem, 1965, p. 18.

113 The resistance to this prayer grew as the Rationalist current gained momentum. For extensive details, see L. Zunz, *Die synagogale Poesie des Mittelalters*, Berlin, 1919, pp. 148-51. The prayer was abolished by the Gaon of Vilna.

late a ritual inspired by Sephardi examples, but that in all other respects did not deviate from the accepted religious codex.[114]

Despite this, the New Community found itself in a cleft stick. In its contacts with members of the Old Community the community was said to be in every respect traditional. Its rabbi was more learned than their rabbi, the prayers more orderly and devout, the ritual bath cleaner, the meat-hall uncorrupted,[115] whereas the members of the Board, who were quite satisfied with being called *Manhigim* (leaders),[116] distinguished themselves by being democratically elected and demonstrated an absence of dictatorial tendencies.

Simultaneously, however, in all its communications with non-Jewish authorities, the differences were both emphasized and exaggerated. C. Asser claimed that the New Community 'made its rabbi preach the true religion of Moses, rather than superstitious superficialities...[that] it had eliminated all prayers that contained curses of those who professed other faiths...[and] that it had permitted the use of several foods forbidden to followers of the other community, which had eased the lot of the poor.'[117]

Following the earlier-mentioned promise to the Chief Rabbi, the differences were amplified even further. The promise was said to play havoc with the freedom of worship. 'Sacrificing the freedom of conscience is something that exceeds human capability,' the twenty-three members wrote in their address to the Board.[118] H. Salomo, who had been appointed spokesman of the majority, continually talked about 'dogmas, rites and ceremonies'. The way he arrived at these 'dogmas' is in itself rather interesting. 'Jews,' he maintained, 'do not have any particular credo or doctrine given by Moses'. Instead they had 613 positive and negative commandments. Nevertheless, he continued, 'even minor ceremonies are of a no less dogmatic nature than the reception of the Bible by

---

114 One of the stipulations is that the rabbi should give a *derasha* every week, and this is also applauded by Lehmans. But what is a *derasha*? A homiletic speech that might contain a moral lesson, or a sermon, which uses Biblical or other ethical texts merely as a springboard for conveying some religious or other moral warning? Lehmans advocates the first approach, but in practice the evolution would favor the second interpretation.

Michael Meyer is of the opinion that – my arguments to the contrary notwithstanding – Adath Jesurun should still be regarded as the first Reform community. (M. Meyer, *Response to Modernity*, Oxford, 1988). In the final analysis this question is a matter of definition. Since Adath Jesurun intended to be a fully Orthodox community, even where its rites differed from those of the Old Community, I do not regard it as a Reform community in the present meaning of the word. Meyer, on the other hand, maintains that the formulation of a singular rite by Adath Jesurun was in itself sufficient to qualify it as a forerunner of the Reform, which in course of time would take a far more radical course.

115 The meat-hall of the New Community also became tainted by corrupt practices. The minutes of the Board of Adath Jesurun during the final years of the community mainly reflect abuses in the meat-hall (these protocols are kept in GAA).

116 The official title of a Parnas was *Parnas u-manhig* (abbreviated '*Pum*'). Even though in Hebrew the word *manhig* (leader) has a more 'dictatorial' meaning than *parnas* (caretaker), the word Parnas had assumed a no less hateful ring than Regent, so that its abolition could be considered a democratic gesture.

117 Colenbrander, *GS* Vol. 5 (1806-1810) II, p. 431. In total only one, unimportant, prayer was removed; this subject will be dealt with further on. Asser does not mention that the permission to eat pulses referred only to the duration of Passover.

118 Petition dated July 13, 1809, by 23 members to the Board of the Community.

Moses from the hand of God'. In other words, expressions to the effect that differences were 'merely ceremonial' contradicted both the meaning and the intention of the author himself (the author referred to being a contributor to the *Koninklijke Courant*, which had written that the differences were of a merely ceremonial nature. J.M.), ' and we repeat that in the Jewish faith ceremonies are also doctrines, as the illustrious Mendelssohn clearly demonstrated in his famous book *Jerusalem*.'[119]

This determined struggle of the majority for the preservation of their synagogue was by no means an exception in Jewish history: throughout all periods far less pressing causes had resulted in schisms in many other Jewish communities, both in The Netherlands and abroad. The problem is that Adath Jesurun failed to come up with arguments that convinced Louis Napoleon that religious freedom was indeed being violated. Instead, sailing even closer to the compass of Asser and Meyer, who would soon be appointed to important official functions, the verbal quibbles about the Jewish interpretation of dogma failed to divert the king from his intention to dissolve the New Community.

However, the New Community activists appeared to be successful in one respect: in his recommendations to the king, Mollerus, the Minister of Religion (who had very little sympathy for the New Community) rejected the demand that both communities should be allowed to see the draft of the new by-laws, arguing that this would only rekindle the conflict and aggravate their mutual alienation. He also agreed that the secret arrangement with the Chief Rabbi should not be honored in its original form, but instead suggested the following slightly amended formulation:

> *Art. 2. The agreed order of ceremonies and prayers shall follow the rules and manners as customary within the High-German Jewish community, except for such changes and improvements as might conveniently be implemented for the sake of reconciling diverging feelings.*
>
> *Art. 3. The High Consistory, at its earliest opportunity following its establishment, shall submit a recommendation to the Minister of Religion as to the manner, and by whom, this conformity of the order of ceremonies and prayers shall be formulated and [by whom] the corresponding by-laws could and should be designed in order to ascertain His Majesty's pleasure about the proposed manner.*[120]

For the time being, therefore, everything was to be arranged as was customary in the Old Community and, secondly, 'the order of ceremonies and prayers' would be uniform – which ruled out the separate existence of a diverging liturgy in another synagogue.

Running slightly ahead of the subsequent developments, I must point out that a procedure was indeed being designed that made the introduction of revisions in the spirit of the New Community illusory. Here too the authorities

119 H. Salomo to Minister of Religion, August 5, 1808.
120 Recommendation Mollerus to the king, August 30, 1808 (ARA, Coll. Janssen, no. 47).

intervened by revising a proposal of the High Consistory in such a way that, at least in the eyes of outsiders, the impression was created that it was not the Chief Rabbi who had the last word. According to the instructions of the Minister, the Chief Rabbi of Amsterdam had to explain his views *in writing*.[121] He did so in a declaration rejecting any changes in the traditional Amsterdam liturgy. The son of the departed Chief Rabbi of the New Community was (also) allowed to submit a memorandum 'defending the reasons why his father had introduced the deviations from and changes in the customary order of the High-German Israelite community'.[122] Both memorandums were to form the basis of an advisory by the Chief Rabbis of Rotterdam and The Hague to the High Consistory. If the three Chief Rabbis were unable to agree, they could invite another two Chief Rabbis, following which the resulting committee would decide by a majority vote.[123] Taking into account that the Chief Rabbis of the two other big cities were no less conservative than their Amsterdam colleague, the outcome of their deliberations was a foregone conclusion. In a rearguard action, the New Community suggested consulting several Christian theologians, but this rather peculiar request was declined.[124]

Neither would the protesting members of Adath Jesurun be consoled by another seeming concession, which turned out to be a mere formality. In fact, if they still hoped to be able to salvage some form of independence for their community, they were in for a rude awakening. On Friday, September 2, Louis Napoleon held an audience at the Dam Palace in Amsterdam on the occasion of his birthday. The Jewish communities of Amsterdam were invited to send a delegation, but shortly before the audience was to begin, the Minister of Religion informed the delegation of Adath Jesurun that the king recognized only two Jewish communities in Amsterdam: the Portuguese and the High-German. They were given two alternatives – to leave, or to join the delegation of the Old Community. It stands to reason that the delegates opted for the latter. A request to the delegation of the Old Community to address the king in

---

121 The High Consistory had proposed a meeting between the three Chief Rabbis for the purpose of discussing Israel Graanboom's defense. The High Consistory believed that speed was of the essence, and that 'only one mode of praying' should be permitted in one and the same community. It did not want to leave the decision entirely to the Amsterdam Chief Rabbi, in order to avoid 'opening up wounds that have only recently healed'. However, the Minister curtailed the authority of the Amsterdam Chief Rabbi even further by forcing him to put down his views in writing, while entrusting the decision – at least in first instance – to the other two Chief Rabbis. (ARA, Letter of the High Consistory to the Minister of Religion, January 14, 1809. Coll. Janssen, no. 65; ARA, Archive High Consistory, Minuut Verbalen van het Verhandelde in de gewone en buitengewone zittingen van het Opperconsistorie – Sessions of January 4 and 15, 1808).

122 This refers to the Memorandum of Apology (Defense) published under the title *Melitz yosher* (see note 104).

123 *Or Ha-emet* (see note 106) should be seen as a reaction of the Chief Rabbi of The Hague, who apparently did not want to be confined to the short letter he sent to the High Consistory.

124 Mollerus' recommendation to the king refers to petitions by Israel Isaecs (= Graanboom), S.M. Metz, treasurer of the former Community, and no fewer than 31 petitions by members of the community requesting the king 'to defer the order of service and prayers determined by a decision of the High Consistory in all the churches of the Dutch High-German Israelite community of the capital until eventually the matter shall have been examined by Christian Theologians'. ARA, Staatssecr. Lod. Nap., 23 Lent Month, 1809.

the name of their congregation as well was rejected, although their spokesman, Elchanan Philip de Jong, was so kind as to mention at the conclusion of his speech that he had also spoken in the name of the four gentlemen who had joined his delegation.[125] The incident had such a profound impact on the Parnasim that they convened the same day and, following a consultation with their legal advisor Brugmans, dispatched a committee to the burgomaster requesting receipt of further particulars. The next day (Sabbath) the burgomaster referred them to Mollerus, but since it was the Jewish day of rest, he personally wrote the relevant request to the Minister. The latter received them forthwith, informing them that he had that very day submitted his advice to the king. A Royal decree was shortly to be expected, but in the meantime business should continue as usual.[126]

The reactions in the Jewish Quarter were less composed. In a letter to the king dated September 3, the Board of Adath Jesurun complained that their 'antagonists' were mocking them, and that they were glorying in their victory and the downfall of their opponents: 'Hardly had your audience come to an end than it was publicly being told in the streets and in the coffee houses, and afterwards in the synagogues, that Your Majesty had completely abolished the New Community, and that the king had finally complied with the most ardent desires of our adversaries during the past thirteen years, but meanwhile being careful not to repeat the conciliating words of Your Majesty with the result that members of our community have been ridiculed, annoyed and molested wherever they appeared in public.'[127]

Mollerus was well aware that the fierce antagonism the king's attitude had provoked within the Jewish community might well become a stumbling block for the establishment of the High Consistory and the unification of the two communities. He realized that for this reason it would be necessary to ensure a more or less controlling influence of the Government on the Boards of the principal Jewish institutions, and – contrary to the recommendation of the Personal Committee – he advised the king to reserve the right to appoint the members of these bodies for himself. Only in this way would it be possible to ensure the implementation of the re-organization of the Jews in the Kingdom of Holland as decided in the Royal decree of September 12, 1808.

The Consistorial System in the Kingdom of Holland

On September 12, ten days after the audience, the Consistorial system was introduced in the Kingdom of Holland. Six months previously Napoleon had imposed a consistorial organization on the French Jews by means of three

---

125 Reports of the audience in the *Protokolbuch*, fos. 317-18 (very extensive), *Bendit Wing*, pp. 92-93, and in a petition by the Board of Adath Jesurun to Louis Napoleon. ARA, Staatssecr. Lod. Nap., September 3, 1808.
126 *Protokolbuch, loc. cit.*
127 Petition Adath Jesurun dated September 3, 1808.

notorious decrees that testified to his low esteem for his Jewish subjects.[128] It is obvious that – as indicated by the use of the word Consistory – Louis Napoleon followed his brother's example, but the differences in content were no less striking. Whereas in France the statutes of the Consistoire had been devised and formulated by the emperor's people, Louis Napoleon permitted the Jews of Holland to formulate their own by-laws. Following the advice of J.H. Mollerus, his Minister of Religious Affairs, he made very few changes in the proposals that were submitted to him.[129] The most important of these, as demanded by Mollerus, was a greater influence of the Government on the High Consistory than that proposed by the Personal Committee.[130] To this end the initial appointments to the main bodies would be made by the king himself – i.e. not only the members of the High Consistory, but also the Parnasim of the Amsterdam High-German Community and even the members of the Welfare Board.[131] The remaining changes were of minor importance. The three draft proposals of the Personal Committee, namely a draft of the by-laws for the High Consistory, by-laws for the (reunited) Dutch High-German[132] Jewish Community of Amsterdam and an outline of the settlement of the conflict between the two existing Amsterdam communities, were in fact accepted in their original form. It is almost certain that the formulation of these lengthy documents was the work of Asser and Meyer, who apparently right from the start of the consultations submitted a previously prepared draft to their fellow members; there is no other way to explain how the Committee succeeded in concluding its task so rapidly. We do not know, therefore, what was the contribution of the other members, especially that of the representatives of the Old Community. It would seem that they were mainly involved with the formulation of sub-paragraphs and various other technicalities.

128 For the three decrees of 17 March 1808, see Schwarzfuchs, *op. cit.*, pp. 123-127 (in the chapter 'The Duped'). For the Jews of France the Consistorial system similarly meant 'a total break with their pre-revolutionary structure and was adjusted with considerable difficulty to their organic needs' (R. Neher-Bernheim, *The Turning Point, The Jews of France during the Revolution and the Napoleonic Era*, Tel-Aviv, Beth Hatefutsoth, 1981, no page numbering).

129 ARA, Staatssecr. Lod. Nap, Mollerus to the king, August 30, 1808 (exh. September 12, 1808, Coll. Janssen, no. 50-52).

130 ARA, Staatssecr. Lod. Nap., Personal Committee to Minister of Religion, August 11, 1808 (exh. September 12, 1808). The committee writes that it in fact welcomes the Government's demand for greater influence.

131 For a discussion of the by-laws, see below. They are cited as follows: A. By-laws for the High Consistory with article numbers; B. By-laws for the High-German Jewish Community of Amsterdam; Chapters indicated with Roman numerals, and Articles with Arabic numerals; C. Compromise between the two communities, indicating the number of the Article.

132 The hybrid name Dutch High-German Jewish Community represented a not very effective solution to a problem that had arisen out of the Committee's proposal to change the name High-German Jewish Community into Dutch Jewish Community. The Committee believed that such a change could also be effective for the purpose of combating the use of Yiddish. The Portuguese Community, which was consulted by Mollerus, objected: they too were Dutch Jews, but because of their Portuguese descent they insisted on a differentiation between them and the Ashkenazi Jews. This resulted in the appellations Dutch Portuguese Community and Dutch High-German Community.

Incontestably the basic design was the work of people bent on carrying through the ideas of the Enlightenment. Not only the organization of the High Consistory, but also the proposed by-laws of the Amsterdam High-German Synagogue were informed by a completely new spirit, as in fact stressed by the Committee itself.[133] The new organization of Dutch Jewry was a construction in the spirit of the times or – as some liked to say – 'a Corinthian building constructed in a strict classical style'. The only deviation from this basic design was a concession to the effect that all officials who had been employed on the basis of the former regulations would retain their positions. This compromise was of course of a temporary nature only, and as such did not mean an infringement of the principles, which entailed: a unitary and centralized organization, a hierarchical structure, an oligarchic administration, uniformity of religion, and subordination of the spiritual leadership to a secular authority.

Organization and Authority of the High Consistory

No vestige remained in the by-laws of the High Consistory of the concept of separation of Church and State.[134] The High Consistory would be subordinate to the Ministry of Religious Affairs; the initial nominations to the principal executive bodies, i.e. the High Consistory itself, the Amsterdam Synagogue Board and Welfare Board, and even the administration of the meat-halls, were to be made by the king. Evidently these direct appointments reduced the authority of the High Consistory, but even so left sufficient power in the hands of this institute, as shown by the organizational chart.

The seat of the High Consistory was in Amsterdam, and all its members were from this city. The High Consistory was responsible for dealing with all current affairs. At least once a year a meeting had to be convened in which outside members could participate, but in practice they attended more often.

These outside members were the representatives of Rotterdam and The Hague and of two other unspecified 'Consistorial Synagogues' – subsequently the communities of Utrecht and Zwolle were nominated. Any community with 1,500 or more members was considered a Consistorial Synagogue. All the Boards of the Consistorial Synagogues were subordinate to the High Consistory, whereas smaller communities were subordinate to the Board of the nearest Consistorial Synagogue. This way the High Consistory was assured of its control of religious practice, education and welfare services. In short, the Jewish com-

---

133 The Committee proudly writes that 'they have drafted entirely new Regulations, as if there never had been any other Regulations – in fact as if we had for the first time established a community'. ARA, Staatssecr. Lod. Nap., n.d. exh. September 12, 1808.

134 Not only that the leaders of Felix Libertate, as members of the Radical faction, regarded separation of Church and State an important plank in their ideology, but as recently as 1802 this principle had been confirmed by Moses and Carel Asser. See p. 108.

munities, which up till then had been completely independent, suddenly found themselves subordinated to and regulated by a supervisory College consisting almost exclusively of Amsterdam residents.

Organizational Chart

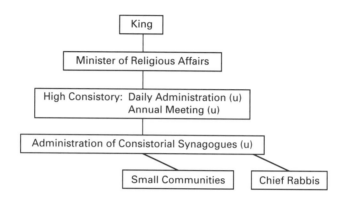

For Amsterdam the plan was as follows

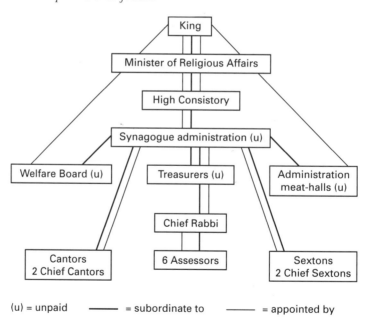

This hierarchic subordination, embarrassing as it was, was further aggravated by the composition of the High Consistory. On December 17, 1808, the day of its inauguration, it consisted of the following persons:

Name	Jewish name	Community
Barend Boas	Ber ben Jakob Boas	Old
Elkan Philip de Jongh	Elchanan ben Lipman Rintel	Old
Isak de Jongh Meyersz.	Itsik ben Meir Rintel	New
Eleazer Herman Keyzer	Leizer ben Manus Keizer	Old
Hartog Abraham van Laun	Hirsch ben Efraim van Loman	New
Benjamin Leemans	Benjamin ben Lima Wing (Wiener)	Old
Hartog H. de Lemon	Herz ben Hirsch Wiener	New
Jonas Daniel Meyer	Jona ben David Rintel	Old
Isaac David Salomons	Eisik ben David Preger	Old
Leonard Davids	Leib ben Shelomo	Rotterdam
Marcus Edersheim	Meier ben Shelomo	The Hague

This means that six of the incumbents belonged to the Old Community and three to the New Community, but since J.D. Meyer in all matters sided with the New Community, and sometimes was even more extreme than the representatives of the latter, the actual ratio was five to four. Davids and Edersheim belonged to the enlightened opposition, meaning that in meetings in which they participated the enlightened faction enjoyed a majority. The fact that Meyer had been appointed chairman meant, that to all intents and purposes, the influence of the representatives of the Old Community was seriously curtailed.

Thus, whereas the overwhelming majority of the Jews and all the Chief Rabbis, rabbis and teachers were averse to Enlightenment ideas, they were ruled by a council in which their sympathizers constituted a minority. The representatives from Rotterdam and The Hague who had been appointed by the king, the physician Dr. L. Davids[135] on behalf of Rotterdam and Marcus

---

135 Leonard (Levie) Salomon Davids (1771-1820) had since 1793 been municipal physician to the poor in Rotterdam. During his student years he had been fined by the Jewish Community for attending a theater performance on a Saturday. This decision of the Chief Rabbi of Rotterdam was confirmed by the burgomaster on September 29, 1788. See E. Slijper, 'Een merkwaardig proces over de haardracht der vrouwen bij de Joden te Rotterdam', *Rotterdams Jaarboekje* 8 (1910), pp. 25-49. In 1797 Davids was a member of a Committee for the purification and improvement of the domestic laws of the [Jewish] Community' in Rotterdam, founded on the same principles as Felix Libertate. At a later stage, under King Willem I, he refused an appointment as Parnas since he was of the opinion that he was the only truly Enlightened person (ARA, Protocollen Consulerende Commissie, probably of August 1815). His appointment would no doubt have irked the Chief Rabbi and the Parnasim.
   Davids was one of the pioneers of vaccination in The Netherlands. About this, see E.A. Rodrigues Pereira, 'Een drietal op de voorgrond tredende Joodse geneeskundigen uit de 19de eeuw', *VA* I, 16 (July 11, 1924), p. 246.

Edersheim[136] for the Hague, similarly belonged to the oppositional minorities in their respective communities. These appointments therefore clearly indicated the direction in which the Government, through the High Consistory, wanted to steer the Jewish communities.

The direct appointments by the king of the Boards of the various governing bodies in Amsterdam must be seen in the same light. It had been a long-standing desire of the enlightened group to wrest control of the Welfare Board from the Parnasim. The fact that the king appointed the nine members of the Welfare Board meant that, although subordinate to the Parnasim, they did not depend on them. Indeed, the appointment of Carel Asser's younger brother Tobie, a lawyer, as chairman of the Welfare Board showed that C. Asser and J.D. Meyer insisted on keeping this key function out of the hands of the Parnasim.[137] In the management of the meat-halls the New Community also achieved considerable influence: three of the directors would look after the big hall of the Old Community, and the remaining two after the small meat-hall that had been established by the New Community.[138] Of the seven Parnasim, two would be from the dissolved New Community which, considering the disparity in membership, also placed the Old Community at a disadvantage.[139]

All this means that the members of the New Community and their enlightened cohorts within the Old Community had not only secured a disproportionate number of seats, but also occupied all the key positions, enabling them to navigate the various administrative organs in the direction they desired. Their position was further reinforced after they jettisoned one of the issues that had been an important plank of their platform of 1796, namely the democratization of the Jewish community.[140] All members who had paid a minimum contribution had the right to vote, but their chances of affecting the composition of the council of Parnasim were extremely limited: all they could do was choose from a list drawn up by the Parnasim and approved by the High Consistory. The Welfare Board co-opted its own members, whereas the Chief Rabbi was elected by the Parnasim and ten members appointed by the Parnasim themselves. The

---

136 Marcus Edersheim was active in the emancipatory club 'Door Vlijt en Eensgezindheyd', established in The Hague in October 1797. (Van Zuiden, *'s-Gravenhage*, p. 94-95 and Bijlage X). Edersheim belonged to the opposition in the Hague Community, and with his support the High Consistory 'attempted to dismiss the incumbent Board of The Hague and replace it by a more enlightened one'. (ARA, Protocollen Opperconsistorie, 9 Wine Month, 1810).

137 With regard to the controversies between the Parnasim and the Welfare Board, M.S. Asser relates that his youngest son: 'fût à la tête de l'établissement pour soulager des pauvres'; the majority of the Parnasim are stiff-necked persons, 'quoique la direction des pauvres restait fidèle aux bons principes' [M.S. Asser to Lebrun, Colenbrander *GS* Vol. 6 (1810-1813), pp. 827-28.]

In 1836, following the death of Carel Asser, his brother Tobias, who was married to Caroline Itzig, succeeded him as a member of the High Committee. A great deal of information about him and his wife is related in Van Eeghen, *Asser, Jeugd*.

138 Regulation B., Chapter VII, Art. 2.

139 And still the New Community complained of prejudicial treatment. 'There also were supposed to be three representatives of each community, whereas as a seventh representative such a person could be chosen by Your Majesty whom Your Majesty knows to be impartial', stated H. Salomo in an (undated) address to the king. (ARA, Staatssecr. Lod. Nap., exh. 129, 1808).

140 All memoranda, letters and publications (incl. the *Diskursen*) emphasize the undemocratic manner in which the Parnasim were elected.

same procedure applied to the election of the Chief Cantors, the only difference being that fifteen members were allowed to participate. One might ask whether this was because Chief Cantors were considered more important than Chief Rabbis, or whether a smaller membership participation reduced the risk that the elected Chief Rabbi would be unwelcome to the Parnasim? Be this as it may, the oligarchic structure of the Synagogue establishment, against which Felix Libertate had fulminated so furiously, was retained – and even reinforced – in the modern structure because the highest authority, the Minister of Religious Affairs, and in last resort the king himself, could always disqualify a candidate who had been chosen despite the wishes of the ruling group.

The Position of the Rabbis

Traditionally the positions of the Chief Rabbis had always been subordinate to the Parnasim, even though the Ashkenazi Chief Rabbi generally carried more clout than his Sephardi colleague.[141] The new by-laws emphasized and reinforced this subservience, and from their formulation it is evident that the authors viewed the Chief Rabbis as a hostile and dangerous element. In contrast to, for instance, the administrators of the Welfare Board and the meat-halls, the Chief Rabbis were to be elected directly by the Parnasim, which made them dependent on the latter rather than on the High Consistory. This does not mean that the High Consistory was not interested in their activities: 'The High Consistory shall pay special attention that the Rabbis and Teachers do not assume positions incompatible with the interests of the State and the fulfillment of the civic duties that are imposed upon Jews just like on any other subject' (A-21); 'rabbis are not to interfere with members' actions "outside the synagogue"' (A-24); 'their main task in their sermons is to encourage love of King and Country, and the defense of the latter, to condemn idleness and to encourage a choice of a profession' (A-25). The High Consistory apparently deemed it unnecessary for the sermons to have any religious content. In the by-laws of the Jewish community of Amsterdam (B) the Chief Rabbi is not mentioned until Chapter 10, where his responsibilities are said to include 'taking decisions on all questions concerning religion about which his opinion is sought' (B-X,7,d). The Chief Rabbi also was 'obliged to appear before the Parnasim as often as required' (B-X,7,g;). For that matter, the Parnasim were supposed to see to it 'that none of the religious functionaries shall in any way violate the laws of this realm, that the Chief Rabbi or others shall not consecrate any marriages that are not performed in accordance with the Political law', and that no other offenses would be committed. A striking aspect of the regulations was their far greater concern with regard to what the Chief Rabbis were forbidden to do than with the positive contribution they might have made to the Jewish community.

---

141 About this, see J. Michman, 'Historiography of the Jews in the Netherlands', in *DJH* 1, Jerusalem, 1984, pp. 22-29.

Everything was done to denigrate the Chief Rabbis and to deprive them of all power, both with regard to the members of the community and vis-à-vis the government.

The Order of Ceremony

The only consolation of the Chief Rabbis was their salvation of the traditional liturgy and sundry religious practices. Thus: 'An identical form of prayer will be introduced in all Synagogues of the Community without exception at the earliest opportunity' (B-XIV,1), and 'Except for such changes and improvements as might suitably be made with a view to conciliating different feelings, the ceremonial order and the prayers shall be arranged according to the customs and usage of the Dutch High-German Jewish Communities' (B-XIV,2).

As we have seen earlier, the High Consistory had committed itself in advance to leaving the decisions on these subjects to the Chief Rabbi of Amsterdam, and although the Royal decree used a more elegant phraseology, both the above-mentioned articles made it clear that no reforms would be introduced in the order of the services.

Carel Asser and his supporters had been compelled to make this concession since the vehement opposition within the Old Community to any changes on points of religion would have caused any attempts at re-unification of the two communities to founder. Even so we should keep in mind that as far as Asser was concerned – and the same applied to J.D. Meyer – yielding to the demands of the Chief Rabbi did not involve any sacrifice of principles. Both regarded the political and social aspects as outweighing the religious aspects, in the same way as organizational structure was more important than content. Religious plurality could only lead to discord and even schisms, and should therefore be avoided at all costs. They too considered *uniformity* a precondition for achieving their goals, and if this required bowing to the demands of the Orthodoxy, any opposition had to be suppressed. For this reason they fully accepted the demand of the Board of the Community that no religious services were to be held outside the synagogues (the so-called 'private minyanim') and that no diverging liturgy would be used in any synagogue (for example that of the formally dissolved New Community).

They stood their ground on one point only, and that was the abolition of the *Birkhat hagoyim* – the prayer about the gentiles. Earlier we mentioned that in one of his reports to the king, Asser had written: 'It (i.e. the New Community) has discarded all prayers containing imprecations against those that profess other creeds'.[142]

This formulation might create the impression that we are dealing here with certain prayers that formed an essential part of the liturgy. Based on this

---

142 'Elle a écarté de ses prières toutes celles qui contenaient des imprécations contre ceux qui professent d'autres cultes.' In his memorandum dated May 5, 1808.

assumption, it has been surmised[143] and even 'determined'[144] that the New Community had abolished the prayer *Lamalshinim* ('About slanderers').[145] This in turn has tended to reinforce the image of Adath Jesurun as a Reform community, even though a man such as Rabbi Yitzhak Graanboom would never have abolished a prayer that had been included in the *Shemoneh esreh* – the 'Eighteen Benedictions' – by Rabban Gamliel II. The by-laws clearly define the *Birkhat hagoyim*: 'The Prayer commencing with the word *hagoyim*, which is recited on the Day of Atonement, shall be deleted' (B-XIV,4). The morning service of the Day of Atonement contains an unusual hymn beginning with the words 'About the Gentiles', in which a large number of nations are cursed.[146] This prayer does not appear in most *mahzorim* (prayer books for the Jewish Holidays), nor – for that matter – in the Amsterdam version. The text was either copied by hand or published as a leaflet. According to S. Seeligmann there exist (or used to exist) three leaflets of this prayer printed in Amsterdam.[147] The integral text, with a translation, was reproduced in Eisenmenger's notorious work *Judaism Revealed* ('Entdecktes Judenthum', Koenigsberg, 1711) to demonstrate how violently the Jews hated their adversaries.[148] In other words, *Birkhat hagoyim* never formed an essential part of the liturgy, and its abolition could not

143 Quoted by Silva Rosa, *Bijdrage*, pp. 19-20.
144 H. Graetz, *loc. cit.* and, among others, Dubnow, VIII, p. 174 and R. Mahler, *loc. cit.* As against this, Petuchowsky, *op. cit.*, points out that there exists no proof whatsoever for Graetz's claim. For that matter, the abolition of the *Birkhat hagoyim* is not mentioned in the *Melitz yosher*, since it had already been included in the by-laws, so that this decision no longer had to be advocated by Israel Graanboom.
145 This prayer had formed an essential part of the liturgy ever since Rabbi Gamliel had included it as the twelfth benediction in the *Shemoneh esreh* (Talmud Bavli, Berakhot 28b). The first attempt to revise the text was made only in 1838 in Germany, followed by an attempt in 1841 to abolish the entire prayer. See Petuchowsky, *op. cit.*, p. 119 and pp. 223-35. See also *Elke Morgen Nieuw*, *Het Achttiengebed*, Folkertsma Stichting, 1978, pp. 98-100, 257-66.
146 The complete text of the prayer is reproduced in Daniel Goldschmidt, *Mahzor layamim hanoraim* II, Yom Kippur, Jerusalem, 1970, pp. 196-97.
147 About this, see I. Davidson–H. Shirman, *Thesaurus of Medieval Hebrew Poetry* (Hebr.), Vol II, New York, 1970, p. 124, no. 178. About the pamphlets printed in Amsterdam, see S. Seeligmann, 'Anti-christelijke gebeden' in *VA* I, 1 (1924), p. 196.
148 Eisenmenger, *Entdecktes Judenthum*, 1711, pp. 142-45. Eisenmenger reported that a pamphlet with the text of this prayer had been distributed in Frankfort am Main on the Day of Atonement. Since the prayer is mentioned in the *Sefer hanizahon* by Rabbi Yomtov Lipmann-Mülhausen, the Chief Rabbi of Prague (end 14th-early 15th cent.), it may be assumed that the prayer was composed in reaction to the persecutions during the middle of the 14th century. However, more recent research ascribes it to Rabbi Kalonymus the Elder who lived in Germany at the end of the 12th-early 13th cent. See Israel Y. Yuval, 'Vengeance and Damnation, Blood and Defamation': from Jewish Martyrdom to Blood Libel Accusation (Hebr.), *Zion* 2, VIII (1993), esp. pp. 52-55.

be called an intervention of any significance.[149] In his desire to impress the king, C. Asser had presented the reforms of the New Community as much more far-reaching and fundamental than they really were.[150]

There were still other stipulations that according to the Personal Committee did not touch upon ritual, but which the religious leadership nevertheless regarded as undermining orthodoxy. These points related to early burial, marriages forbidden by law and the use of Yiddish.

Early burial (burial on the same day a person had died) was a well-known bone of contention between the Orthodoxy and the Enlightenment. Because of the theoretical possibility that a person only appeared dead, enlightened Jews contended that immediate burial was perilous, in which opinion they were supported by Moses Mendelssohn.[151] Adherents of the New Community obviously followed the views of the enlightened Jews. The Orthodoxy, on the other hand, continued to be guided by the Mishna (Sanhedrin 6:5), according to which it was forbidden to leave a corpse above ground overnight. This viewpoint was heatedly defended by Rabbi Ya'akov Emden, the uncle of the Amsterdam Chief Rabbi, whose rulings bore great authority in Amsterdam.[152] The particular by-law stipulated that a burial could only take place twenty-four hours after death and following the issue of a death certificate by a physician (B-XV,3). On this point the Orthodoxy was by necessity defeated since the ruling applied to all the citizens of the realm.

Another problematic issue was the consecration of marriages between uncle and niece, that were halakhically permitted but forbidden under the laws of the Republic and subsequently also by the Napoleonic Code. Thus far such ceremonies had either been performed illegally or the authorities had chosen to turn a blind eye – in exchange for a bribe. From then on the Jewish authorities acted

---

149 The prayer was replaced by another one that similarly begins with the word '*Hagoyim*'. Of this prayer, too, only the uneven strophes were printed, since the even strophes included highly uncomplimentary expressions about the Gentiles. The degree to which this problem of Jewish-Gentile relations exercised the contemporary mind is attested by a foreword written by Rabbi Avraham Prins, an orthodox Parnas, for a Pentateuch with Rashi commentary and prayers financed by him. The concluding words of this foreword read – in translation – 'Important announcement for anyone reading this book, that in every place where the word *goy* is mentioned, or idolator, or stranger, this always refers to earlier nations who did not believe in the Creator and His Providence, as mentioned by Rambam in his book *Yad hahazakah*, as well as in the *Moreh nevukhim*, but that this in no way refers to the contemporary nations in whose midst we reside; on the contrary, about them our Sages have said: pray for the welfare of the Government, like we are accustomed to pray every Shabbat for the Emperor and the Empress and the entire imperial dynasty, their advisors and ministers, and may the God of Peace bless us with peace. Amen.' (*Hamisheh humsheh torah*, ed. Proops, Amsterdam, 1811).

150 This is after all a prayer that was recited only once a year, and therefore did not belong to the nucleus of the liturgy.

151 For a review of this issue and an exposition of the views of Moses Mendelssohn, see Altmann, pp. 288-93. See also Graetz, Leipzig (2nd. ed., no date), Vol 11, pp. 29-30, 153-54. The two foremost halakhic authorities, Rabbi E. Landau of Prague and Rabbi Jacob Emden prohibited delaying a funeral, except on the specific instructions of the authorities.

152 About his correspondence with Mendelssohn, see Altmann, *loc. cit.* and A. Bik, *R. Jacob Emden* (Hebr.), Jerusalem, 1974, p. 25. There exists a bibliography of the issue of funerals during the Enlightenment period: M. Pelli, *Bekhavlei masoret*, Jerusalem, 1972, see under *Halanat metim*.

to prevent these marriages, threatening anyone involved – in particular the rabbis – with punishment.

However, the most virulent opposition of the enlightened group was directed against the use of Yiddish. The High Consistory went all-out in this struggle, using all the means with which it had provided itself in the by-laws. All teachers had to be able to read and write Dutch; the Bible was to be translated into Dutch (A-32,b,e); from now on minutes of the meetings of the Parnasim would have to be taken in Dutch (A-40); and public announcements in the synagogues had to be made in the manner as determined by the High Consistory (i.e. in Dutch). Besides this, Chief Rabbis would either have to be native Dutchmen or have been resident in The Netherlands for at least six years, and they had to be able to read and write Dutch (B-/x,1). All these requirements clashed with the existing situation. Hardly any of the Jewish teachers spoke Dutch and Tenakh explanations were given in Yiddish. The majority of teachers hailed from abroad, as was also the case with rabbis and Chief Rabbis. In Amsterdam the meetings of the Parnasim were recorded in Yiddish. It is therefore clear that the struggle for the supremacy of Dutch would be fought along a very wide front and – given the fact that all functionaries involved would remain in their positions – promised to be a prolonged affair.

Social and Political Issues

The Dutch supporters of the Enlightenment also aspired towards the amelioration of the conditions of the Jews through education and the acquisition of professional skills.[153] For this reason the High Consistory assumed the 'superintendence' of the entire Jewish educational system, besides – as already mentioned – instructing the Chief Rabbis and teachers to urge the Jews to try and support themselves by means of some business enterprise (retailing) or craft. However, contrary to the situation in Germany, they saw themselves confronted with a problem that made immediate intervention imperative, namely the excruciating poverty of thousands of Jews in Amsterdam and hundreds of others elsewhere in the country.

As they had discovered earlier, professional training was hardly a palliative.[154] The struggle against mendicancy, which both the spiritual and secular leadership was committed to pursue, barely contributed to alleviating poverty.

---

153 About the views of the 'Aufklärer' concerning education and vocational training, see M. Eliav, *Jewish Education in Germany in the Period of Enlightenment and Emancipation* (Hebr.), Jerusalem, 1960, pp. 25-70, 280-81. Besides Mendelssohn and Weisl, David Friedlander also had considerable influence on the leaders of the New Community.

154 In 1798 twenty-seven Jewish citizens founded the association 'Voor Arbeid en Vlijt', with the purpose of 'educating indigent youths in all kinds of handiworks, crafts and sciences and following the conclusion of their courses and after they have mastered the crafts they have learned, fully to establish them in these.' The membership of the association expanded considerably, up to 446 members in 1807 – in stark contrast to the trifling number of pupils in the same year: no more than eight students and three graduates. See Belinfante, *Bijdragen*, p. 313.

The Jewish community could not shirk its obligation to support the indigent, both directly, by means of handouts, and indirectly by supporting hospitals, orphanages, physicians for the poor, nurses, midwives, pharmacists and free medicines. For more than a century the Welfare fund (*Kupat hatzedakah*) had provided the enormous amounts needed for this purpose. By far the most important source of income of the Welfare funds had been profits from the meat-hall, for which the Community had obtained a monopoly from the Amsterdam municipality. Yet it was this obligation for Jews to patronize the meat-hall – and the penalties for failing to do so – that had been a thorn in the side of Felix Libertate. Much of the propaganda among the members of the Old Community and complaints to the authorities related to this monopoly. The cancellation of the monopoly also conformed to an article in the by-laws, according to which the Jewish communal establishment had no right to interfere in the personal lives of its members.[155] However, the inevitable result was that the Jews of Amsterdam started buying meat from private ritual butchers, or ordered meat from outside the city. Apart from this, it was impossible to verify whether everyone purchased kosher meat to begin with. The obvious result was a serious decline in income for the meat-hall – and thus the Welfare fund. Actually, the Personal Committee had foreseen this danger. One of its solutions was a drastic reduction in the number of welfare recipients and the amounts paid (B-VI). Another was the imposition of members' surtax over a period of ten years (an additional ten pennies to the guilder), which was paid into a special fund for the establishment and maintenance of orphanages for boys and girls and the vocational training of children (B-VI, 9-11).

In addition to reducing the number of welfare recipients in order to counter begging, the Personal Committee introduced another article into the by-laws that had long been on the New Community's list of desiderata: the barring of foreign Jews (A-42-44).[156] This point was initially opposed by the Minister of Religious Affairs, who reminded the members of the Committee that they were in fact forcing the government to discriminate between Jews and non-Jews (for whom there existed no immigration barriers). In reply, the Committee pointed out the danger of the Kingdom of Holland being flooded with hordes of homeless Jews, due to 'the measures taken against many of them in the Alsace

---

155 B-III,8,e: 'Any actions contrary to the religion that take place outside the synagogue are not subject to the authority of the Board of Parnasim.'

156 In the detailed memorandum submitted to the authorities by advocate Fannius Scholten in the name of the New Community (ARA, Staatsbewind, exh. July 6. 7, 1802), the claim that the New Community shirked its responsibilities towards the maintenance of the poor was rejected with the following argument: 'If one would take the trouble to look closely into the position of the Jews of Amsterdam, one would come to the conclusion that the reason why they are forced to apply to the Welfare Board is often due to the persons concerned. If the Parnasim had not themselves been the reason why many of them resorted to begging and vagrancy rather than attempting to establish a proper existence, if one had not put an end to the indiscriminate entry of all alien Jews from Germany or Poland, and if the organization of the Welfare Board would have been placed on a firmer footing – one of the complaints that led to the separation in the first place – there would not have been any reason to worry about the subsistence of the poor in the first place.'

(by Napoleon's notorious decree of March 17, 1808, J.M.), forced conscription and the poverty in parts of Germany and Poland which by necessity will drive them hither'.[157] The violation of Jewish equality was regarded as less serious, since the proposal originated with the Jews themselves, besides which the committee saw it as a temporary measure. The Minister yielded to these arguments, but nevertheless recommended that the matter be referred to the Minister of the Interior.[158]

The Committee made several other requests, not concerning the internal affairs of the Jewish community, but the improvement of its position within the Kingdom. First of all it asked that any 'distinctions' (i.e. discrimination) still existing in several towns be abolished; secondly that Jews in all localities with Jewish communities should be allowed to conduct collections, in the same way that other denominations were permitted; and thirdly, that the existing special oath formula for Jews should be replaced by the formula applicable to all other citizens, except that Jews would take the oath with their heads covered.[159]

Mollerus did not comment on any of these requests, but advised the king to consult the Minister of the Interior.[160] Louis Napoleon, however, granted all three requests,[161] thereby initiating the fulfillment of his promise to help improve the situation of the Jews once a re-unification of both Amsterdam communities had been achieved. But he did more than this. Around the same time he caused the Saturday markets to be moved to another day, in order to enable the Jews to participate in them. He also forced the Amsterdam municipality to admit Jews to the Civil Guard[162] and appointed J.D. Meyer and C. Asser to important governmental offices,[163] a precedent in the history of The Netherlands that would remain an exception for many years to come.

Undoubtedly Louis Napoleon would have done a lot more for the Jews, had he been granted the time and the means. But the growing financial and political difficulties, the exacerbation of the conflicts with his powerful brother, as well as the military and financial commitments he was forced to assume, would – his good intentions notwithstanding – have disastrous consequences for the Jews as well.

Implementation Difficulties of the Royal Decree of September 12, 1808

There were many problems to be solved before the Royal decree of September 12, 1808, could be implemented and the High Consistory could begin function-

157 In the above-mentioned document dated August 11, 1808.
158 Mollerus to the king in the above-mentioned memorandum of August 30, 1808.
159 See note 157.
160 See note 158.
161 At the time of the decision to establish the High Consistory. See also Wolff, pp. 65, 97.
162 See J. Michman, 'De Emancipatie van de Joden in Nederland', in *Bijdragen en Mededelingen betreffende de Geschiedenis der Nederlanden*, 96, (1981), p. 80. See also ARA, Coll. Janssen, no. 25.
163 J.D. Meyer was appointed Director of the *Koninklijke Courant* (Royal Gazette) and C. Asser Head of the 2nd Division of the Ministry of Religion.

ing. Even the final composition of the High Consistory appeared undecided, and the Council was not nominated until December 17, 1808. But for two delegates, S.Z. Philips and J. Littwak,[164] whose place was taken by E.H. Keyzer[165] and I.D. Salomons,[166] the Amsterdam representation coincided with the Personal Committee. The installation took place on January 4, 1809, and that same day the High Consistory held its first meeting.

Opposition by Members of the New Community

A number of things happened in the period between the publication of the Royal decree and the installation of the High Consistory. We have already discussed the futile attempts of certain members of the dissolved New Community to be given the right to conduct their own synagogue services. Another matter that created considerable commotion was the future of the personnel of the New Community. In the re-unification arrangement (C) several dispositions had been made with regard to the property and the employees of the New Community. Its property – together with the Community's debts – was transferred to the Old Community, which meant that the latter acquired the synagogue building and the adjoining rooms. These rooms, however, were immediately handed over to the High Consistory, which also appointed the New Community's former beadle, M.S. Alexander, as its secretary. All other employees were transferred to the united community.

Even so, there remained two problems. The re-unification arrangement also included a settlement for the widow of Rabbi Yitzhak Graanboom. Besides receiving an annual pension of Df. 1,575, she was granted free occupancy of the ground floor apartment adjoining the synagogue (C-7,8). No provisions were made for the Chief Rabbi's son Israel, indicating that the members of the Personal Committee, who obviously were quite familiar with the New Community's affairs, did not consider him a legitimate functionary. The opposition, however, led by H. Salomo, tried to prove that he had succeeded his father as a teacher and therefore should be assigned a post within the new system.[167] Besides consideration for the Chief Rabbi's family, the members' concern was probably also due to the fact that the appointment of Israel Graanboom to some

---

164 As we have seen, J. Littwak opposed a reunification, which may have been the reason why he was shunted aside. As a result, the proponents of the merger, although constituting a minority within the New Community, were represented in the High Consistory by two members (C. Asser and H. de Lemon), and the minority by one member (H.A. van Laun). However, it is also possible that his financial circumstances prevented Littwak from accepting this honorary office. Soon after he was appointed as Advisor and Translator for Hebrew and Chaldean at the High Consistory (ARA, Notulen en Verbalen etc., Session 30, Lent Month, 1809).

165 As early as the beginning of the 18th century members of the Keyzer family were included among the Parnasim. Lion Hermanus Keyzer (Leib ben Manus) was Parnas in 1796; Eliazer (Leizer) Hermanus Keyzer was a member of the College of former Parnasim.

166 Isaac David Salomons (= Eisik ben David Preger). About the Preger family, see G. Yogev, *op. cit.*

167 Letter from H. Salomo, ARA, Staatssecr. Lod. Nap., Inv. no. 158, dated September 29, 1808: Salomo claimed that the son of the departed Chief Rabbi was discharging his father's duties.

religious function or other would ensure a continuation of his father's ideas and decisions, and we may assume that the authorities regarded this as potentially disruptive. In any case, the request was turned down on the grounds that Israel Graanboom had at no time been a salaried official of the community.[168]

The second problem concerned Leizer ben Mendele Shohet, the ritual slaughterer of the New Community, who also acted as Chief Cantor and buyer of livestock. He was allowed to stay on as cantor (at a remuneration of Df. 1,500 annually) while continuing to fulfill his function as *shohet* and buyer of livestock (at another Df. 1,400 per year) (C-10). Surprisingly this arrangement turned out to be the most controversial, and to understand this we must clarify the situation which existed within the Old Community.

Opposition within the Old Community

The Royal decree of September 12, even though the Parnasim regarded it as a victory for the Old Community, created serious anxiety among many members. The decision was published on September 24 in the *Royal Gazette*, and four days later the Parnasim held an urgent meeting, to which J.D. Meyer was also invited. It was decided to send a letter to the Minister of Religious Affairs, informing him that there were 'poorly enlightened and less perceptive individuals in the community who perceived in some of the articles of this law an intention to effect changes in the religion'. The Minister was requested to issue a statement that there 'would be no affront whatsoever to the religion'.[169] It would seem that the Chief Rabbi also belonged to these 'poorly enlightened individuals', since L. Rintel (E.P. de Jongh) had been summoned to the burgomaster, who had informed him that the Chief Rabbi and certain members of his community were campaigning against the decree of September 12.[170] The Chief Rabbi denied the accusation, but admitted he had suggested that a number of concerned members go to the '*Kaals Stub*' (the meeting hall of the Parnasim) to ask for clarification.

The Parnasim informed the burgomaster about this, requesting him to exert his influence, while at the same time 'persuading His Majesty to appoint as members of the High Consistory and the council of Parnasim such persons who, because of their known devotion to the Jewish religion and its tenets, are esteemed and honored by the majority of the members of the Community'.[171]

---

168 In his commentary on Salomo's letter (*loc. cit.*, October 6, 1808) Mollerus writes that Israel was at one time employed by the New Community as 'assistant butcher' at a salary of Df. 50, but that he had resigned this position 'since he apparently preferred his vocation as a merchant or shopkeeper'. He never was a rabbi or teacher, 'and whenever he occasionally had intended to act in such a capacity, the [Board of the] Community had prohibited him.' This suggests the existence of frictions within the Community, and thus it is possible that Israel was cultivated by the more radical current.

169 *Protokolbuch*, September 29, 1808.

170 *Op. cit.*, fo. 329.

171 *Loc. cit.* It was said that the Chief Rabbi denied 'wanting to criticize His Majesty's decisions or to lend himself to any conspirational attempts at changing the Royal decree.'

The Minister actually wrote a letter in which he confirmed that the by-laws would be applied '*zonder di geringste aynbrukh tsu velen makhen in eynige zakhen velkhe gerekhnet kenen veren das vesoures hayehudim zu betrefen*'.[172] It was decided to write a letter thanking the Minister and the king, while once again emphasizing the concern of the members.[173]

The entreaties of the Parnasim were effective to the extent that the composition of the High Consistory turned out to be more favorable for them than that of the Personal Committee (six to three, as against of five to four), and the Parnasim were no doubt gratified and reassured by this reinforcement.[174] Not so the Chief Rabbi and his supporters. The Chief Rabbi had agreed to the new arrangements on the condition that he alone would determine the 'order of ceremony' of the Community. No doubt he regarded this breach of promise as both a threat and an insult, whereas the new by-laws, which seriously curtailed his authority, must also have caused him considerable concern. This explains why, when following the installation of the High Consistory and the new Board of Parnasim, the first steps were taken towards the implementation of the re-unification scheme, the Chief Rabbi seized the only remaining instrument of power left to him: a refusal to issue a ritual slaughterer's certificate to the *shohet* of the former New Community. Even though the individual concerned had been a *shohet* before the schism, the Chief Rabbi decided to withhold his certificate as long as no 'order of ceremony' had been determined. All the meat slaughtered by him (in the small hall of the former New Community) was declared *treyfa* (ritually unfit) and thus forbidden for consumption by Jews. The Chief Rabbi even refused to examine the *shohet*.[175] This refusal led to a violent argument with the new Parnas J.J. Jacobs, a former member of the New Community, during which the latter grievously insulted the Chief Rabbi.[176] As a result the Chief Rabbi refused to enter the Great Synagogue, while his followers organized themselves to assist him in his struggle. The commotion within the community caused serious concern among the High Consistory and the Parnasim, and it explains why a final decision on the liturgy suddenly became a matter of the utmost urgency. The High Consistory gave the Chief Rabbi of Amsterdam, as well as the son of Rabbi Yitzhak Graanboom, eight days to submit their memoranda, whereas the Chief Rabbis of Rotterdam and The Hague were given a fortnight to submit their opinions, however without enter-

---

172 'Without wanting to impinge in any way on matters that might be regarded as pertaining to the religion of the Jews.' *Loc. cit.*

173 The Parnasim carefully wrote 'qu'ils ne peuvent avoir aucun doute sur l'interprétation de quelque articles un peu obscurs, sur la manière dont Votre Majesté fera examiner les rites religieux et sur les nominations que Votre Majesté s'est réservé', *op. cit.*, fo. 335.

174 The Board of Parnasim had been decimated by the death of several members, as a result of which only Benedictus Lemans was appointed to the High Consistory, whereas all members of the Committee of Former Parnasim had been appointed. J.D. Meyer also was the sixth member of the Old Community in the High Consistory.

175 *Bendit Wing*, pp. 97-98.

176 *Loc. cit.*

ing into explanations.[177] Meanwhile the tumult within the Amsterdam community continued. Even after a visit of the *shohet*, in the company of two former leaders of the New Community, Joel Stokvis and S.M. Metz, the Chief Rabbi persisted in his refusal to examine him; even worse, he ordered an announcement in his name to be made in the synagogue during the Sabbath service that only meat slaughtered by ritual butchers authorized by him may be eaten.[178] This, by the way, was the first time he appeared in the synagogue following the insult by Parnas Jacobs, and he was cheered as if he had achieved a great victory.[179]

However, the rejoicing was premature, for the following Monday the Parnasim called an urgent meeting and decided that the *shohet* would be allowed to slaughter in the small meat-hall only, and that the Chief Rabbi would be obliged to examine him.[180] On Wednesday the High Consistory also met in a special session. Besides issuing a serious warning to the Chief Rabbi, it invoked the Parnasim to urge the members of the community to maintain peace and quiet, particularly during synagogue services.[181] Prior to this a committee from the High Consistory had consulted the Minister of Religious Affairs, who similarly decided to bring his authority to bear. In brief succession the Chief Rabbi's son Naftali and the leaders of the opposition were summoned to the Minister, who beseeched them to convince the Chief Rabbi to moderate his views.[182] The final discussions took place on Thursday, but by Friday a new development had already occurred. The replies from Rabbi Arieh Breslau of Rotterdam and Rabbi J.A. Lehmans of The Hague had arrived, and that same morning the High Consistory met and decided that the matter of the 'order of ceremony' had now been settled. The Parnasim were duly informed, as a result of which they were able to inform a gratified Sabbath synagogue congregation that the remaining issue had been solved and that, consequently, the warning against disturbing the peace in the synagogue no longer applied.[183] The *shohet*, the

---

177 How quickly all this was implemented is shown by the instructions of the High Consistory. The session during which the instructions of the Minister of Religion about the order of service were discussed took place on January 24, 1809.
  The answer of Rabbi J.A. Le[h]mans was received on 21 Shevat (February 7), and that of Rabbi Arie Breslau on 22 Shevat (February 8). Following this, the High Consistory met on the morning of February 10.

178 *Bendit Wing*, p. 98. There is an incorrect date given for the visit, i.e. February 11 instead of February 4.

179 *Op. cit.*, p. 99.

180 *Protokolbuch*, February 4, 1808, fo. 34.

181 ARA, Notulen en Verbalen, etc., February 8, 1808.

182 *Loc. cit.* and *Bendit Wing*, p. 99. This is the first time that supporters of the Chief Rabbis are mentioned by name. Among them was the noted Avraham A. Prins. It is no coincidence that in the same year the latter, together with Itzik Berklau and Hirsch Lehren, acted on behalf of the collection for Eretz Israel, a function that traditionally had been a responsibility of the Jewish Community.

183 *Bendit Wing*, p. 100. The Board of Parnasim met on Saturday night for the purpose of formulating the proclamation that was to be read the next morning in the synagogue of the former New Community. The Parnas J.J. Jacobs protested against this, stating that the decision of the High Consistory contravened the decree of September 12, 1808, and that he reserved the right to take all steps 'necessary to prevent a new schism'. *Protokolbuch*, February 11, 1808, fo. 7.

innocent object of the entire controversy, was examined by the Chief Rabbi and found to be competent.

Notwithstanding the many intimations, the High Consistory's decision remained a heavy and unexpected blow to the former members of the New Community. It appears that they had continued their services on the old footing, even after the installation of the High Consistory, but now the day of reckoning had come. On Friday, February 10, the day of the High Consistory's decision, Rabbi Yitzhak's son, who now called himself Israel Isaacs, petitioned the king to postpone the decision, which in his view clashed with the decree of September 12, 1808.[184] The following Sunday, Samuel Moses Metz, the former treasurer of the New Community, disallowed the reading of the official announcement of the Parnasim in their synagogue. He even attempted to prevent a subsequent recitation by addressing a petition to the king that very morning.[185] However, all this was to no avail.[186]

So intense was the dismay among the remaining members of the New Community that the king was swamped with dozens of letters beseeching him at least to allow them to rent their own premises, where they would be able to practice their religion according to their own convictions.[187] Their theatrical style and sentimentality notwithstanding, these letters nevertheless evoke a feeling of profound loss. We are dealing here with the hard core of the former New Community, and it looks as if these people were prepared to make great sacrifices in order to preserve their distinctive, modernized brand of Judaism.[188] However, they were never given a chance: neither the king or his counselors, nor the High Consistory, intended to risk the arduously contended peace and unity for the sake of a few dozen conscientious objectors. Besides, several other issues concerning the new structure, which were far more important in the eyes of the decision makers, and which were expected to arouse

---

184 Req. Samuel Moses Metz. All petitions, 33 in total, were referred to the Ministry of Religion for advice.

185 Req. Samuel Moses Metz, dated Februariy 12, 1809. He requested the king, who happened to be in Amsterdam during that week, to grant him an urgent audience.

186 *Bendit Wing*, p. 101.

187 Contrary to previous actions, during which large numbers of persons had signed the same petition, all members this time submitted their own petitions, even though – with a few exceptions – they were identical. The first batch was sent on Febuary 21, the second between March 6 and 17.

188 One example of the sentimental tone in which many of these petitions were worded: 'Reasons why the supplicant reverently turns to Your Majesty, and humbly cries, prays and supplicates' Interesting is the claim of most of the petitioners that 'they are bereft of a sacred place of congregation' – or even 'a church' – but three of them (A. de Jong, E.M. Calff and J. Wertheim) write that they lack 'a Temple'. The first Reform Temple would be inaugurated in July 1810 by Israel Jacobson in Seesen (in the Kingdom of Westphalia-Brunswick) (*EJ*, 9, col. 1241). Could the use of the word 'Temple' possibly indicate contacts between the German and the Dutch 'enlightened' currents?

The petitions also include three from children of members of the New Community (Daniel Metz, 13 1/2 years old; S.M. de Jong, 14 1/2 years old; and S.M. Muller, 16 years old). Contents, style and signatures show that these letters were drafted by one of the leaders of Adath Jesurun rather than by the children themselves. The children concerned formed part of a generation that had grown up in the atmosphere of the Adath Jesurun liturgy.

opposition, were awaiting implementation. One of these was the struggle against the use of Yiddish. According to the by-laws, all publications and announcements, whether produced by the government, the High Consistory or the Parnasim, were to be phrased in Dutch. This instruction turned out to be unenforceable. In addition to provoking angry reactions in the synagogue, the announcements in the vernacular also missed their point, since most of the congregation knew too little Dutch to understand them. Reluctantly the High Consistory was forced to allow announcements not seemingly related to religious matters, such as the sale of seats or appeals for charitable contributions, to be made in Yiddish.[189] This was yet another indication that the moving forces within the High Consistory, especially J.D. Meyer and C. Asser, had underestimated the opposition that their modernization program had provoked.

Conclusions

The High Consistory was not the culmination of an organic or evolutionary development among the Jewish population. Nor was it what the supporters of Felix Libertate had intended. Their view had been focused on the large High-German community in Amsterdam, and even their contacts with like-minded groups in other places were incidental to this larger purpose. The High Consistory was a French fabrication – a product of French centralism and formalism, and as such diametrically opposed to the federalism and particularism of the Republic, where compromises with existing laws were not necessarily regarded in a negative light.

Yet, despite the French dominance, the unification of all High-German Jews within a national framework would have failed, had not Louis Napoleon taken the initiative and placed the full weight of his royal authority behind his brainchild. He acted out of sympathy for the Jews, whose miserable economic situation he attempted to improve, while showing sincere consideration for their religious feelings.

Even so, when it came to practical implementation, he could not avoid deferring to the small 'enlightened' minority among the Jewish community. It comprised an intellectual *avant garde* which was interested in supporting the king's efforts to integrate the Jews into Dutch society, but – unlike Louis Napoleon himself – was sufficiently unscrupulous to employ coercive measures against their intractable co-religionists.

The simultaneous introduction of the Consistorial system in France and in Holland was, of course, no coincidence, but this fact only tends to highlight the

---

189 Highly characteristic is an early request by the Parnasim, dated 19 Grass Month (= April) 1809 to the High Consistory objecting to the use of the Dutch language 'because of the adverse feelings this is likely to arouse among the majority of the members of the Community, whose mentality we know better than anyone else, and whose consequences would be immeasurable.' The Parnasim write that 'they only half understand the Dutch language', and that recitations in this language would be considered an insult, 'quite apart from the fact that erroneous interpretations would render these announcements ineffectual and entirely illusory'.

discrepancies between the two systems. In France the system was conceived and enforced by Napoleon and his government for the purpose of controlling the Jews and harming them economically. Louis Napoleon allowed the Jews to conceptualize their own structure, and the far-reaching intervention by his Government did not conflict with the views of his Jewish advisors; they had long ago abandoned the ideal of a democratization of Jewish society with which they had started their struggle in 1795. Realizing that they would never succeed in getting the overwhelming majority of the Jews on their side, they chose to impose their minority views on the masses and such other persons as were considered to represent this majority, including Avraham Prins of Amsterdam and Moshe Lehren of The Hague, who were deliberately excluded from leading positions.

The subordination of the spiritual to administrative authority also fitted very well into this scheme. During the Republic the Parnasim had already become more powerful than the Chief Rabbis – in the same way that the Regents dominated the Christian clergy – but the Parnasim had been more considerate of the rabbis' authority in religious matters, as well as in the acceptance of their halakhic decisions. Under the Consistorial system the subordination of the Jewish clergy to the administrative bodies had simply been institutionalized, as shown, for instance, by the obligation of the Chief Rabbi to answer the summons of the Parnasim to appear at their meetings.

The Chief Rabbi had emerged victorious on one very momentous issue: existing religious traditions would not only be maintained, but had been declared mandatory for the entire organization; alternative rites were no longer tolerated. From the Orthodoxy's point of view this situation was in fact preferable to the one that had existed before. Yet the Orthodoxy paid a high price for this one, undoubtedly very important, achievement, for from then on it was virtually ignored in the national Jewish representation, which as such was subordinate to a Minister, but in practice was subordinated to a civil servant.

The leading personalities in the Orthodox camp, particularly the Chief Rabbi of Amsterdam and his supporters, had only themselves to blame for this turn of events. The management of their opposition to the plans of the authorities had been devoid of any vision, without the slightest feeling for the drastic changes that were taking place in the surrounding society.

Of course they protested, but without any underlying constructive plan of action. Once it had become clear that under the new constellation no deviations from the traditional ritual were to be accepted, they did not consider it necessary to study the new construction to ensure that their highest authority, the Chief Rabbi, would not be shifted backstage. Whereas the Chief Rabbi and the rabbis in the French *Consistoire* occupied prominent positions, in The Netherlands not a single rabbi or even Chief Rabbi ever occupied a seat in one of the higher administrative organs.

The Consistorial system of Louis Napoleon was a rigid structure that failed to survive the incumbency of its architect. Following the annexation of The Netherlands to France, it was for a brief period replaced by the French system. But even after the establishment of the Kingdom of The Netherlands under William I, it proved impossible to re-establish the High Consistory. Too little consideration had been given to ancient traditions and the typical Dutch particularism. Nevertheless, Louis Napoleon's concept of a national organization and the outlines of the structure created by him continued to form the basis for the organization of Dutch Jewry. With good reason the Personal Committee prided itself on having formulated a set of by-laws without taking into account the pre-existing synagogue regulations. In addition, all subsequent by-laws can be traced back to the High Consistory, which was the forerunner and prototype of the present Dutch Israelite Synagogue Association.

7 Haskalah – but Orthodox

Haskalah is the Hebrew term for the Enlightenment. Yet, although the underlying ideology is the same, Haskalah has had its own history and evolution. For one thing, the Haskalah started later – during the 1770s, when the Enlightenment had already reached its zenith. It also lasted longer – in Eastern Europe until the 1880s. Moreover, there are considerable differences in terms of content, for reasons relating to the Jewish religion and way of life, the structure of Jewish society and the geographical dispersion of the Jewish communities.[1]

The great precursor of the Haskalah movement was Moses Mendelssohn, whose philosophical writings, written in Berlin, propagated a different approach to Judaism.[2] Mendelssohn adhered to the orthodox way of life, but his views demolished the walls of the Jewish spiritual ghetto. He was the father of a movement that aspired towards a renaissance of the Jewish people by the dissemination of the vernacular and the suppression of Yiddish, and through a more tolerant attitude in religious matters. All of this was aimed at a more harmonious adjustment to the Gentile society and would, at a later stage, result in a striving towards integration. The Jews had to be released from their isolation and lifted out of their state of spiritual narrow-mindedness and economic deprivation.

Mendelssohn had considerable influence on the non-Jewish proponents of the Enlightenment,[3] and his ideas aroused considerable interest in the Dutch

---

1 There exists extensive literature about the *Haskalah*. See, for instance, *JE*, Vol. 7, cols. 1433-1452. A good insight is provided by Katz' books *Ghetto* and *Tradition*. The latest contribution is Shmuel Feiner, *Haskalah and History*, Jerusalem, 1995 (Hebr.), with an extensive bibliography (pp. 469-504). As far as I am aware, not a single study exists on its reception in The Netherlands.

2 The standard text about Mendelssohn is Alexander Altmann, *Moses Mendelssohn, A Biographical Study*, Philadelphia, 1973.

3 Mendelssohn had *i.a.* an important share in the preparation of C.W. Dohm's epoch-making brochure *Über die bürgerliche Verbesserung der Juden* (1781); see also Altmann, *op. cit.*, pp. 449-71.

Republic.[4] However, in Jewish circles in the Republic the Haskalah only made its weight felt at the end of the 18th and the beginning of the 19th century.

This is in itself rather surprising, for ever since the middle of the 17th century, the walls separating Jew and Gentile in the Republic had not been as high and impenetrable as elsewhere. The Jews had become accustomed to living in a more or less 'neutral' environment which enabled them to shed their orthodoxy, but without being forced to join one of the Christian denominations.[5] The most famous example was Spinoza who, despite being expelled from the Jewish community, was otherwise left in peace. The wealthy Portuguese Jews, who included ship-owners and army victuallers, and some of whom held diplomatic positions, lived in a style comparable to their Christian colleagues. Jews had even joined Freemasons' lodges.[6] Isaac de Pinto, a renowned 18th-century writer of political and economic tracts, as well as holding several positions in the Portuguese-Jewish community, maintained contacts with Prince William IV.[7]

---

4   Mendelssohn's works *Über das Erhabene und Naive*, and his *Letter to Lavater* (1769 and 1770) were translated into Dutch by Professor Rijklof Michael van Goens (1748-1810) of the University of Utrecht. Van Goens's friend Tetsch also translated one of Mendelssohn's treatises: *Onderzoek der redelijke gevoelens* (1769). The Orthodox Calvinist journal *Nederlandsche Bibliotheek* condemned Van Goens' translation as a flagrant denigration of the Christian faith. The latter replied by means of a 'Bericht van Professor van Goens rakende de Recensie van zijn vertaling van de verhandeling van Moses Mendelssohn over het verhevene en naive in de fraaie wetenschappen' ('Declaration by Professor van Goens concerning his translation of the treatise by Moses Mendelssohn about the Exalted and Naive in the Fine Arts'; Utrecht, 1771). Van Goens was forced to resign from the university and in 1776 took up permanent residence abroad. See M. Weytens, *Nathan en Shylock in de Lage Landen*, Groningen, 1971, pp. 66-68. Another of Mendelssohn's Dutch correspondents was the Amsterdam Baptist minister Allard Hulshof (1734-1795). The first Jew to translate one of Mendelssohn's writings, viz. *Phädon* (1769) was a certain David ben Phoebus Wagenaar of Amsterdam; Altmann, *op. cit.*, pp. 192-93, 790. Sigmund Seeligmann's thesis, according to which Mendelssohn had only limited influence in The Netherlands, is refuted by the expressions of admiration of all Dutch *maskilim*. About this, see J. Michman, The Impact of German Jewish Modernization on Dutch Jewry, in Jacob Katz (ed.), *Toward Modernity*, New York, 1987, pp. 178, 184.
5   About the 'neutral' society, see Jacob Katz, *Exclusiveness and Tolerance*, Oxford University Press, 1961, pp. 156-81. Yoseph Kaplan, in his study of the *herem* (excommunication) in the Portuguese community of Amsterdam, states: 'The Portuguese Jewish community of seventeenth-century Amsterdam had to confront problems which were to characterize the other Jewish communities of Europe from the time of the Emancipation.' ('The Social Function of the Herem in the Portuguese Jewish Community of Amsterdam in the Seventeenth Century', *DJH* 1, p.152).
6   See R.J. van Pelt, 'De loge als speel- en oefenplaats der joodse emancipatie in Nederland', *Toth, Tijdschrift voor Vrijmetselarij* 30 (1979), pp. 67-76. A practical problem for Jewish Freemasons was that they were expected to participate in the communal meals. Only at the beginning of the 19th century, when High-German Jews began to join the Freemasons, was an accommodation requested. This suggests that the Portuguese Jews, who had been members ever since the 18th century, had not previously objected.
7   J.S. Wijler's dissertation about Isaac de Pinto from 1923 has been superseded by the Ph.D. thesis of I.J.A. Nieuwenhuis, *Een Joodse Philosophe Isaac de Pinto (1717-1787) en de ontwikkeling van de politieke economie in de Europese Verlichting*, Amsterdam, 1992. See also the articles by B.H. Popkin about De Pinto: 'Hume and Isaac de Pinto', *Texas Studies in Literature and Language* XII (1970), pp. 417-30; 'Hume and Isaac de Pinto II, Five New Letters', in W.B. Todd (ed.), *Hume and the Enlightenment*, Edinburgh, 1974, pp. 99-127; 'Isaac de Pinto's Criticism of Manderville and Hume on Luxury', *SVEC* 154 (1976), pp. 2705-14.

Hebrew writing, one of the ideals of the Haskalah, could look back on a long tradition within the Sephardi culture in Amsterdam.[8]

Neither were Jewish contacts with the gentile population restricted to the elite. Certain indigenous robber bands included quite a few Jews,[9] and if we believe one Amsterdam author, there were even Jewish prostitutes.[10]

In light of the above, one would expect the process of adaptation and integration within the Republic to have advanced further than in Germany, for instance. Yet this was not the case. Most of the above-mentioned phenomena remained more or less confined to the Portuguese Jews, who nevertheless remained loyal to their own community, out of pride for their ancestral heritage and their links with the exalted Iberian culture. Many High-German Jews also maintained contacts with a cross-section of Dutch gentile society, but the Jewish masses clung to their religious traditions, using a Dutch form of Yiddish as their vernacular. This phenomenon was by no means restricted to Amsterdam alone: outside the capital violations of the religious code similarly were exceptions, and offenders were punished.

These and other subjects formed part of the discussions about whether, and to what extent, the Jews of the Batavian Republic should be recognized as enfranchised citizens. Both religion and language were involved in the debate. The same had been the case in Germany and France, but two factors tended to accentuate these aspects in the Batavian Republic. First of all the Dutch National Assembly included quite a few Protestant theologians who were well informed about Judaism. According to them the Jewish faith, by its own admission, regarded the Jews as a separate nation, whose sojourn outside the Holy Land was a temporary expedient, pending the coming of their Messiah, a 'King' who would take them back to Zion.[11] The same argument had been used in Germany and France, but there advocates of emancipation such as Dohm and Abbé Grégoire had countered it by stating that the Messiah was a purely spiritual concept. For in saying this, they could refer to Mendelssohn, who had

---

8   Earlier historians of modern Hebrew literature, all of whom originated from strictly orthodox Jewish milieus in Eastern Europe, regarded the secular poetry of the Sephardim in Amsterdam and Italy as a precursor of the Haskalah. In reality the Amsterdam Hebrew poets, including David Franco Mendes and Isaac Cohen Belinfante, continued the genre, but were also its last exponents. With the publication of the collection *Shir emunim* (1793), which contained both religious and secular poetry, this current came to an end. See my dissertation, *David Franco Mendes*, Amsterdam-Jerusalem, 1951, pp. 9-19.

9   Florike Egmond, *Banditisme in de Franse tijd*, Soest, 1986. Despite their collaboration in hold-ups, the Jewish conspirators basically continued to observe the traditional Jewish way of life – and not only for religious reasons: '...religious observance was only one among the many external (although by no means superficial) characteristics, such as rituals, names, and language.' (Florike Egmond, 'Contours of Identity: Poor Ashkenazim in the Dutch Republic', *DJH* 3, p. 221).

10 *De ongelukkige levensbeschrijving van een Amsterdammer*, Amsterdam, 1965, pp. 60, 103-5.

11 See in particular the address by Prof. Y. van Hamelsveld (1743-1812) during the debates in the National Assembly about the emancipation of the Jews. The subject would continue to exercise him, as evidenced by his book *Geschiedenis der Joden sedert de verwoesting van Jerusalem tot den tegenwoordigen tijd*, Amsterdam, 1807. See also Bolle, pp. 138-44 and A. Halff, 'The Discussions in the National Assembly of the Batavian Republic on the Emancipation of the Jews' (Hebr.), *SDJ* 1, pp. 201-40.

given the Messiah-idea only the most cursory attention.[12] Messianism was a completely alien concept to him, his Utopia being a society in which people of different views and beliefs could live peaceably together.[13] In such a world there was no room for a 'King-Messiah', who would place himself at the head of the 'nations streaming to Mount Zion' (Isaiah 2:2; Micah 4:1). In the course of time Liberal Judaism was to adopt this line of thought by tucking the Messiah safely out of sight behind a vaguely humanistic façade.

A second factor in the Batavian Republic, not present elsewhere, reinforced the viewpoint of the Protestant theologians. This was the very large, and in terms of religious custom and language quite distinct, Jewish community in Amsterdam, whose existence complicated the religious aspects of the debate even further.

One of Mendelssohn's disciples, David Friedrichsfeld, joined the emancipation debate with a brochure called *Republikanische Gesinnung und Judenmessias*. Being a child of the Republican age, and to counter any suspicion that the Jews were monarchists, he naturally described the Messiah not as a king, but as a superhuman being.[14] In fact, in the same way as only an insignificant number of Jews had returned to the Holy Land from the Babylonian exile, the majority of the Batavian Jews would, if and when the Messianic era arrived, elect to stay in The Netherlands where they had built up and created a livelihood – provided of course they were recognized as equal citizens.

In this respect Friedrichsfeld was entirely correct. Even though the High-German Jews were not yet as well-adjusted to Dutch society as their Portuguese brethren, they definitely felt at home in The Netherlands, and as such were exposed to the prevailing mentality, mind-set and customs of their environment. In 1772 Rabbi ben Issahar Bar poured out his heart in a lengthy Hebrew essay entitled *Olam hadash* ('The New World'), in which he deplored the rampant neglect of even the most basic religious precepts and the adoption of alien cultural habits such as reading French books and visits to the opera and theater.[15] Jews even adopted gentile clothing habits, such as the wearing of tie-wigs. In 1788 the Chief Rabbi of Rotterdam also railed against this effeminate habit in one of his sermons.[16] The daughters of Parnas Benjamin Cohen

---

12 See Isaac Eisenstein-Barzilay, 'The Jew in the Literature of the Enlightenment', in Abraham G. Duker, Meir Ben-Horin, *Emancipation and Counter-Emancipation*, New York, 1974, p. 106. Altmann completely disregards the Messianic idea in his biography of Mendelssohn. See, however, Bolle, pp. 74-75.

13 Katz, *Exclusiveness*, pp. 177-81.

14 About David Friedrichsfeld, see D. Michman, 'David Friedrichsfeld – A Fighter for Enlightenment and Emancipation of the Jews' (Hebr.) *SDJ* 1, pp. 151-99. Other brochures by Friedrichsfeld in the struggle for emancipation were *Beleuchtungen über den Vortrag des Bnr. v. Swinden bey den Stellvertretern des Volks von Holland in den Haag, die Stimmgerechtigkeit und Bürgerrecht der Juden betreffend*, December 14, 1795, and (possibly) *Emanzipationsforderungen der Juden an die National-Versammlung von Holland* (see D. Michman, *op. cit.*, p. 155-56).

15 The unpublished manuscript is in the collection of M.H. Gans. For the contents, see Bolle, pp.66-67.

16 About this, see E. Slijper, 'Een merkwaardig proces over de haardracht der vrouw bij de Joden te Rotterdam', *Rotterdams Jaarboekje*, 1910, pp. 25-49.

were accused of indecent conduct,[17] notwithstanding the fact that even girls from well-to-do families behaved in a markedly different way from their German sisters. There girls from established families were the first to abandon their Jewish heritage and convert to Christianity. Several of the ladies concerned gained considerable renown because of their salons, frequented by prominent literary figures. Nothing like this existed in The Netherlands, and regardless of a girl's education, once she was married she retired into her husband's shadow.

The Reception of the Haskalah – the Initial Period

Despite being a disciple of Mendelssohn, the earlier-mentioned Friedrichsfeld already belonged to the second Enlightenment generation. Amsterdam had made an important contribution to the first period thanks to two notable personalities, both of whom spent some time in this city. The first was Naphtali Herz Weisl (Wessely), a Hebrew grammarian and poet and a pioneer of educational reform.[18] The second was Salomo (of) Dubno, a Torah-commentator, poet and one of the foremost authorities of the Hebrew language.[19] Both men

---

17 In Jacob Preger's letters to his brother in London he impugns the way of life of the Cohen family (May 21, 1785; Sept. 18, 1785). On August 13, 1785 his brother David writes that Gompertz had arrived in London to arrange a marriage between Leib Preger and a daughter of Benjamin Cohen: '...*kenen ale di tekhter nit, ober wir heren zayn liderlikh.*' Yogev, p. 144.

18 Weisl – also called Wessely (1725-1805) – is the pivotal figure of the first Haskalah period. His great-grandfather, Joseph Abraham Reis, was a leading personality in the Amsterdam High-German community at the end of the seventeenth century (D. M. Sluys, 'Bijdrage tot de geschiedenis van de Poolsch Joodschen Gemeente te Amsterdam', in *Feestbundel ter gelegenheid van den zevenstigsten verjaardag van L. Wagenaar*, Amsterdam, 1925, pp. 140-156). He moved to Copenhagen, where his great-grandson also eventually settled. Weisl lived in Amsterdam from 1755 till 1766 (or 1767). About him, and his stay in Amsterdam, see J. Melkman, *David Franco Mendes, A Hebrew Poet*, Amsterdam-Jerusalem, 1951. I have argued that when writing Divrei shalom ve-emet Weisl was inspired by the atmosphere of openness among the Amsterdam Portuguese Orthodoxy, and which which, although conservative by nature, he found it easy to associate. Pelli contests this point of view (The Age of Haskalah, Leiden, 1979, p. 114), without explaining why. Weisl himself wrote in his second letter of Divrei shalom ve-emet: In Amsterdam I have seen with my own eyes that their leaders were men of virtue and honor, and I know that if my letter reaches these men, they will not consider this strange and that they will praise me for my candor and honesty. This is confirmed by D. Franco Mendes, who informed Weisl in a letter that Haham Selomoh Salem, the Portuguese Chief Rabbi of Amsterdam, admired him [letter dated 1 Tammuz 5531 (1771)]. While in Amsterdam, Weisl published a two-volume philological work called *Yain Levanon* (Wine from the Lebanon; 1765-66) with approbations of the Chief Rabbis of Amsterdam and The Hague, which also included poems by Isaac Bashan and the corrector and poet Isaac Hacohen Belinfante. A first biography about him, *Zekher Zaddik* written in Hebrew by Friedrichsfeld, was published in Amsterdam in 1809. Weisl was buried in the Portuguese-Jewish cemetery of Altona (*Zekher Zaddik*, p. 1).

There exists extensive literature about Weisl, but no detailed biography. See, for example, M. Waxman, *A History of Jewish Literature*, III, New York, 1945, pp. 107-19; Jacob S. Raisin, *The Haskalah Movement in Russia*, Philadelphia, 1913; P.M. Pelli, *Struggle for Change: Studies in the Hebrew Enlightenment in Germany at the end of the 18th Century* (Hebr.), Tel-Aviv, 1988. For his impact in The Netherlands, see Frederique P. Hiegentlich, 'Reflections on the Relationship between the Dutch Haskalah and the German Haskalah', *DJH* 1, pp. 207-18.

19 About Salomo (van) Dubno (Dubno, 1738 – Amsterdam, 1813), see E. Carmoly, *Revue Orientale* III (1843-44), pp. 310-12; Raisin, *op. cit.*, pp. 81-82; G. Kressel, *Encyclopaedia of Modern Hebrew Literature* (Hebr.), Merhavia, 1965; I, see under Dubno.

Salomo Dubno, 1738-1813

were profoundly influenced by their contacts with the Portuguese Jews, mainly because of the forthright kind of Portuguese orthodoxy, which did not shrink from contacts with foreign cultures. Weisl was also impressed by the 'dignity' of the synagogue services – so much so that for the remainder of his life he used only the Sephardi pronunciation in his prayers.

There can be no doubt that Weisl's revolutionary scheme for Jewish educational reform, including his suggestion to introduce general subjects into the curriculum, was in large measure inspired by his experiences in Amsterdam. His plea for educational reforms, contained in his brochure *Divrei shalom ve-emet* ('Words of Peace and Truth'; Esther 9:30) created a tremendous stir within the Jewish world and, as we shall see, served as a guide for the educational policy of the Dutch *maskilim*.

Salomo Dubno lived in Amsterdam from 1767 till 1772. Chief Rabbi Saul remembered him from his studies in Dubno. During his residence in Amsterdam Dubno discovered an extremely rare copy of a play called *Leyesharim tehillah* in the library of Etz Haim, the Portuguese rabbinical seminary, written in 1743 by the famous Rabbi Moske Haim Luzatto on the occasion of a marriage in the De Chavez family. It was republished in Berlin in 1780, with an introduction by Dubno, emphasizing that this publication would encourage young people to study the Holy tongue and assist them to learn and teach pure and unadulterated Hebrew.

In 1772 Dubno moved to Berlin as private tutor to the Mendelssohn family. From then on he began his cooperation with Mendelssohn in the preparation of a Jewish translation and commentary of the Bible in German (the *Biur*), for which Dubno supplied the exegesis. That Dubno retained his connections with Amsterdam is evident from the fact that the prospectus for the translation (written in German, but with Hebrew letters) was published in Amsterdam by Proops (1778) under the title *Alim literufah* ('Pages for Healing'). The prospectus was signed by Dubno, and although Mendelssohn's biographer is of the opinion that the text was mainly written by Mendelssohn,[20] it may safely be assumed that the pages regretting the loss of the purity of Biblical Hebrew came from the hand of Dubno.

In 1780 a rift developed between Mendelssohn and Dubno. The details of their quarrel are not relevant to this narrative, but it appears fairly certain that Dubno was alarmed by the fierce criticism Mendelssohn's Bible translation had aroused among leading rabbinical personalities. In his commentary on Genesis (the only book in which he had actively cooperated) he had restricted himself to summarizing the traditional commentaries, and it seems that he wanted to disassociate himself from the by now highly controversial enterprise.[21] Next he attempted to publish his own commentary on Mendelssohn's translation of the Pentateuch, under the name *Netivot hashalom*, in which effort he was encouraged by the foremost rabbinical authority of the time, Rabbi Ezechiel Landau of Prague. In the course of time he returned to Amsterdam, famous but penniless, eking out a living by lending books and manuscripts from his remarkable

---

20 Altmann, *op. cit.*, pp. 369-70.
21 The conflict erupted about the subject of copyright, but it seems that Dubno's break with Mendelssohn was precipitated by a discussion in Berlin with his former teacher from Dubno. Dubno promised his teacher that he would stop collaborating with people, who according to such halakhic authorities as Rabbi Ezechiel of Prague, were guilty of undermining Jewish tradition. See B.H. Auerbach, *Die Geschichte der Israelitischen Gemeinde Halberstadt*, Halberstadt, 1866, pp. 179-80.

private library. Dubno, who always maintained his orthodox way of life, also gave Bible instruction to youngsters, in whom he instilled a love for pure and grammatically correct Hebrew – the original language of the Bible rather than the Hebrew of later rabbinical literature.[22]

There were other German connections during this first period of the Haskalah. The philosopher Naphtali Herz Ulmann from Mainz lived in The Hague, where he wrote his many philosophical works and, among other things, corresponded with Mendelssohn.[23] A book by a certain Yehuda ben Mordekhai (Amsterdam, 1766) contains an approbation by Mendelssohn.[24]

Yet the most interesting expression of the spirit of the Haskalah is to be found in a manuscript by Yekel (Jacob Michael) Weil (1776-1856), a physician whose father, brother and brother-in-law were also physicians.[25] He had received a thorough Talmudic education, and just like the other members of his family, remained orthodox all his life. He began to copy texts that interested him when he was very young, and at the age of fourteen undertook the translation of the *Disticha Catonis*, a 3rd-century book of Latin proverbs that was often used as a teaching manual.[26] In his foreword Weil expresses his fondness for the Talmud on the one hand, and his love of unadulterated Hebrew, on the other. The translation and accompanying commentaries were completed in 1798, the same year that he and his younger brother graduated from Leiden University. Another Hebrew work from his hand, written at about the same time, deals with among other subjects zoology and physics. This interest in the

22 M. de Wulft, a student at the Amsterdam rabbinical seminary, tells about him: '...accompanied by one Salomo Dubno, whose extensive Israelite theological knowledge all of us will no doubt remember'. M. de Wulft, *De zwakke en onbeduidende stem of billijke aanvraag aan den heer S.I. Mulder*, Amsterdam, 1827, p. 6. Already during his first stay in Amsterdam, in 1771, Dubno prepared a catalogue of his library (HS Ros. 469).

23 About him, see S. Seeligmann in Van Zuiden,'s *Gravenhage*, pp. 59-63, and the unpublished dissertation by A. Even-Chen (Hebr.), Univ. of Jerusalem, 1992. His son, Leon Jacob Ulmann (1793-1856) was a prominent *maskil* and *i.a.* a member of *Hanokh lana'ar 'al pi darkho*.

24 *Sefer amudei beth Yehuda* (Hebr.), Amsterdam 5526 (= 1766), in the unpaginated foreword. The author had come from Vilna to Amsterdam. About Yehudah ben Mordekhai Halevi Horowitz, see Y. Zinberg, *Toldoth Sifruth Yisrael*, Tel-Aviv, 1958 (Hebr.), pp. 310-14; Mahler, I, Book 4, pp. 37-40.

25 About him, see L. Hirschel. 'Iets over Dr. Jacob Michael Weil (1776-1856) en zijn familie', *NIW*, 1933 (August 1, 25; Sept. 1). The father, who originated from Mannheim, received a doctorate in medicine at Leiden University in 1774. In his dissertation his son Jacob praised the medical knowledge of the post-Biblical Jewish sages. The manuscript also contains a Hebrew poem in his honor. Jacob became a physician in Nijmegen and married a daughter of another physician, Levie Isaac de Wolff. Eventually he settled in Nijkerk, where he became the focal point of the community. He also gave lessons in Talmud.

    His younger brother Isaac Weil (1779-1855), who also studied medicine in Leiden and graduated simultaneously with him, established a practice in Amersfoort, where he became a parnas and town counselor, as well as treasurer of the Holy Land collection campaign. Their scientific training notwithstanding father and sons all remained strictly orthodox.

26 The collection *Disticha Catonis*, consists of four volumes. The proverbs are of a monotheistic but humanistic tenor without any outspoken Christian imprint. The attitude towards women and slaves is similarly tolerant. This may be the reason why Weil was attracted to these texts. See W.S. Teuffels, *Geschichte der Römischen Literatur*, Leipzig, 1882, pp. 37-38. The manuscript *Minhat Ya'aov-mat'amei Ya'acov* is in the Bibliotheca Rosenthaliana (HS Ros. 168).

general sciences, particularly mathematics and physics, coupled with a preoccupation with pure Hebrew and an adherence to the traditional beliefs, is characteristic of the Dutch Haskalah. In Germany too, people scarcely deviated from the orthodox way of life during this first period, which explains the interest in the Republic for the Haskalah journal *Ha-meassef* ('The Collector'), initially published in Koenigsberg and later in Berlin; in 1785 there were fifteen subscribers in Amsterdam, among whom David Franco Mendes.[27]

Even Naphtali Löwenstamm, the son of the strictly orthodox Amsterdam Chief Rabbi J.M. Löwenstamm, was infected by the Haskalah bug,[28] which indulged him to write both religious and love poems. To the accusations that he also read Gentile treatises, Naphtali responded:

> *And still I was asked: Why did you indulge in learning the sciences, and studied books and theories?*
>
> *I answered them: About this the sages of previous generations said: Know how you should answer [the heretic].*

Nothing is known about Orthodox criticism of the purist Hebrew zealots, until in 1808 the then twenty-three-year old Moses Lemans, or Moshe Treitel as he calls himself in his brochure, put the cat among the pigeons with the *Ma'amar imra zerufa* ('Article about a Pure Diction').[29] In it he argued that the Hebrew pronunciation customary among Sepharadim was more correct than the Ashkenazi pronunciation. During his early youth in Naarden, Lemans had become accustomed to the Sephardi pronunciation, and he continued to use it

---

27 In 1809 there were only eight subscribers in Amsterdam, but 17 in Rotterdam. Franco Mendes contributed several short biographies about Amsterdam Sephardim, for which reason he was – wrongly, as it happens – regarded as a member of the *Ha-meassef* group. See my evaluation in *Franco Mendes, op. cit.*, pp. 9-19.

28 Naphtali married a girl from Koenigsberg, an important center of the Haskalah. He himself settled there, but eventually returned to Amsterdam. His manuscript *Imrei shefer* ('Fine Words' – Bibl. Rosenth. HS 94) contains poems as well as letters and prayers. He started writing in 1798, but remained strictly orthodox.

29 Moses Lemans (Naarden, 1785 – Amsterdam, 1832) was the second most important Hebraist in the Dutch Haskalah after Mulder. He studied mathematics (among others with Judah Litvak), but – besides Hebrew – was also conversant with Greek, Latin, Arabic, Syriac, Chaldaic, German, English, French, Italian and Spanish. He settled in Amsterdam in 1802, where he earned a living as a simple schoolmaster, and afterwards headmaster, before being appointed teacher of mathematics at the Municipal Lyceum (1828). In 1807 he was co-founder of 'Mathesis Artium Genetrix', and in the same year of the association 'Tot Nut en Beschaving'. The combination of mathematics and literature was very popular among the maskilim. He also contributed to *Ha-meassef*. In addition to occasional poetry, he translated Ovid's idyll *Philemon and Baucis* into Hebrew. He corresponded in Hebrew with Professor J.H. van der Palm. Shortly before his death in 1832 he wrote the epic *Pesha' Belgi* (or: *De seditione Belgarum*), a typical example of 'citadel poetry'. He wrote on a wide variety of topics, including an essay called *Een proeve van Talmoedische Wiskunde* (1816).

  Lit.: J. Teissèdre, 'L'Ange', *Konst en Letterbode* (1833), vol. II, pp. 115-19, 130-35; G. van de Vijver, *Jaarboek van Amsterdam* (1832), pp. 100-04; L.J. U(lmann), 'Levensschets van Mozes Lemans', *Jaarboeken der Israëliten in Nederland* (1836), pp. 297-312; Meijer, *da Costa*, pp. 40-47, 138-145. The exchange of correspondence with Van der Palm was published by E. Slijper, *Achava* (1906), 1.11, 1.12), (1907), 1.1, 1.2); *Pesha' Belgi* was rediscovered by the author and published in *SDJ* 1, pp. 241-84. The archives of the Leidse Maatschappij der Letterkunde contain letters to various scholars.

after he moved to Amsterdam.[30] He was able to support his thesis with many confirmations from Jewish sources. Despite his emphatic claim that he did not mean to abolish the existing Ashkenazi pronunciation, his brochure immediately invited a fierce counter-attack in the form of two brochures, both of which were rebutted in the same year. David Friedrichsfeld, the black sheep of Orthodoxy, who was accused of having encouraged Lemans, also joined the fray.[31]

Education

This literary skirmish was a mere incident compared to the far more serious conflicts about education that were to erupt in the same year. All available information indicates that the educational situation of Jewish children was backward in the extreme.[32] Communities in smaller towns usually had a schoolmaster with uncertain qualifications, who eked out a living by accepting a variety of additional occupations such as cantor or synagogue beadle. In larger towns the children of well-to-do families were taught privately, and the wealthiest families even had live-in tutors. In a number of towns, such as Rotterdam, Haarlem, Leeuwarden and Appingedam, the Jewish community maintained schools for indigent children, but in Amsterdam – with the largest concentration of Jews – the situation was nothing less than deplorable. There were only two Jewish schools, the *Talmud Torah* and the *Lomedei Torah*, with (in 1807) rosters of 150 pupils and seven teachers, and 130-150 pupils and five teachers respectively.[33] Together with the Jewish orphanages, which had their own

---

30 The last remaining Portuguese inhabitants of Naarden had handed over their synagogue to the High-German Jews on condition that services would be conducted according to the Sephardi ritual and using the Sephardi pronunciation. This Sephardi island in a High-German sea continued to exist until 1885, when the community changed to the High-German rites and pronunciation. See H. Heinrichs, *De Synagoge van Naarden 1730-1945*, Amstelveen, 1985. The Board of the Naarden community obliquely refers to this fact in a letter to the Consistory of the Zuiderzee region: '...the synagogal and ritual arrangements in this city...differ in several respects from those of other communities and cities.' ARA Bi.Za. (March 2, 1813).

31 The author of the counter brochure *Divrei mesharim* had accused Friedrichsfeld of inciting Lemans to heresy ('...it surely is a temptation by that evil heretic, so perfectly acquaintanted with all heretics and Christian writings, David Friedrich F. Do not make peace with the wicked, says God.'). Friedrichsfeld replied by means of an essay called *Ma'aneh rakh* ('A Gentle Answer'; Prov. 15:1). He had left Amsterdam the previous year and only a month before its publication, he received a letter from Lemans about *Ma'amar imra zerufa*. The opponents' answer was published in a pamphlet *Meishiv heima* ('Turns away anger' – the continuation of Prov. 15:1). About Lemans the first-mentioned brochure stated: 'Who would dare to do something so abhorrent to God as abolishing the pronunciation?' About this polemics, see S. Morag, 'Planned and Unplanned Development in Modern Hebrew', *Lingua*, Vol. VIII (Sept. 3, 1959), pp. 248-49; A.R. Malachi, 'Ben Yehuda and the Sephardic Pronunciation' (Hebr.), *Bizaron* 19, 1957/8, pp. 15-20.

32 An extensive study about Jewish education is D. Michman, 'Jewish Education in the Early 19th Century: from Independence to Governmental Supervision' (Hebr.), *SDJ* 2, pp. 89-138, with a detailed scientific apparatus. An abbreviated version without notes was published in Dutch: D. Michman, 'Joods onderwijs in Nederland, 1606-1905', Stichting Joodse Scholengemeenschap, Amsterdam, 1973, pp. 13-29.

33 GAA, *Protokolbuch* 1807, fo. 219.

educational facilities, there were fewer than 350 pupils.[34] At the end of the eighteenth century some Jewish children began to attend non-Jewish schools, an in itself highly unusual phenomenon, particularly taking into account that they were excused from attending lessons in Christian religious subjects.[35] We have no way of knowing what kind of Jewish education these children received – if at all. It is possible they attended one of the numerous private Jewish schools. According to a report from 1811 there were 60 such institutions in that year with an average of 11.4 pupils each.[36] Together this means an enrolment of 700 children – a fraction of the total number of Jewish children in Amsterdam.

Many of the teachers came from Poland, having exchanged a wretched life in that country for an indigent existence in Amsterdam, even though they were at least free to profess their religion. One item not in short supply was Hebrew textbooks and grammars, both of which were produced in remarkably large quantities in the Republic.[37] Unfortunately they were unsuitable for children, if only because of the language: the schoolmasters and children spoke Yiddish, and their knowledge of Dutch was limited in the extreme.

The first step towards the renewal of Jewish education was taken by Moses Cohen Belinfante, a young teacher at the Portuguese school in The Hague.[38] In 1786 he had given evidence of his modern ideas by placing boys and girls in the

---

34 *Ibid.*, fo. 220. For lack of money the number of wards in the Boys' Orphanage had been reduced from 33 to 21. Only six girls remained in the Girls' Orphanage.

35 In 1797 two of the ten indigent schools in Amsterdam had Jewish pupils. In one school 100 out of the 250-280 pupils were Jewish, and in the second, supervised by the Dutch Reformed Church, 120 out of 400 children. Other towns where Jewish children were accommodated in ordinary schools were Kampen, Enter, Ommen and Rijssen. See D. Michman, *op. cit.*, pp. 124-27.

36 According to S.R. Rodrigues de Miranda, *Amsterdam en zijn bevolking in de negentiende eeuw*, Amsterdam, 1921, p. 66.

37 Johan Leusden (1624-1699) commented that as many Hebrew grammars had been published in the seventeenth century alone as there were weeks in the year. (L. Hirschel in an unpublished dissertation. Bibl. Ros.).

38 Moses Cohen Belinfante (The Hague, 1761 – Amsterdam, 1827). During 1775 and 1776 he tried to study medicine in Copenhagen. His father, Sadic, commented that 'he was a good-for-nothing, and should preferably become a schoolmaster'. After his father's death in 1786 he was appointed principal of a school for indigent children – the first Dutch school in which the Bible and the prayers were taught together with a Dutch translation. Moses Belinfante knew eight languages, and also was a sworn translator. He was co-founder of 'Door Vlijt en Eensgezindheid' ('Through Industry and Solidarity' - 1797). In 1804 he and his brother established a printing business in The Hague. He published a journal, *Bijdragen betrekkelijk de verbetering van den Maatschappelijken toestand der Joden* (1806-07), as well as the *Hollandsche Almanak* (1806-1810). In 1808 he relocated to Amsterdam in order to devote himself to the Bible translation project. Following its collapse and the failure of his bookshop in Amsterdam, he returned to The Hague. During his later years he continued his publishing activities, particularly in the field of Jewish textbooks.

About Belinfante, see H. Somerhausen, *Israelitische Annalen*, May 10, 1840; idem, 'Sur quelques Israélites Hollandais, Souvenirs sémi- seculaires', *Archives Israélites* (1847), pp. 339-47; 398-406; Salo W. Baron, 'Moses Cohen Belinfante, A Leader of Jewish Enlightenment', *Historia Judaica* V, April 1943, pp. 1-26; idem, *Yivo Bletter* XIII (1939), pp. 429-59; Da Silva Rosa, *VA* 5b (Febr. 6, 1929, pp. 300-02); J. Meijer, *Maandblad voor de geschiedenis van de Joden in Nederland*, pp. 22-29, 50- 57, 279-85.

same class. In the same year he and several friends founded the association *Talmidei Sadic*('Disciples of Sadic') in memory of his father, the rabbi of the Portuguese community who had died in the same year.[39] No doubt under the influence of Mendelssohn's Bible translation, the association took the momentous initiative of translating the Hebrew prayers into Dutch. The enterprise was brought to a successful completion, and the entire prayer book was published in four volumes between 1791 and 1793.[40] In 1793 the industrious Belinfante issued yet another publication, a booklet called *Geschenk voor de Israelitische jeugd* ('A Gift for Israelite Youngsters'), that began with several reading lessons and continued with an exposition of basic religious morality – without, however, any references to Jewish religious beliefs or precepts.[41]

The feverish political activities of the members of Felix Libertate contributed nothing towards the advancement of Jewish education. Not until 1806 were any suggestions made for education reform; surprisingly enough these came from within the Old Community. A committee under the chairmanship of J.D. Meyer submitted a comprehensive plan to the Parnasim for 'The Improvement of Education', including the following points.

1. The establishment of a type of school common in Germany and other countries, in which the pupils would be taught 'the fundamentals of faith and morality, as well as arts and sciences'. This school was intended for pupils from well-to-do families, but a small number of 'youngsters of the lower classes who showed signs of superior intellectual capacities' were to be accepted without having to pay.

2. Schools for children from the lower classes, so-called 'normaalscholen' ('normal', or 'normative' schools), with a curriculum consisting of a grounding in religion and morality, reading and writing in the vernacular, elementary mathematics and several handicrafts.

3. The establishment of training courses in arts and crafts, 'not against payment as such, but against the work in kind and certain refunds out of future earnings'.[42]

The reference to Germany proves that the Dutch *maskilim* closely observed the developments in Jewish eduation in that country. We shall return to this relationship later in this chapter.

Interestingly enough, the proposal contained absolutely no reference to Jewish subjects, and neither did the Parnasim in their (evasive) reply mention

39 About *Talmidei Sadic*, see M. Henriques Pimentel, *Geschiedkundige Aanteekeningen betreffende de Portugeessche Israëliten in Den Haag en hunne Synagogen aldaar*, The Hague, 1876, pp. 63-64. The founders were seven young members of the community, 'lovers and practitioners of the Hebrew and Dutch languages'. In course of time they were joined by another five members, including Chief Rabbi David Leon (Bayonne, 1740 – The Hague, 1826). The association existed from 1787 till 1793. Its archives are kept in the Amsterdam Municipal Archives (GAA 334, no. 1307).
40 The publisher was Lion Cachet of The Hague.
41 A revised edition was published in 1810; subsequently several other reprints appeared.
42 GAA, *Protokolbuch* (1806-07), fo. 90-91. For more details about the Committee, see Ch. 6, notes 49-51.

such education. Obviously this did not signify indifference to the teaching of Pentateuch, Mishna and Talmud, and possibly the initiators were drawing a comparison with the public schools in which Jewish children received – or were supposed to receive – lessons in Jewish subjects outside the general curriculum. This rigid separation between general, or secular, and 'sacred' subjects was entirely in the spirit of the time: as far as the initiators were concerned the officially legislated separation of Church and State in the Batavian Republic forbade anything of a religious nature to impinge on public life. A striking illustration of this are the Articles of Association and accompanying 'pledge' of the association 'Door Vlijt en Eensgezindheid', founded in October 1797 in The Hague. Even though all members were Jewish, there is not a hint that it concerns a Jewish organization.[43] Naphtali Herz Weisl, in his programmatic brochure *Divrei shalom ve-emet*, also dealt separately with Jewish and secular subjects, even though he was mostly concerned with the 'sacred' aspects, since the other subjects were taught mainly to enable the pupils to make a living.[44]

Nothing came of this proposal by Meyer *et al.*, although soon after Meyer would have another and more practical opportunity to influence the education of Jewish children. On August 20, 1808, yet another educational association was established, called '*Hanokh la-na'ar al pi darkho*'(Prov. 22: 6 – 'Train a child in his way' – i. e. according to his capability). It was aimed at 'promoting the thus far deficient and unpedagogic education of Israelite youth by means of an appropriate translation of the Bible and the prayer books, as well as the production of suitable textbooks'.[45] Founders were the already mentioned M. Lemans and M.C. Cohen Belinfante, together with Jacob Belinfante[46] (a younger brother of

43 Van Zuiden, 's *Gravenhage*, Annex X.
44 For an analysis of the educative aspect of *Divrei shalom ve-emet*, see Fréderique P. Hiegentlich, 'Een onderzoek naar Filantropijnse elementen in Naphtali Herz Wessely's Divrei shalom ve-emet', in *Neveh Ya'akov*, Assen, 1982, pp. 118-132. Hiegentlich identifies three sources of the educational reforms proposed by Weisl: earlier Jewish reforms, such as the Freischule, the educational system of the Portuguese Jews in Amsterdam, and Philanthropinism. The last-mentioned current, called after the Philanthropinum school that was established in 1774 in Dessau, was utilitarian in nature. The school, which also admitted Jewish children, aspired towards a pedagogic approach of education, besides propagating the publication of suitable textbooks. All these tendencies had a profound impact on the school system in The Netherlands in general, and they are recognizable in the reform attempts within the Jewish community.
45 Meijer, *Problematiek*, p. 37
46 J.J. Belinfante (1780-1845). He was editor of the *Official Gazette* under J.D. Meyer, and continued in this function till 1835.

Moses), Hirsch Somerhausen,[47] I.M. de Solla and Benedictus van Emden as secretary.[48] It was the second attempt by the two brothers Belinfante to publish textbooks for children, the first attempt having been suspended for lack of capital. This raises the question of how they were suddenly able to embark upon such a costly enterprise as publishing a translation of the Bible – the more so since neither they nor their co-founders were very affluent. Lemans and Somerhausen were schoolmasters and Van Emden was an impecunious printer. Little is known about De Solla, except that he was definitely incapable of bankrolling the enterprise. What kind of support had the group been promised, and by whom, when they decided to go public?

The answer to this question is fairly simple. At the moment that '*Hanokh la-na'ar al pi darkho*' was founded, the introduction of the Consistorial system in the Kingdom of Holland was a foregone conclusion, as was the fact that J.D. Meyer would be appointed president of the High Consistory. The by-laws, a draft of which already existed on August 20, included a paragraph about the publication of a Bible translation, and the publication of the Royal decree of September 12, 1808, elevated this part of the program to official Government policy.

Neither the rabbis, nor the assorted schoolmasters in the employment of the Jewish communities could be relied upon to implement the educational policies that the High Consistory, and especially its President, had in mind. For the young *maskilim* on the other hand – enlightened Jews, and as such fervent proponents of teaching pure Hebrew as well as Dutch – this was the chance of a lifetime. The aim of *Hanokh*, namely a pedagogic approach to education according to the principles of Philanthropinism, was entirely in the spirit of Weisl's *Divrei shalom ve-emet*. Contrary to the traditional system, which compelled children from a tender age to struggle with the dialectics of Talmudic law, Weisl advocated a graduated pedagogic approach adapted to the mental absorption capacity of the students. Following this, the German Haskalah journal *Ha-meassef*, which as mentioned earlier had a number of Dutch subscrib-

---

47 Hirsch (Zvi) Somerhausen (Sommerhausen; Niederwehren, 1781 – Brussels, 1853). His father was President of the Jewish community in his birthplace. He spent several years in Berlin and was friendly with Moses Mendelssohn, with whom he also conducted a correspondence. Being bankrupted by the invasion of the French army, the family decided to emigrate to The Netherlands (1797). Both father and son became teachers. Hirsch at first taught in Nijmegen and afterwards in Amsterdam. Until his eighteenth year he knew only Hebrew and (mediocre) German. Even so he would eventually master ten languages, and contribute articles in Dutch, French and German to the major Western-European Jewish journals. Following the establishment of the Kingdom of the Netherlands he settled in Brussels (1817), where he remained, notwithstanding an offer by King William I of a function in The Netherlands. He organized Jewish education in Brussels, taught Dutch and was one of the first fighters for the recognition of Flemish as an official language – which earned him the enmity of the Belgian government. Among the numerous organizations of which he was a member were the Freemasons, in which he rose to the thirty-third (the highest) grade. Among his Hebrew works were a '*Haggada for Purim*' and the *Michtamim, Epigrammata*. See S. Cahen, Archives Israélites 1853, no. 14, pp. 186-93; , Michman, 'Hirsch Somerhausen, author of Michtamim, Epigrammata', *Michmanei Yosef* (Hebr.), pp. 263-71.

48 Benjamin Joachim van Em(b)den was a son of Dr. Joachim van Embden, and his partner in the publishing business.

ers, also began to publish articles about education.[49] In general, the Amsterdam *maskilim* were well aware of the educational developments in Germany, if only through the contacts of the Asser brothers. Tobias' father-in-law, Izak Daniel Itzig[50] had been the founder (in 1781) and long-time director of the 'Freischule', the first modern Jewish school in Berlin,[51] and Carel, through his wife Rose, the daughter of the banker and jeweller Levin Markus, also had contacts with a number of wealthy Berlin families.

The first issue of *Hanokh* was published in 1809 by the firm of Belinfante under the title *Bikurei hinukh* ('First Fruits of Education').[52] In actual fact, it was rather an expanded prospectus of the publishing plans of the firm. The idea was to publish a series of booklets of three or four sheets each, totalling some forty sheets per year, to which people could subscribe for six guilders per year. Each booklet would contain articles in Dutch [or Low-German, as it was called – as

49 Eliahu Morpurgo was an Italian Hebraist and pedagogue. In 1786 he published a plan for a gradual approach to Hebrew eduation in *Ha-Meassef*, according to which boys would not begin studying Talmud and Mishna before their 13th year. Weisl, on the other hand, had recommended that they should start at the age of eight. See M. Eliav, *Jewish Education in Germany during the period of the Enlightenment and Emancipation* (Hebr.), Jerusalem, 1960, pp. 53-59. *Ha-Meassef* continually pleaded for the production of textbooks that were adapted to the curriculum. The fact that the members of *Hanokh* adopted this concept does not reflect any antagonism to the Talmud, as was at times claimed about the first *maskilim* in Germany. Dubno and his Dutch followers accepted the authority of the Talmud. Mulder used Talmudic material for his epic *Bruria*, and he and Lemans frequently quote Talmudic sayings in their Biblical dictionary. See also Moshe Pelli, 'The Attitude of the First Maskilim in Germany towards the Talmud', *LBY* XXVII (1982), pp. 243-60.
50 Isaac Daniel Itzig (1750-1806) was the son of Daniel Itzig (1723-1799), the wealthiest Jew in Berlin. Almost all his descendants were baptized. About the family Itzig, see Steven M. Löwenstein, 'Jewish Upper Crust and Berlin Jewish Enlightenment: the Family of Daniel Itzig', in *East and West, Jews in a Changing Europe*, edit. F. Malino-D. Soskin, Oxford, 1990, pp. 182-201. Tobias was married to Rosa Levin, a sister of the renowned Rahel Varnhagen von der Ense-Levin. Rahel and her brother Robert were baptized and called themselves Roberts. Between 1770 and 1833 no fewer than 1,200 Berlin Jews were baptized, and on average the Jewish community amounted to no more than 360 members. Apostasy on such a large scale was unknown in The Netherlands. The first Asser to convert to Christianity was the Nobel prize recipient Professor T.M.C. Asser (1838-1913), and even he kept his apostasy a secret. About the baptism epidemic in Berlin, see Peter Honigman, 'Jewish Conversion – A Measure of Assimilation?', *LBY* XXXIV (1989), pp. 3-39; Steven M. Löwenstein, *The Berlin Jewish Community, Enlightenment, Family and Crisis, 1770-1830*, Oxford, 1994; H.T. Tewarson, 'German Jewish Identity in the correspondence between Rahel Levin-Varnhagen and her brother Ludwig Robert', *LBY* XXXIX (1994), pp. 3-29. This shows their close contacts with their sister and brother-in-law Asser.
51 The *Freischule* was founded in 1781 by Daniel Itzig and his brother-in-law, the noted David Friedlander. For Itzig's role in the conception of the curriculum, see Eliav, *op. cit.*, pp. 71-79. Other similar schools were established in Breslau (1791), Dessau (1799) and Seesen (1801). In 1804 Mayer Amschel Rothschild founded the Philantropin School in Frankfurt. See Arthur Galliner, 'The Philantropin in Frankfurt', *LBY* III (1958), pp. 169-86. Asser and Meyer were of course familiar with developments in Germany, as evidenced by frequent references in their memoranda. The *Freischule* was an essentially philanthropic project, and its curriculum did not specifically accord with the views of the *maskilim*. This is the conclusion of Dr. S.Feiner of Bar-Ilan University in an as yet unpublished study. Meyer's proposal of 1806 is similarly philanthropic in concept, and therefore may have been inspired by the *Freischule*.
52 See my article 'Bikurei hinukh' (Hebr.), *Leshonnenu la'am* 18 (1967), pp. 76-90, 120-35. Reprinted in *Michmanei Yosef*, pp. 263-71.

opposed to (High-)German] and Hebrew, dealing with subjects such as language, religion, morality, behavior, and so forth. It is interesting that the chapter on Religious Education contained a paragraph about the expulsion of the Jews from Spain, which the editors rationalized as follows:

> *Some would reason that a story denigrating adherents of a religion that preaches peace has no place in this booklet, but in our era, now that tolerance has been enshrined in laws and treaties, the beneficial aspects will be the more obvious to the formerly so frequently persecuted Israelite.*

Nothing came of these grandiose plans. In 1810 four booklets of *Hanokh* were published, which were to be the last. However, it was the Bible translation that would deal the *coup de grace* to this entire short-lived project.[53]

The Bible Translation

The Haskalah era had started in a dramatic fashion with Mendelssohn's translation, which – although not intended as such – had also proven to be an effective instrument in the fight against Yiddish.[54] In The Netherlands this 'Jewish language', also pejoratively referred to as 'gibberish', had struck even deeper roots than in Germany, not only as a language of communication, but as a literary vehicle.[55] The High Consistory regarded the resolute struggle against Yiddish as one of its main objectives. Given the success of Mendelssohn's translation, the High Consistory hoped that a Dutch translation would prove equally effective in the struggle against Yiddish, and its support of *Hanokh* was in the first place intended to help implement the Bible project.

The High Consistory had also won over the king to its plan. Obviously Louis Napoleon could have instructed the Jews to use the Protestant *Statenvertaling*, which was still in general use, and this would have been very much in the spirit of his brother. It is characteristic of the king's attitude that he refused to impose

---

53 These publications were: 1.*Yesodei hamikra*, 2 vols., by H. Somerhausen; 2. *Leket tov*, anthology of translations from English into Dutch; 3. List of Hebrew characters; 4. Collection of Dutch literature.

54 Initially Mendelssohn intended to prepare the translation for his son, who was more familiar with Hebrew characters than with Latin script. This is why it was published in Hebrew transcription. This aroused the ire of the traditionalists, since it enabled every Jew to read the German text. Graetz writes: 'So hat er...absichtslos die geistige Befreiung seiner Stammesgenossen herbeigeführt, von der sich ihre Wiedergeburt datiert' (Graetz, *Geschichte*, Vol. 11, p.38.) See also J. Meisl, *Haskalah*, Berlin, 1919, p. 13: 'Nicht mit Unrecht und ohne Übertreibung ist gesagt worden, daß seit den Tagen der Septuaginta keine Bibelübersetzung so gewaltige Wirkungen ausübte als die Mendelssohnsche.'

55 According to a study covering only the first century of Yiddish book printing in Amsterdam (i.e. up till and including the first half of the 18th century) no fewer than 220 Yiddish books were published, including the two Bible translations. This publishing activity continued until the 19th century. See Chava Turniansky, 'On Yiddish Didactic Literature in Amsterdam (1669-1749)' (Hebr.), in *SDJ* 4, pp. 163-177, and 'Khone Shmeruk, Yiddish Historical Songs in Amsterdam in the 17th and 18th Century', *idem*, pp. 143-61.

something on his Jewish subjects that was of Christian origin, and instead
agreed to a Bible translation according to their own tradition. The result was a
decision that may well be unique in Jewish history: not only were the Jews
permitted to prepare a translation conforming to their own beliefs and usage,
but its use would be declared compulsory in Jewish education.

Because of the fierce opposition to Mendelssohn's Bible translation in German,[56] similar protests on the part of Dutch rabbis and religious teachers were
anticipated in Holland. For this reason the Royal decree included certain
provisions aimed at nipping such obstruction in the bud. The memorandum
accompanying the new law explained that 'the thus far sorely neglected use of
the Dutch language among them [the Jews] must be encouraged and the use of
the so-called Jewish language [i.e. Yiddish] abolished.' Article 1 of the law stated
that the translation was to be 'the sole authentic translation for use by Jews'.
Article 3 stated that those High-German Israelites who were teachers by profession were obliged to use this translation in school as well as for private lessons.
Use of the 'Jewish language' would be proscribed and the punishments imposed
on infractions were draconian in the extreme: six months suspension from their
post for a first offense, and a permanent loss of their teaching license ('Patent')
in case of a recurrence.

In Article 4 of the law, the High Consistory was instructed 'in the name of the
King' to order all Chief Rabbis, rabbis and teachers actively to encourage their
co-religionists to speak Dutch and refrain from using alternative Bible translations. The High Consistory was expected to inform the Ministries of Religious
Affairs and the Interior concerning which rabbis had obeyed this ruling and
who had failed to cooperate to the desired degree.[57]

Article 5 of the law determined that teaching 'patents' would in future be
issued only to people with full mastery of the Dutch language who had passed
an examination by the local Board of Education. Anyone who wanted to become
a religious instructor would need an authorization by the High Consistory.

The Royal decree left no doubt that the Dutch Bible translation was intended to serve as ammunition in the fight against Yiddish. Consequently
rabbis as well as teachers were subjected to considerable pressure, and schoolmasters were threatened with the loss of their livelihood. Since the majority
were barely able to express themselves in Dutch, and the transition from one
vernacular to another is a gradual and time-consuming process, this portended
almost certain dismissal. However, gradual was apparently an unknown word in
the High Consistory's lexicon.

As already mentioned, the translation was placed into the hands of the editors
of *Hanokh*, and the firm of Belinfante was to be responsible for printing and
distribution.[58] The project was begun with the utmost dispatch. The names of

---

56 Altmann, *op. cit.*, pp. 381-98; Graetz, *op. cit.*, pp. 40-45.
57 ARA, Staatssecr. Louis Nap., 10 Hay month 1809, no. 6.
58 The High Consistory had budgeted Df. 12,000 for the translation and publication, a
    considerable sum in those days.

the contributors were unknown, but we may assume that Lemans and Somer-hausen were responsible for the lion's share. Within a short time the translation of Genesis was completed, but at that moment the first difficulties arose.

A copy of the text was sent to all Chief Rabbis in the Kingdom of Holland, requesting their comments. Most refused to react, using a variety of pretexts: Berenstein of Leeuwarden and Hertzfeld of Zwolle were too busy; Löwenstamm of Amsterdam was unfamiliar with the Dutch language, and only Rabbi J.A. Lemans (Rebbe Lemmel) of The Hague was prepared to admit that he objected to the translation on principle.[59] After having been submitted to considerable pressure, Berenstein finally sent a letter containing a few trifling comments, adding that he could not possibly judge the translation due to his insufficient knowledge of Dutch.[60] This was enough for the High Consistory to announce that none of the Chief Rabbis except one had made objections – a somewhat skewed representation of the facts, to say the least – after which the time had come to put pressure on the Jewish teachers – simple schoolmasters and private teachers alike – to sign a declaration that from now on they would only use the Dutch translation.

Faced with the dire threat of losing their 'patent' – and thus their principal or even sole means of existence – the majority chose to sign the declaration. Even so fourteen teachers in Amsterdam plucked up the courage to refuse, and twelve of them sent a lengthy petition to the Minister of the Interior requesting an exemption on the grounds that their religious instruction also included the Bible commentaries of Rashi, the explanations of the 613 positive and negative commandments, and even the Talmud, subjects that could not possibly be taught – or, for that matter understood – in a language in which neither they, nor their pupils were proficient. Besides, how could they be compelled to use a translation they had never even seen, and which so far had not been approved by the Amsterdam Chief Rabbi and his assessors?[61] The complainants were supported by the Parnasim, who reminded one and all that the commotion in the great Synagogue following announcements in Dutch had made it only too clear what the masses thought about the High Consistory's scheme.

The Minister forwarded the petition to the High Consistory for advice. This placed the Old Community's representatives in the High Consistory before a dilemma: supporting the schoolmasters was tantamount to opposing the Royal decree and opposing a body that had been established by the king. Against this stood the severity of the sanctions demanded by J.D. Meyer, the president of the High Consistory, which, if they went along with him, would almost certainly put

---

59 Meijer, *Problematiek*, pp. 36-37.
60 The letter is dated Leeuwarden, 27 Summer month (June) 1810. ARA Arch. Opperconsistorie no. 11. The letter does not mention whether Berenstein saw the complete text of the Pentateuch, since his comments are restricted to several passages from Genesis and Exodus. He compared the Dutch translation with that of Mendelssohn, preferring at times the Dutch and sometimes Mendelssohn's translation. However, the material is too limited to enable us to draw conclusions about either the quality of the Dutch translation or Berenstein's evaluation.
61 ARA Bi. Za., 7 Flowering month (May) 1810. On May 10 the Minister forwarded the petition to the High Consistory for a preliminary recommendation.

them on a collision course with their community. In the end the High Consistory adopted the following decisions with the smallest possible majority (five votes against four), which were submitted as recommendations to the Minister:

1. The petition should be turned down.
2. All synagogue announcements not directly connected with religion or ceremonial aspects had to be made in the Dutch language, as well as posted in Dutch, or announced in proper Hebrew besides being posted in Dutch.
3. The Parnasim of the capital had to be reminded of their duty and due obeisance by means of a serious warning and other suitable means.
4. The Chief Rabbi of the Capital should similarly be reminded of his duty and obeisance in the strictest possible terms, and he should be instructed forthwith to devote a sermon to the introduction of the Dutch language.

Even these strictures failed to satisfy Meyer and two former members of the New Community (Van Laun and De Jonge Meyersz.). Although voting for the contents of the recommendation, they objected to its phrasing, so that the deciding votes were cast by two other members of the former New Community, De Lemon and Carel Asser. This was the first token of a more tolerant attitude on the part of Asser, who thus far had invariably presented a common front with his colleague Meyer.[62]

Eventually, after having issued a severe admonition to all concerned, the High Consistory, on July 20, 1810, agreed to allow the rabbis and teachers who had admitted their guilt, as well as those who had earlier surrendered to the High Consistory's dictate, to sign the declaration that they would use the new Bible translation.[63] By forcing the recalcitrant clergy and teachers to surrender, the High Consistory had once again emerged victorious.

Nevertheless, the High Consistory would not be able to savor its victory. Three weeks previously, on July 1, the emperor Napoleon had forced his brother to resign the throne, and the Kingdom of Holland was annexed to France. On November 20, 1810, the High Consistory sent a memorandum to the Governor-General of the annexed territories, Charles F. Lebrun, which – among

---

62 On May 15 the High Consistory decided to appoint a committee consisting of Meyer, De Lemon and Boas to formulate the Minister's answer. The committee's draft was accepted with a few changes, which turned out to be sufficiently contentious to cause Van Laun, De Jonghe Meyersz. and Meyer to vote against the formulation of para. 2. ARA *ibid.*, May 20, 1610.

63 The extremely condescending and humiliating manner in which the High Consistory treated the rabbis is shown by the report to the Minister. After having received authorization from the Minister 'the High Consistory, informed by a desire on its part to do everything to promote peace and harmony, made it emphatically known that it was as yet prepared to accept the submission of our rabbis. Due to this manifest intention, four of the said rabbis appeared at the session held on the 19th of the Summer month, and having admitted their guilt, requested to be allowed to sign the required declaration, whereas the remainder applied in writing to the High Consistory indicating their willingness to sign.... The High Consistory would be inclined to accept the first four as such, and the others after having given them a strict reprimand.'

other subjects – touched upon the forthcoming Bible translation.[64] It now appeared that not only had contracts been signed with the translators, and special fonts cast for use in this publication, but that even the paper had been ordered – all of this involving a considerably higher expense than originally estimated. Considering that one thing and another was a direct consequence of a Royal decision, the High Consistory assumed that Lebrun would kindly agree to cover the deficit. Unfortunately Lebrun was not so inclined. In fact, he saw no reason, as he put it, 'to translate the Bible from one dead language into another dead language (i. e. Dutch!)'.[65] In other words, the High Consistory was saddled with the financial responsibility. The situation was even worse for the Belinfante brothers, who were so deeply indebted that they had to close their printing business.[66]

The Revival of Hebrew Literature

Lebrun's comment is characteristic of the mind-set during the annexation period of The Netherlands. 'We are now French Israelites,' concluded Meyer and Asser, who apparently had no difficulty adapting themselves to their new circumstances and masters.[67] Meanwhile, it was not only the Bible translation that fell victim to the new French orientation: the ambitious scheme for producing Dutch textbooks for Jewish youngsters also had to be suspended. Hebrew, the other 'dead language', nevertheless fared slightly better. This was an era in which the Classics were being rediscovered, and Cicero's Latin once again

---

64 Colenbrander *GS* Vol. 6 (1810-1813), pp. 872-75. This lengthy memorandum reviews the developments between 1795 and 1808, as well as the views of the High Consistory. It concludes with a number of concrete recommendations. The Bible translation is discussed within the framework of the struggle against 'jargon'. The entire Pentateuch has been translated and the editing of the book of Genesis has been completed, but due to the political situation printing has been suspended. According to the same document, the instruction to permit only Dutch-language announcements in the synagogue had been completely ineffectual due to the opposition of a number of Synagogue Boards, people who regarded this as a threat to their religion, as well as 'due to the little energy the Government had invested in supporting the Consistory'.

65 Meijer, *Problematiek*, p. 43. In the Protestant Netherlands the Dutch Bible translation formed an integral part of the Dutch cultural heritage, a viewpoint that a Roman Catholic Frenchman could hardly be expected to share, or even understand. This is why Lebrun was able to say: 'Vous voulez donc, messieurs, traduire la Bible d'une langue morte dans une autre langue morte.'

66 Already at the end of 1809 Van Emden and Belinfante were unable to pay the supplier of the specially cast Bible fonts. See Meijer, *Problematiek*, p. 44. Between 1805 and 1810 the Belinfante Company published 39 publications, not all of them by Jewish authors or on Jewish subjects. In 1811 and 1812 only two publications appeared.

67 See Carel Asser's letter of December 1, 1812 to Chief Rabbi Berenstein: '...and since all distinctions between Israelite and Israelite have been cancelled and [since] we are now French Israelites...' Carel Asser is referring to the distinction between Portuguese and High-German Jews, whom he now wanted to see united within one organization. The letter was published by I. Mendels, *VA* 2 b (1925), pp. 130, 132, 148-50.

achieved normative status.[68] This created opportunities for a rekindling of interest in classical Hebrew, an inherent part of the *triplex lingua* Greek, Latin and Hebrew, which had been declared fundamental languages by the humanists during the early 16th century. In The Netherlands, too, a revival of Latin was evident, and this spurred the *maskilim* to make a similar effort to revive pure Biblical Hebrew. This striving towards a pure, normative Hebrew, patterned on the language of the Bible, although indeed yielding a number of lofty literary creations, particularly poetry, had its shadow side. There are different kinds of Hebrew, and for example mishnaic Hebrew differs from Biblical Hebrew in vocabulary as well as morphology. But the Aramaic of the Talmud and Kabbalah has also attained legitimacy in several literary genres. The devotion of the *maskilim* to Biblical Hebrew put an end to the Dutch Sephardi literary tradition and to rabbinical literature as a source of new creativity. It evidently was a dead-end street, symbolized by Moses Lemans' gesture of submitting his epic work about the Belgian insurrection to the Royal Dutch Institute of Sciences, Literature and the Arts, where he believed the most competent judges of his work were to be found. The results of this event would only become visible following the Restoration, which period falls outside the scope of this book. Even so, the foundations were laid during the French era.

The flourishing of Dutch Haskalah literature is due to one individual in particular: the author, poet, pedagogue and organizer Samuel Israel Mulder (1792-1862).[69] His father had imbued him with a love of Hebrew literature, and to this end had invited David Friedrichsfeld as live-in tutor. In 1808, at the young age

---

68 'Even more characteristic is the revival of Latin as the language of higher education, the restoration of a dignity that had begun to fall into disuse even before 1795.' (J. Huizinga, *De Nederlandse Natie*, Haarlem, 1960, p. 109.)

   A. van der Heide believes the criticism of the absolute choice of a normative Biblical Hebrew to be anachronistic, since according to him the criticism was predicated on the revival of Hebrew as a spoken language. However, he forgets that the choice of the *maskilim* meant the break with a rich literary past, which severed modes of expression and in turn caused impoverishment of the language. See A. van der Heide, 'Problems of Tongeleth Poetry', *Stud. Ros.* XIX (1985), pp. 264-74. For the text of Lemans' letter, see *SDJ* 1, pp. 283-84.

69 Samuel Israel Salomon (or Schrijver) in 1811 adopted the name Mulder. He was by far the most active Jewish personality in the religious, cultural as well as pedagogic field. He was highly influential for many years in a variety of capacities: as a teacher, inspector of Jewish education, author, translator, Hebrew poet and lexicographer, organizer and community leader. It is therefore regrettable that we lack a fitting biography, or even a bibliography of his writings. After his death various obituaries and summaries were published: *Ned. Israëlitisch Jaarboekje*, 1863, pp. 64-67; address E.B. Asser, Letterkundig Genootschap Tot Nut en Beschaving (March 19, 1863); J.J. Belinfante, *Nederlandsche Spectator* (Aug. 7, 1863); Van der Aa, see under Mulder. Among later literary recollections the following are worth mentioning: Van Zuiden, 'Dr. S.I. Mulder en het Jiddisch', *VA* 8 (Oct. 23, 1931), pp. 63-64; H. Boas, 'De leraar Hebreeuws van Eduard Asser', *Jbk. Amstelodamum* (1965), pp. 126-36; J. Meijer, *H.J. Koenen, Geschiedenis der Joden in Nederland (1843)*, Heemstede, 1982, pp. 50, 84-102. The latter gives a rather negative evaluation of Mulder, not only as a historian (never regarded as his strongest suit), but also as a person. Recently he has gained increased appreciation as an outstanding Haskalah poet; see, for example, Y. Friedlander, S. Mulder, 'Beruria bat rav Hanina ben Tradyon – a Critical Edition' (Hebr.), *SDJ* 3, pp. 125-65. Also J. Bar-El, *The Hebrew Long Poem from its Emergence to the Beginning of the Twentieth Century* (Hebr.), Jerusalem, 1995,

of sixteen, Samuel became a founder-member of the association 'Tot Nut en Beschaving' (Utility and Culture), which aspired towards 'the practice of literature and the arts, the promotion of the moral civilization [and] everything capable of ennobling the human heart.'[70] Other members of the association included Moses Lemans and Hirsch Somerhausen, who at this juncture had already been chosen to collaborate on the new Dutch Bible translation. In 1815 Mulder united the activist Hebraists into another scientific and literary circle, similarly – and almost inevitably – carrying the word 'Utility' in its name, albeit in Hebrew: *Le-to'eleth* – which in the course of time changed into *To'eleth*.[71]

This fashion for Hebraization permeated even the pietist association '*Reshit hokhma*' [The fear of the Lord (...is the beginning of wisdom); Ps. 111:10], which was entirely devoted to Talmud study. It is known that its president used to open the annual meeting with a Hebrew speech, a custom that continued until the middle of the 19th century.[72] The spiritual father of both organizations was Salomo Dubno, who even after his death in 1813 remained a highly revered figure to all the members.

Even though *To'eleth* existed for only twenty years, it has the distinction of having rekindled the flame of Hebrew as a literary language. This had indeed been one of the ideals of the Haskalah – but in the case of The Netherlands it was an Orthodox form of Haskalah. For the country continued on the course charted during the first Haskalah period, opposing all reformist tendencies that were spreading hand over fist in Germany during the same period. This means that *To'eleth* could boast contributions, both essays and poetry, by Ortho-

70 The association was established in 1807, among others, by H. Somerhausen, J. Benedictus van Em(b)den, and D.S. Boas, a son of the Parnas. Eventually it merged with the mathematicians' society 'Mathesis Artium Genetrix', which also had a predominantly Jewish membership. 'Tot Nut en Beschaving' had a number of distinguished gentile members, including the well-known poet Willem Bilderdijk. See J. Meijer, *da Costa*, pp. 142-43. Throughout the 19th century the association remained a bulwark of the assimilatory current, 'the meeting place of the Amsterdam Jewish academe that rejected any dogmatic faith'. In 1864 the Board permitted Dr. J.H. Dünner, then rector of the Theological Seminary in Amsterdam, who had been invited as a guest speaker, 'to keep his head covered' (*Weekblad voor Israëlieten*, April 22, 1864).

71 Officially *To'eleth* was founded in September 1816. The initiators, besides Mulder, Moses and Meir Loonstein, were Saul Koster, David Lissaur and David Tall. In 1817 there were 27 members, which number increased to 47 in 1820, but even so the membership never exceeded 50. Its history is described by I. Maarsen, '*Tongeleth*, een Joods letterkundige kring uit de XIXde eeuw', *VA* Ia (1924), pp. 390-93; *ibid.*, pp. 135-37, 146-48, 199-201 (also published as a brochure). See also the extensive doctoral dissertation by P. Tuinhout-Keuning, *To'eleth en de Hebreeuwse Haskala in Duitsland* (Groningen University, 1986), which contains a contextual and literary analysis of the writings of *To'eleth*.

72 *Reshit hokhma*, an association for study of the Bible, Mishna and Talmud, was founded in 1813 by students of Dubno. One of the founding members was Simon Ephraim Heigmans (born 1790), at that time – in other words at the age of nineteen – one of the contributors to *Hanokh*. Later on he published Hebrew poems, textbooks and translations (of the apocryphal book Judith). In *Reshit hokhma* a large group of Eastern-European Jews objected to the *Biur* by Dubno, but they remained a minority. See Benzion J. Hirsch, 'Bijdrage tot de geschiedenis van de Bioer', *VA* 2b (1926), pp. 338-39.

dox rabbis.[73] *To'eleth*. Yet another orthodox Hebraist was M. de Wulft (see note 22). There exists a manuscript of his hand called *Keter Torah Ha-Me'assef* (Coevorden, 1815) with an approbation by no less than A. Susan, De Wulft's teacher at the Amsterdam Beth Hamidrash and subsequently deputy Chief Rabbi (HS Ros. 196). In 1812 De Wulft wrote a Purim parody: *Neta' Sha'ashuim* (HS Ros. 318). Yet another of Mulder's great contributions was that he succeeded in completing, single-handedly, the project that had defeated the High Consistory and *Hanokh*. He translated a large part of the Bible, published a complete Bible for young people, as well as translated the daily prayer book. At the same time, Mulder was a poet of some distinction and, all in all, doubtlessly the worthiest exponent of the Dutch Haskalah.[74]

The Holy Land and the Origins of Pekidim ve-Amarkelim

The fact that several rabbis were members of *To'eleth* did not mean that the ultra-orthodox 'righteous' Jews who had spearheaded the opposition to the Haskalah and, among other things, had spurred the riots in November 1813 necessarily approved of its ideas. The struggle of these zealots was directed against any kind of innovation, and as such was of a mainly negative and barren nature. During the period that King William I was organizing the Jews in the Kingdom of the Netherlands, they made no constructive contributions, even though the vast majority of Dutch Jewry stood behind them. The reason for this must be that the social integration of Jews within the surrounding society was a completely alien idea for most, with which they were conceptually unable to cope. This assumption is strengthened by the fact that in a sphere that was close to their heart the leaders of the Orthodoxy evinced remarkable ingenuity, with one remarkable success.

Support by Jews for their co-religionists in the Holy Land has traditionally been a prime religious duty, equal or even superior to assisting the local poor, since Torah study in Eretz Israel was regarded as more sacred than comparable studies in the lands of the Dispersion. For this reason the Amsterdam Jewish community collected funds that were routinely transferred to the Portuguese

73 Including the Leeuwarden Chief Rabbi Joakhim (Haim) Löwenstamm. The most intriguing foreign contributor was Hyman Hurwitz (1755-1846) from London. He was addressed with the rabbinial honorific of *Moreh*, but he was the principal of the first modern Jewish school in London (1799-1821). See Todd M. Engelsman, *The Jews of Georgian England 1714-1830*, Philadelphia, 1979, pp. 158-59. Jona Hena Benjamins, although belonging to the strictly orthodox 'genuine' Jews, was also very active in *To'eleth*. Yet another orthodox Hebraist was M. de Wulft (see note 22). There exists a manuscript of his hand called *Keter Torah ha-me'assef* (Coevorden, 1815) with an approbation by no less than A. Susan, De Wulft's teacher at the Amsterdam Beth Hamidrash and subsequently deputy Chief Rabbi (HS Ros. 196). In 1812 De Wulft wrote a Purim parody: *Neta' sha'ashuim* (HS Ros. 318).

74 Mulder and Lemans jointly composed the *Hebreeuws-Nederduits Handwoordenboek* (Amsterdam, 1831). It is an excellent and as yet to be recommended work. Its numerous Talmudic references characterize it as typical of the Dutch Haskalah.

community, the oldest Jewish community in Eretz Israel, which also had a central office in Constantinopel.[75]

At the end of the 18th century a number of untoward events took place in Eretz Israel, including several natural calamities and repressions by various local administrators, resulting in increased poverty of the local Jews. Coincidentally the religious freedoms granted to the Jews resulted in the collapse of the Amsterdam Welfare Fund. Since the transfers to Eretz Israel were partially financed from the Welfare Fund, the contributions of the Amsterdam Jewish community to the Holy Land started to lag behind, a situation aggravated by the fact that this item was low on the list of the emancipatory movement's priorities.

The second half of the 18th century saw an exacerbation of the tensions between Sephardim and Ashkenazim concerning the collections for the Holy Land. By the end of the century growing numbers of Ashkenazim were settling in Eretz Israel, and demanding a say in the division of the funds,[76] until, in 1789, a rabbinical delegation from Brody visited Amsterdam to conduct negotiations concerning a separate collection on behalf of the Ashkenazi Jews. They also suggested an end to the current practice of transferring funds via the Sephardi community. The Parnasim were loath to enter into such an arrangement, but agreed to exert pressure on the delegates from Eretz Israel to achieve an equal division between Sephardim and Ashkenazim.[77] The transfer system via the Portuguese community continued to exist until 1809, with occasional exceptions whenever a delegate from Eretz Israel visited Amsterdam. Yet it was this method in particular that aroused growing opposition, due to the high overhead involved in the use of middlemen and occasional doubts about the reliability of the delegates.[78]

Most of the contributions for Eretz Israel consisted of earmarked pledges by individuals who were called up to the reading of the Torah during the weekly synagogue services. Whenever these pledges were insufficient the *Kupat zedakah*, the Welfare Fund, came to the rescue. After 1806, for the reasons mentioned earlier, the Welfare Fund was no longer able to pay its regular allocations, or

---

75 About these contacts, see Gérard Nahon, 'Les Relations entre Amsterdam et Constantinople au XVIIIe siècle àprès le Copiador de Cartas de la Nation juive portugaise', *DJH* 1, pp. 157-84; idem, 'Amsterdam and Jerusalem in the 18th century. The State of Sources and some Questions', *DJH* 2, pp. 95-116.

76 At the end of the eighteenth century the Ashkenazi community in Eretz Israel underwent a rapid growth in three waves: 1764, 1774 and 1794. Serious frictions arose between the old-established Sephardi colony and the new arrivals. See M. Eliav, *Eretz Israel and its Yishuv in the 19th century, 1777-1917* (Hebr.), Jerusalem, 1978, pp. 57-82.

77 GAA *Protokolbuch*, Menahem Av 5549 (1789). Although the two rabbis were received with due honors, they were subsequently fobbed off with a mere 2 ducats for expenses. About the origins of the institute of the Pekidim ve-Amarkelim in particular, see my article in *Michmanei Yosef*, pp. 229-44.

78 For the assistance to the Jews in Eretz Israel by Jewish communities in the Diaspora, see Jacob Barnai,*The Jews in Palestine in the Eighteenth Century under the Patronage of the Istanbul Committee of Officials for Palestine*, Alabama, 1992. The standard work about the delegates is Awraham Yaari, *Sheluhei Eretz Israel* (Hebr.), 2nd. ed, Jerusalem, 1977, which also deals with the various delegates who visited The Netherlands.

even the salaries of its permanent staff. Consequently the community could no longer honor its commitments towards the Jews in Eretz Israel, among which an annual payment of Df. 100 for the Jews of Hebron. By 1815 the community owed Df. 800 in back payments.[79]

It seems that the interested parties in Eretz Israel, especially those in Jerusalem, were looking for ways and means of stimulating the collection activities in Amsterdam. An indication of this is found in a note in the *Protokolbuch* of the Amsterdam community. Following a dispute about whether or not the community owed money to Jerusalem, 'we requested the expert testimony of three prominent members of our community, the *ketzinim* (wealthy men) Isaac ben Nathan Berclau,'[80] Avraham ben Aharon Prinz[81] and Hirsch ben Moshe Lehren.[82] Following their testimonies it was decided to pay 300 guilders to Messrs. Texeira de Mattos, to be transferred via Constantine (Constantinople?).[83] We see, therefore, that even in 1809 the community was still using the Portuguese Jews as intermediaries. It is impossible, therefore, that the subsequently illustrious Pekidim ve-Amarkelim foundation already existed at this time. In fact, the impulse for the decision to establish an Ashkenazi aid association for the Holy Land of the three Amsterdam notables came from Jerusalem.

Even in 1810 the list of associations supported by the Jewish community of Amsterdam did not include any association dealing with the Holy Land.[84] The year 1809, commonly assumed to have been the year in which the Pekidim

---

79 'Having heard the request of the Honorable Baruch Maestro, delegate from the Holy Land, specifically Hebron, for the payment of Df. 800 for an allowance of 8 years for the poor of the city of Hebron.' It is decided to pay the arrears by transferring the money to the 'Central Israelite Board at Constantinople on behalf of the city of Hebron.' GAA, *ibid.*, May 11, 1815. See also Yaari, *op. cit.*, p. 706.

80 According to the sources one of the founders, and first President of Paku"am was Itzik ben Nathan Breitbart (or Braatbard), also called Guteinde. Could he have been identical with the Berclau mentioned in this document? Many Jews were known by several different names. The same Breitbart was recommended as a member of the advisory committee in the petition of the 'righteous' Jews; see Ch. 9, p. 221.

81 Awraham Aron Prinz(s), (Alkmaar, 1768 – Amsterdam, 1851) was one of the wealthiest members of the community. He was rated in category A for communal tax purposes. He left a kind of diary that passed into the possession of the bookseller Salo Mayer. When I was allowed to peruse it, I found a passage on p. 46 which reads (in translation): 'Delegates from Eretz Israel Jacob David Jekutiel Rappoport and Raphael Jacob from Ophir appoint him and Isaac Braatbaart [and] Hirschel Lehren. This appointment has been confirmed by Rabbi Jacob Moses Löwenstamm.' Jacob David Jekutiel and Raphael Jacob (Matalon) left Jerusalem in 1806 on a fund raising mission. Yaari writes that the historian A.M. Luncz states in his book *Jerusalem* that during their stay in Amsterdam the two delegates founded the 'Pekidim ve-Amarcalim' – without, however, mentioning his source. The note by Prinz confirms this information. Yaari, *op. cit.*, pp. 704-08.

82 Zvi Hirschel Lehren (1784-1853) was the son of the Hague Parnas Moses Lehren, an active opponent of the High Consistory. He was the son-in-law of the banker David Hollander of Altona. So far three volumes of his correspondence on behalf of Paku"am have been published: *The Letters of the Pekidim and Amarcalim of Amsterdam* I-III, Jerusalem, 1965, 1970, 1978.

83 GAA, *Protokolbuch*, 20 Heshvan 5669 (1810).

84 A 'Memorandum of Pious Institutions that have submitted regulations for approval by the Parnasim' (January 1810) contains 69 names. Insofar as they permit us to draw conclusions, it appears that they are mainly social and communal organizations, including several aimed at the study of the Scriptures and several women's associations. Not a single association for the Holy Land is mentioned, from which we may conclude that the triumvirate Braatbaart-Prinz-Lehren had not yet established a separate foundation. GAA, *Protokolbuch*, January, 1810.

ve-Amarkelim was founded, is therefore merely the date in which the three above-mentioned persons organized themselves as a lobby on behalf of the Ashkenazi Jews in Eretz Israel. Since all were wealthy in their own right, it is reasonable to assume that they contributed sizeable amounts for the purpose privately.

Until 1815, and possibly somewhat later, the Jewish community remained officially in charge of the collections. However, in light of the above-mentioned initiative by the three Amsterdam notables, who eventually would constitute the Board of the foundation, 1809 may be regarded unofficially as the year of the formation of *Pekidim ve-Amarkelim* (abbreviated Paku"am) for financial support of Jews in Eretz Israel. Hirsch Lehren, a strictly orthodox and mystically inclined figure, was to become the predominant personality of the three. With his banking house as its center, he established a network of collection agents extending from the smallest Jewish community in The Netherlands and into Belgium, France and Germany. Eventually these contributions, carefully administered and transferred to the last penny to representatives in the Holy Land, effectively maintained the Jewish community residing there. In the process, Hirsch Lehren intervened repeatedly with regard to the division of these funds, and as such wielded considerable influence on the lives of Jews in a country that he himself never had the good fortune to visit.

8   Jewish Soldiers in the Batavian Republic and under French Rule

As long as Jews lived within their closed communities and were regarded as aliens, both by themselves and by the non-Jewish population, the question of their military service was hardly relevant. Jewish soldiers could not observe their religious obligations; nor were military commanders interested in Jews. During the 18th century, however, and particularly during its second half, the walls that separated Jews from their gentile environment began to come down. The authorities, too, began to look at them with a different eye. By way of preface I should like to present a striking incident that profoundly influenced subsequent developments.

In the late 18th century the Dutch Republic was suffering from a serious lack of military personnel, particularly in the navy. The glorious days of de Ruyter and Tromp were long past, and a maritime career no longer attracted ordinary citizens. The neglect of the navy became painfully evident during the Fourth English War (1780-1784). In order to fulfill the country's obligations to the French ally, the Dutch navy needed refurbishing at short notice. No fewer than 9,500 sailors were needed, 5,000 of whom had to be provided by the city of Amsterdam.

We have seen that Amsterdam possessed a large reservoir of young Jewish men, who lived in dire poverty because most of the customary professions were closed to them. It seemed a logical idea to try to tempt them to enlist in the navy. At the initiative of the physician Jacob de Leon Arons, the naval authorities began negotiations with the Parnasim, without whose permission no Jew could enlist.[1]

The agreement signed may well be unique in Jewish history. The navy accepted the dictates of the Parnasim, who set forth extremely strict conditions on behalf of the seamen. The discussions resulted in the following regulations:

---

1   See Eduard van Biema, 'Het Nederlandse zeewezen en de Amsterdamse Joden in het einde der 18de eeuw', *Amsterdams Jaarboekje 1901*, p. 76-91.
   Jacob Lion (or de Leon) Arons (Jacob Rofeh), b. 1709, graduated as a physician in Leiden (1728); he also was a certified translator (Hes, *Physicians*, p.11). As a descendant of Uri Halevi he was allowed to attend religious services in the Esnoga, but only after first having obtained permission from the High-German Community against payment of 25 guilders (July 6, 1777). See S. Seeligmann, 'Het Nederlandse zeewezen en de Amsterdamse Joden in het einde der 18de eeuw.' CBIN, Dec. 7, 1901. On January 30, 1781 the advocate Jan Deth approached him with the suggestion that he talk to Capt. (later Admiral) Van Kinsbergen, together with one or two of the Parnasim.

Regulations to be observed in order to enable Jews to sail with the Admiralty or the East India Company:

1. *All foodstuffs for use by the Jews shall remain separate from those of the non-Jews in a special place aboard the ship under the supervision of a Jew, who will keep the key. This Jew may also be appointed as the cook.*

2. *All meat to be carried on the ship for consumption by the Jews shall be provided by the Israelite Meat Halls, unless the shohet (ritual slaughterer) of our Community kills the cattle in the houses or at another place that has been destined for this purpose by the owners; the meat of the ritually fit animals shall be porged [the removal of forbidden fatty and other parts] by a Jew, and he himself shall soak it in water and salt it as well as pack it in vats. These vats shall be sealed with a double seal, brought to the ship and handed to the keeper, to be locked away as earlier decided.*

   In the event that ships at sea enter a port because of a shortage of food in order to take on supplies for Jews, all the above should be observed in these places as well. For this reason the Jew who supervises the food supplies must be licensed to act as a ritual slaughterer and to pronounce on the ritual fitness of cattle; alternatively, a shohet from here should be taken on board.

3. *In the bakery in which bread and rusks are baked for consumption by the Jews, a Jew shall act as a supervisor; and in the event cheeses for Jews are carried on board, these must be purchased from Jewish cheese merchants and duly stamped with the marks of ritually permitted cheeses.*

4. *When the ships depart from here at such a time that they will find themselves at one place or another outside our commonwealth during the Passover festival, sufficient Passover cakes will have to be baked for them by a Jew prior to their departure. These Passover cakes shall be carefully kept at a previously arranged place, so that Jews shall not – God forbid – be guilty of eating forbidden leavened food at the Passover festival.*

5. *The Jew who acts as a cook shall be allocated spacious accommodation in the kitchen, called the galley, where he can prepare and cook food for the Jews in such a way that this will not come into contact with any forbidden food.*

6. *The Jews shall always conduct their prayers separately. They shall be allowed one half hour after sunrise and in the evening one half hour before sunset at a place on the ship set aside for this purpose in order properly and without interference to say their morning, afternoon and evening prayers.*

7. *That the Jews shall not perform work of any kind whatsoever, either at sea or on land, on the Sabbath and Israelite festivals; however, during a heavy storm or at moments of danger, they may assist in saving human life.*

8. *When a Jew falls ill, or has an accident in the course of his work aboard the ship, and it is impossible to heal him on the ship, the captain shall have him put ashore at his*

expense and see to it that he is lodged with Jews. In the event that there are no Jewish residents in that place, the captain shall allow one of his Jewish shipmates to stay with him in order to attend to him and provide food and medicines for him for as long as his illness will last.

9. *That it shall be written in the document signed by the captain and the crew, known as the 'muster-roll', that all these conditions will be implemented without exception; and in order to lend them force, the captain shall be required to display these conditions, written on parchment, aboard the ship.*

10. *Finally, in order to ensure the gravity and authority of these conditions, and to prevent their non-observance, the Government – may God enhance its glory – shall be requested to designate supervision over the above described and explained regulations.[2]*

The first Jewish sailors began their service in the year 1782, and before setting sail they were addressed by the Amsterdam Chief Rabbi R. Saul, who also pronounced a blessing for their physical and spiritual welfare.[3] The number of Jewish sailors on that first voyage is not known, but cannot have been very large.

A naval career does not appear to have solved the employment problems of the Jewish youths of Amsterdam; as a precedent, however, the affair would prove to have far-reaching consequences. The same was the case with the permission granted by the rabbi of Prague, Ezechiel Landau, for Jewish soldiers to join the army of Emperor Joseph II; he too had blessed each Jewish soldier individually.[4]

The Jews did, however, represent an obvious potential, which may have convinced the Amsterdam Deputy Chief-Constable Papegaay to hire forty young Jews to protect his home in 1787.[5] Similar considerations played a role with the commander of the Amsterdam garrison, Count van Golowkin, when in

---

2 See E. Biema, *op. cit.*
3 Later publications repeatedly refer to this fact. See, for example: *Tweede Brief van H.L. Bromet* (Amsterdam, 1795), p. 18: 'During our last English War in the year 1782, when several armed merchant ships were sent to Surinam and, for lack of able seamen, it was decided to accept Jews as sailors, Chief Rabbi Saul Levie, the father of the present Chief Rabbi, Moses Saul, not only granted permission for accepting these naval commissions; but prior to the departure of the mustered sailors, after having cautioned them to observe to the best of their ability the laws concerning the Sabbath and [ritually permitted] foods, the aforementioned, having placed his hand on the head of each and every one of the sailors, gave them the Lord's blessing and wished them a successful journey.' (Da Silva Rosa, *Bibliografie*, no. 27).
4 The Amsterdam *maskilim* probably derived their knowledge of R. Ezechiel Landau's from the enthusiastic description in *Ha-meassef 5549*, p. 252. In fact he had no choice but to acquiesce in the Emperor's decree regarding the Jewish community. With tearful eyes he beseeched the recruits to observe their Jewish obligations, explaining that obeying the authorities might promote an end to all discriminatory measures. See Katz, *Emancipation*, p. 249. The question of guard duty on the Sabbath was also raised in 1797 in Mantua, but the local rabbi saw himself obliged to grant his permission. In many other communities Jews unsuccessfully tried to be exempted from guard duty in the National Guard on the Sabbath. See Gil Graff, *o.c.*, p. 67, 162.
5 See above, pp. 5-10.

1794 he suggested that Prince William V recruit Jews to defend the city against the expected French attack:

> *It shouldn't be too difficult to establish a kind of native [militia] drawn from among the Jewish nation in order to defend their own town; if His Excellency does not consider this idea completely ridiculous, I could get someone to sound the Parnasim.*[6]

Evidently the Prince assented, since Van Golowkin, who was making every effort to reinforce the city's defenses, did indeed approach the Parnasim with a request for soldiers and money. In return he had something to offer the Jews: emancipation![7] Thus the first offer of Jewish emancipation originated with a representative of the *Ancien Régime*, rather than with the bearers of Enlightenment ideas, the Patriots.

We do not know how the Parnasim, who in 1787 had proven to have effective control over the 'Jewish street', reacted to this proposition. In any event, by the autumn of 1794 it was too late for a decision: on January 18, 1795, the city of Amsterdam surrendered, and Van Golowkin turned over his command to Dr. Krayenhoff, the nominee of the Committee of Patriotic Clubs.

Krayenhoff was ordered to replace the existing local civil guard companies by a 'National Guard' – national in name only, since its jurisdiction did not extend beyond Amsterdam. The title of one document in the Krayenhoff collection of documents is (in English): 'Reflections on the military status of the Israelites.' Judging by its contents and style, it was almost certainly written by H. L. Bromet.[8] Although the task of the Civil Guard units was essentially limited to maintaining public order in the city, during the Patriotic revolt of 1787 they had been heavily involved in street fighting, skirmishes in which Jews had played an important role. The 'Reflections' do not address the question of whether Jews were permitted to perform guard services, but they do contain an extensive historical review of the military prowess of the Jewish people, as shown by the introduction:

> *That the Israelites have since ancient times been proficient in warfare and tended towards military service needs very little argument beyond the ample proof that we find in the Bible.*

The problem of the Jews centered on their having to keep the Sabbath, although only in a 'war of choice' – in other words a self-initiated war – for in a compulsory war *halakhah* permits the use of any means to ensure victory. According to his own words the author based himself in particular on Maimonides' Laws of the Sabbath,[9] as well as invoking Rabbi Ezekiel Landau:

---

6   'Il ne serait pas non plus difficile de créer des espèces de Landzaten ('natives') tirés de la nation juive pour défendre la ville: si Elle ne trouve pas cette idée absolument ridicule, je pourrais faire sonder les Parnasim.' Colenbrander, *GS*, Vol. 5, (1806-1810), pp. 378, 418. Van Golowkin's letter is dated Oct. 2, 1794.
7   Schama, *Patriots*, p. 176. Schama does not cite his source for this information.
8   'Gedachten over den militairen stand der Israeliten,' ARA, Inv. No. 151 cc.
9   Maimonides, *Mishneh Torah*, 'Laws of the Sabbath', Ch. 2, §§ 23, 24, 25, and Laws of Kings, Ch. 8, § 1. Obviously Maimonides was referring to Jewish armies, rather than to individual Jews serving in foreign armies.

> *On the 19th of the month of Iyar of the year 5549 of the Creation, the famous*
> *Rabbi Ezekiel of Prague addressed the Israelites, earnestly counseling them to*
> *comport themselves like loyal and brave soldiers.*

This memorandum was obviously not meant to convince Krayenhoff; the halakhic and historical arguments were intended rather to defuse objections that had already been sounded by the Orthodox. The author does not seem to have expected to encounter any opposition from the non-Jewish side. From 1795 onwards, Jewish names appear on the Guard rosters of Amersfoort;[10] the Groningen regulations, dated June 19, 1795, no longer exclude Jews.[11] In The Hague, a Jew, M. Ephraim, was only a few votes short of being elected as an officer.[12]

The case was quite different in Amsterdam. There tensions between Jews and Patriots had reached the boiling point. We should not forget that the only pogrom-type assaults that ever took place in The Netherlands occurred in Amsterdam under a Patriot administration – on October 11, 1787, as well as on April 1, May 18, August 9 and 25, and September 25, 1795. No Jews were killed during the clashes of 1795, but a considerable amount of property, including market stalls, was destroyed; the fighting on August 25 claimed eighteen Jewish wounded. As usual in other, more pogrom-prone countries, the authorities claimed they had been forced to maintain public order against provocative Jewish actions.[13] However, as soon as the authorities decided to intervene, for instance in 1787 when the anti-Patriots regained power, or in 1795, thanks to the intervention of the burgomaster Visscher, the riots came to an end. It is not surprising, therefore, that the members of the Civil Guard units for areas adjoining Jewish neighborhoods (Districts 14 and 15) fiercely opposed the admission of Jews to the National Guard. The petition by the 315 citizens of District 15 leaves no doubt about this:

10 List of conscripts for the local Guards, Bloemendaal quarter, showing four Jewish names. GA Amersfoort, Inv. no. 444.
11 Chapter V of the 'Reglement voor de Gewapende Burgermacht der Stad Groningen' (Groningen, 1795) lists those who 'may be excused'. Paragraph 7 reads: 'All those who are of the Jewish persuasion. Even so all persons referred to in the above chapter shall be admissible, provided that they enlist according to the conditions stated with regard to persons above 55 years of age.'
    In Rotterdam Jews had repeatedly been refused (for instance in 1786 and 1788), but as of June 17, 1796, they were obliged to enlist in the 'armed Civil Guard'. 'Reglement voor de gewapende Burgermacht der Stad Rotterdam,' Ch. 2, art. 13, (Rotterdam 1796). For Leeuwarden, see NNJB, 1795, p. 2371; for Haarlem, *ibid.*, p. 2144.
12 See NNJB, March 1795, p. 1575: 'The Commissioners charged with the organization of the Hague citizenry are so dedicated to the purposes of Liberty and Equality that they have mobilized the Jews, like other citizens, for the Civil Guard; this action of the Commissioners merely constitutes an interpretation of the freedom-loving sentiments of The Hague. Proof of this is that in one of the companies the Citizen M. Ephraim lacked merely a few votes for his election as an officer.' Moses Ephraim (The Hague, March 14, 1767, Amsterdam Nov. 16, 1845) was, together with the two brothers Belinfante, the first Jew to enroll in the Civil Guard. He was 'a determined opponent of rabbinical Judaism' and his three sons converted to Christianity. See J. Zwarts, 'De familie Tilanus en Ephraim', *VA* Vol. 4, no. 7 (May 13, 1927), pp. 109-110.
13 Bloemgarten, *St. Ros.* 1 (1967), pp. 89-92.

This rumor [that Jews want to serve in National Guard units] has created a violent sensation among the Christian residents of this area; for, citizen representatives, do you realize how the Jews have unceasingly played havoc with the citizens of District 15? We still shudder because of the ghastly murder committed in 1787 of one of our dearest friends, after they had separated him from our patrol. We tremble at the thought of all those persecutions, molestations, yes, even the total ruin wreaked on some of us, following that cursed revolution…and daily intercourse with them causes us, more even than others, to perceive their inbred hatred against all decent-minded persons, which explains our extreme aversion to the idea of having to guard together with Jews.[14]

The events of 1787 had struck deep wounds within both parties. The Guards of Districts 14 and 15 stuck to their refusal to accept Jews in their midst. But the vast majority of the Jews, too, understandably showed little enthusiasm for joining the National Guard, while the Parnasim and rabbis frowned upon the idea. Their opposition was based on religious motives, specifically the fact that membership in the Guards would lead to desecration of the Sabbath. They could not argue publicly that Jews were loath to serve together with Guards from other, hostile districts, but this consideration no doubt played a role.

Under the circumstances, the uphill struggle of Felix Libertate to gain admission of Jews to the National Guard was foredoomed. A municipal committee (Breukelaar-De Wilde), ordered to draft a recommendation on the issue, asked

the Citizens Chief Rabbi Daniel Cohen d'Azevedo of the Portuguese, and Moses Saur (sic, should be Saul) of the High-German Jewish Nation…whether it was permissible for Jews to bear arms, whether on the Sabbath or not? To which the above-mentioned Citizen Chief Rabbi d'Azevedo answered: No! The Law forbids this! Which was confirmed by the other Citizen–Chief Rabbi Moses Saur.

Seeing that both Christian and Jewish circles had voiced opposition, the committee concluded that Jews should not be admitted to the National Guard.[15] As soon as the Municipality accepted this advice, Felix Libertate launched a campaign to reverse the decision. Bromet wrote two pamphlets (March 22 and 26) whose contents correspond closely to the Krayenhoff document, in addition to a violent attack on Chief Rabbi Moses Saul, whose famous father had already permitted Jews to serve in the armed forces.[16] Directors and members of Felix Libertate submitted petitions (March 23 and 27) that Jews nevertheless be

14 GAA, N. St.B. 404. Annexes to the Dagblad van de Vergaderingen der Representanten van het Volk van Amsterdam, Vol. I, pp. 267-277 (Oct. 10, 1795).
15 GAA, N. St.B. 391, pp. 171-279 (session of March 23). The petition of Felix Libertate is dated March 12, 1795.
16 H.L. Bromet, *Vrijheid, Gelijkheid en Broederschap*, March 22, 1795, (Da Silva Rosa, *Bibliografie*, no. 25) and *Tweede Brief van H.L. Bromet, lid en commissaris van de Volks-societeit Felix Libertate*, March 26, 1795.

admitted to the National Guard, as well as an Open Letter to the Armed Provisional Guard (March 26) demanding an end to their '*chimérique*' reservations.[17]

It was all in vain. More petitions followed, on May 13 and October 5 of the same year, addressed this time to the Committee for the Organization of the National Guard. The committee agreed that it had no mandate 'to exclude Jews directly', but neither was it empowered to accept them. As the Guards of the Amsterdam Districts 14 and 15 had observed, the issue could not be resolved at a local level, but would have to be addressed for the Batavian Republic as a whole. This was merely an excuse, of course, for Amsterdam took no steps to initiate discussions at the national level. The committee did comment that

> *In the meanwhile it had heard several oblique references to the unfavorable mood among the Christian inhabitants of the city about being armed and guarding together with Jews – an unfavorable attitude to which undeniably the earlier behavior of this 'Nation' must have somehow contributed.*[18]

Thus the Jews remained excluded from the Civil Guard, even after the Emancipation decree, and despite the fact that they had meanwhile received the suffrage. This situation continued until 1807, when King Louis Napoleon personally intervened by issuing a Cabinet resolution instructing the Minister of the Interior to order the relevant authorities 'not to discriminate between Jews and other residents of the country.'[19] A special deputy, F. van Hoogstraten, was sent to Amsterdam to inform the City Council of the king's express desire. According to his report, the councillors promised every cooperation, assuring the deputy that:

> *we have acted with the same circumspection as the Government of this large and populous city has been accustomed to proceed with excellent results since times immemorial in many, indeed, almost all, cases involving policy, namely by consulting and communicating with the Parnasim of the High-German Nation about all affairs concerning Jews, in this case with the result that the above-mentioned Parnasim have submitted a list.*[20]

The most suitable of the nominees were accepted.

This lack of enthusiasm for the employment of Jews as Civil Guards, eleven years after the emancipation, is also evident from a report submitted by Lt. Col. Alewijn. 'How many Jews there were (in answer to a question by the Minister) he couldn't say, for some of them had been approached in the street, but in total

17 The three documents that were sent simultaneously were: (a) Missive aan de Commissie tot Organisatie van de Nationale Garde deezer Stadt en Jurisdictie; (b) Aan de Provisioneele Representanten van het Volk van Amsterdam; and (c) Commissarissen en leden der Volks-Societeit Felix Libertate aan de Gewapende Provisioneele Schutterij deezer Stadt en Jurisdictie (GAA, N. St. B., p. 278).

18 October 7, 1795. Annexes of the Dagblad van de vergaderingen van de Representanten van het Volk van Amsterdam (GAA, N. St. B.).

19 ARA, Collectie Janssen No. 25 (Jan. 29, 1807).

20 Ibid. Report by F. van Hoogstraten (Feb. 4, 1807).

there were fewer than fifty.' The list submitted by the Parnasim had yielded only a few suitable candidates,

> *since many of them had been too small of stature, even crooked or misshapen,*
> *and others had been refused because the companies had been almost complete,*
> *or because the Christians (mainly in the Districts 15 and 16, that is the 6th*
> *Company) had submitted no fewer applications than the Jews.*[21]

The Jewish Corps

Civil guards were not soldiers: they lived at home and their duties were not overly exhausting. This explains the readiness of Jews to implement their right to enfranchisement – and consequently their public acceptance as equal citizens – via their service in the Guard Companies. The fierce resistance this aroused in Amsterdam shows how large a gap still divided Jews from the general population.

The experience with the naval enlistment in 1782 and the known aversion of Amsterdam Christians to serve alongside Jews may have inspired Louis Napoleon's idea that the only way to achieve a large-scale enlistment of Jews would be the formation of a separate Jewish unit: an Israelite Army Corps. This is an extremely rare phenomenon in Jewish exilic history, probably comparable only to the regiment established by Berek Joselewicz in Warsaw in 1794, which participated in the defense of the Warsaw suburb of Praga. Propagandists for the Jewish Corps eagerly cited this example, although there was one essential difference: the Polish Jewish regiment had been raised at the initiative of Joselewicz himself, whereas the Dutch corps was established by the king.

Contrary to the situation in the Civil Guard Companies (*Burgerwacht*) Jews had long been accepted in military units; but – as Koenen remarked[22] – this was more a result of the low esteem in which army service was held than a proof of the liberal views of its commanders. A certain Joseph Jacob van Lier claimed that he had joined the army in 1797.[23] Due to the threat of an English invasion in the Batavian Republic that year, twenty-five Jewish boys were called up in Amsterdam, followed by additional mobilizations in September and October. Two informers took the recruiting captain to the Jewish boys who appeared the most suitable. There was considerable weeping and wailing in the Jewish quarter, and eventually most of the Jewish boys were sent back home.[24] In fairness, it should be added that the mobilization order applied to all citizens, not only Jews.

---

21 Ibid. Report Lt.-Col. Alewijn, at the request of Col. H. van Slingelandt (Jan. 31, 1807).
22 Koenen, p. 382.
23 Meijer, *Problematiek* , pp.30-31.
24 On August 1, 25 persons aged 18-35 were called up; additional call-ups followed on September 6 and October 6. In the Jewish quarter, two informers showed the recruiting captain whom to choose. Several were compelled to leave at once, but most were allowed to go back home. *Bendit Wing, IL*, Vol. 3 (1877-1878), pp. 68-69.

It is noteworthy, though, that so few Jews enlisted. After all, here was an opportunity for the poorest among them to earn a living. Perhaps this is why Louis Napoleon's decree of '8th Hay month' (July 8), 1809 refers so pointedly to the choice between the idleness of mendicancy and an honorable vocation. The king wanted to try and retrain the *armée des bandits*,[25] as a high French official had characterized the Jews, as professional soldiers. This was emphasized by the king's promise, in his decree about the Israelite Corps, that he would establish a special training college for Jews, provided enough of them enlisted. Like the naval authorities in 1782, the king wanted to quash any fears that Jews would be unable to fulfill their religious duties.[26] According to the instruction issued by Van der Capellen, the Minister of Religion and Interior Affairs, to the High Consistory (19th Hay month 1809):

> *One or more spiritual leaders will be appointed, one or more butchers will be employed; in addition, they will be guaranteed and granted the fullest facilities to observe all of the precepts of the Jewish religion, in so far as only the most urgent situations do not prevent this.* [27]

But the venom was in the tail: Articles 6 and 7 established a connection between enlistment in the Corps and the dole. The High Consistory was told to submit an accurate list of all persons who received poor relief or other social support, not only from municipal funds, but also from one of the many Jewish charitable funds – and not only the adults concerned, but their children too. Also required was a list of persons who, although indigent, were not on the dole. All social benefits, whether in money or in kind, paid to all those who were suitable for military service, had to be withdrawn forthwith if they failed to report for military service.[28] In all publications, the Corps was presented as perhaps the greatest privilege the king had ever bestowed upon the Jews. As Bromet had insisted in his pamphlet, the latter were now able 'to demonstrate the same courage as their illustrious forefathers, from Moses till Berek Joselewicz.' Bromet's arguments in favor of military service were derived from the religious codex, and famous decisors were also once again cited.

---

25 This is the characterization of State Councillor Réal in his report on his visit to the Amsterdam Jewish quarter. Colenbrander, *Inlijving*, p. 97.

26 The proposal submitted to the king by the Minister of Religion and Interior Affairs (G.A.P.J. van der Capellen) shows that the initiative for the establishment of the Corps came from Louis Napoleon himself. The Minister had consulted the High Consistory, which was enthusiastic about the plan. It was the High Consistory that suggested applying pressure by 'reducing, or even canceling, the all-too-generous social relief allocations...' Van der Capellen commented that a special Israelite Corps actually contradicted the promotion of interfaith tolerance. He also doubted the military capacities of the Jews, but – keeping in mind the Polish example – this might turn out not as bad as he feared. He considered it necessary, however, to exert considerable pressure on the Chief Rabbis. Strict measures would have to be taken against idlers, and 'the Church and its officials should not be permitted to support them'. Conversely, families of Corps members had to be favored. The advice is dated 3 Summer month (= July) 1809.

27 'Publicatiën in de Hollandsche Hoogduitsche Kerken gedaan betrekkelijk het oprigten van een Corps Troepen, Amsterdam 1809.' The full text is also printed in Amsterdam Yiddish.

28 *Ibid.*, pp. 11-12.

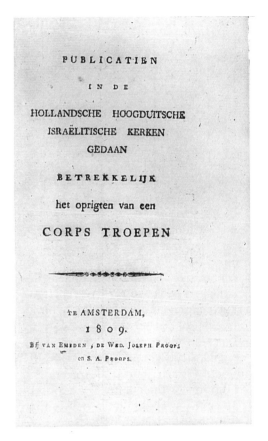

The propaganda brochure for the Jewish Corps, with text in Dutch and Yiddish. Universiteitsbibliotheek, Amsterdam.

As recently as 1795 the two Amsterdam Chief Rabbis had voiced their unequivocal opposition to Jewish participation in the Guard Corps – a duty far less likely than army service to lead to transgression of religious precepts. At the time, they had received the full support of the governors of the High-German and Portuguese communities. What was their position now about enlistment in the Israelite Corps?

Many changes had taken place during the intervening fourteen years. The position of the rabbis had been undermined; after the establishment of the High Consistory, their formal subservience to the governors of the community and the High Consistory had been set forth in an official constitution. The Parnasim were no longer so strictly orthodox as in 1795, and integration and assimilation had made inroads even within their own families.

Thus the rabbis were in fact powerless against a government that imposed its will upon the Jews and received the full support of the High Consistory – and in practice of the Parnasim as well. The Minister instructed the rabbis to praise the Corps in their sermons; the High Consistory demanded that such sermons should be given on each day that the Torah was read, i.e. every Sabbath, Monday, and Thursday. The Minister warned that:

> the Government will pay special attention to the behavior of those concerned, [to see to what extent] they will forcefully promote this beneficiary measure or indirectly contravene it.[29]

Rabbi Moses Saul, the Amsterdam Chief Rabbi, had evidently not changed his mind, at least initially. The Parnasim had approached him for a halakhic decision. Neither the wording of this request, nor the Chief Rabbi's answer is known; but there is a letter from the Parnasim, in reply to this answer, which shows that no halakhic ruling had been made (neither for nor against), but that the rabbi and his *dayyanim* had expressed themselves against enlistment. To this the Parnasim replied that they had asked for a decision, not for advice.[30] The High Consistory, too, put heavy pressure on the Chief Rabbi: its president, Dr. De Lemon, drafted a letter of support for the Israelite Corps, which the Amsterdam Chief Rabbi was compelled to sign.[31]

Following his capitulation, the Chief Rabbi gave a sermon in the Great Synagogue on the Sabbath, August 5, in the presence of the entire High Consistory. After the service, all its members accompanied the Chief Rabbi back to his home. According to Bendit Wing, many people either stayed away from the synagogue or left before the start of the sermon.[32] The Chief Rabbi of The Hague, Rabbi Lehman Simons (J. A. Lehmans), the acting Chief Rabbi of Rotterdam, Rabbi M. Philip, and the Portuguese Chief Rabbi, D. d'Azevedo,[33] also delivered their compulsory discourses; copies of their letters of support were circulated as part of a large-scale propaganda campaign on behalf of the Corps.[34] The official publications about the Corps, including the letters of

---

29 Ibid.
30 See the Hebrew letter of the Parnasim, dated 14 Teveth 5570, in answer to the letter (dated 2 Heshvan) sent by the Chief Rabbi and his *Beth Din* to the Parnasim: '...we saw in this neither a religious commandment nor a statement of the Torah, but merely that the *Gaon* (i.e. the Chief Rabbi) and his *Beth Din* have set themselves up as advisors with an advice that we had never asked them to give...We shall therefore refuse to heed what is written in this letter, for we requested Torah (i.e. a halakhic ruling) rather than advice during our discussion on 11-21 Kislev in our conference room. The *Gaon* and several *dayyanim* (judges, members of the *Beth Din*) were silent at the time and failed to express their permission or prohibition, whereupon we stated expressly that we interpreted their silence as a permission, and we have answered the Minister accordingly...' (GAA, *Protocollen van de Joodse Gemeente van Amsterdam 1809*, fol. 291, Dispositie 5).
31 See J. Zwarts, *De gefingeerde brief van R. Jacob Mozes Löwenstamm* (1809). *VA* 5 (Dec. 7, 1928), pp. 156-158.
32 *Bendit Wing, IL* 4 (1878- 1879), pp. 106-120; 186-187.
33 Hakham Daniel d'Azevedo's sermon (like all other sermons) was given on August 5, and was published (with a Dutch translation) under the title *Sermão Heroico*.
34 Dep. van Erediensten, Inv. nos. 69 - 116.

support, were issued in the form of a pamphlet, in both Dutch and Yiddish. The use of the latter language must have caused the High Consistory considerable soul-searching, but it proves how important a medium the Corps was considered for the integration of the Jews into Dutch national society. Although the Modernists regarded Yiddish as the principal enemy of such integration, they realized that only through Yiddish could they reach the vast majority of Amsterdam Jewry.

The services of the noted propagandist of integration M.C. B(elinfante) were also enlisted. He wrote a brochure entitled 'Encouragement of the Dutch Israelites to Exploit the Possibilities Now Available for a Military Career'.[35] With regard to the halakhic and historical arguments, he referred to the pamphlets by Bromet. In a lengthy introduction he sketched the adverse circumstances under which the Jews had lived in the Republic, and how these conditions were now much improved, mainly thanks to King Louis, who had opened for the Jews:

> *the glorious profession of the military trade, even ensuring the preservation and observation of the religious duties....This last benefit of the king exceeded, if one could at all dare to measure its value, all previous ones, since there exists no greater honor for a person than to help defend his fatherland.*

The High Consistory did not restrict itself to verbal and written propaganda; it had recourse to the use of press-gangs as well. In Amsterdam they were headed by the hated Jacob Marcus. Everyone who enlisted was paid six ducats (one ducat was worth approximately Df. 5.50/US $3). According to an article in the German magazine *Sulamith*, the Rotterdam recruiter Lieut. Mayer Simons paid every candidate an extra six ducats out of his own pocket.[36] Recruits had to sign on for at least six years. According to the official decree, the Corps would initially consist of one battalion of 883 men; as soon as this was complete, a second battalion would be formed. The two together would compose a regiment.

Things never got that far. As early as October the king realized that not even one battalion was in the offing. In a secret decree dated 17 Wine month (October), 1809, he disbanded the battalion. At the insistence of the High Consistory, particularly J. D. Meyer, implementation of the decision was deferred for three months (on 13 Slaughter month 1809).[37]

---

35 M.C. Belinfante, *Aanmoediging aan de Hollandse Israëlieten tot het betreden van de voor hun geopende loopbaan van den krijgsdienst*, Amsterdam, 1809.

36 *Sulamith* 3 (1810), pp. 81-87. According to the magazine, the establishment of the Corps enjoyed 'den ungetheiltesten Beifall. Es zeichnete sich sowohl durch gute Mannszucht als auch durch schöne Haltung aus...In Rotterdam ist Herr Mayer Simons als Werbeleutnant ernannt worden. Das sogenannte Handgeld ist zu 6 holländischen Dukaten bestimmt. Der erwähnte Herr Simons gibt aber noch besonders einem jeden Israëliten, der sich bei ihm engagiert, 6 holländische Dukaten Handgeld aus seinem eigenen Mitteln. Die Dienstzeit ist auf 6 Jahren festgesetzt...Der Sonnabend ist Synagogenparade. Das Corps marschiert dann in Compagnien dahin und zurück.' This item fits very well in the propaganda campaign of the High Consistory. *Sulamith*, founded in 1806, was the first German Jewish journal.

37 ARA, Collectie Janssen, No. 122.

The High Consistory decided to make one last all-out effort to attract the required number of recruits. On November 6, the 2nd-Lieut. Moses A. Daniels (or Nijmegen), a son of one of the Parnasim, died.[38] He had been persuaded to join the Corps by Parnas Barend Boas, mainly because of his insecure financial position. On his deathbed, Daniels declared that he did not want to be buried with military honors, and his family, too, was opposed to a military funeral. However, the High Consistory recognized a first-class opportunity to boost the reputation of the Corps. True, the departed was not a war hero who had died for King and Fatherland on the field of honor – but he was a Jewish officer nevertheless. Bendit Wing describes the funeral:

> *The kabranim [gravediggers] carried the body out of his home, placed it on a stretcher, and placed across the coffin an arch or burrie [litter J.M.], covered with a black cloth, on one side of which was affixed the drawn sword of the deceased, and on the other his scabbard and epaulettes. After this, he was taken by the kabranim to the front of the synagogue building of the former so-called New Community, where the Consistory currently holds its meetings, and where the body was awaited by many Christian soldiers and officers. Here the body was left for about half an hour in front of the building, while people were treated to refreshments inside. Suddenly the noted Jacob Marcus gave his marching orders. At this the Christian soldiers, and only two soldiers of the Jewish corps, one of them a cohen, lifted the bier onto their shoulders. In front went someone with a collection box, followed by the orphanage children, and behind these a detachment of soldiers beating a mourning march on a muffled drum. Before the procession moved off, the soldiers fired a salvo. Behind the bier walked Tevele Lemoeneman, the usher of the High Consistory, wearing his badge, but without a mourning cape. He was followed by the President of the Consistory, H. De Lemon, with on his right the Vice-President of the Parnasim, Philip Izak de Jongh, and on his left the President of the Welfare Board, Samuel Moses Metz.[39] After him came the celebrated brigand Jacob Marcus with Captain Boas of the Jewish Corps and 1st-Lieut. Cantor; and behind these the Christian officers, etc. Having arrived at the barge, the military once more handed the body over to the kabranim, after firing another salvo. The kabranim placed the body in the barge. When this was about to start moving the soldiers fired a third salvo. This brought the ceremony to an end.[40]*

The account clearly shows to what extent the High Consistory identified itself with the Corps and how it exploited the funeral for propaganda purposes. The military ceremonial honoring the deceased was simultaneously a salute to the High Consistory, intended to boost its reputation.

---

38 *Bendit Wing, IL* 4 (1878-79), pp. 118-120.
39 Samuel Mozes Metz succeeded T. Asser as president of the Relief Board. The honors shown De Metz at this funeral were intended to raise the status of the Relief Board. For details about De Metz, see: Els van Wageningen, Metz & Co., OA 39 (1987), p. 92.
40 The story ends with the following words: When the people had returned home, they lamented in a loud voice: 'Woe to us for having been present at such an occasion...that the final tribute to a departed had to be rendered in a Christian manner.'

The results proved to be counterproductive. Here, for all to see, was what a Jewish boy could expect in the Israelite Corps: a Christian funeral, with only two Jewish pallbearers – one of them a *cohen*, forbidden to go near a corpse by Jewish religious law! Nor had the highest Jewish authority seen fit to respect the last wish of the deceased and the pleas of his family. How could any self-respecting Jew join such an army?

The High Consistory was not satisfied with propaganda alone. It forced the leaders of the communities and the welfare funds to strictly implement the instructions about withholding support from families whose sons failed to enlist. The revolutionaries of 1795, who had risen against the 'aristocratic despots who called themselves Parnasim', and who had been so incensed about the repression and exploitation of the 'common man', now showed that they could behave far more despotic and mercilessly than the Parnasim, even though they represented only a small minority. The High Consistory and the mayor of Amsterdam wrote the Parnasim, instructing them to 'cooperate forcefully with the voluntary enlistment, and to cease payments to families whose subject members are capable of army service.' The Parnasim replied that they had issued proclamations on a number of earlier occasions, and had also contributed 300 ducats towards cash bonuses for volunteers. They further informed the mayor that 'already yesterday they had made a start on withholding the monthly allowances, however embarrassing and heartrending it was for us to hear the wailing and groaning.'[41]

The Consistory demanded that even the free distribution of matzot for the Passover festival be regarded as charity support; but here the Parnasim drew the line, since this was a religious matter 'governed by the Mosaic and Talmudic laws.'[42] They also protested the fact that the 300 ducats they had contributed from the poor fund as bonuses for volunteers had been used for propaganda purposes; they were not authorized to change the destination of funds intended for the indigent. Through their contributions they had also hoped to prevent more severe measures, but this expectation had been in vain.[43]

---

41 These 300 ducats had been made available by the Parnasim as a contribution towards the cash bonuses, which in turn were intended to avoid forced conscription and other more stringent measures. Since the High Consistory had used the money for other purposes, the Parnasim demanded its return 'since we do not consider ourselves authorized to spend the funds that have been entrusted to us in an arbitrary manner, unless they are clearly spent for the relief of the poor." (GAA, *Protocollen van de Joodse gemeente te Amsterdam*, 1809-1810, 19 Slaughter month (November) 1809, fol. 253, Dispositie 2, and 15 Lee month (January) 1810, fol. 315, Dispositie 4.

42 The Parnasim had called up all children over 16 years of age of relief recipients, 'in order to persuade them to enlist voluntarily.' Matza does not fall under the rubric of payments, for its distribution is part of the 'Israelite customs under the Mosaic and Talmudic laws.' Thus persons who receive only matza are not necessarily to be regarded as relief recipients. Letter to Maire, *ibid*, fol. 288, Dispositie 3.

43 Letter to the High Consistory, dated 6 Lee month (January) 1810, *ibid*, fol. 315, No. 4. Despite the cold winter, the Relief Board even wanted to deprive indigents of peat rations (letter to T. Asser, 31 Lee month 1810, *ibid*., fol. 323, No. 4). The exchange of letters between the Parnasim and the Relief Board shows that it was mainly the latter that wanted to put pressure on the indigents.

The High Consistory could not be budged. The captain of the Corps, L. S. Boas, was instructed to investigate the conduct of the Parnasim with regard to peat coupons. The Parnasim in turn protested that they had given rations to 'credible' indigents, particularly independent or physically handicapped children who consequently were unfit for army service.[44]

Meanwhile, complaints had begun to come in from conscripts who had experienced difficulties in observing their religious duties. The Parnasim asked the High Consistory to see to it that these complaints were solved.[45]

These complaints were of course grist to the mill of the Orthodox opposition, centered around the Chief Rabbi, who secretly incited against conscription. On November 20, a number of the main opponents of military service by Jews, including Parnas Awraham A. Prins, Bendit Wing (author of the chronicle), Joseph Fride and Wolf Waag, were summoned to the head of the First Division of the Ministry of Police and Justice because of complaints that these influential persons had dissuaded people from registering for army service. According to Wing:

> All of us answered in more or less the same way, namely that we were now being oppressed by several so-called Jews who are intent on abrogating the Jewish laws, and by a certain ill-famed fellow, Jacob Marcus, and others who act in concert with them. We are against all of them; but we do not obstruct the king's orders. We have a good and noble king, and we are aware that already three weeks ago the king canceled the plan for a Jewish Corps; but the ill-famed Jacob Marcus and his henchmen, whose only purpose is to exalt themselves, not as Jews but as Christians, succeeded in convincing the king to reconsider the scheme. This is contrary to human nature, in particular for Jews.[46]

Despite the intensive propaganda, the pressures exerted on the rabbis and Orthodox leaders, and the withdrawal of all social support, including the peat that the poor needed to ward off the winter cold, enlistment remained insignificant. On December 20, those who had been receiving poor relief from the *kehillah* in the form of peat or matzot were summoned to appear before members of the High Consistory, the Council of Parnasim and the Welfare Board, who informed them that all their children of service age were required to report the next day at the recruitment office. Of the 81 persons concerned, only five appeared, and even these refused to enlist.[47] Outside Amsterdam the situation was no better. Parnas Rood of Haarlem reported that there was not a single family or youth in his community who lived off welfare.[48]

---

44 Parnasim to High Consistory, 11 Gleaning month (February) 1810, *ibid.*, fol. 331, Dispositie 6.
45 Parnasim to High Consistory, 28 Lee month (January) 1810, *ibid.*, fol. 319, Dispositie 3.
46 Bendit Wing, IL 4 (1878-79), pp. 117-18.
47 *Ibid*, pp. 186-187.
48 M. Wolff, *Haarlem*, Vol. I, p. 51. In other towns recruitment was similarly unsuccessful. In Zwolle, for instance, it yielded only three boys, one of whom was physically incapacitated; in Deventer there was only one, and he was near-sighted; in Steenwijk the campaign resulted in one boy of 19. See H. Poppers, *op. cit.*, pp. 138-139.

How many persons signed up, all told? On 8 Flowering month (May), 1810, the High Consistory submitted a petition to the king. It should be mentioned that Louis Napoleon had just spent four months in Paris (he had left Amsterdam on November 27, 1809, and returned on April 11, 1810), as a virtual prisoner of his brother the emperor, who had already decided to depose him. In other words, the king had more pressing problems than the Jewish Corps. His absence also explains why the three-month grace period granted to the High Consistory turned into more than six months. In its petition, the Consistory wrote that a total of 360 persons had been recruited. It is interesting that Jonas Daniël Meyer, in a memorandum he wrote a year later for the controller of the Ministry of the Interior, Baron F. J. B. d'Alphonse, mentioned the figure 300, although we would have expected him to round off his figures up rather than down. Meyer claimed that the figure would have been higher had the king not dissolved the Corps for reasons of economy.[49] Whatever the case may be, we see that the number of Jewish soldiers failed to reach even half the strength of the planned battalion.

The final decision to disband the Jewish Corps was taken on the 10 Hay month 1810, nine days after King Louis Napoleon's abdication and one year after the royal decree mandating its formation.[50]

The much-advertised scheme, touted as a major benefit for Dutch Jewry, turned into a resounding fiasco. The soldiers who had enlisted were given a choice of having their passports returned or transferring to the First Rifles Regiment.[51] The recruits seemed to feel that they had been victimized; at a meeting of the High Consistory president J. D. Meyer informed his fellow members that:

> *there were rumors to the effect that several of the riflemen who had served in the Jewish Corps were planning to disturb general law and order and attack members of the High Consistory.* [52]

A corporal had already been assaulted in the Jodenbreestraat. A number of soldiers had shouted obscenities near the premises of the High Consistory, departing only because none of its members had been present at the time.

The High Consistory's behavior during the campaign to establish the Jewish Corps merely intensified the existing hatred for this body. The annexation of The Netherlands by France made the situation even worse, for the Jews and for all other inhabitants. Louis Napoleon had genuinely tried to defend his subjects, and in particular had taken the interests of the indigent Jews to heart. He

---

49 Letter from J.D. Meyer to Baron d'Alphonse (June 19th, 1811): '...ont parvint – à bien peu de temps – à trouver 300 volontaires, et on avait tout lieu de croire que ce nombre se serait augmenté de beaucoup si des motifs d'économie n'eussent porté le Roi à supprimer ce corps, dont deux officiers, l'un capitaine, l'autre premier lieutenant sont encore sans emploi.' ARA, Bi.Za vóór 1813, Inv. No. 1005 (1-61).

50 ARA, Coll. Janssen, 123.

51 In Dutch they were called 'Jagers', but they were also referred to as 'Vélites' (from the French *Vélites*).

52 Meetings of the High Consistory, 3 Hay month (May) 1810. Inv. Vol. III (1930), p. 129.

had probably seen the Jewish Corps as a means of ameliorating the living conditions of the Jewish population and raising its social status. But his French outlook and ignorance of the conditions and mentality of Dutch Jewry effectively doomed this endeavor.

In any case, after the annexation all efforts in this direction were abandoned. The French Governor-General, Lebrun, however amiable a man he may have been, had no choice but to follow Napoleon's orders.[53] What is more, Dutch Jewry was incorporated into the Organization of French Jews, the *Consistoire Central*, subordinating them to the same rules to which French Jewry was subject. As regards military service, this meant that the Jews were obliged to report any youth whose situation made him liable for conscription – something which applied to no other religious denomination. In addition, the infamous decree of March 17, 1808, forbade Jews to provide replacements for their sons of military age, as was customary in France. Fortunately, the High Consistory persuaded Governor Lebrun to use his influence with the emperor to annul this regulation as far as Holland was concerned; and much to everyone's surprise, he succeeded.[54]

Conscription

But conscription of Jews could no longer be evaded. The implementation led to serious disturbances all over Holland, among Dutchmen as well as Jews, as early as 1811, even before the serious losses of the *Grande Armée* had become known.[55] That the emperor was serious about reinforcing his army with troops from the occupied territories had become clear from Lebrun's audience with the emperor, about which he reported to the High Consistory on November 3, 1810. Lebrun insisted that the rabbis preach in favor of rearmament; the Chief Rabbis and religious teachers received a letter from the Prefect ordering them

---

53 *Ibid.*, 6 Slaughter month (November) 1810.
54 On March 12, 1811 d'Alphonse writes to the French 'Directeur général des revues et de la conscription militaire' that the prefects in Holland want to apply the French law to Dutch Jews. He argues that the annexation (euphemistically called *réunion* – see S. Schama, *Citizens*, Toronto, 1990, p. 643) cannot cancel existing rights, and that this had been confirmed by Lebrun on January 23, 1811: in Holland Jews had the same rights as all other citizens. [Colenbrander *GS* Vol. 6 (1810-1813), p. 1047]. On March 13, Lebrun approached the emperor directly to protest the application to Holland of the French decree of March 17, according to which French Jews may not provide substitutes (Colenbrander *GS* Vol. 6 (1810-1813), no. 196, p. 126). On April 8, he addressed a second letter to the emperor, to inform him that recruits have departed without having been given an opportunity to appoint replacements (not even Portuguese Jews). This had caused a great deal of trouble with the families concerned (*ibid.*, No. 218, pp. 140-141). On April 11 he thanked the emperor for his permission to provide substitutes (*ibid.*, p. 141).
      Particularly troublesome was the prefect of the Maas estuary region. In order to find out which Jews were liable to conscription, he instructed the burgomaster of Rotterdam to demand that the Jewish community submit its circumcision registers (in translation, of course), but without divulging the purpose for which they were going to be used. See E. Italie, 'De Conscriptie en de Rotterdamse Joden,' *Rotterdamsch Jaarboekje* X, Rotterdam ,1912, pp. 81-89.
55 Schama, *Patriots*, pp. 623-625.

to instill a love for the emperor in their congregations and encouraging them to enlist. Copies of the relevant sermons were to be sent to the Prefect.[56]

Thursday, April 1, was the day on which the Jewish conscripts had to report. While they were being taken through the Jodenbreestraat on their way to their barracks, riots broke out, similar to those that had taken place in other parts of the country. In the Zandstraat, the military escort was attacked and seven soldiers were wounded; one of them subsequently died. Lebrun, who that same day had reported to the emperor that the Jews appreciated his permission to allow them to provide replacements, was outraged. He immediately informed Napoleon about the riots in the Jodenbreestraat. The very next day, April 12, the Parnasim were summoned to appear before the Chief of Police and Lebrun himself.[57] Lebrun fiercely denounced the insurgents and demanded that they be apprehended. In addition, the residents of the Jodenbreestraat were to be disarmed and the Parnasim were to see to it that all eligible recruits reported forthwith. The Parnasim convened a meeting the same day, at which they decided that: (1) orderlies would be instructed to seek out the 'aggressors'; (2) the conscripts who had not yet left Amsterdam would be summoned to a meeting; and (3) these resolutions would be read out in the synagogues that very night, and the public would be cautioned to maintain the peace and desist from molesting anyone.

Carel Asser, who attended the meeting, wrote to Lebrun in the following terms:

> *I cannot but credit the goodwill that almost all those present have shown. I would only except two persons, whose answers were ambiguous.*

He added a list of 900 potential conscripts, and did not forget to mention the names of the two persons who had given 'ambiguous answers.'[58]

The transport of the conscripts occurred during Passover, and parents insisted on bringing their sons matzot for the holiday. But the authorities refused to allow this and reinforced their argument by summoning the Chief Rabbi on the first day of the festival. Since the Chief Rabbi was indisposed, the assistance of J.D. Meyer was called on to spare the invalid the long walk to Lebrun's office. Eventually three people were sentenced to death for having instigated a rebellion.[59]

56 See note 54.
57 Lebrun to the emperor, April 11-12, 1811 (Colenbrander *GS* Vol. 6 (1810-1813), pp. 141- 143). He enclosed a letter from Asser to Lebrun, praising the goodwill of the Parnasim, as well as a list of names of 900 recruits including their replacements.
58 See previous note.
59 During the meeting of the Parnasim on Friday, April 12, the president informed the College that he had visited the Secretary-General of Police, who had demanded that the rebels be apprehended. J.D. Meyer appeared at the meeting to inform those present that Lebrun had agreed that the conference he had demanded with the (ailing) Chief Rabbi on the Sabbath would be cancelled. On April 21, C. Asser and J.D. Meyer were once again forced to intervene to protect the Chief Rabbi. The riots were partly due to the fact that the conscripts had been told to report during the Passover week. Their families had wanted to bring them matzot, but this had been forbidden. GAA, *Protocollen van de Joodse Gemeente van Amsterdam*, 1811, fol. 80, Dispositie 2.

As already mentioned, the resistance to military service was not limited to the Jewish quarter of Amsterdam; there were riots in many other places, but they did not lead to a general insurrection. This does not mean that the population acquiesced to French rule. Understandably the discontent grew even worse after the fate of the *Grande Armée* became known. The dead and missing included large numbers of Dutchmen. French authority sank to such a low ebb that the Parnasim found it necessary to issue a special warning before Purim, cautioning the Jews not to ridicule the French military, let alone the even more despised French *douaniers*.[60]

By present-day standards the number of conscripts was low. This is reflected in the efforts of the Board of the Jewish orphanage to exempt its wards from military service. Again it was Jonas Daniel Meyer who exerted his influence; seven of the eight boys concerned were exempted because their mothers were still alive; only the eighth, a full orphan, was conscripted.[61]

We may therefore conclude that the overall number of Jewish recruits was small. Both the efforts at mass enlistment in the Navy in 1782, and the recruitment for the Israelite Corps in 1809 ended in failure. Even the prospect of exchanging dire poverty in freedom for a square meal as conscripts failed to attract the Jewish proletariat. As regards Amsterdam, its citizens' hostile attitude, demonstrated during the efforts to secure the Jews' admission to the Civil Guard, had been sufficient to scare the latter off. In addition, the strictly orthodox lifestyle of most Jews effectively precluded a military career.

This situation did not change materially following the establishment of the Kingdom of The Netherlands. The Constitution stated that a militia would be formed to defend the national territory, but its size was to be limited and it was to be composed 'mainly of volunteers.' In practice this meant that most Jews remained outside the army until general conscription was introduced.

---

60 The Parnasim warned the members of the community not to instigate riots, and in particular to refrain from molesting French soldiers, either verbally or physically. Before Purim the Parnasim had issued a public warning to the effect 'das obschoynt le'oniim (the poor) tsu geshtanden ist bimey purim mit iren shpilen [in] die hayzer geyen zikh tsu divertiren okhayn das lumas zey (notwithstanding this) zikh keyner untersteyen zol um zikh in militeyr oder duane kleydung tsu vayzen un peshite (naturally) um nit zolkhe shpilen tsu makhen oder zolkhe verter tsu eksplitsiren (or use such words) di als eynige beshpotung kenen konsidderirt veren'. *Ibid*, fol. 63, Dispositie 3.
61 See I. Maarsen, 'Hoe J.D. Meyer erelid van het Nederlands Israelietisch Jongensweeshuis te Amsterdam werd,' *VA* 8 (Dec. 18, 1931), pp. 178-180.

9 Finale: the Establishment of the Jewish Denominational Structure by King William I

A Royal decree by William I provided the Jews with a legally constituted organizational framework ahead of any other religious community in The Netherlands[1] – even before the official Constitution was promulgated and adopted.[2] Although this decision has been attributed to the king's wisdom and friendly disposition towards the Jews,[3] we are not doing him or his close advisors an injustice by suggesting that the Jews were not uppermost in their mind while preparations for the return of Prince William to The Netherlands and the administrative organization of the Kingdom were in hand.

To understand the real reason for the sudden and compelling concern for the Jews, we must go back to September 12, 1808, the day of the establishment of the High Consistory, which brought about a radical and revolutionary change in the structure of the Jewish community. The centralized organization created at this time had crushed the power of the Parnasim and thus ensured freedom of conscience (i.e. the rabbis or Parnasim were no longer able to control the private lives of the members of their communities, as had previously been the case). Also gone were the fines and other punitive measures that the local authorities had previously allowed them to impose.[4]

---

1   The Dutch Reformed Church was not officially constituted until January 7, 1816 (H.T. Colenbrander, *Willem I, Koning der Nederlanden,1,* Amsterdam, 1931, p. 375).
2   The Constitution was ratified in March 1814 by the Plenary Session of notables.
3   Van Zuiden makes only a passing mention of the conflicts in 1813 and 1814. '…For in particular the ban on the use of Yiddish in the synagogue, and the ruling that those who were called up to the reading of the Torah must be called by their surnames, created bad blood. In November and December 1813 these rulings even provoked disturbances in the synagogue in Amsterdam.' [*Stud. Ros.* II (1968)], p. 83]. He confuses the Consistory of the Zuyderzee Department with the High Consistory: 'These incidents were disagreeable (sic!) to the High Consistory, for which reason it stepped up its countermeasures.' *Ibidem.* Sluys and Hoofien even write: 'The Sovereign Monarch now made it one of his primary concerns to annul the French organization of the Jewish Denomination and bring the relationships between the latter and the Government closer in line with the new state of affairs.' (*Handboek voor de Geschiedenis der Joden*, Vol. 3, Amsterdam 1873, p. 634). The only detailed description is to be found with D.M. Sluys, 'Uit woelige dagen' in: *Programma van het Koninklijk Bezoek aan de Grote Synagoge te Amsterdam van April 1, 1924,* Amsterdam 1924, p. 7-17. The article is based solely on the protocols of the Jewish community, and essentially reflects the viewpoint of the Parnasim.
4   Article 25 of the by-laws of the High Consistory. Fines as such were not mentioned in the general regulations, but before the High Consistory approved any local by-laws, it checked that no articles were included empowering the Parnasim to impose fines.

The large Amsterdam community had cause to rejoice about the dissolution of the competing New Community, whose members – albeit reluctantly – returned to the parent community. Although most of the latter were economically better situated than the average member of the Old Community, their preparedness to pay contributions was minimal. For that matter, the same applied to the orthodox opposition which, although most of its adherents were poor as church-mice, also included a few extremely wealthy families who had been avid supporters of the old regime – the negative consequences of which the High Consistory had experienced earlier.[5]

The Meat-Hall

A far more serious setback for the community was the financial decline of the meat-hall. Freedom of conscience also meant that Jews could buy meat outside the meat-hall, which meant that its income declined precipitously.[6] Since the revenues from this source were used for subsidizing the community's social welfare system, for which huge sums of money were required, the consequences were catastrophic. According to the Parnasim the community had 18,000 welfare recipients, and even if this figure is exaggerated, it shows the enormous burden borne by a thin upper layer in order to satisfy even the minimum requirements of these indigent masses.[7] In the year 1806 – in other words, prior to the introduction of the Consistorial system – the community's monthly welfare disbursements amounted to more than Df. 7,000. The Parnasim complained that even this amount was insufficient, and that the schism in the

5   In a letter to the Ministry concerning a dispute between the Parnasim of the Amsterdam community and the Welfare Board, the High Consistory notes that welfare collections are low due to the economic situation and 'that the dissatisfaction induced by new institutions and fed by malevolence could only exacerbate this consequence.' ARA, Minuut Verbalen van het behandelde in de gewone en buitengewone vergaderingen van het Opperconsistorie, Wine month (September/October) 1810.
6   See above.
7   The figure of 18,000 has been derived from a letter sent by the Parnasim to the 'Illustrious Representatives of the Batavian Republic' (February 27, 1806). This figure is merely an approximation. As such it is obviously far from exact and it seems exaggerated, but still it appears regularly (*Protokolbuch* 1806-1807). A letter to the Welfare Board dated September 4, 1804 also mentions a figure of 17,500-18,000 (*ibid.*, 1804-1805); in 1805 the Welfare Board even raised the number to 19,600. The figure becomes more realistic when considering the general situation in Amsterdam around 1800. J. Goldberg, the Agent for the National Economy, established that 80,000 – or three-eighths – of the population of Amsterdam were in receipt of relief (Schama, *Patriots*, p. 372). Among these were 18,000 Jews, i.e. 22.5 percent, or twice the percentage of Jews in the general population, which amounted to approx. 210,000.

community was responsible for the fact that they were unable to raise more.[8] However, in 1810, when the effects of the new arrangements had made themselves felt, the community could afford no more than Df. 700 a month – one-tenth of the previous amount. The community no longer derived any income from fines, and the revenues from the meat-hall had declined to one-third.[9] The administrators bore their share of this malaise: their salaries had been slashed by half, the remainder being paid in the form of promissory notes of dubious value.[10] We may therefore conclude that it was the Jewish proletariat that paid for the emancipation and freedom of religion. If only the local authorities or the government had taken care of the destitute Jewish poor, who had been so badly hit by the newly imposed laws and regulations, Emancipation could have been a blessing. But the Amsterdam Municipality was totally opposed to this solution and turned a blind eye to the horrendous scenes of the half-naked and homeless men and women roaming the Jewish quarter in search of food and alms.[11]

---

8   Our calculation of 7,000 guilders per month is based on data from the above-mentioned letters:
    1) Peat for approximately 1,700 families, comprising a total of 6,800 persons.
    2) Monthly allowance ('*kitzva*') of Df. 2 for nearly 1,000 families, comprising approx. 4000 persons (total Df. 2,000).
    3) Additional financial support for another 500 families (2,000 persons).
    4) Shirts and coats for approx. 1,200-1,300 persons.
    5) Matzot for Passover for about 18,000 persons.
    6) Care for the sick, including remunerations of physicians, surgeons and midwives.
    Df. 7,000 is therefore a conservative estimate, especially since the disposition of corpses has not been included in our calculation.
9   The figures for the revenues of the meat-hall were as follows:
1806	Df. 65,000
1807	Df. 60,000
1808	Df. 51,700
1811	Df. 37,170
1812	Df. 26,400
1813 (est.)	Df. 23,300

    By this time the monthly allowance (*kitzva*) of Df. 2, already reduced to Df. 1, had been suspended. The number of persons eligible for financial assistance was drastically reduced, and at times payments were two months overdue.
10 The Parnasim informed the Welfare Board of this measure and requested it to act likewise with regard to its own officials (*Protokolbuch*, August 5, 1810). The High Consistory also had no choice but to acknowledge that the Parnasim could not possibly meet Art. 4 of the decision of the Ministry of Internal Affairs regarding payments to the Welfare Board.
11 See the report of Staatsraad Réal quoted on p. 43. The community records similarly mention naked and half-naked men and women. Prefect De Celles decreed that any person found wandering the streets naked was to be brought immediately to the poorhouse (March 16, 1813). The police requested the directors of the poorhouse for assistance in carrying out this difficult task (March 20). However, the latter replied that they could not possibly carry out De Celles' instructions, since only an institution twice the size of the poorhouse would be capable to cope with such a job. (GAA Notulen van de Regenten van het Werkhuis, April 22, 1813.) At that time there were 1,300 beggars in the poorhouse. See E. Boekman, 'Demografische en sociale verhoudingen ong. 1800', *VA* 6a (1929), pp. 104-105.

The Consistorial Arrangement

Even before the annexation by France the majority of the Jewish population of Amsterdam was incensed at the ruling emancipatory clique, and the annexation only intensified their hatred. In addition, the consistorial system which existed in France was introduced in The Netherlands, too.[12] The High Consistory did attempt to gain recognition as a Consistory for the entire annexed territory, but the Consistoire Central in Paris refused.[13] Instead it established four 'Consistorial synagogues', located in Amsterdam, Rotterdam, Zwolle and Leeuwarden.[14]

The gentlemen in Paris were of course entirely ignorant of the specific conditions of the Jews in The Netherlands, and they insisted that the French system be applied lock, stock and barrel.[15] They even refused to grant the Portuguese community of Amsterdam a status other than a constituent synagogue of the Amsterdam consistory. Even though the French regulations recognized the existence of a 'synagogue particulière' with its own Board of management subordinate to the local consistory, Paris rejected this alternative as well.[16] Fortunately this displeased the French authorities in Holland, who considered it inconceivable that such a venerable community as the Portuguese

12 Colenbrander's description of the introduction of the Consistorial system in the annexed territories is entirely false: 'The Jews had been left out, as the French laws for the Jewish Synagogue Administration had already been promulgated in The Netherlands (January 1812, J.M.), and it seemed they could easily be implemented as soon as it had been agreed that the Portuguese Jews did not have to amalgamate with the High-German Jews and were permitted to keep their own synagogue.' (Colenbrander, *op. cit.*, p. 37). This mistaken view of events also explains the strange choice of documents in his *Gedenkstukken*.

13 In a letter to Lebrun dated November 27, 1810, the High Consistory explains the situation of the Jews in The Netherlands. Since this was radically different from that of French Jewry, the French consistorial system was not suitable. One difference was the overwhelming influence of the rabbis on the Jewish masses, due to which – contrary to the French situation – no Dutch rabbi should be appointed to the Consistory! As an interim measure, the High Consistory proposed to appoint a committee of three to five persons 'qui pendant quelques années sous l'autorité de S.E. le ministre de l'intérieur serait chargée de toutes les fonctions actuelles du Consistoire et serait sous les ordres du Consistoire Central à Paris.' Colenbrander GS Vol. 6 (1810-1813), p. 874.

14 Under the French system the seat of the 'Consistorial Church' (i.e. synagogue; the expression was borrowed from Christian terminology, but it referred to the Jewish community or *kehilla*, J.M.) was located in the city with the largest number of Jewish inhabitants. Thus Leeuwarden was chosen rather than Groningen – which also aspired to a seat – and Rotterdam over The Hague. The Hague Parnasim were convinced that this was the High Consistory's way of taking revenge.

15 'Le Consistoire Central des Israélites à Paris insiste pour que l'application du réglement du 10 decembre 1806 reçoive son application aux Juifs de la Hollande' (Bigot to Lebrun, June 3, 1812) Colenbrander, *op. cit.*, p. 799.

16 In a letter to J.D. Meyer, dated September 10, 1811, the Consistoire Central contended that in general they did not favor the establishment of a 'synagogue particulière', nor was it considered necessary in this case. The appointment of 'Commissaires-surveillans est plus simple et plus économique.'

ARA, Erediensten. (Here too the word 'synagogue' refers to the Portuguese-Jewish community.)

Jews would be incorporated into the High-German establishment.[17] Eventually the French officials won out, and on July 14, 1812, during his stay in Vilna, in the middle of his Russian campaign, Napoleon signed a decree recognizing the Amsterdam Portuguese community as a 'synagogue particulière'.[18] This tug-of-war considerably delayed the introduction of the French consistorial system in the Dutch territories, so that only on February 21, 1813, shortly before the end of the French occupation, was the Amsterdam Consistory finally inaugurated. Its composition clearly betrayed the sympathies of the powers that be: of the five members, two were Portuguese Jews (A. Mendes de Leon and Rabbi Abendana de Britto), although the Portuguese community constituted only 10 percent of the entire Amsterdam Jewish population. Mendes de Leon was also appointed chairman. The three other members were J. D. Meyer, Carel Asser and Chief Rabbi S. Berenstein.[19] This composition reflected the French regulations, which required two rabbis on a Board of five, but it conflicted with the prevailing tradition in The Netherlands. The fact that Asser and Meyer were to represent the large High-German community, of which they merely represented a small oppositional faction, indicates that, like its predecessors, the French administration preferred the Dutch Jewish community to be dominated by the emancipatory camp.

As soon as the Amsterdam consistory had been inaugurated, it lost no time in trying to implement the instructions received from Paris. This is not so surprising when we realize that in general terms French policies corresponded with those that Asser and Meyer, both dominating personalities on the Board, had been pursuing for a number of years. During its first session, on February 21, the Consistory took several decisions that on the surface did not seem overly radical, but which, given the tense situation and the pent-up resentment against the Jewish leadership, explain the violent reaction they provoked.

---

17 Already on September 28, 1810 Lebrun wrote in this spirit to Napoleon (Colenbrander, *GS* Vol. 6 *(1810-1813)*, p. 81). See also Lebrun's letter to Bigot (November 28, 1811): '.quoi qu'on fasse, les Portugais croiairent se dégrader par la réunion et les Allemands ne s'enlèveraient pas' (*ibid.*, p. 791). Bigot agreed, and he would have preferred the establishment of two Consistories in Amsterdam, but this was against the regulations. It was his idea to establish a 'Synagogue Particulière' (Bigot to Lebrun, June 3, 1812), *ibid.*, p. 799-800.

18 Eventually the Consistoire Central tried to save face. On March 17, 1813, it dispatched the Imperial Decree, with the following addition: 'Telle est la mesure que d'après les représentations du Consistoire Central le gouvernement a adopté pour concilier les différents interêts'.(Archives Nationales F19, no. 1204).

19 In conformity with the regulations of the Consistoire Central, each consistory had to be composed of two rabbis and three laymen. In Paris the Grand-Rabbin was the president, but in the Dutch circumstances this was unthinkable. The position of Grand-Rabbin was given to S.B. Berenstein, the rabbi of Leeuwarden, who was considered the most progressive (or rather sole progressive) rabbi in The Netherlands – for one thing because he was the only one to react to the High Consistory's request to comment on the Dutch Bible translation. Later Berenstein would claim that he had only accepted the appointment of Grand-Rabbin at the insistence of his father-in-law, the Amsterdam Chief Rabbi J.M. Löwenstamm (see his letter dated Dec. 23, 1813 to King William I, ARA Staatssecr. I, exh. Febr. 26, 1814, no. 90).

The rabbis and teachers no longer had any choice but to express their support of the decisions of the Grand Sanhedrin.[20] Since they were all dependent on the Jewish authorities, there was almost no solution for them, although even so there was some initial resistance. However, the Jewish masses were in a different position, and the measures concerning them encountered far stronger resistance. The adoption of family names had been compulsory since 1811, but now these names also had to be used in the course of religious ceremonies.[21] The Consistory did not hesitate to impose severe punishments on those who refused to comply with this ruling, as the following example will demonstrate. E.J. Benjamins, a member of a prominent family, refused to be called up to the reading of the Torah by his civil surname on the day of his son's circumcision. The authorities accused him of seditious behavior and the Consistory demanded an exemplary punishment.[22] Eventually he recanted, and the threat of punishment was retracted – fortunately for him, since imprisonment and even branding would have been in store for him.

A similar decision concerned marriage ceremonies. The Consistory had determined that marriages had to be consecrated in the synagogue; one reason was to prevent unions that were forbidden by the Code Napoléon – such as

20 The decisions were translated into Dutch and published by the publishers J. Belinfante, J. van Embden, S.A. Proops and D. Proops Jr. under the title 'Decisien van den Grooten Sanhedrin in 1807 te Parijs vergaderd geweest. Gedrukt op last van het Consistorie der Israëlieten, in de Circumscriptie van Amsterdam.' (no year). It included the following text addition: 'I, the undersigned _____ Rabbi (or Teacher of Religion) domiciled at _____ Department _____ herewith declare, pursuant to the stipulations contained in Art. 26 of the Regulations of the Assembly of the Israelites of December 10, 1806, ratified by Imperial Decree of March 17, 1808, and reading as follows:
"Every Rabbi (or teacher of the Religion), who, after the present regulations shall have come into force, and who, regardless of his employment, wishes to retain his domicile in France or in the Kingdom of Italy, will be required to declare his adherence to the Decisions of the Grand Sanhedrin by means of a formal declaration signed by him."
I hereby declare my complete and unconditional loyalty to the doctrinal decisions of the Grand Sanhedrin; – for which reason I pledge in the name of the Religion, that I shall teach nothing, either, publicly or in private, that fails to accord with the spirit of above-named Decisions. In witness of which I have signed the present document at _____ , date _____.
21 About the introduction of surnames, see H. Beem, 'Joodse Namen en namen van Joden', *Stud. Ros.* III (1969), p. 82-94. Even those Jews who had already taken surnames objected to their use in the synagogue or in the course of any other religious ceremonies.
22 The Consistory wrote a letter on the subject to the Chief Constable of Amsterdam (May 16, 1813), claiming that Eleazer Jonas Benjamins and Hartog Abraham Erdingen 'se sont opposés publiquement dans la synagogue.' The letter specifically demanded 'de prendre telles mesures principalement contre le Sr. Eleazer Jonas Benjamins.à fin de assurer la tranquillité dans les synagogues et l'observance des lois.'
Benjamins publicly expressed remorse for his behavior, and on the Sabbath he requested that a blessing be pronounced for all members of the Consistory. Evidently the Consistory wanted to neutralize one of the members of the opposition.

those between an uncle and a niece – from being contracted.[23] Any official caught violating this law – whether a rabbi, cantor or sexton – was to be dismissed immediately.

And finally, on May 11, the Consistory decided to eliminate the linguistic distinctions between people of the same country and religion:

> *One of the principal obstacles that cannot be removed too soon is that thus far for publications, public documents, receipts, etc. the Portuguese language, as well as Hebrew and High- and Low-German [Yiddish] were used; especially this last so-called language has contributed in no small amount to subjecting our former High-German co-religionists to ridicule and scorn in the eyes of their fellow citizens.*[24]

The Parnasim, who – just as in France – were now called 'Commissaires–surveillans', were instructed 1) from this moment on to use only French or Dutch in all official documents and proclamations; 2) to abolish any distinctions between Portuguese and High-German Jews in all official documents; and 3) to see to it that these instructions were also followed by all other officials and subordinates.

The foregoing makes it clear that Portuguese, still extensively used within the Portuguese community, was similarly swept away in the struggle against Yiddish. Asser and Meyer's craving for unification attempted to eradicate the age-old separation between Portuguese and High-German Jews, but for all practical purposes they failed to eliminate the existing divisions and enforce a 'reconciliation'.[25] In the High-German community too, the vast majority resisted the abolition of Yiddish, and even during the annexation period Yiddish remained the main language used for synagogue announcements – simply because there was no other way to communicate with the members of the community.[26]

---

23 The Consistoire Central had circularized all communities that marriages could only be consecrated in a synagogue, in areas specially designated for this purpose (Jan. 20, 1812, AN, F 19, no. 1032). In a memorandum to the communities (Sept. 14, 1813) the Amsterdam Consistory referred not only to the Napoleonic Code, but also to the 'Political Statute' of 1580 and the decision of the Councils of Holland and West-Friesland of September 30, 1656, which forbade certain kinds of marriages that were quite customary among Jews. Persons consecrating such marriages could be dismissed on the spot, and any children resulting from such a union were deemed illegitimate and excluded from inheriting from their parents. (ARA, Circumscriptie van Amsterdam, Minuutverbaal en relatieven 27.)

24 *Ibid.*

25 The Consistory wrote to the Administrators of the Synagogue Particulière that no time was more salutary for effecting a reconciliation than the initiation of a new ecclesiastical authority. The *Mahamad* was not convinced and objected to this innovation. (May 23, 1813); GAA, Notulen van het College van Administrateuren, 1813/1814).

The actions of the Consistory conflicted with both Portuguese and High-German Jewish tradition, and they only demonstrate the extremity of the measures the Consistory was prepared to take in order to enforce assimilation in the shortest possible time. However, the Consistory was not in the least perturbed, and following a lengthy correspondence, the use of Portuguese was permitted only for '*avelut*' (the mourning ceremony). It is highly surprising that the two Portuguese members of the Consistory, Mendes de Leon – who was also the President – and Rabbi Abendana de Britto did not object to Asser's and Meyer's radical behavior.

26 Between 1809 and 1813 the Parnasim and the Commissaires-surveillans repeatedly requested approval for publications in Yiddish, and this was permitted whenever it was a matter of reaching all the members of the community.

These ukases of the Consistory merely exacerbated the already rebellious mood among the Jewish masses. Napoleon's military debacles further contributed to the erosion of the authority of the Consistory, now generally regarded as lackeys of France, to the point that open resistance against the tyrants could no longer be avoided. In October 1813 riots erupted in the synagogues in Amsterdam concerning the appointment of cantors, but insiders pointed out that these were in fact the result of the prevailing hostility against the Consistory.[27]

During the second half of November 1813 Amsterdam witnessed a series of dramatic events, but both the authorities and the Jewish leadership chose to react with the utmost caution.[28] On November 15 a new, revolutionary City Council was elected in Amsterdam, which included two members of the Consistory, Mendes de Leon and J.D. Meyer.[29] On November 15 the French troops withdrew from Amsterdam, and from this moment on there were incessant riots in the Jewish quarter and in the synagogues. The Commissaires-surveillans hired fifty men to maintain order, while trying to convince the Consistory to meet some of the demands of the people. The only concession they were prepared to make was to cancel the prayer for the Emperor,[30] while meanwhile Asser and Meyer started negotiations with a view to ensuring the continued existence of the Consistory under the changed circumstances. In a subsequent proposal Asser changed the hated name 'Consistory' to 'Great Synagogue Council',[31] which would presumably include the Portuguese Jews also – and at any rate this was believed by the leaders of the 'synagogue particulière' ('...that secret moves are afoot to legalize the Consistory and incorporate us in this institution').[32] It would not take them long to find allies in their struggle against the Consistory.

27 This was written by David S. Boas in a letter to the Commissioner-General of the Department of the Zuyderzee (February 20, 1814). ARA, Commissariaat Kerkelijke Zaken, 1813-1815, Tiende Portefeuille Omslag 135.
28 See Brugmans, pp. 83 ff.
29 For the objections against the appointment of J.D. Meyer, see pp. 46-48.
30 The Commissaires-surveillans made a last attempt to make the Consistory change its mind via the burgomaster (November 25), but it insisted that its announcement that all regulations remain valid be read out in the synagogue. On the Sabbath, November 27, rioting broke out in every synagogue, and in the Great Synagogue the Grand Rabbin and the Commissaires-surveillans did not have the courage to read out the publication of the Consistory; they were also forced to yield to the demand of the public not to use the surnames of those called up to the Torah. The same evening acting chairman A.B. de Metz was summoned by Meyer, who reproached him for not calling the police to help restore order. At this point the Commissaires-surveillans requested that the Governors-General for the Department of the Zuyderzee intervene with the Consistory. It was decided that the publication would be read out after all – but in Yiddish.
31 On December 1, the Consistory decided to continue on the same basis and try to extend its authority to the remainder of the country (ARA, Netverbaal van het verhandelde in de vergaderingen van het Consistorie voor de Circumscriptie van Amsterdam).
32 ARA, Governors-General of the Department of the Zuyderzee to Mr. de Metz, president of the Commissaires-surveillans of the High-German Israelite Synagogue (dated December 9, 1813).

The Restoration

The entry of Prince William in Amsterdam on December 2, 1813, on which occasion he was proclaimed Sovereign Monarch, effectively ended the French rule of The Netherlands. It also tended to convince the Jewish population that all remaining French-inspired institutions and decrees – including the hated Consistory – were automatically abolished; those who thought differently would, if necessary, be convinced by force.

This seemingly reasonable assumption would soon be proved mistaken, for most of the newly appointed government officials belonged to the established bureaucratic elite that had earlier served under Louis Napoleon and the French administration, people who were totally lacking in revolutionary élan or inclined to meet the demands of 'commoners'. The election of Mendes de Leon and Meyer to the Amsterdam Municipal Council also pointed in the direction of a continuity in people and conceptions. It is therefore understandable that the new regime regarded the fracas in the synagogues as a dangerous omen.

Even so, it had underestimated the enormous disaffection in the Jewish quarter. The Commissaires-surveillans, i.e. the former Parnasim, despite their desire to display loyalty to the regime, were unable to control the voluble protests of the crowd whenever announcements were made in Dutch, or when worshipers were called up by their secular surnames to the reading of the Torah. They implored the recently appointed Governor-General to make concessions to the people, but the Consistory refused to comply, leaving the Governor-General no choice but to order the High-German community to abide by the rules of the Consistory:

> *Meanwhile we request you, and if necessary order you, duly to inform the Community that all by-laws and administrative regulations existing at the time (i.e. on November 21, 1813) shall remain in effect, until such time as new dispositions shall have been made, [and] that the existing regulations concerning the afore-mentioned Consistory shall remain in effect, and since therefore no decision has as yet been taken by His Royal Highness, the respective Israelite Communities are hereby requested, and if necessary ordered, to submit to the Laws of said Consistory in the meantime, it being the desire of our Sovereign that no person, no matter who shall act on his own authority against, or refuse to obey the Laws or Regulations that are presently in force, something which to our regret seems to have occurred in the High-German Synagogues.*

The Consistory lost no time in pursuing the issue, and the following day it met and adopted a number of decisions liable to intensify the agitation, to wit:

Art. 2

All arrangements concerning the reading of announcements in the Dutch language; the consecration of marriages, the use of surnames, etc., will remain unchanged, and in accordance with the Publication of the Consistory dated February 23, 1813.

Every rabbi and official was expected to obey the written instructions of the Commissioners-General, on pain of being fired and having charges brought against him:

Art. 4

Anyone obstructing [the implementation of] the aforementioned written instructions, will be dismissed forthwith and charged before the competent authorities as opponents of the Supreme Government and its orders.

The Consistory was particularly outraged by Chief Rabbi Löwenstamm's flaunting of the Consistory's decision by consecrating a marriage in a private home, assisted by two cantors and several other officials. Even though deserving of being punished with immediate dismissal, the Consistory decided for once to overlook his transgression.[33] However, the opposition did not sit still either. On December 12, forty-three members of the community submitted a petition requesting the dissolution and abolition of the Consistory, founded as it was 'on the principles of the French Constitution, the separation of religion from the state, and the assumption that every person could or could not serve God as he saw fit, principles that revealed their morally corrupting and godless aims as clearly as the midday sun.' From this it followed that the pre-1795 situation, when during the reign of the Sovereign Monarch's forefathers the Jews had enjoyed complete freedom of religion, should be restored. Former members of Adath Jesurun (including Bromet, M.S. Asser and I. de Jonge Meyersz.) objected, while a third petition submitted by supporters of the incumbent Parnasim argued that the former religious customs must be re-instated, but that simultaneously Jews should retain their civil rights – this in contrast to those who preferred the restoration of the 'ancien regime'.[34]

Far from restoring peace and quiet in the Jewish Quarter, the decisions of the Consistory so inflamed the populace that A.L. de Metz and B. Boas, the two most hated Commissaires-surveillans, no longer dared to attend synagogue services for fear of being assaulted. However, on December 18 Boas' son persuaded his father to pluck up courage, arguing that a refusal to go to the synagogue countered the instructions of the Government, which wanted life to continue as usual. The arrival of Metz and Boas signaled the outbreak of the most serious disturbances ever known in the synagogue. After having been pushed and shoved about, Boas was thrown out of the *shul*; while crossing a bridge on his way home, someone tried to throw him into the water. Fortunately his two sons turned up just in time. L.S. Boas, who, following his frustrating experiences with the Jewish corps was on his way to Admiral Verdooren to request a commission in the navy, attempted to extricate his father, but instead

---

33 ARA, Extract uit het Register der deliberatiën van het Consistorie. Extraordinary meeting of December 10, 1813. Rabbi Löwenstamm, the Chief Sextons and Chief Cantors also received a copy.
34 ARA, Staatssecr. Koning Willem I, exh. February 26, 1814.

was himself attacked and had his sword taken away.[35] His brother, D.S. Boas, was in even bigger trouble: he was kicked, thrown to the ground and dragged through the mud. He succeeded in reaching his father's house, where in the meantime the windows had been broken. And as if all this was not enough, he was arrested and taken to prison in chains. His wife suffered a nervous breakdown.[36]

However, Boas was not the only one to be taken into custody. The riots were a cause of great concern to the still insecure government. Fannius Scholten, the Commissioner-General of the Zuyderzee Department (who had been the New Community's lawyer), decided to institute vigorous disciplinary measures against the Jews who had so maltreated their lawful leaders. He ordered a thorough investigation, whereas Boas lodged a complaint against his attackers. However, the following day the authorities realized that strong measures would only exacerbate the situation, and thus all those arrested were freed and the investigation was called off. D.S. Boas was prepared to withdraw his complaint, on condition that he, his father and his brother would receive full satisfaction.[37] He demanded the same for the sons of De Metz, who had also been molested. Nothing ever came of the promised satisfaction.[38]

How can we explain this sudden turnabout? By now it had become clear to the powers-that-be that hostility to the Consistory was so intense and widespread that it was inconceivable to continue supporting a leadership which was so abhorrent to the vast majority of the Jews. Even in non-Jewish circles voices

35 In 1811 L.S. Boas became a cadet and later a captain in the navy. He died in 1827 in Den Helder.
36 Letter from D. Boas dated February 20, 1814. All documents received by or originating from the office of the Commissioner for Religious Affairs are in the Algemeen Rijksarchief under: Commissariaat van Kerkelijke Zaken 1813-1815, Tiende Porte-Feuille, Zaken der Israeliten A. This portfolio includes six folders. Each folder has an introduction, usually a short description of the contents. The titles of the folders are:
– 135. Behandeling van het geschil over de organisatie van het Israëlitisch Kerkbestuur tengevolge van de omwenteling van 1813. Tot op het Staatsbesluit van 26 Februari 1814.
– 136. Bijdragen tot de geschillen over de Israëlitische organisatie.
– 137. Besluit van 26 Februari 1814 en werkzaamheden dientengevolge tot vaststelling der nieuwe Israelitische organisatie.
– 138. Israelitische Organisatie van 12 Juni 1814 en handelingen dientengevolge.
– 139. Benoeming van Notabelen tot ontwerping van de Reglementen der Hoofd-Synagogen en Handelingen deswegens.
– 140. Reglementen der Hoofdsynagogen.
Any documents mentioned in this chapter not referred to by any other source are from this Tenth Portfolio. The introductions to the collections of documents numbered 135, 137 and 139 are reproduced *in extenso* in Anton E.M. Ribberink, 'Overheid en Eredienst rond 1813', Neveh Ya'acov, Assen, 1982, pp. 58-60.
37 *Ibid.*
38 The Commissaires-surveillans also put in a demand for satisfaction, and when no reaction was forthcoming, turned directly to the king. Their letter described the heavy financial burdens on the one hand, and the plunge in income on the other. They expected the king to promulgate such 'laws and institutions that would protect the community against all kinds of dissolution' and requested him to 'grant the undersigned fair redress'.
On March 10, Van Stralen replied that they had welcomed the decision of February 26, and presumably did not expect 'further compensation for the unpleasantness one suffered in times of confusion.'

were being raised in favor of turning back the clock. P.A. Brugmans, a member of the Amsterdam municipality (and previously legal advisor of the Old Jewish community) defended the Orthodox point of view in a lengthy memorandum.[39] Should the 'real Jews', so he asked, be ruled 'by those who are not Jewish, but actually Deists, who had only caused problems in Europe. They were Jews merely because they had been circumcised. They don't attend Synagogue services, nor do they keep the Day of Atonement, or fast during the prescribed times, and they live among the secular society without abstaining from impure meat and anything that is deemed impure by the Jew.' The Amsterdam Municipality went even further, by advocating a complete return to the pre-1795 situation, when the Parnasim had wielded unlimited power over the members of their community: 'Religious authority [shall] be established in the manner existing up to 1795 according to the by-laws prevailing at the time'.[40]

At the same time it became apparent that the aversion to the Amsterdam Consistory, which most people regarded as a continuation of the High Consistory, was not confined to the Capital only. Suddenly the Government was deluged with complaints from the provinces, and was forced to take action. The Amersfoort community, one of the most orthodox in The Netherlands, wrote: 'every Dutch community, and even every single individual wants to be rid of this arbitrary and despotic body, whose conduct so clearly characterizes the French system of government'.[41] The community of Utrecht, which had been forced to dismiss its cantor due to lack of funds, complained about the fact that the Consistory employed officials, while 'neither we nor other Israelites are interested in the existence of the Consistory'.[42] A tumult broke out in the synagogue in Weesp when the decision of the Consistory of December 13 was read out.[43] Den Helder,[44] Veenendaal,[45] Nijkerk,[46] and Kampen[47] also demanded the abolition of the Consistory.

The Rotterdam Consistory had only been appointed on October 20, 1813, and had not yet started functioning, but in January 1814 the elders of the Rotterdam community wrote to King William I, complaining that they had suffered a great deal under French legal jurisdiction, for which the 'Supervisory Consistory' of Amsterdam (an obvious allusion to the High Consistory) was to a

---

39 Letter dated February 12, 1814. Pibo Antonius Brugmans (1764-1851) was an influential lawyer. He was the brother-in-law of F. van Maanen, and in 1829 he was appointed Counselor of State.
40 Burgomasters of the City of Amsterdam to His Excellency the Secretary-General of the Ministry of the Interior (dated January 14, 1814).
41 Petition dated December 27, 1813. Only with the greatest difficulty was Amersfoort persuaded to instruct the teachers of religion to sign the decisions of the Sanhedrin.
42 Letter dated January 5. It was discussed at a session of the Consistory on January 11 and answered on January 12. Sessions of the Consistory etc. ARA, Bi.Za.
43 Information by Commissaires-surveillans of Weesp on December 13, *ibid.*
44 Moses Abraham Groen complained that the Commissaires-surveillans in Den Helder failed to behave according to Jewish law. Session of the Consistory on February 1, *ibid.*
45 Petition by A. van Creveld of Jan. 18, 1814. ARA, Archieven Bi.Za.
46 *Ibid.*, December 31, 1813.
47 Petition by Jewish community of Kampen, December 29, 1813, *ibid.*

large extent responsible 'by having introduced various new religious ceremonies and institutions.'[48]

The Parnasim of the Hague community, chaired by Moses Lehren (the father of the three famous brothers), who had been at odds with the High Consistory for a long time, decided unilaterally that they no longer owed any allegiance to the Consistory.[49] The fact that M. Edersheim,[50] who belonged to the opposition in The Hague, had been appointed their representative to the High Consistory, had from the outset adversely affected relationships. Under these circumstances the demand of the Hague Parnasim 'that all superiority and usurpatory powers assumed by the Consistory be abolished' is understandable. Chairman Lehren and Secretary Dr. S. Stein also wrote to William I (December 12, 1813), stating that the Consistory had been established as a result of local disagreements in Amsterdam and through the pressure that certain persons, acting solely out of self-interest and their desire to improve their own standing, had exerted on King Louis Napoleon. The High Consistory had merely aggravated the life of the Jewish communities.

The Portuguese Jews, who traditionally could count on more sympathy from the authorities than their High-German co-religionists, made it known that they urgently wished to re-establish their independence. The 'amalgamation of all Jews' had merely served 'to sacrifice religious happiness, which the Portuguese Jewish Community had always enjoyed, to the dissenters within the High-German Jewish Community'.[51]

On December 29, Abraham Mendes de Leon wrote that he disagreed with the decision of the Consistory – of which he was president – to establish a Central Consistory in Amsterdam. He had indeed signed the decision, but he now wished to relinquish his position.[52] Finally, the Portuguese Jews of The Hague also requested to reinstate the previously existing administrative system.[53]

This widespread discontent made the position of the Amsterdam Consistory untenable. Government intervention by the authorities was unavoidable, but what direction should this take? Did it mean, for instance, that the Emancipa-

---

48 Letter to King William I, dated January 7, 1814.
49 The conflict with The Hague was discussed during the sessions of the High Consistory of October 2 and 9, 1810 (ARA Minuut verbalen van het verhandelde in de zittingen van het Oppercosistorie). Immediately following the arrival of the Crown Prince, the Parnasim decided 'that all superiority and usurpatory powers...assumed by the Consistories are null and void.' Van Zuiden, *'s Gravenhage*, pp. 107-108.
50 Marcus Edersheim had been a member of the society 'Door Vlijt en Eensgezindheyd', founded in The Hague in October 1797 along the pattern of Felix Libertate, *idem*, p. 94.
51 On December 20 the lawyers J. Bondt and A.J. Cuperus asked to see the Commissioner-General for Internal Affairs and proposed to remove the Portuguese community from the authority of the Consistory (ARA, Bi. Za.) The Administrators had already registered a protest.
52 Admittedly Mendes de Leon had signed Asser's proposal for the reorganization of the Jewish denominational structure, but – as he wrote on December 29 – 'he did not concur with the decision to establish the Central Consistory in Amsterdam.' His suggestion that Asser would submit the proposal in his personal capacity rather than on behalf of the Consistory was defeated by a majority vote (January 11, 1814). His repeated requests to be relieved from his responsibilities were turned down.
53 Petition dated 1Dec. 17, 1813. ARA Bi.Za.

tion decree of September 2, 1796 that had been proclaimed under French pressure should be revoked, as actually happened in other countries formerly occupied by France[54] – a measure to which, judging from the text of their letters to the authorities, many Dutch Jews professed not to object?

The New Organization

That no such drastic remedy was adopted doubtlessly benefited the Jews of The Netherlands. Apparently it was never even seriously considered, which is understandable since many of the high officials who had been responsible for implementing Louis Napoleon's policies continued to be instrumental in the decision-making process under William I. G.A.G.P. van der Capellen,[55] who had served as Minister of Religion and Internal Affairs in the Kingdom of Holland, was Commissioner-General of the Zuyderzee Department in 1813, and as such responsible for Amsterdam. The king was well-disposed towards Van der Capellen, as well as to Reinier Falck, a friend of J.D. Meyer's, who had been appointed Secretary-General (of State).[56] The only one among William's close advisors to support a return to the former situation was Gijsbert Karel van Hogendorp, but he allowed Falck to persuade him.[57] In actual fact, William's advisors were all guided by the advice of J.D. Janssen – the senior official of the Ministry of Internal Affairs, who had already been involved in the formulation of Louis Napoleon's decisions with regard to the High Consistory, and who in the same capacity continued to exert a decisive influence on the religious policies of the Kingdom, especially those with regard to the Jews.[58] The Secretary (i.e. Minister) of Internal Affairs, H. van Stralen (similarly a minister under

54 At the Congress of Vienna the Jews almost succeeded in retaining the rights granted to them in the areas conquered by France. At the last moment a formula was adopted according to which the Jews would retain the rights granted them *by* (instead of *in*, as printed in the original text) the states. With the exception of Prussia, this had not been the case in any state. But even in Prussia the reforms on behalf of the Jews were curtailed in many places and in many different ways. (Graetz, Vol. 11, p. 314-16.)

55 About Van der Capellen's status with the king, see Colenbrander, *Vestiging van het Koninkrijk (1813-1815)*, Amsterdam, 1927, p. 115.

56 A.R. Falck had held important positions under Louis Napoleon. Van Stralen had been in charge of the Ministry of Religious Affairs during the period of Schimmelpenninck. Mollerus, who under Louis Napoleon had been deeply involved in Jewish affairs, occupied important offices under William I.

57 See the introduction to folder 137 of the Tiende Porte-Feuille: 'Since it appeared as if Minister van Hogendorp was inclined to protect the "oudgezinde" (conservative) party of the Jews, it seemed doubtful that the middle course suggested by Janssen would be adopted, but the deft management of Secretary of State Falck, the friend of the Liberal party among the Israelites, persuaded Mr. van Hogendorp, and the matter was referred to the Council of Ministers followed by the constitutional decree of February 26, 1814, no. 90.'

58 J.D. Janssen exercised considerable influence on the religious policies under Louis Napoleon and William I. See, for instance, Brugmans, *op. cit.* Vol. 5, p. 181: Most of the contemporary measures from and about the church originated with him. The formal organizational structure of the Reformed Church adopted in 1816 was in fact the work of the Department at The Hague. On February 10, 1814 he (Janssen) visited Amsterdam and had a meeting with the Commissaires-surveillans. Sluys, *op.cit.*, p. 16.

Louis Napoleon) had requested Meyer to submit a proposal for resolving the problems among the Jews of Amsterdam. Even before this proposal was received, on December 16, a memorandum arrived from Janssen containing his reaction to the documents submitted by various Jewish parties. In addition to a clear explanation of the issues at hand, this memorandum also elucidates the policy that he suggested should be followed:

> *Initially the conflict seemed to revolve around certain specific issues, such as the continued existence of the Consistory in its present form, the use of the Dutch language, [the form of] certain public announcements, and the consecration of marriages in the Synagogue. It is now evident that the supplicants' desire is the complete abolition of all changes effected since the Revolution in the Jewish religious administration and the complete re-establishment of the old system.*
>
> *On the one hand this is the desire of the vast majority of the old Parnasim, who used to hold absolute sway over their nation; – as against this, the most prominent, perceptive and enlightened Jews wish to retain the present institutions, albeit with certain modifications....*
>
> *Maintaining the existing institutions in their present form will no doubt displease the vast majority of the Jews; but dismantling them would quash the institutions, at least some of which are extremely beneficial to civilization, enlightenment and the moral betterment of thousands [of persons] who at the present time are in effect a useless and even harmful ballast to Society. No Government, especially not a new and as yet untried administration, should decide to destroy such institutions supported by the most talented among the Jews without due consideration, lest it be condemned by revolutionaries and for spiritless indulgence.*

Janssen concluded that a decision had to be taken, since what was involved here was not a matter of religion, but of 'external administration', while this decision would also determine how the Government saw the Jews: if the old 'institutions' were reinstated, 'then the Jews cannot be regarded as citizens of this country, as Dutchmen'; instead they would constitute a 'separate nation, with a separate, semi-civic, semi-ecclesiastical administration, under the protection of the Sovereign of the Land'. If, on the other hand, the new 'institutions' were preserved, albeit with certain modifications, 'then the Jews are also Dutchmen and they merely constitute yet another denomination.' Janssen's attitude was clear, namely the continuation of Louis Napoleon's policy which, although contrary to the wishes of most Jews, had been devised by the 'most prominent, perceptive and enlightened Jews', i.e. Asser and Meyer. At the same time he was willing to accept certain changes, but on this score he met with no response from these same gentlemen, who had no intention of yielding on even a single point. On the contrary, they proposed that 'the Amsterdam Consistory...be declared a *Central* Consistory for the entire Netherlands.and that the beneficial institutions...be retained'. Yet a draft proposal submitted by Asser on January 7, 1814 contained one concession: the name 'Consistory' would be abolished and replaced by 'Great Synagogue Council'. In all other respects he maintained the existing French structure: the Great Synagogue Council would also have seven members, two of whom were to be rabbis (appointed for life) and five laymen. The draft regulations for the Jewish communities included an article committing the communities to obey all regulations issued by the High Consistory.

Even this proposal barely contributed to assuaging pent-up emotions. Janssen realized that Asser's proposal offered no solution to the difficulties facing the Government. Doubtlessly he also appreciated that the opposition to the Consistory was not only rooted in the changes it wanted to introduce, but also – and possibly most of all – in the attendant hierarchical structure that had robbed the communities of their independence – one aspect that Asser's plan intended to retain. In a detailed report, dated January 21, Janssen revised his opinion on this point. He challenged the stand of the Amsterdam municipal authorities who wanted to return to the pre-1795 situation and grant the Parnasim the same unlimited power they had previously held. At the same time he made a new and far-reaching proposal: the existing synagogal administrative structure would be canceled, and all Jewish communities in The Netherlands would be allowed to *resume their separate and independent existence* (underlined in the original) – including the New Community in Amsterdam. For purposes of liaison with the authorities, several of the principal communities would be designated 'correspondent' or 'main' synagogues, without, however, having any authority over the other, smaller communities. An advisory committee, made up of members of the Portuguese, High-German and New Communities would be established to assist the directorate of the Department for Religious Affairs. With regard to the remaining three disputed points, he determined that calling people up by surname and the celebration of marriages in the synagogue were not sufficiently vital issues 'to justify donning armor'. However, as far as the use of 'jargon' (Yiddish) was concerned, he was of the opinion that the struggle should continue and that at the very least all synagogue announcements had to be made in Dutch. Further, in the Jewish schools the use of 'Lower German' (i.e. Dutch, as against 'High-German' = German) should be encouraged.

Janssen's proposals were approved by Van der Capellen[59] and subsequently by Van Stralen. Only with regard to marriages did both remain of the opinion that these could be consecrated following a civil ceremony. Van Stralen had already drafted a resolution for the king's signature when a new proposal arrived on February 16.

Its originator was Dr. E.S. Stein,[60] Secretary of the Jewish community in The Hague, whose President, Moses Lehren, was strictly orthodox. However, in his

---

59 Van der Capellen received the report on January 22 and replied on February 5. He was of the opinion that Janssen had discovered the proper middle course, adding merely that the Parnasim should see to it that no marriages were consecrated in conflict with the law.

60 Dr. Samuel Elias Stein (1778-1851) was the son of the famous chess master E.S. Stein (1748-1812). The latter had taught William V as well as his sons Frederick and William, the future king, to play chess. He wrote *Essai sur le jeu des échecs avec réflections militaires*, The Hague, 1789, subsequently also published in Dutch. See also Van Zuiden, *'s Gravenhage*, pp. 66-67; *VA* 5 (6July 6, 1928), p. 223. His son studied medicine in Leiden and received his doctoral degree in 1799. On January 18, 1809, he had become honorary secretary of the Jewish community of The

accompanying letter Dr. Stein stated that he had been a supporter of the High Consistory and the Jewish Corps, and of all matters benefiting Jewish culture, but that everything had changed for the worse under the French regime. His detailed proposals clearly made a great impression on Janssen and undoubtedly helped to propel Stein to the pivotal position he was to occupy during the following years in the organization of the Jewish communities. His plan actually presented a clear outline for restructuring the Jewish communal framework in The Netherlands, which was to form the basis for the ultimate organization and regulation of Jewish life. Stein proposed the establishment of ten 'Main Synagogues' – a construction that would seem to have been chosen to prevent once and for all one community, namely Amsterdam, from attaining a dominant status. After all, this had aroused the ire of the other communities during the existence of the High Consistory and the Consistory of the Zuyderzee. All synagogues (i.e. communities) situated within a Main Synagogue's jurisdiction would be subordinate to it, and all communications with the authorities would be conducted solely via the Main Synagogue. The Board of each Main Synagogue would, depending on the number of Jews within its jurisdiction, consist of at least three and at most seven Directors or Parnasim. These, together with one representative from each subordinate community (whose administrators were called *manhigim*)[61] would annually convene a *Main Assembly* to discuss affairs pertinent to the district, including the elections of the Parnasim and the Chief Rabbi. In turn, the Parnasim would hold a national *General Meeting* each year to discuss matters concerning Dutch Jewry as a whole. The Hague was proposed as a venue for this meeting, a choice that was obviously not coincidental. Whereas Louis Napoleon had governed from Amsterdam, the new Government had transferred its seat to its traditional location in The Hague. This meant the elimination of Amsterdam as the principal administrative center, notwithstanding the fact that it contained the largest Jewish population concentration in the country. Incidentally, whether Stein realized that the nature of his proposals might also propel him into a high and influential office cannot be ascertained – but this would soon prove to be the case.

The Government was so preoccupied with its efforts to quell the riots in Amsterdam that Janssen had no time to consider Stein's proposals directly after they were received. Even so, it is clear that Janssen had already read the document and stood behind its general contents. In fact, Art. 6 of the Royal decree published on February 26, 1814 (two weeks after the submission of Stein's proposals, and entitled: 'Concerning the Dissolution of the present Organization of the Israelite Synagogue Administration, and the Determination of further Relevant Provisions') contains the following formulation:

> *In order to maintain the relations between the large number of High-German Jewish Communities in The Netherlands, and to facilitate correspondence with*

Hague. Isaac da Costa called him a 'devilish intriguer' (see Meijer, *Problematiek*, p. 90). In 1843 he was appointed town physician.

61 The Hebrew term for the administrators was *Parnas u-Manhig* (abbrev.: *Pum*). Stein split the term in two. The heads of Adath Yesurun had called themselves *Manhigim*.

> *the Government, some of the most prominent communities will be nominated as*
> *Corresponding or Main Synagogues according to a definition to be determined*
> *by the Commissioner-General for Internal Affairs.*

We see, therefore, that the term Main Synagogue suggested by Stein was immediately assumed in the Royal decree, a clear indication that the idea had fallen on fertile soil. The remainder of the Royal decree dealt with the concessions recommended by Janssen that the Government had been prepared to make: the cancellation of the compulsory use of surnames during the Torah reading in the synagogue, and the ban on the consecration of marriages outside the synagogues (but following a civil ceremony). The use of Dutch remained compulsory only for announcements in the synagogues on behalf of governmental authorities and for the minutes and similar documents of the synagogue Boards (Art. 5). The annulment of the Consistorial system also meant the end of the centralized organizational system:

Art. 2

All presently recognized Jewish communities in The Netherlands, both High-
German and Portuguese, are from this day on reinstated in the same separate
and independent form.

The second clause in this article indicates the sympathy of the authorities for the enlightened faction: Supporters of the 'new institutions' (i.e. also non-members of the New Community) as well as the members of the former New Community could join either the Portuguese or the High-German Community or, alternatively, establish yet another separate community. Although the New Community had ceased to function only six years earlier, just one person requested the authorities for it to be re-established.[62]

Even though it seems as if the Royal decree met most of the demands of the Orthodox opposition and the majority of synagogue Boards, this was more appearance than reality. The sting was in the tail: the Commissioner-General for Internal Affairs was supposed to issue the necessary regulations for the implementation of the Royal decree, in which he was to be assisted by a 'Consulting Committee'. The big question was *how* was this committee to be constituted?

> *One representative each of the Portuguese communities of Amsterdam and The*
> *Hague; one member each from the High-German communities of Amsterdam,*
> *The Hague and Rotterdam, and one member of the Board of the former New*
> *Israelite community at Amsterdam.*

The two Portuguese communities (again, inevitably mentioned first!), which between them constituted less than 10 percent of Dutch Jews, were allocated two out of six seats – which ratio became even more absurd when Dr. Immanuel

---

62 Actually the member involved, Samuel Salomo, wanted to join the Portuguese community and
   he argued that the text of the Royal decree permitted this, but Janssen rejected this
   interpretation (May 29, 1815).

Capadoce,[63] known as a progressive individual, was appointed president of the committee and requested a second representative of his community to be added, who was soon co-opted as a member.[64] At this point the Portuguese occupied three of the seven seats, including the Presidency. The allocation of a seat to the non-existent (nor re-established) New Community had merely been a ploy to ensure a place for Carel Asser. Even if all representatives of the High-German communities had belonged to the Orthodox camp, there would still have been an 'enlightened' majority (the Portuguese were considered to belong to this group) of four to three. Initially yet another 'enlightened' personality had been considered as representative of Amsterdam, the choice being between Boas or De Metz – both hated Commissaires-surveillans.[65] However, two prominent members of the Amsterdam High-German community had submitted a petition contending that the Consulting Committee could only function properly if 'authentic' Jews were appointed as members. They added a list of eighteen persons who, in their opinion, met this requirement. Probably on the strength of this reaction it was decided to appoint Elkan Philip de Jong. He had already been proposed by the opposition and, as a former member of the High Consistory, was an obvious choice.[66]

The representational as well as personal composition of the Consulting Committee turned out to be the more important aspect since, although intended to be of a transitional nature only, it soon received a permanent status, eventually culminating in the establishment of the Supreme Committee ('Hoofdcommissie') for Israelite Affairs in The Netherlands – the most important Jewish representative body during the 19th century (until 1870). Initially the fear for the resurgence of an authoritarian power structure was so deep-seated that Janssen deemed it necessary to accompany his recommendation to approve the Consulting Committee's request for permanent status by an emphatic declaration to the effect that the Committee could make inquiries with the communities, but was forbidden to impose its will.[67] The only person to

63 We recall the struggle waged by Dr. Immanuel Capadoce for the participation of the Portuguese community in the Grand Sanhedrin in Paris against the decision of the *Mahamad* and in the spirit of Adath Jesurun (see pp. 95-98).

64 The substitute, eventually a permanent member, was Jacob de Ishac Teixeira de Mattos.

65 Initially even the name of J.D. Meyer was mentioned, but Janssen decided against him; most probably it was realized that his appointment would constitute a provocation and create renewed unrest.

66 The two signatories of the letter were D. Abrahams and A.A. Prins. They write that they were acting 'by virtue of a responsibility assigned to us', but they do not mention the names of those who had asked them to accept this task. The list of nominees included several former Parnasim, including J. Prins and M.R. Keizer.

67 In a letter to Willem van Hogendorp about the dispute between Zvi Hirsch Lehren and the Supreme Committee, Isaac da Costa gives the following characterization of the various members: 'The Supreme Committee for Israelite affairs is, as you know, comprised of my uncle Capadoce, as President. Furthermore Salvador, Teixeira, De Jongh, Asser and Stein, and another member from Rotterdam whose name I do not recall. Among them Stein, a devilish intriguer, is particularly hostile to him (i.e. Lehren, J.M.). Asser essentially agrees with Stein, but he is less inimical against the person of L., [but] no less on the subject of faith and religion. Salvador is an honorable fellow, but he lacks religion and has an English semi-liberal mind, and he can easily be influenced. De Jong is a religious Jew, but he belongs to the party of the

possess this authority was the Minister of Internal Affairs, who was invariably guided by Janssen's advice. Thus Louis Napoleon's policies, aimed at the integration and 'Netherlandization' of Dutch Jewry, continued unchanged during the regime of William I, supervised and guided by a permanent civil servant, J.D. Janssen, and supported by a royally appointed committee of Jews who were far from representative of the Jewish religious and organizational concensus. Dr. S.E. Stein, who as a result of his many proposals and suggestions gained considerable influence on Janssen, became the dominant figure in the committee. Janssen even proposed granting Stein a small salary (Df. 500 per annum) for the large amount of work he performed. The other members of the committee received no remuneration: after all, they had been chosen from among the cream of the Jewish notables.[68]

According to the Royal decree of February 26, the Secretary of State for Internal Affairs was responsible for formulating by-laws for the administration of the Israelite Communities, which were published on June 25, 1814.[69] These determined that there were to be twelve Corresponding or Main Synagogues in The Netherlands, whose leaders were to be called *Parnasim*. These Parnasim would in turn be responsible for the smaller communities or 'rings', whose leaders, the *Manhigim*, could only communicate with Government departments via the Main Synagogues. The promised concessions of the Royal decree were reiterated, as well as the proscription of burials taking place within twenty-four hours after the determination of death. The by-laws also included rules for the election of Chief Rabbis, as well as another enlightenment perennial: the Chief Rabbis pledged to give a sermon at least once a month, aimed – among other things – at 'instilling love for the country and the Sovereign, diligence in its defense, the fulfilment all social responsibilities, and the pursuance of an

---

Parnasim who are fearful for the interests of their Welfare Fund. However, my uncle Capadoce has always held him in high esteem.'

The letter is dated December 19, 1822 (J. Meijer, *Problematiek*, p. 90). Willem van Hogendorp characterized the members of the Supreme Committee 'the most dedicated opponents of their own Church,' and he continued: 'And all this happens with the best of intentions and in good faith, in the belief that in this way the Jews may be converted to Christianity.' Quoted from J. van Gelderen, *Veilige Stad in Honderd plus tien*, Kampen, 1975, p. 162.

68 In his recommendation (May 1814, no precise date), Janssen writes that 'in general, matters concerning the Israelite denomination are of such an exceptional nature that without advise from intelligent and influential Jews, even the Government runs the risk of being misled.' There is no need to ask whom Janssen regarded as 'intelligent and influential.'

On June 2, a circular letter was sent out which was typical of the manner in which the authorities dealt with Jewish matters. From now on the Parnasim or Board members were to direct their correspondence to the 'Committee for matters of the Israelite denomination, acting under the direction of the Commissioner for Religious Affairs.' The Committee (i.e. no longer the Advisory Committee) did not even have an address, since the envelopes were to be addressed to the: 'Commissioner for Religious Affairs at the Department of Internal Affairs, The Hague.' The official decision by the Secretary of State for Internal Affairs Roëll was published on June 14, 1814 (no. 38).

69 The Constitutional Decree of June 25 is entitled: 'Reglement op het Kerkbestuur der Israelitische Gemeente in de Vereenigde Nederlanden.'

honest vocation'. Conversely, these sermons had to 'disparage idleness and vagrancy'. Not a word was said about the religious content of the sermons.

In conclusion it is worthwhile to analyze a decision made by the Secretary of State for Internal Affairs dated August 13, 1814, referring to the formulation of by-laws for the Main Synagogues and which led to two incidents. The by-laws were to be drawn up by the Parnasim, in cooperation with a certain number of notables from each Main Synagogue, to be nominated – how else – by the Secretary of State.[70] The appointees from Amersfoort refused to accept their nomination because the new by-laws had annulled the *herem*, the religious ban, besides which the Parnasim no longer had the right to supervise the everyday behavior of the members of their community. The authorities had no patience with the recalcitrant, strictly orthodox community; they peremptorily sacked its leadership and replaced them by others. The recognition of Amersfoort as a Main Synagogue (rather than Utrecht) was deferred until such a time that Amersfoort would decide to toe the line.[71] Which is exactly what the new notables did.

A greater problem for the various authorities was J.D. Meyer's unexpected refusal to accept his appointment. When Meyer failed to arrive, E.P. de Jong and Carel Asser, the representatives of the Consulting Committee who were

---

70 The idea of approval – besides the Parnasim – by certain prominent figures was not invented specifically for the Israelite denomination. The Constitution itself was ratified by notables appointed by a committee proposed by the Commissioners-General of the Departments.

   At the recommendation of the Commissioner for Israelite Affairs (i.e. Janssen), the Secretary- General of Internal Affairs appointed the Jewish notables according to the following key:
   Portuguese Main Synagogue, Amsterdam 9
   High-German Main Synagogue, Amsterdam 10
   Portuguese Main Synagogue, The Hague 4
   The Hague 7
   Rotterdam 7
   Amersfoort 5
   Middelburg 5
   's Hertogenbosch 7
   Nijmegen 5
   Zwolle 7
   Leeuwarden 5
   Groningen 7

   Once again the deliberate slight to the High-German community in Amsterdam is conspicuous: they were represented by only 10 notables, as against the Portuguese communities 9, and most other synagogues 7. Two of the ten notables, J.D. Meijer and T. Asser, belonged to the 'enlightened' group.

71 The three dissidents were reprimanded by Roëll: their behavior had made them unworthy of further consideration. B.M. Schaap, a member of the Municipal Council, was admonished even more severely for 'not having shown a clearer sense of duty'. The fourth notable, who had not refused, was Dr. Isaac M. Weyl (1778-1855). Eventually he became a member of the Municipal council of Amersfoort, as well as a corresponding member of the Supreme Committee. Roëll now appointed Jacob van Minden (in his letter mistakenly called Van Monden), Salomon Cohen and Isaac Hartog Herschel (letter dated November 9).

   On November 20 Dr. Weyl reported that, in compliance with his commission, he had installed the notables and 'that all notables had assumed their assigned positions without evidencing the slightest objection.'

expected to install the Parnasim and notables of the High-German Community of Amsterdam, canceled the ceremony.[72] Ostensibly Meyer claimed to be dissatisfied with the new state of affairs, but there can be no doubt that he was piqued that not he, but his colleague Asser had been appointed to the Consulting Committee. Meyer was subjected to considerable pressure to make him change his mind. W.F. Roëll, the new Secretary (and later Minister) of Internal Affairs wrote him a sharp letter stating that he 'could not imagine how, following the restoration of Dutch freedom and independence under the rule of a Dutch monarch, Meyer should declare himself unwilling to render those services that he had not refused to a foreign oppressor'.[73] Unable to resist such outright blackmail, Meyer yielded and he was duly honored at his installation.[74] The rejoicing was of short duration: soon afterwards, Meyer resigned, and thus the man who for a number of years had occupied the most exalted positions in the Jewish community was eclipsed from the Jewish scene as suddenly as he had first appeared in 1806.[75]

The final arrangements for the establishment of the 'Dutch Israelite Church' whose by-laws were to be drafted by the Parnasim in cooperation with the notables of the various regions and towns, were to incorporate several principles dictated by the authorities. Two aspects in particular illustrate the difference with the situation under the Republican regime: the prohibition to interfere with the private lives of members of the community (and implicitly the prohibition of excommunication), and the subordination of the Chief Rabbis and rabbis to the Parnasim, who at all times could summon them if they refused to obey their directives. Paramount among the latter was the duty to instill love of King and Country, obedience to the laws of the land, and so forth.

At long last peace and tranquility within the Jewish communities had been restored. In addition the Jews had achieved a constitutionally regulated organization ahead of all other Dutch religious denominations. Needless to say the

---

72 De Jongh and Asser deferred the entire inauguration 'because one of the most capable members was missing'. They also wrote that the reasons why Meyer had refused his assignment were unclear to them, 'since the said Gentleman had never before withdrawn from activities on behalf of his co-religionists, either by order or at the Government's request.' (August 30)

73 Letter from Roëll to J.D. Meyer, dated September 1. At first Meyer persisted in his refusal, following which Roëll wrote him another letter on September 12. He conceded that there might be certain difficulties with the 'activity', but he could not imagine Meyer being unable to overcome his objections.

74 Minutes of the meeting of Parnasim and Notables of September 19, 1814.

75 In the petition that had been sent to Schimmelpenninck in 1806, his name had been added at the last moment, and this was the first time he became involved in the community (see p. 31). At that moment his colleague Carel Asser, who was the same age, had been active in Jewish affairs for almost ten years. Three years later Meyer was appointed to the highest position in Jewish public life: President of the High Consistory. Earlier the king had appointed him as director of the *Royal Gazette*, besides which he was one of the eleven members of the Royal Institute of Science responsible for Dutch language and literature. Some of his colleagues were luminaries such as Bilderdijk, Rhijnvis Feith, Prof. J.H. van der Palm and M. Siegenbeek (De Beneditty, p. 21).

  Besides his activities as lawyer (his most famous case being his appearance for Louis Napoleon in 1820 when the latter sued King William I for the return of his possessions in The Netherlands), he gave scholarly lectures for the Institute of Science.

developments leading up to this situation were not due to a voluntary initiative on the part of the authorities, but through force of circumstances, namely the fear of uncontrollable agitation. Thus, it is worthwhile to cast a retrospective view at the situation immediately following the Restoration, as reflected in a plaintive letter dated January 16, 1814, by the Commissaires-surveillans of the Amsterdam community:

> *A populous and self-opinionated community whose individual members do or do not subject themselves to the existing laws and regulations as they see fit. A community burdened by a large number of indigent members, which necessitates substantial expenditures, if only to maintain them in their diseased state and provide with the bare necessities of life, and to inter their corpses. [It is] a community whose finances have declined to a most deplorable state, while its funds are totally depleted and its sources of income are diminishing daily and are practically exhausted. A community, finally, whose leaders, being publicly slandered and scorned by certain individuals, are so infirm that they barely manage to carry out their functions.*[76]

Firmness of purpose returned after six months or so, and people no longer ignored the existing laws. Thanks to the basically insignificant concessions and the newly established authority of the monarchy, there were no more riots in and around the Great Synagogue of Amsterdam. However, the financial situation of the community had not improved. The new by-laws did indeed contain a clause to the effect that the meat-hall of the Jewish community was allowed to collect a surcharge for the Welfare Fund, but this was insufficient to relieve the wrenching poverty of the Jewish poor. It goes without saying that the thousands of raggedly clothed and continually hungry Amsterdam Jews were totally uninterested in how the community was administered or what it said in the dozens of clauses of the newly drafted by-laws.

We might ask what happened to the strictly orthodox elders of the community who from 1795 onwards had spearheaded the struggle against the Modernists, the wealthy Parnasim and their families, and the established spiritual authorities led by the Chief Rabbis and rabbis? They were conspicuous by their absence. Chief Rabbi Jacob Moses Löwenstamm of Amsterdam had for some time proven unequal to the task of providing leadership and preserving the exalted status of the rabbinate under trying circumstances.[77] His colleagues in The Hague and Rotterdam were equally silent.[78] Grand-rabbin S.B. Berenstein who

---

76 Copybook Jewish Community of Amsterdam, folio 125, no. 2. Letter to Consistory. In a letter to the Commissioner-General of the Zuyderzee Department dated March 2, 1814, it was emphasized that 'the entire existence of our community is dependent on the revenues of the meat-hall.'

 Admittedly the new regulations of 1809 provided for a direct as well as an indirect tax, but with few exceptions 'individuals' simply evaded payment. Consequently the community was forced not only to defer its debt repayments, but to refuse welfare allowances and postpone payments to its salaried staff (*ibid*. fo. 137, no. 2).

77 In addition, the Chief Rabbi had been ill for several years, and he died soon afterwards.

78 Rotterdam had no Chief Rabbi between 1809 and 1813, in which year Elias Casriel was appointed Chief Rabbi. He had been assessor of the Amsterdam Chief Rabbi, but nothing is

had been a willing pawn of Asser and Meyer in the Consistory of the Zuyderzee, was at the present juncture mainly concerned about preserving his livelihood.[79] Although he was indeed properly looked after,[80] any fight on behalf of the principles – or even the preservation – of rabbinical authority was not to be expected of him.

Where then were the champions of the Amsterdam Chief Rabbi, for example Avraham Prins, Bendit Wing and other activists in the struggle against the High Consistory? Apart from a timorous, but successful, attempt to have one of their trustees appointed to the Consulting Committee, they failed to take a single initiative. Neither did they raise a single constructive proposal that, despite the changed circumstances in the Kingdom, might have been acceptable to the new Government. This is the more surprising in view of their solid backing by the

known about any activities on his part during this turbulent period in Amsterdam. The newly appointed 58-year-old Chief Rabbi could scarcely be expected to develop a different leadership style at such short notice.

   The Chief Rabbi of The Hague, J.A. Lehmans (1766-1842; also known as Leman Symons or Rabbi Lemmel) had made vigorous efforts during the establishment of the High Consistory to try and prevent the legitimization of the order of service of the New Community. However, he stayed on the sidelines throughout the preparation of the new Jewish denominational structure. According to S. Seeligmann relations between him and Amsterdam Chief Rabbi S.B. Berenstein were 'hardly congenial', although it is not clear whether and to what extent this was a result of Berenstein's attitude towards the 'enlightened' current. (See Van Zuiden, *op. cit.*, p. 71).

79 On December 23, 1813, while the Amsterdam Consistory, of which he was a member, used his vote to try and extend its sway over the whole of Dutch Jewry (which would have made him Chief Rabbi of the entire Kingdom) Grand-Rabbin Berenstein sent the king an abjectly fawning letter begging the monarch to enable him to continue in his position 'with a salary that will allow me to support my family and ensure a proper education for my children.' Even though Berenstein had to support a family of nine, this was by no means the style to be expected from the potentially highest spiritual leader of the realm. Berenstein's annual salary amounted to Df. 2,000, compared to the Df. 1,100 he had earned as Chief Rabbi of Leeuwarden; as against this, life in Amsterdam was indeed expensive, and in Leeuwarden he had enjoyed certain fringe benefits that were absent in Amsterdam. The rabbi also found it necessary to apologize at great length for having accepted the position of Grand-rabbin.

   The following quote, which begins with a reference to his sermons, bears out the style in which his letter was written:

'...in which he mainly urged the performance of the duties to the legal Monarch and the Country, which so fully accords with the pure learning of the Israelite religion and the heartfelt sentiments of the undersigned. And with how much enthusiasm he had done this, after the yoke of the tyrant had been shaken off. In fact, the Israelites had been given every reason for feeling this way because of the attitude of the exalted Government, for who can doubt the fatherly concern of Your Royal Highness for all his subjects, due to which the Israelites who have the benefit of being able to call themselves Dutchmen are assured, under such a benevolent Government as that of Your Royal Highness, of being guaranteed their civil rights'... etc., etc. (ARA, Staatssecr. Koning Willem I, exh. Febr. 26, 1814, no. 90).

80 On July 1 the position and the conditions of the Chief Rabbis and rabbis were established by Constitutional decree (no. 24). They were reinstated in their former functions, with the Chief Rabbis and rabbis who had held positions with the Consistories benefiting from an additional salary or pension. Berenstein was to be paid Df. 2,000 per annum for life, as long as he did not hold any other rabbinical position; in such a case his extra salary would be deducted. He did not have to wait long. In 1815 his father-in-law died, and as promised in the earlier-mentioned Constitutional decree, he was appointed Chief Rabbi of the High-German Main Synagogue in Amsterdam (1815-1838) – without a doubt against the wishes of the Orthodox majority of the community. According to Sluys there was a story to the effect that Chief Rabbi Löwenstamm's function had first been offered to his son Naphtali, but that he had refused the honor. (D.M. Sluys, 'De installatie van den Opperrabbijn Samuel Berenstein', *NIW*, July 22, 1917, p. 4.)

Jewish masses, and their awareness of the bitterness in many communities outside Amsterdam concerning the dictatorial behavior and domestic intervention by the Consistory. The Orthodoxy proved itself socially inept, and thus its modest expectations could be satisfied with a few paltry concessions by the authorities.

The 'Dutch Israelite Church' during the reign of King William I was henceforth controlled by a civil servant, i.e. Janssen, assisted by a Consulting (eventually Supreme) Committee appointed by the king and composed of representatives of a small minority in the Jewish community. The founders of Felix Libertate had emerged victorious. By now they were established in influential positions, from where they could try to push through further reforms. Even so, they had not been spared disappointments: the changes had taken a long time, and the hated Yiddish 'jargon' would remain the vernacular of the Jews of Amsterdam for many decades to come. Apart from this, the leaders of the *Neye Kille* (the New Community) had forfeited their leading position among Dutch Jewry, and the center of gravity had shifted to The Hague – to the Government and the Supreme Committee, with Dr. S.E. Stein as its Permanent Secretary. In effect, the Jews no longer elected their own leadership organs: the 'enlightened' group, who realized only too well that they constituted a tiny minority, did not wish to do so, whereas the Orthodox were unable to adapt themselves to the structure of a modern state.

One can hardly blame the Dutch Government for any insensitivity to the needs and religious attitudes of the Jewish masses. This was the responsibility of a leadership intended to be chosen by the Jews themselves. However, the events of 1813-14 proved that they were incapable of governing themselves. Neither did this situation show any improvement during the 19th century. Who knows how much longer the Jewish religious establishment would have continued to exist under this 'exceptional' and essentially unconstitutional tutelage if in 1870 the Government had not exerted heavy pressure on Dutch Jewry to display a more responsible attitude and start taking charge of its own affairs?[81]

---

81 About the problems related to the establishment of an independent Jewish Denomination after 1848, see J. Michman, 'Centrum en Periferie', pp. 210-11.

A Amsterdam

On october 7, 1795 the Amsterdam City counsil commissioned a census, to be carried out during the same month. According to this census the population of Amsterdam amounted to 217,024 persons, among whom 20,335 Jews. However, wih regard to the Jews the committee charged with the implementation of the census commented: 'The population density in certain sections of the Jewish Quarter is so great, [with] every place, including the attics, so crowded, the indecorousness of many of this Nation [living] in these kinds of houses, was such that many of the District Superintendents could not vouch that a number of persons, particularly children, were not overlooked.' For this reason the committee decided to round off the number of Jews upwards to 21,000. (Rapport over de Telling van het volk van Amsterdam, 20 october 1795, overgegeven door J.P. Parret, A.G. Verster, J.H. van Swinden, GAA N. St, B. vrl., inventarissen 130A.)

In April 1797 a special census was conducted of the religious denominations not belonging to the main Dutch Reformed Church. This resulted in the following numbers of Jewish inhabitants:

High-German Jews	20,304
Portuguese Jews	2,800

The total was therefore 23,104 Jewish individuals.

Since the total number of High-German Jews is almost identical to the head count in 1795, it must be assumed that, either, due to the prevailing hurry the Portuguese Jews were counted with the Christians, or that a far greater number of Jews was overlooked than originally assumed by the committee. Whichever is the case, the Jewish population of Amsterdam around the turn of the 19th century may safely be put at 23,000.

The above means that there were far more Jews residing in Amsterdam than in any other city in the contemporary world.

B Total jewish population in The Netherlands during the annexation

The following statistic represents the number of Jews residing the Dutch territories annexed by France[1].

Siège de Synagogue	Département	Population	Population de la siège de la Synagogue
Amsterdam	Zuyderzee	24,395	22,241
Rotterdam	Bouches de la Meuse	5,278	
	Bouches du Rhin	600	
	Bouches de L'Escoute	219	2,129
	Deux Nettes[2]	245	
Zwolle	Bouches de L'Yssel	1,677	
	Yssel supérieur	1,758	372
Groningen	Frise	1,022	
	Eems Occidental	2,281	
	Eems Oriental	1,500	
Emden	Bouches de Weizer	1,129	
	Eems Superieur	1,076	
Hamburg	Bouches de L'Elbe	7,092	6,299
	Total	48,272	

For the Jewish population per town or village, see *Pinkas*, 1992, pp. 587-594.

1 From: Organisarion Consistoriale de Six Nouvelles Conscription(!), GAA, Parnasim aan Opperconsistoire, October 31, 1811.
2 West-Brabant, with its capital Antwerp, also belonged to the province of the two Nethen.

Abbreviations

Archives:

ARA	Algemeen Rijksarchief, The Hague
Bibl. Ros.	Bibliotheca Rosenthaliana, Amsterdam
CAHJP	Central Archives for the History of the Jewish People, Jerusalem
GAA (PA)	Gemeente Archief, Amsterdam (PA = Private Archive)
Protokolbuch	*Protokolbuch* 1787/8, Minutes of the Board of the High-German (Ashkenzi) Jewish Community of Amsterdam (in GAA, PA = Private Archive)

Books and articles:

Van der Aa	A.J. Van der Aa, *Biografisch Woordenboek der Nederlanden*, (repr.), Amsterdam, 1969.
Altmann	Alexander Altmann, *Moses Mendelssohn, A Biographical Study*, Philadelphia, 1973.
Anchel	R. Anchel, *Napoléon et les Juifs*, Paris 1928.
Beem, Jerosche	H. Beem, *Jerosche*, Assen, 1970.
Beem, Leeuwarden	H. Beem, *De Joden van Leeuwarden*, Assen, 1974.
Beem, Mokum	H. Beem, *Uit Mokum en Mediene*, Assen, 1974.
Beem, Sheerith	H. Beem, *Sheerith, Resten van een taal*, Assen, 1967.
Beem, Yiddish	H. Beem, 'Yiddish in Holland, Linguistic and Socio-Linguistic Notes,' in Uriel Weinreich (ed.), *The Field of Yiddish*, New York, 1954.
Belinfante, Bijdragen	*Bijdragen betrekkelijk de verbetering van den maatschappelijken staat der Joden*, The Hague, Belinfante, 1806-1807.
Bendit Wing	*Kroniek Bendit Wing*, published by M.M. Roest als 'Uittreksel uit ene Kronijk van de jaren 1795-1812', in *De Israelitische Letterbode* (IL), I-VI (1875-1880).
Beneditty	N. de Beneditty, *Leven en Werken van Mr. Jonas Daniel Meyer*, Haarlem, 1925.
Bloemgarten	S.E. Bloemgarten, 'De Amsterdamse Joden gedurende de eerste jaren van de Bataafse Republiek', in *St. Ros.* I, 1 (1967), pp. 66-96; I, 2, pp. 45-70; II (1968), pp. 42-65.
BMGJW	Bijdragen en Mededelingen van het Genootschap voor Joodse Wetenschappen in Nederland.

Bolle   M. Bolle, *De opheffing van de autonomie der Kehillot in Nederland 1796*, Amsterdam, 1960.

Breen   Johan C. Breen 'De regeering van Amsterdam gedurende den Franschen tijd', *Jbk Amstelodamum* 12, (1914), pp. 111-120.

Brugmans   H. Brugmans, *Geschiedenis van Amsterdam*, (6 vols.), Utrecht, 1972/3.

Brugmans-Frank   H. Brugmans and A. Frank, *Geschiedenis der Joden in Nederland*, I, Amsterdam, 1940.

Centraalblad   *Centraalblad voor Israëlieten in Nederland.*

Colenbrander, GS   H.T. Colenbrander, *Gedenkstukken der algemeene geschiedenis van Nederland, 1795-1840*, The Hague, 1905-1922.

Colenbrander, Inlijving   H.T. Colenbrander, *Inlijving en Opstand*, Amsterdam, 1941.

Disk. A.K.   *Diskursen fun di Alte Kille*, Amsterdam 1797-98.

Disk. N.K.   *Diskursen fun di Neye Kille*, Amsterdam 1797-98.

DJH   *Dutch Jewish History* (ed. J. Michman) Vols. 1-3, Jerusalem, 1984-1993.

Dubnow   Dubnow, *Die neueste Geschichte des jüdischen Volkes*, Berlin, 1930.

Duker/Ben-Horin   Abraham G. Duker, Meir Ben-Horin, *Emancipation and Counter- Emancipation*, New York, 1974.

Van Eeghen, Asser Autobiografie   I.H. van Eeghen, 'Autobiografie van M.S. Asser', *Jbk Amstelodamum*, Vol. 55 (1963), pp. 130-165.

Van Eeghen, Asser Jeugd I. H. van Eeghen, *De Jeugd van Netje en Eduard Asser 1819-1833*, Amsterdam, 1964.

EJ   *Encyclopaedia Judaica*, Jerusalem, 1972.

Eliav   M. Eliav, *Jewish Education in Germany during the period of the Enlightenment and Emancipation* (Hebr.), Jerusalem, 1960.

ESN   J. Meijer, *Encyclopaedia Sephardica Neerlandica*, Amsterdam, 1949-1950.

Falck, Brieven   *Brieven van A.R. Falck, 1795-1843* (ed. D.J. van Lennep), 2 vols., The Hague, 1861.

Falck, Gedenkschriften A.R. Falck, 'Gedenkschriften' (R.G.P., kleine serie 13), The Hague, 1913.

Franco Mendes   see Fuks.

Fuks   R. and L. Fuks: Een Portugese kroniek over het einde van de Patriottentijd door David Franco Mendes, *St. Ros.* VII (1973), pp. 8-39, quoted: with reference to introduction: Fuks; with reference to text: Franco Mendes.

Geyl, GS   P. Geyl, *Geschiedenis van de Nederlandse Stam*, Amsterdam, vol. VI (1792-1790), 1962, Amsterdam-Antwerp, 1972.

Geyl, Medespeler	P. Geyl, *Geschiedenis als medespeler*, Utrecht-Antwerp, 1958.
Geyl, Revolutie	P. Geyl, 'De Bataafse Revolutie', in: *Verzamelde Opstellen*, vol. 2, pp. 106-126, Utrecht-Antwerp, 1978.
De Gou	L. de Gou, *Het Ontwerp van Constitutie van 1797*, The Hague, 1983.
Graetz	H. Graetz, *Geschichte der Juden von den ältesten Zeiten bis auf die Gegenwart* (2nd. ed.), 11 vols., Leipzig, 1900.
Graff	Gil Graff, *Separation of Church and State, Dina de Malkhuta Dina in Jewish Law, 1750-1848*, University of Alabama, 1985.
Hess, Physicians	Hindle S. Hess, *Jewish Physicians in the Netherlands*, Assen 1980.
Hess, Printers	Hindle S. Hess, 'The Van Embdens. A Family of Printers in Amsterdam', *Quaerendo*, vol. XI/I (1981), pp. 46-52.
Jaarboeken	*Jaarboeken voor de Israëlieten in Nederland* IV, 4 vols., The Hague, 1835-1838.
Jbk Amstelodamum	Jaarboek Amstelodamum, series.
De Jong	L. de Jong, *Het Koninkrijk der Nederlanden in de Tweede Wereldoorlog* (14 vols.), The Hague, 1969-1991.
Katz, Emancipation	Jacob Katz, *Out of the Ghetto, The Social Background of Jewish Emancipation*, Cambridge, Mass.-New York, 1973.
Katz, Exclusiveness	Jacob Katz, *Exclusiveness and Tolerance*, Oxford, 1961.
Katz, Tradition	Jacob Katz, *Tradition and Crisis, Jewish Society at the End of the Middle Ages*, New York, 1961.
Kleerekooper	S. Kleerekoper, 'Het Joodse proletariaat in het Amsterdam van de 19e eeuw', *St.Ros.* I (1967), pp. 97-104.
Koenen	H.J. Koenen, *Geschiedenis der Joden in Nederland*, Utrecht, 1843.
Kossmann	E.H. Kossmann, *The Low Countries*, Oxford, 1978.
Livro de Resoluçoens	*Livro de Resoluçoens* (Minute Book) of the Spanish-Portuguese Jewish Community of Amsterdam.
Livro de Segredos	W.Ch. Pieterse, *Livro de Segredos – Inventaris van de archieven der Portugees-Israëlitische gemeente te Amsterdam*, 1614-1870, Amsterdam 1964.
LYB	*Leo Baeck Yearbook*, I-XXXIX, London, 1955-1994.
Mahler	R. Mahler, *History of the Jewish People in Modern Times*, (Hebr.), Vol.I, Merhavia. (transl.: *A History of Modern Jewry*, 1780-1815, London, 1971.)
Meijer, da Costa	J. Meijer, *Isaac da Costa's weg tot het Christendom*, Amsterdam, 1946.
Meijer, J.D. Meyerplein	J. Meijer, *Het Jonas Daniël Meyerplein*, Amsterdam, 1961.
Meijer, Problematiek	J. Meijer, *Problematiek per Post*, Amsterdam, n.d.
Meijer, J.D., Wetenschap	J. Meijer, *Joodse wetenschap in Nederland*, Heemstede, 1982.

Meijer/Slagter	J. Meijer en Jet Slagter, *Versteend verleden, de Joodse begraafplaats te Overveen*, Haarlem, 1983.
Melitz Yosher	Israël Graanboom, *Melitz Yosher,* Amsterdam, 5569 (1809).
Memorboek	M.H. Gans, *Memorboek*, Baarn, 1972.
Mendels	I. Mendels, *De Joodse gemeente te Groningen,* 2nd. printing, Groningen, 1910.
Mevorach	B. Mevorach, *Napoleon utekufato* (Hebr.), Jerusalem, 1969.
Michman, Centrum en periferie	J. Michman (Melkman), 'Centrum en periferie, Amsterdams dubieuze positie als centrum van Joods Nederland', *St. Ros.* XIX (1985), pp. 203-20.
Michman, Michmanei Yosef	J. Michman (Melkman), *Michmanei Yosef, Studies on the History and Literature of the Dutch Jews* (Hebr.), Jerusalem, 1994.
Nieuwenhuis	I.J.A. Nieuwenhuis, *Een Joodse Philosophe Isaac de Pinto (1717-1787) en de ontwikkeling van de politieke economie in de Europese Verlichting*, Amsterdam, 1992.
NIW	*Nieuw Israëlietisch Weekblad*, Amsterdam.
NNJB	*Nieuwe Nederlandse Jaarboeken*, Leiden-Amsterdam.
Petuchowsky	Jakob J. Petuchowsky, *Prayerbook Reform in Europe*, New York, 1968.
Pieterse, Bijlagen	Bijlagen bij de Notulen van de President, 1789 and 1806; see also Livro de Segredos.
Pinkas	*Pinkas hakehillot – Holland*, J. Michman, H. Beem and D. Michman (Hebr.), Yad Vashem, Jerusalem, 1985 (Dutch ed. 1992).
Poppers	H. Poppers, *De Joden in Overijsel van hunne vestiging tot 1814*, Utrecht-Amsterdam, 1926.
Prinz	Losse Bijdragen tot de Geschiedenis der Joden in Nederland, Kronijke van de jaren 1787/8 in *Israëlische Letterbode*: I (1875), nrs. 2-6.
Raisin	Jacob S. Raisin, *The Haskalah Movement in Russia*, Philadelphia, 1913.
Rijxman	A.S. Rijxman, *A.C. Wertheim*, Amsterdam, 1961.
Roth	Cecil Roth, *The History of the Jews of Italy*, Philadelphia, 1946.
Schama, Citizens	Simon Schama, *Citizens*, Toronto, 1990.
Schama, Patriots	Simon Schama, *Patriots and Liberators*, New York, 1977.
Schatzky	J. Schatzky, *Presse Sammelbuch zum 250-ten Joweil fun der jiddischer Presse*, New York, 1936.
Schwarzfuchs, Sanhedrin	Simon Schwarzfuchs, *Napoleon, the Jews and the Sanhedrin*, London, 1979.
Schwartzfuchs, France	Simon Schwarzfuchs, *Les Juifs de France*, Paris, 1975.
SDJ, 1-5	*Studies on the History of Dutch Jewry* (ed. J. Michman), Jerusalem, 1975-1988) (Hebr.).

Silva Rosa, Bijdrage   J.S. da Silva Rosa 'Bijdrage tot de kennis van de econo-
                           mische en politieke toestand der Hoogduitsche Joden
                           te Amsterdam in het begin der vorige eeuw', *Centraal-
                           blad voor Israëlieten in Nederland* 31 (1916), nos. 50, 51,
                           52; 32 (1917), nos. 2, 4, 6, 9.
Silva Rosa, Bibliographie J.S. da Silva Rosa, *Bibliographie der Literatur über die
                           Emanzipation der Juden in Holland*, Frankfurt, 1912.
Silva Rosa, Geschiedenis   J.S. da Silva Rosa, *Geschiedenis der Portugese Joden*, Am-
                           sterdam, 1925.
Slijper   E. Slijper, 'Een merkwaardig proces over de haar-
                           dracht der vrouw bij de Joden te Rotterdam', *Rotter-
                           dams Jaarboekje*, 1910.
Sluys, Bange dagen   D.M. Sluys 'Uit bange dagen', *VA* IV (1927), pp. 324-
                           27, 340-43, 371-74, 386-88, 407-09, 420-23.
Sluys, Protocollen   D.M. Sluys, 'De Protocollen der Hoogduitsch-Joodse
                           Gemeente in Amsterdam', *BMGJW* IV, 1928, pp. 110-
                           29.
Stud. Ros.   *Studia Rosenthaliana* I (1967).
Tama   Diogène Tama, *Organisation civile et religieuse des Is-
                           raélites de France et du Royaume d'Italie*, Paris, 1808.
VA   *De Vrijdagavond*, Amsterdam, 1924-1932. Proefnummer
                           (11. 1. 1924); 1a (1924); 1b (1924/25); 2 (1924/25); 3
                           (1925/26; 4 (1926/27); 5 (1927/28); 6 (1928/29); 7
                           (1929/30); 8 (1930/31); 9 (1932).
Wolff, Lod. Nap.   M. Wolff, 'De betekenis van de regering van Lodewijk
                           Napoleon voor de Joden van Nederland', *Bijdragen
                           voor Vaderlandse Geschiedenis en Oudheidkunde*, 7 (1920),
                           pp. 51-110.
Wolff, Haarlem   M. Wolff, *Geschiedenis der Joden in Haarlem 1600-1815*
                           (2 vols.), Haarlem, 1917).
Yaari   Awraham Yaàri, *Sheluhei Eretz Israel* (Hebr.), 2nd. ed,
                           Jerusalem, 1977.
Yogev   G. Yogev, *Hape'iluth Hakalkalith shel hapatriat hayehudi
                           beanglia bamea hashemoneh-esre* (Hebr.), doctoral thesis,
                           Hebr. Univ. Jerusalem, 1962. Condensed English ver-
                           sion: *Diamonds and Corals. Anglo-Dutch Jews and Eight-
                           eenth-Century Trade*, Leicester, 1978.
Van Zuiden, Lod. Nap.   D.S. van Zuiden, 'Lodewijk Napoleon en de Franse
                           Tijd', *St. Ros.* II (1968), pp. 66-88.
Van Zuiden,   D.S. van Zuiden, *De Hoogduitsche Joden te 's-Gravenhage
's-Gravenhage ii   vanaf hunne komst tot heden*, The Hague, 1913.
Van Zuiden,   D.S. van Zuiden, 'Het doorvoeren van de emancipatie
Emancipatie   in het Departement van de Neder-Rhijn', *VA* 1b, pp.
                           143-44.

Index